DIVA

The New Generation

DIVA

The New Generation

The Sopranos and Mezzos of the
Decade Discuss Their Roles

Helena Matheopoulos

LITTLE, BROWN AND COMPANY

A *Little, Brown* Book

First published in Great Britain in 1998
by Little, Brown and Company

A CIP catalogue record for this book
is available from the British Library.

ISBN 0 316 64720 9

Typeset in Perpetua by M Rules
Printed and bound in Great Britain by
Clays Ltd, St Ives plc

Little, Brown and Company (UK)
Brettenham House
Lancaster Place
London WC2E 7EN

CONTENTS

Introduction   xix

Sopranos

Barbara Bonney   3

Jane Eaglen   20

Renée Fleming   36

Barbara Frittoli   55

Angela Gheorghiu   73

Galina Gorchakova   91

Maria Guleghina   104

Elena Kelessidi   121

Catherine Malfitano   140

Karita Mattila   162

Deborah Polaski   181

Ruth Ann Swenson   196

Carol Vaness   210

Veronica Villarroel   233

Contents

Mezzo-Sopranos

Cecilia Bartoli	247
Olga Borodina	263
Susan Graham	274
Denyce Graves	289
Vesselina Kasarova	304
Jennifer Larmore	319
Dolora Zajick	332

To the memory of

Lucia Popp
Tatiana Troyanos
Lucia Valentini Terrani

Friends who cast long shadows . . .

ACKNOWLEDGEMENTS

I SHOULD LIKE to thank the following people, each of whom has contributed in a different way, towards making this book a reality:

William Frohlich, Director, and Editor in Chief, Northeastern University Press, whose idea it was to embark on a new volume on the female singers of the decade after the considerable success of *Diva: Great Sopranos and Mezzos Discuss Their Art*; Philippa Harrison, Chief Executive and Publisher, Little, Brown & Co; Alan Samson, Editorial Director, Little, Brown & Co, for believing in the project and proving *the* most supportive, encouraging and patient of editors: I didn't think there were still people like him and Philippa in publishing, but blessedly there are; Linda Silverman, the most enthusiastic and imaginative Picture Researcher I've ever worked with; Joanna Macnamara, Assistant to Alan Samson, whose forbearance and resourcefulness knew no bounds! Being cossetted and sustained by a team exuding such warmth and commitment is manna from heaven to an author, especially during the very lonely and emotionally draining months of writing.

My thanks to my agent and friend Gillon Aitken of Gillon Aitken

Associates, for many years an essential part of my professional 'life sup-port system'; Edmund Forey of the Grove Dictionary of Music, who edited the book with tact and sensitivity, usually within a hectic time schedule; Maestro Christoph von Dohnanyi, Music Director, the Cleveland Orchestra and Principal Conductor, the Philharmonia Orchestra; Sir Charles Mackerras; Dr Jonathan Miller; Elijah Moshinsky; Peter Katona, Artistic Administrator, the Royal Opera House, Covent Garden; Matthew Epstein, Artistic Director Designate, the Lyric Opera of Chicago, and Vice-Chairman Columbia Artists Management Inc; Brian Dickie, General Director, European Union Opera; Dr Alexander Pereira, General Director, the Zurich Opera; Pál Christian Moe, Director of Programming, the Paris Opéra; Pierette Chastel, Attachée de Press, the Paris Opéra; Jonathan Tichler, Press Assistant, the Metropolitan Opera; Mary Serantoni, Director of Public Relations and Marketing, the Lyric Opera of Chicago; Melissa Labbe, the Metropolitan Opera Press Office; Suzzanne Stephens, Public Relations Director, the Washington Opera; Leo Boucher, Press Associate, the Houston Grand Opera; Helen Anderson, formerly Director of Press Relations, the Royal Opera House, Covent Garden, a wonderfully warm, super-efficient presence sorely missed at the Opera House; Ann Richards, Press Officer, The Royal Opera House, Covent Garden; Rita Grudgeon, Press Assistant, the Royal Opera House, Covent Garden; Miss Tia Schutrupps, Press Officer, The Netherlands Opera; Signor Andrea Vitalini, Archivio Fotografico, Teatro alla Scala; Tom Graham, Managing Director, IMG Artists; Barbara Sigal, IMG Artists; Stefania Almansi, IMG Artists; Helen Palmer, Assistant to Stefania Almansi, IMG Artists; Nicola Fee Bahl, Lies Askonas Ltd; Caroline Woodfield, ICM Artists Ltd, New York; Nalo McGibbon, Assistant to Caroline Woodfield ICM Artists Ltd; Edgar Vincent of Vincent and Farrell, New York; Alan Green and Jean Fréderic, Green/Zemsky Division, Columbia Artists; Jennifer Bredtmeyer, Kursidem and Lewin, Berlin; Frau Gehringer, Frau Sienel, Frau Kathrin Geisler, Germinal Hilbert Theateragentur,

Munich; Didier de Cottignies, Director of Marketing, Decca Records; Monyene Kane, Assistant to Didier de Cottignies, Decca Records; James Lock, Chief Engineer, Decca Records; Katherine Howard, Press Officer, EMI; Lester Smith, Chief Engineer, EMI Abbey Road Studios; Terri Jayne Griffin, Press Officer, Deutsche Grammophon; Carol Lowrie, Press Officer, Sony Music; Alfred Goodrich, Press Officer, Nimbus Records; Cathy Tyler, Press Officer, BMG Conifer Records; Liz Griffin, International Press Officer, Warner Classics.

Finally, those friends whose kind and generous hospitality rendered the countless trips to interview the artists in this book such fun and so memorable: Dr Christine Warnke in Washington; Mr and Mrs Panagiotis Lemos in New York (where their telephone suffered from acute telefonitis!); Alexis Gregory in Paris, in whose lovely West Bank apartment several of these interviews took place; Irene Sculi Logotheti in Paris; Nada Geroulanos in Zurich, in whose lakeside apartment the interview with Cecilia Bartoli took place; Ioanna Tsatsos for performing an invaluable favour; John Karaiosifoglou, without whose toing and froing on my behalf I would have finished this book much later; Eduwigis R. Angeles, my invaluable help around the house who became an expert faxer in the process; and George Karamanos, Head of Marketing, Virgin Atlantic, Athens who kindly delivered the corrected proofs for this book.

GLOSSARY

appoggiatura: a term derived from the Italian verb 'appoggiare' (to lean or support). A grace note inserted before a note but to be sung equal length, to support or emphasize a melodic or harmonic progression

bel canto: literally 'beautiful singing'. A term associated with singing in the eighteenth and early nineteenth centuries when a beautiful vocal performance was more important than the dramatic. *Bel canto* composers most often referred to in this book include Bellini, Donizetti and Rossini

cabaletta: in nineteenth-century opera, the fast concluding section of an aria or ensemble. In the early part of that century, a separate aria in lively tempo

cantabile: literally 'songful' – denotes *legato*, expressive singing

da capo: return to the beginning

a cappella: unaccompanied singing

cavatina: technically a short aria but now used to describe widely differing types of song and therefore virtually meaningless

coloratura: elaborately embellished singing. The term later came to apply to singers specializing in roles needing great vocal agility

'*covering*' *a note*: singing it with a 'closed' throat, i.e., allowing the larynx to float downwards rather than upwards

fioritura: florid vocal embellishment

legato: from the Italian verb 'legare', meaning to bind or tie. Refers to the smooth passage from one note to another, as opposed to *staccato*

lirico-spinto: from the Italian verb 'spingere', meaning to push. Identifies a lyric voice leaning towards the dramatic

messa di voce: a crescendo and diminuendo on a phrase or note

mezza voce: literally 'half voice'. Denotes singing softly, but not as softly as piano. A special way of singing as if under the breath, referring not only to the amount of volume but to a different quality from that when singing full voice

passaggio: the notes E, F and G which lie between the head and the chest registers

piano: term applying to volume meaning soft; also

   pianissimo: very soft

   forte: loud

   fortissimo: very loud

portamento: from the Italian verb 'portare', meaning to carry. A practice by which singers slide from one note to another without a break.

recitative: declamatory passages imitating speech which precede arias, duets and ensembles. Particularly common in eighteenth-century opera

register: a term used to denote a certain area or vocal range – 'chest', 'middle', 'head'

rubato: literally 'stolen time'. A way of performing without adhering strictly to musical time

solfège: an elementary method of teaching sight reading and ear training whereby the names of the notes (*do, re, mi* . . .) are pronounced while the notes are sung unaccompanied. The intervals have to be learned by ear. A common teaching method in France and Italy, known in English as 'tonic sol-fa'

tessitura: literally 'texture'. A term used to designate the average pitch of an aria or role. A part can be taxing despite the absence of especially high or low notes due to the prevailing *tessitura*

verismo: literally 'realism'. The opposite to *bel canto*, where drama is as important as beautiful singing. A term applied to the works of Italian composers after Verdi including Puccini, Mascagni, Leoncavallo, Zandonai and Giordano. Can also be used as an adjective, *veristic*, meaning realistic and applied to the way in which the works of these composers are sung – i.e. more freely and less precisely than those of composers such as Mozart

vocalize: exercise the voice. Can be a specifically composed wordless song or exercise

AUTHOR'S NOTE

CONSIDERATIONS OF TIME and space alone have forced the omission of a few artists whom I would very much like to have included in the book. First and foremost, *Deborah Voigt*, whose recent account of the title role in Strauss's *Die aegyptische Helena* for Covent Garden at the Festival Hall left everyone spellbound. Unfortunately the book was then in its closing stages and Miss Voigt left for America immediately, so there was no time to arrange a meeting. *Nathalie Dessay* is a coloratura soprano of infinite promise and potential whom I wanted to include: but she was at the last stages of her pregnancy and gave birth to a baby during the only period possible for me to travel to her. *Christine Schaefer*, the German light lyric soprano could not find the time within the book's time schedule. *Larissa Diadkova*, is a mezzo with a voice of top quality and a technique so accomplished that she will, I feel sure, shine in the Italian repertoire she is now embarking on as much as she does in the Russian. The wonderful Finnish soprano *Soile Isokoski* also deserves mention. Her Fiordiligi at Covent Garden was one of the most accomplished in the history of the House, but I have not seen her in any other role.

Among young artists, others who should have a bright future are the

Danish soprano *Inger Dam Jenssen*, the Italian *Nuccia Focile*, the Italian mezzo *Sonia Ganassi* and the Swedish dramatic soprano *Catarina Dalayman*.

But a book of a size that would allow the inclusion of all these artists is, sadly, not a practical possibility!

The chapters have been conceived to be read individually as well as consecutively. For this reason, the titles of people such as Music Directors, General Managers of specific organizations are repeated the first time they are mentioned in each chapter (i.e. Matthew Epstein, Artistic Director Designate of the Lyric Opera of Chicago and so on).

Every opera is given its full official title the first time it is mentioned in each chapter. Then, in conversational reference, it is abbreviated in the usual conversational manner, to avoid tedium. (For example, the first time *Un ballo in Maschera* is referred to in each chapter, it is with its full title and hence forth it is referred to as *Ballo*).

HM
London, July 1998

INTRODUCTION

WHAT IS A diva? What makes some very good singers create an instant buzz around them wherever they go while others, equally good or maybe better, fail to ignite the public imagination? And what makes audiences scream with adulation and throw remarks like 'Just come back and stand there and let us love you' to a diva who had just fled from the stage because when she opened her mouth nothing, no sound, came out — as they did to an aging Renata Tebaldi at a sold-out concert in Salzburg?

'I think it's an aura that some of them exude,' says Sir Charles Mackerras. 'Something which many good, even excellent singers may not necessarily possess. There has to be something unusual as well as competent about a diva, something compelling about her personality, whether you like it or not, whether it be charming or repellent — and I *can* think of some with the latter quality — or both at the same time! Personally I prefer the good sort, even though they may not qualify as divas because they are too *normal*.' (In this context it is worth remembering Jennifer Larmore's description: 'Divas are a little bit like witches. Just as there are black witches and white witches, so there are bad divas and good divas.)

To Sir Charles's list I would add glamour, a larger-than-life personality (both on stage and off), an innate communicative gift that enables them to touch 'their' public at a very deep level – and of course a great and, most importantly, an instantly recognizable voice.

The 1990s has been a bumper decade for female singers of very high quality. Unlike the 1980s, which despite the presence of 'divas' such as Dame Kiri Te Kanawa and Jessye Norman, were dominated by the Three Tenors on one hand and on the other by baritones and basses of exceptional star quality, who outshone their female counterparts. The past eight years have seen the steady rise of divas capable of drawing mass audiences as well as enthralling the cognoscenti, and who deliver performances to rival those of the great singers of the past.

The message of the decade is: forget nostalgia. For, as far as top quality female voices are concerned, both sopranos and mezzos, we have seldom had it so good. Most of the voices in this book (plus a few who are omitted solely for practical reasons), can hold their own and in several cases even surpass some of their illustrious predecessors. This was not the case eight years ago, when *Diva: Great Sopranos and Mezzos Discuss Their Art* was published. In fact the scene was still depressing enough for me to print the pessimistic introduction I had written five years previously for my book on male opera singers.

In fact, the 80s was a decade strewn with vocal corpses: prematurely ruined singers who had done too much, sung the wrong roles, or even the right roles at the wrong time. No more. The singers of the 90s seem to have taken collective note of what happened to those before them, and to be determined to prevent it from happening to them. Contrast the shrewd, conscientious caution of the greats of today's singers – Mattila, Gheorghiu and Kasarova, to name but a few – with the reckless abandon of the 80s: a time when mezzos became sopranos seemingly at a stroke, when light lyric sopranos sang Turandot and lyrics sang Wagner.

The result was a dramatic dearth of quality voices for very large sections of the repertoire. As James Levine, Artistic and Music director of the Metropolitan Opera said at the time, whereas earlier 'a good performance of *Madama Butterfly* could be taken for granted, today [the 80s] it would be the exception rather than the rule.'

But in the 90s the situation has improved significantly. As Matthew Epstein, Artistic Director Designate of the Lyric Opera of Chicago, vice-president of Columbia Artists and also a world authority on voices explains: 'It's very reassuring that once again we can cast parts which a few years ago we had great trouble casting. Now we can say again, "whom shall we have as Sieglinde?" for example, and come up with names such as Karita Mattila, Deborah Voigt, Nadine Secunde and Katarina Dalayman, and that's just four off the top of my head. This gives you choice once again, it gives you room for thought. The same is true of Brünnhilde: Jane Eaglen is wonderful, Polaski's wonderful, Schnaut is interesting and maybe Voigt will grow into it too. We also have a fabulous crop of mezzos, both in Europe and America. It's just fantastic. This adds up to a very optimistic picture for the future.'

The chief characteristic of female singers of the 90s is that they are *artists* first and divas second. They are musically well educated, vocally well trained, excellent actresses and good-looking to boot. In the 80s this was still considered too absurd and excessive a combination of gifts to demand. 'Perhaps we have come to expect too much from our opera singers,' said Janine Reiss, the distinguished French vocal coach who has worked with most of the singers of the last quarter century. 'Instead of letting them concentrate on their vocal development and the need to sing as beautifully and perfectly as they can, we also demand that their acting be of a standard comparable to that of the Comédie-Française or the Royal Shakespeare Company, that their dancing matches that of the starlets of *A Chorus Line* and that their looks compare with those of matinée idols in other branches of show business. It's a lot, you know.'

Now this is the norm. With very few exceptions today's top singers combine all of those qualities as well as brains: a strong *mind* as well as the proverbial strong will of the archetypal diva, plus self-knowledge and a concern for self-preservation. This is true even when, like Renée Fleming, they happen to be 'flavour of the month' and in demand everywhere. 'We keep having to say no, even to the most important conductors,' says Matthew Epstein, currently Fleming's agent. 'She just can't be everywhere, even though in these days of the Concorde, people get very upset at such refusals. I'm proud to have worked with people of her calibre throughout my career at Columbia Artists: singers such as Catherine Malfitano, Samuel Ramey and Neil Shicoff, all of whom have had long, sustained and lucrative careers, as well as integrity as artists.

'For, as I keep trying to make singers understand,' continues Epstein, 'it's not in the first five years of the career that the money's made – it's in the *last* ten years. Their aim should be vocal longevity, to be singing thirty or even forty years after the onset of their career. Look at Leontyne Price, Christa Ludwig, Leonie Rysanek and Birgit Nilsson, as well as Sutherland and Caballé. They all sustained great careers for *decades*. That's what a career is supposed to be about – not about cashing in fast! Because the end of your career is also when you can bring your whole life experience and consummate artistry to your work.'

These are almost the exact words of Christa Ludwig herself, who in the midst of the rampant commercialism that first afflicted the operatic world like a tidal wave in the 80s, contrasted this to her own slow ascent to fame and fortune: 'My career began slowly. And my money also came slowly. Today it seems to come so quickly – and such a lot of it – that many singers feel, "what if I can only manage a ten-year career if by the end of it I will have made enough to last for the rest of my life?" But I, guided by my mother who *had* ruined her voice prematurely, always hoped I would still have my voice intact when I was mellow enough to *know* what it's about, what's inside the music. This can only come with age and eludes all those who make quick careers and burn themselves out before they reach this ripe state of *knowing*.'

Certainly a decade ago few singers would have had the guts to say no to the late Herbert von Karajan (whom I idolize as a conductor but hold responsible for luring more voices than one cares to name to their ruin). Today, Barbara Frittoli said no – in a very nice, gentle and roundabout way as she describes in her chapter – to Riccardo Muti, who wanted her to sing Leonora in *La forza del destino* at La Scala. *And* she's Italian. That's guts.

Yet it's not from Italy or indeed Germany – the main sources of our musical and operatic heritage – that the singers set to dominate the next millennium come from, but from Russia and the United States. Today's Russian singers are certainly luckier than their predecessors who languished behind the Iron Curtain, limited not only geographically but artistically and spiritually as well. For they are the only generation of Russian singers both to benefit from the state-funded and very thorough system of musical education that prevailed under Communist rule *and* to enjoy the new-found freedom to travel, sing any repertoire they please and polish their gift to Western standards. The only danger facing them is the temptation to do too much, motivated on the one hand by financial gain (but who can stand in judgement of people who until recently had so little in the material sense) and on the other by the dynamic head of the Kirov (now Mariinsky) Theatre, Valery Gergiev, who works his singers like a slave-driver, seemingly oblivious to their vocal health. As for American singers, the world seems to be their oyster at the moment. And with good reason. For while there have always been some superlative American opera singers – Beverly Sills, George London and Richard Tucker, to name but three – there have never been so *many*, and for every area of the repertoire. Their characteristics are consummate professionalism, an infinite capacity for hard work, punctuality, poise and all the qualities stemming from what Barbara Bonney rightly calls 'the American ethos': 'We are all steeped in a specifically American morality and work ethic which permeates our professional attitude, and has to do with the way we carry ourselves, with being punctual, respecting our colleagues and trying not to let the other side down.'

There are four main reasons for the number and quality of American singers to have made it to the top. Firstly, there is the superb quality of musical education and vocal training available in the United States, from the Juilliard and the Manhattan School of Music to the musical faculties throughout most of its universities. Secondly, the infrastructure that exists in many of the top American opera houses now provides singers with a platform between their graduation from college and the beginning of their career. There is the San Francisco Opera's famous Merola Program, which proved the launching pad for Carol Vaness, Dolora Zajick, Ruth Ann Swenson, Deborah Voigt and Susan Graham, among others. Similar programmes exist at the Houston Grand Opera, where Denyce Graves was first launched. (The only comparable establishment in Europe has been the Zürich Opera studio, founded by the late lamented Robert Belford, also an American. Thirdly, there is the valuable work done by great musical organizations such as the Richard Tucker Foundation and the George London Foundation, which provide financial support for young singers at precisely this crucial point in their lives. Lastly, there is the enormous contribution to the operatic scene and the art of singing by James Levine, the charismatic conductor at the helm of the Metropolitan Opera for over twenty-five years, which can hardly be overestimated. Although a top symphonic conductor, he is also a born conductor for the voice, with a passion for singers and the knowledge, patience and humility to work *for* rather than against them, both in management and in the pit. As a manager he listens to them, nurtures, guides and even mounts new productions to take account of their particular repertoire needs and wishes. Never does he miscast or try to lure them into the wrong rules. In short he is big enough to admit that 'singing counts for eighty percent of operatic performance'.

Eight years ago, when asked whether conductors had changed during her long career, Christa Ludwig answered: 'No. Conductors are very funny people. They *have* to have a big ego, otherwise they couldn't do their job. They are the only autocrats in the world, they can do whatever they want. They have us singers completely in their hands. Barring Third World dictators, this degree of power doesn't exist in any other profession anymore. Coming to think of it, even dictators depend on their armies or palace guard or something. But conductors can have it all their own way. They can set the tempo, decide on dynamics and choose their casts. They are like emperors.' Eight years later, Galina Gorchakova states that one thing that hasn't changed in Russia is that as in the West, 'the power of the conductor in an opera house is like Stalin's'. Levine, however, has been an undoubted exception to this rule, someone who sees flexibility as an operatic conductor's most important quality, and values the ability to shape a performance to get the best out of any particular singer. His sterling work at the Met has produced rich results in improving the quality of singing in the United States. He is not alone in that country in providing optimum conditions for singers: Terry McEwen, for many years General Manager of the San Francisco Opera has also been responsible for nurturing many a famous talent; and the late Ardis Krainik of the Lyric Opera of Chicago, much beloved of singers, also contributed a great deal to the development of American artists. Her heritage is safe in the expert hands of Matthew Epstein, who moves to Chicago next season.

So today's operatic scene is dominated by singers with two completely different musical traditions and national temperaments: on one hand by well-schooled, soulful Russians in the process of acquiring the Western style and patina, and on the other by the equally well-educated, polished Americans who seemingly have it all. Each group has its champions and detractors. Director Elijah Moshinsky finds some of the American singers a bit bland: 'They tend to hide behind a technique and are a bit cool, a bit distant, more concerned with efficiency than with dramatic truth or intensity. Efficiency is a real value to them and they are indeed very efficient in their singing. Their voices never portray *strain*, whereas the Russians are always on the point of portraying strain and doing the unsingable — which is exactly what Callas did!'

'The Russians have made, and are making, giant strides,' agrees Peter Katona Artistic Administrator of the Royal Opera, Covent Garden. 'Gone are the days of their wobbly basses, yelling tenors and screeching sopranos. They are now looking to the world market and picking up fast. The Americans, on the other hand, have all the skills but less *character*. Their voices don't have such an immediately recognizable personality.' I'm not sure I agree with those statements — or rather, I'm sure I don't! I think Renée Fleming's celestially beautiful instrument *is* instantly recognizable, and I don't think the ultra-committed, involved performances of American artists such as Carol Vaness, Deborah Polaski or Catherine Malfitano are bland. But, *chacun à son goût*. We are extraordinarily lucky to be living in an operatic decade that can boast such rich and varied talents. I would not wish to do without either group. Opera being such a universal, international art form, I am sure these two traditions will influence and stimulate each other in a fascinating way.

The problems and concerns facing female opera singers are also universal. One of the main ones is how to combine a career of such high and constant mobility with any kind of personal or family life. This is one of the reasons why the casualty rate of diva marriages is very high. Then there are the peculiar lives and psychological idiosyncrasies of the species itself. For, away from the electricity, excitement and high tension of the operatic stage, a diva's life boils down to a peripatetic existence in hotel rooms and rented flats; on top of this is a daily routine requiring discipline, training, careful living and the stamina of an athlete. Moreover, divas live in a state of permanent preoccupation with their health, the slightest variation in which can affect The Voice, this volatile and unpredictable instrument, so bound up with their physical and emotional state. 'Singers live on an emotional tightrope. All they have to do sometimes when they're having a small problem is realize that the public probably won't know it. If, on the other hand, the problem is more substantial, they need someone close to them to say, "look, you're having a problem. Fix it. Fast!" And if they're smart, they'll fix it,' says Matthew Epstein.

For all these reasons, I suspect that the unsung heroes of this book – as indeed of my previous book on the subject – are the members of that long-suffering breed, the diva husbands. As Teresa Berganza's husband, Jose Rifa put it, they are doomed to live in 'a permanent *ménage à trois*: my wife, myself and The Voice.' For many, there is a clash between marriage and career (though this is, of course, also true for many modern women).

So what are these modern, fitness-conscious and intelligent divas really like? Certainly light years away from the traditional visions of fur- or feather-boa-trailing prima donnas, imposing their imperious wills on kowtowing managements. Or are they? According to Peter Katona, 'they may not look like divas – in fact when you see them backstage, sometimes they can look more like cleaning ladies – but they are still very strong, very choosy, very difficult and very demanding, because they wish to achieve the best in their careers which, they realize, will not last all that long. So, a modern-day diva is somebody who doesn't *look* like a diva anymore, but who nevertheless still has both the claws and ultimately, the clout, to throw her weight around.'

SOPRANOS

BARBARA
BONNEY

I FIRST MET Barbara Bonney in 1985 at a dinner party given by mutual friends in London during the rehearsal period for the Covent Garden production of *Der Rosenkavalier*, conducted by Sir Georg Solti and directed by John Schlesinger. Blonde, pretty and petite, she came across as charming and remarkably collected, despite the imminent approach of such an important international début. So important, indeed, that her mother, who had never before seen her perform on stage, flew over from Maine. In the event, her performance was judged to be an unqualified triumph and she went on to become the definitive Sophie of the next decade and longer.

It was therefore poignant that the interview for this book, in November 1997 in Paris, happened to coincide with her farewell to this role: Herbert Wernicke's production of *Der Rosenkavalier* at the Opéra Bastille. This was dubbed 'the American *Rosenkavalier*' because, apart from Bonney, it featured Renée Fleming as the Marschallin and Susan Graham as Octavian. The cast, as Hugh Canning rightly remarked in the *Sunday Times*, was 'unbeatable in the international opera scene today, with three of the best-looking, most musicianly and histrionically convincing singers before the public today'. Bonney's 'silvered soprano' was judged to be 'in peak condition, ethereally beautiful in "Wie himmliche".'

Why then has Bonney, whose crystalline, light lyric voice is still in top form, decided to turn her back on the role one had come to consider her calling card?

'When you are a light lyric soprano and you turn forty, you have a problem: you have literally nowhere to go in opera. You can't keep reproducing these young girls forever and ever,' she explained, displaying an almost ruthless self-critical faculty that would become apparent throughout our conversation. 'Sophie is supposed to be fourteen and I am forty-one. And although the theatre is about illusion, dramatically it gets harder and harder to get into the right frame of mind. Vocally, parts like Sophie need a very young fresh voice, but with good carrying power. I would love to be able to sing the Countess. I would love to be able to sing Fiordiligi and Mimì. But I can't. So I have decided to shift the emphasis of my career. At the moment, my time is split fifty–fifty between opera and Lied. In the future the balance will shift to seventy-five per cent in favour of Lied. In any case, Lied has always been my real love, the reason why I became a singer in the fist place.'

Just as Lucia Popp, 'the greatest Sophie of her generation', passed the mantle of this role on to Bonney when she graduated to the Marschallin with the words 'Barbara, I have been singing Sophie for seventeen years and now I give her to you', so does Bonney now feel that, 'the time has come for me to pass her on to a younger singer. So, this Paris production is definitely going to be my last Sophie'. Luckily there are two videos of *Der Rosenkavalier* (one conducted by Solti, the other by Carlos Kleiber) which will enable posterity, as well as fans disgruntled by her apparently premature decision to give up the part, to experience Bonney's radiant Sophie.

Whilst Bonney's farewell performances of this role took place in ideal conditions vocally, dramatically Herbert Wernicke's production left a lot to be desired.

The cast, who were acutely aware of these limitations (as Renée Fleming and Susan Graham also explain in their chapters), had to work hard to make up for a production which was, in Bonney's words, 'rather cool, with glassy floors, lots of mirrors and precious little human warmth. The way it was staged made intimacy between the three characters very difficult and conversation – central to this opera – near impossible. All three of us fought hard to reach a compromise that would allow us to project the nature of the relationship between the characters.'

She stresses that Sophie is much more difficult than is generally assumed, both vocally and dramatically. 'She is hugely underestimated and usually cast as a whimpering little girl with a voice you can barely hear, which is completely wrong. She *has* to have guts, because she is an adolescent on the verge of womanhood, fighting for what she wants, fighting against parental authority. As a character, I find her a spoilt little brat, a dreadful, *dreadful* person. In fact I can't stand myself as Sophie. I think she's *awful*, utterly obnoxious. OK, she's cute enough for a few moments. She's rather sweet and demure, but only for as long as it takes for her to get what she wants. So, as I don't like myself as Sophie, I understand full well that she and Octavian are not going to work out at all. Basically, they are very mismatched. Octavian has much more stature than she has. So, although it all seems wonderful for the moment, I don't feel it's going to last.'

She explains that her point of view is corroborated by the music, in particular the sadness of the moment when the Marschallin replies 'Ja, ja' to Faninal's remark that 'this is what young people are like'. 'That's when I realize that yes, Octavian is marvellous and I'm very lucky to have got him. But I also realize that I'll never be happy because I will always know that he will leave me the way he left her. And for this reason I don't feel that theirs will be a fulfilled destiny. Something will always be missing . . . because when a man leaves another woman for you, it means that he's also capable of leaving you. This is why, when the Marschallin sings 'Ja, ja' I always feel deeply sad. And the way

Felicity Lott sang it, with an eloquent, simultaneous gesture of the hand, moved me so much that I nearly burst into tears on stage. I could almost feel them welling up in my throat. Because at that moment it became clear to me, as Sophie, that I would never be completely happy with Octavian. And finding the right way of suggesting this to the audience is not at all easy.'

As far as the vocal demands of the role are concerned, the main challenge is to project the text, every shade and nuance of the words, as expressively as possible. Playing with the language is absolutely crucial to singing Strauss. Otherwise, as Lucia Popp explained to Bonney when they performed this opera together he can easily become boring. Popp also passed on some of her other secrets to her younger colleague, such as how to sing triplets, how to go up and down with the language, stressing certain syllables or emphasizing certain words in phrases such as 'und ich bin ganz allein'. 'This goes beyond singing the musical notation. If you did just that, you could never hope to arrive even at an approximation of what Strauss wanted. In this sense, singing Strauss is the closest you come in opera to singing Lieder. But this can create vocal problems. Because so much of your physical energy must go into getting the text across over a very dense orchestration, Sophie's pretty musical phrases become much harder to sing. Small opera houses are not a problem. But in bigger theatres, the projection of the text takes so much physical, diaphragmatic energy that it can leave you vocally tied up in knots. Overcoming this takes up even more energy.

'The other obvious vocal challenges in the role are those very high phrases which you have to float. I have always found the beginning of "Wie himmliche" quite difficult. I don't think I've ever done it terribly well. I've *pretended* to do it, I've convinced people that I can do it, but I know I can't. I fooled everybody and almost fooled myself . . . but I suppose theatre is about illusion, and as long as people are happy, that's all that matters. Even Carlos Kleiber, who can never be fooled, was almost happy. He said, "OK, there are some things missing, but yours is still the best-characterized Sophie I know at the moment."'

Carlos Kleiber was the conductor of the one performance of *Der Rosenkavalier* from among the 255 that she has sung in her career that Bonney would single out as a real 'Sternstunde', to treasure and remember forever. It was the fourth of a run of performances during the Vienna State Opera's Japanese tour of 1994. 'Felicity Lott was the Marschallin, Anne Sofie von Otter was Octavian and Kurt Moll was Ochs. And it took off in such a magical way that we all felt, "This is *it!*" Now we can all be run over by a truck because we have done it. This evening we made this work come alive in the way we feel Strauss wanted! Nothing can ever be like this performance. Even the remaining performances of the run, under the same near-ideal conditions, were a disappointment after what we had experienced on that fourth evening. There and then, I decided I never wanted to sing Sophie again. The time had come for me to pass her on to another singer. [This run was incidentally the last time to date that Carlos Kleiber has conducted opera.] The Paris production was already booked for November 1997, so I determined to make it my farewell to *Der Rosenkavalier*. Henceforth I would concentrate on a handful of operatic roles and devote much more time to concert singing and Lieder. As I mentioned earlier, Lied was the reason why I decided to study music.'

Bonney was born in Maine to parents who were not musical. The only other musical person in the family was her grandmother, who had studied the piano at the Juilliard. But when Barbara was three, her parents noticed that she had perfect pitch. The family had a clock, and the child could imitate its chimes, the little tune it chimed on the hour, before it struck, with total accuracy. As soon as she was old enough, she began taking piano lessons. 'But the piano was not my thing. So I swapped it for the cello, the most vocal of all instruments.' She continued studying the cello throughout her childhood and adolescence, while also singing in various local choirs. In 1974 when the time came for her to enrol in the music faculty of the University of New Hampshire, her chosen subjects were the cello and singing, 'but only Lieder, never operatic singing.'

While at university she began to sing in various Renaissance ensembles. 'Renaissance singing interested me a lot, as did composers such as Poulenc and Stravinsky, who share the same "intellectual" rather than Romantic approach. Romanticism didn't interest me at all at the time. I had also begun to be fascinated by languages and by all things Northern – cool weather and so on. That's what turned me on. So I decided to focus on German.' She took the option of spending her junior and senior years at Salzburg University as part of a student exchange programme. Incredible though it seems, she didn't realize at the time that Salzburg was Mozart's birthplace or that it had a conservatoire called the Mozarteum! But somebody alerted her to the fact and suggested that, as a music student, she should do something about attending classes there as well. As she was paying for her entire university education herself, by doing odd jobs ('anything', she says, not without a trace of bitterness at the memory of how hard it must have been), and could 'barely afford to get myself over to Europe', she didn't think this would be possible. But she didn't think there was any harm in auditioning. So she auditioned with a Schumann song, and they took her.

'So, all of a sudden, I was a vocal student. I thought to myself that this was all right as long as I could concentrate entirely on Lied, the only thing that appealed to me. So I started studying Lieder and my German began to improve dramatically. After about two and a half years an agent happened to be passing through Salzburg and asked to audition some Mozarteum students. I was part of this group. As this was the end of the summer term, I left shortly afterwards for my summer holiday in Switzerland, with my boyfriend. In the middle of our vacation, there was a call from this agent: "Do you remember me?", he asked. "Yes", I answered, and he went on: "Get on a train tonight. You have an audition at the Darmstadt State Theatre at ten o'clock tomorrow morning! Sing just anything. They are desperate *now*, immediately, for a soprano for this coming season starting next month, September".'

'So I got on the overnight train. I didn't have a bra or a skirt with me. Just a pair of trousers and a top. I got off at Darmstadt and found a hairdresser to wash my hair so I wouldn't look a sight after my hiking holiday, then I made my way to the opera house. My teacher at the Mozarteum had insisted that I learn at least two operatic arias, just in case I ever needed to audition. One was Anna in Nicolai's *Die lustigen Weiber von Windsor* and the other was Susanna in German. So I offered the only two operatic numbers I knew. And they took me! They said, "OK. Come back in two weeks. Your first engagement will be *Die lustigen Weiber von Windsor* so you will have to learn the part right away."' Back in Salzburg, Bonney had to explain to the Mozarteum that she would not be coming back to complete the course for her diploma; but she had time to perform in the Festival Chorus with which she was singing in *Aida* under Karajan – with Carreras, Freni, Cappuccilli and Raimondi.

'All of a sudden, I was an opera singer. I had no diploma. (I still needed another year's study for that), nothing. So I moved my few belongings to Darmstadt, found somewhere to stay and threw myself at it.' Her New England upbringing had prepared her well: 'American singers come to Europe well prepared musically, knowing the language and prepared to work very hard. And we tend to go for it because we are allowed to. In Europe that attitude of going out and getting what you want has always been frowned upon, whereas in America it's instilled in us: it's the New World philosophy. But it takes a lot of energy and time. You have to learn everything from scratch and, for a time, performing in a language that isn't your own is a bit hairy. The first time I sang in Italian was terrifying. I didn't know what I was doing, but I just kept working away and eventually I amassed a huge repertoire. It takes a while to learn your trade on the public stage.'

Bonney is in fact one of the few contemporary sopranos who, like their great predecessors of earlier years, learnt their job step by step and whose vocal development rests on very secure foundations. During her first years she sang a total of about 120 performances encompassing ten different roles, among them Adina (*L'elisir d'amore*), Gilda (*Rigoletto*), Aennchen (*Der Freischütz*), Cherubino, Manon, Gretel and Marzelline (*Fidelio*). Over the next seasons she would learn another thirty-five roles. 'You could say I overdosed on opera during those years.'

After about two and a half years it had become apparent to everyone in the theatre that she was highly talented and had great potential. She also auditioned for the Frankfurt Opera, where she was accepted and subsequently spent a year. Kurt Horres, the Intendant at Darmstadt, was moving on to Hamburg, he suggested that she move there too. Initially she agreed. But meanwhile, her agent had arranged for her to audition for Sir Georg Solti and Carlos Kleiber, both of whom were interested in working with her. Solti wanted her for his Covent Garden *Rosenkavalier* and Kleiber for Munich, but Hamburg refused to grant her leave of absence. So she told Horres, 'Sorry, Herr Professor, but I shall not be coming to Hamburg after all.' And from that moment on (in 1984), she has been freelance.

After her Covent Garden début in *Rosenkavalier* her international career took off. She made her début at the Vienna State Opera and the Bavarian State Opera in 1984 as Sophie, at La Scala in 1985 as Pamina, and made her Metropolitan Opera début in 1988 as Naiad in *Ariadne auf Naxos*. In 1989 she made her Lyric Opera of Chicago début as Adele in *Die Fledermaus*, and in the same year made her début as Nannetta at the Grand Théâtre de Genève. The Artistic Director at Geneva was the exceptional Hugues Gall, now Director at the Paris Opéra, which he is re-establishing as one of the world's leading opera houses. Shortly after his arrival he invited Bonney to make her Opéra début, in 1997, as Susanna.

Now, having come full circle, Bonney admits to having become very choosy about which roles she accepts. 'I only want to sing roles I really, really love, such as Susanna, Pamina, Ilia, Nannetta (in America if not in Europe, where they want a different kind of voice for Verdi), Zdenka in *Arabella*, which I will do at the Metropolitan Opera in 2001 and Hanna Glawari in *Die lustige Witwe* in 1999 in Vienna. I would also love to sing Cleopatra in Handel's *Giulio Cesare*, if someone would give me the chance. As I already mentioned, I can't sing roles such as Fiordiligi, the Countess or Mimì, which require a heavier lyric voice than mine, much as I would love to. I have sung Despina, but don't like the part; Zerlina, which I do like, I have sung only on record. Like Susanna in *Le nozze di Figaro* – one of my favourite roles – it's an interestingly ambiguous part. Zerlina would love to fool around with Don Giovanni, just as Susanna would love to fool around with the Count. What could be more delicious? But both realize the risks involved.'

Bonney first sang Susanna in Zürich under Nikolaus Harnoncourt, who subsequently became one of the greatest musical influences in her career. 'Apart from being a genius, he is also stimulatingly un-predictable. However hard you try to figure out what he'll want in advance, you can be sure that when you come face to face with him, he'll want something totally different. And when you ask why, he'll explain, on the spot, exactly why he wants it done utterly differently. He is completely and constantly surprising, which is wonderful. Doing my first Susanna with him was a deeply enriching experience.' Bonney has recorded *Figaro* with Harnoncourt for Teldec.

Since that Zürich *Figaro* she has performed Susanna all over the world, notably in Jonathan Miller's vintage Vienna Festival production in 1991. She describes the role as hugely long and extremely tiring. 'It's a real killer, but very rewarding because by the end you feel you have earned your keep and also because, as Susanna, you have been through quite a lot psychologically. For Susanna has to help everybody in the opera and basically make all their decisions for them. The action hap-pens within one day, and Susanna has to manage everything and keep it moving as opposed to just letting it happen. She has to change the course of the river, so to speak, and to think of everyone else simulta-neously, *and* revolve furniture, *and* run up and down stairs, *and* make the beds! I tell you it's a killer role!' The brilliant revolving set of Miller's Vienna production, which allowed characters to walk from room to room during their recitatives and thus set the stage for the next scene at a very fast pace, enabled the audience to realize this hectic one-day time span better than any other production in living memory.

'As a character, Susanna is a very clever girl. She wants a better position in life than the one she holds and knows she's capable of getting it. The Count knows this, too, and it's what makes her so attractive to him. The Countess, on the other hand, is a real mess. She has the greatest music ever written, she has "Dove sono", but she's a mess of woman. In fact the Countess's life is acted through Susanna's will. So Susanna has to be two people and this is what takes so much energy.

'As far as her relationship with Figaro is concerned, I think she's fond of him, but not in love. I think he's all she can get. He's a powerful man in the household. He's the Count's personal valet. He has got quite far with his abilities, as far as they go. I don't think he's particularly smart, in fact I don't think he's smart at all. And when she slaps him quite hard two or three times in the opera she really means it. If she were truly in love with him, she wouldn't do that. Cherubino's attentions she quite enjoys but she knows he's a waste of time. Basically I think that she fancies herself . . . and she fancies the Count. She feels terribly guilty about this. You see, there are so many layers behind the notes and between the lines, I think the music tells the story very well. It's up to us as interpreters to clarify the ambiguity, and convey these layers by exuding the right kind of energy on stage.'

She confides that she has, momentarily, been 'sexually attracted to all the Counts with whom I have performed this opera. I don't mean that I have wanted to pursue the attraction off stage but that on stage, as Susanna, I have been massively turned on by my Counts. And it *has* to be like this. The singers who perform the Count – such as Thomas Allen, Ruggero Raimondi, Thomas Hampson and Bo Skovhus, most of whom also sing Don Giovanni – tend to be sexy enough to make the onstage attraction seem real to the audience. I repeat, it *has* to be like this. You *have* to let the *juice* flow on stage, otherwise the performance doesn't mean anything. It becomes just empty music.

'Take the scene at the opening of Act III, for instance, where the Count sings "Crudel, perchè finora farmi languir così". Now if *that*'s not teetering on the verge of doing it behind the nearest bush, I don't know what is! And if you didn't convey this to the audience, it would mean nothing. It's got to be like this. It's in the music and you have to show it and wake up the audience. The music also suggests that when Susanna sings "Deh, vieni non tardar" we don't know if she's thinking of Figaro or the Count . . . Who knows? No conductor or producer has ever really known and I'm not sure whether Mozart himself knew, either. Maybe she's just singing it to the audience. Because after all the complex music that has gone before, after all the ensembles, a simple little number such as "Deh vieni" is sure to captivate the audience. It's a release, both musically and dramatically. Everybody can come back to normal and there is only one more hurdle before the finale. Only a genius such as Mozart would write such a simple little number at the end, to bring everybody back to earth and prevent the whole thing from exploding, as it was on the verge of doing.'

Bonney points out that Susanna is as tiring vocally as it is dramatically because the tessitura can be problematic. 'Susanna carries the melody, she's always above the Countess in their duets. In the ensembles she's always hovering on the passaggio, and with six people belting away under her, she has to be heard.' Yet Bonney looks forward to performing Susanna again at the Metropolitan Opera in November 1998 and December 1999.

She was headed for the Metropolitan Opera in February 1998 shortly after our Paris meeting to perform another favourite role, Pamina in *Die Zauberflöte*. Pamina has been an important role both in her career and her personal life. She first sang it in 1985 for her début at La Scala, where she met her first husband, the distinguished Swedish baritone Håkan Hagegård, who was singing Papageno. Maybe this also explains the importance she places on the character of Papageno in the opera.

She points out that Pamina is certainly not the easy role it is sometimes portrayed to be vocally. 'Mainly because of all the dialogue, which although not difficult in itself, keeps breaking the vocality, just as it does for Constanze in *Entführung*. And it's very, very hard to go from singing to speaking and vice versa. On top of this, it's a terribly exposed role. Every time I have to sing 'Ach, ich fühl's' I feel terrified and wish it to be over as soon as possible.'

'Dramatically, Pamina is certainly not her mother's daughter. The character I feel she's most linked to is Papageno, who has real stature and is so human, unlike Tamino who is quite spoilt, in the sense that he is always told what to do and does it. Papageno, on the other hand, is quite ready to put his life on the line and hang himself when he thinks that it is not worth living anymore. Pamina's the same. They are the only true humans, while Tamino represents a sort of ideal with a destiny to fulfil. (Sarastro, whose hostage she is, she finds frightening, but she realizes that he has a very important message which she must understand in order to be freed.)

'Pamina is a stronger character than Tamino, the one who throughout the opera does what her heart tells her. It is she who leads Tamino through the ordeals of fire and water, not the other way around. It is she who says, "Come, let's go now"; and not he who says "Come Pamina, let me take you through the ordeals". He just agrees to follow through the fire and the water. Just like real life where women have much more courage in the face of adversity or any kind of unpleasantness. Men always try to evade it. So Pamina is a wonderful person, *honest*, direct and upright, who says what she thinks. In this sense she resembles another of my favourite parts, Ilia in *Idomeneo*, who also has a great deal of moral sense and fibre. She also has a *huge* tenderness, a huge willingness to give and to sacrifice herself. She is a true blue female in the best sense of the word: the tender, nurturing sense that can make such women the salt of the earth. She is the Mother Teresa of operatic characters because she gives without wanting anything back. It's all in one direction, it's all give. And that is something very, very special.'

Bonney, who sang *Idomeneo* first in Darmstadt, and more recently in

Madrid, will repeat the role again at the San Francisco Opera for her début there in November 1999. She points out that if Ilia seems vocally easier than Pamina this is an illusion. "Zeffiretti lusinghieri", Ilia's gorgeous aria, is, she stresses, very, very difficult to bring off, 'especially in a big house where you have to give a lot of voice. It's full of long, long phrases with nowhere to breathe, and you have to be able to take this on board. I hope that the more I sing it, the easier it will become. But it's definitely one of those roles that can easily be vocally underestimated. They appear easy, because they're by Mozart, but in fact they're very, very difficult. Mozart is *the* most difficult composer. Strauss is much easier. His orchestration is like having a mattress underneath you. The expressiveness you have to place on the words lets you a bit off the hook, vocally. But in Mozart, as with all Classical composers, such as Schubert, you are totally exposed.'

Bonney likens singing music of the Classical period to 'being on a horse and never being allowed to canter. All you can do is trot. And that's it, that's the limit. It goes without saying that you are not allowed to gallop, either. You have to keep reining yourself in. So, the moment you get to a group of Strauss songs or a Strauss aria you feel "Oooph, now I can run, I can jump, I can fly!" But in Mozart there's nowhere to hide, you can't muffle anything. He demands utter perfection.'

Bonney will get a chance to try a new Strauss role, Zdenka in *Arabella*, at the Metropolitan Opera in November 2001, with Renée Fleming in the title role and Christoph Eschenbach conducting. She greatly looks forward to the experience, firstly because she loves working with Renée Fleming ('a lovely girl and a gorgeous colleague'), and secondly because Zdenka is a trouser role, something she hasn't had a chance to sing since her first Cherubinos in Darmstadt all those years ago. She feels that the Strauss trouser roles in particular have a piquancy which can be very intriguing.

'Zdenka is vocally very similar to Sophie, though not quite as long nor as demanding or exposed. There are some wonderful duets but, as in Sophie, the most important thing is singing it on the word. The expression of the language is crucial. But it is definitely easier than Sophie. Nothing in my whole repertoire is quite as scary as the Presentation of the Rose! Dramatically, Zdenka is a very rewarding role, a wonderful character: tender and sweet and self-effacing, yet totally honest with herself. She knows what she wants, she knows what she lacks, and would throw herself under a train for her sister, which is so gorgeous. There is a bit in the aria in Act I, where she sings "I love you so much, my sister," which I used to think was a bit corny. But now this capacity to love with no holds barred is something I have come to admire and prize above everything in life.'

When asked which of her heroines she loves best, she replies that she doesn't think she loves any of them, or rather, that somewhere inside, she loves all of them equally, especially when performing them. 'I have now honed down my group of girls so much that I think that, in order to exist at all, they must share equal billing.'

This select little group will soon be joined by Hanna Glawari in *Die lustige Witwe*, which she is due to sing at the Vienna State Opera under John Eliot Gardiner, with Bo Skovhus as Danilo. She knows full well that operetta, which she first got to perform in Darmstadt, is 'very, very difficult to pull off'. Everything – the singers, the conductor, the director, the sets and the costumes – has to be of the highest quality so that the thing sparkles in way that appears light-handed and effortless. 'Performing Hanna Glawari should be great fun. She is every woman's dream. She has a super song to sing, she has power, she has money, she has beautiful clothes, sex appeal and men eating out of her hand. All the same, she feels that something's missing, and wonders why she doesn't also have happiness. Then of course, she meets, or meets again, the man who can make her happy. Hers is a privileged lifestyle, a privileged existence, and singing her will be great fun.'

As she has previously stated, Lied will enjoy star billing in her career during the coming years. She feels that she has paid her 'operatic dues', and emphasizes that opera was not something she ever really wanted to do. The world of Lied is inherently much more satisfying for her.

'Seeing your audience, being able to look them in the eye and watch the shifts in the exchange of energy between you during the evening; and also seeing how this changes *my* life: this means a lot to me. Lieder singing is very self-exposing, like standing naked in front of a mirror. There is no fictitious character to hide behind. You have to show these people who *you* are. And I find this deeply gratifying. In addition, the world of Lied is an untapped treasure trove, a repertoire so endless that a singer can learn as many as one hundred new songs a year. And if I choose them judiciously, there is no reason why I shouldn't be singing at sixty-five.' Opera, on the other hand, she finds 'very difficult, very hard work. All those clashing egos . . . very draining.' This is why she particularly relished the blissful working relationship between herself, Renée Fleming and Susan Graham during the Paris run of *Der Rosenkavalier*. Far from being competitive, the three were even planning a joint celebration for Thanksgiving, which coincided with the performances. In any case, Bonney considers that the traditional diva-rivalries and diva-bitchiness are a thing of the past, especially among American singers, as is 'divadom' of the old school itself.

'We are all steeped in a specifically American morality and work ethic which permeates our professional attitude. It has to do with the way we carry ourselves, with being punctual, respecting our colleagues and trying not to let other people down. Of course, there are always exceptions. But there is bound to be a backlash sooner or later in such cases, especially as you ride over the crest of your career. That's when you need your colleagues most. That's why loving and respecting your colleagues is very important, and it's what I like to think we, this generation, are about.'

So after twenty years on stage, Bonney will be moving away from opera. 'I won't be giving it up altogether, but I will gradually start shutting the door to it. I'm not saying "Never, never". I shall be doing some exciting things, as I mentioned. Maybe doing less opera might make me miss it and rekindle my interest. But let's face it, my voice isn't big enough for the women I want to sing, and most of the women

I *can* sing no longer satisfy me psychologically. But I want to avoid the mistake so many people make of taking on parts for which they are not suited. I understand it in a way because giving up the theatre is hard, very hard, hard on the ego. This is what it's about, because without a sizeable ego you can't do this job.'

Bonney is fortunate in having found an understanding, supportive partner in her second husband Matthew Whittaker, a former violinist whom she met in Tokyo when she flew in to replace Arleen Auger. She explains that at that time her marriage to Håkan Hagegård was 'crumbling', because their respective careers kept them so busy that they hardly ever saw each other. They had been together for eight years, since they first met at La Scala in *Die Zauberflöte*, and had been married for three. Through Hagegård, Bonney came to love Sweden passionately. She misses it, and her garden there to this day. Nevertheless, by the time she went to Tokyo, she had decided to get a divorce and move to England.

'Because of my career I have to live in Europe, and I thought England would be the best place. It's still a northern country and London is a big musical centre. So, as I was busy singing all over the place, I hired Matthew as my personal assistant, to help me get settled quickly and organize everything. Two weeks after I moved into my house in Barnes, he cooked me a meal so sensational that, there and then, we decided we were made for each other. And that was it. We have now been married for three years and I have been incredibly lucky because Matthew [who now works as an agent in the orchestral department of IMG, the agency that also looks after Bonney] is a very cool, clever and a supportive husband.' She agrees that being a diva's husband is much harder than the other way round. Successful diva-husbands are often as much in love with the whole operatic scene as with the diva herself. So, when a diva's career comes to an end, this can be almost as hard on the husband as on the diva herself. The task facing both of them is to find ways of living a fulfilling life away from the stage.

Acutely aware of the problem and of how difficult such a transition can be, Bonney has already started preparing for it by giving master-classes. She has taught two at Tanglewood and at Ravinia; and one at the Royal Academy of Music, the San Francisco Conservatory of Music, the Juilliard, the Cleveland Institute of Music, and the Wigmore Hall. There is talk about doing another which would be televised. In fact, whenever she does recital tours now in the United States, she tries to link them to masterclasses.

'Teaching will not only fill my life after I eventually retire, it's already filling it so much that I almost feel like quitting right now! I know, I *know* I am a much better teacher than I am a singer. As a teacher I'm utterly confident, whereas I'm never utterly confident as a singer. Quite the reverse. I'm completely and utterly *un*confident. Because every time we open our mouths, everyone expects 100 per cent perfection. And once a concert is finished, it's gone. You cannot go back to correct or improve anything. This is why when I sing there is always self-doubt and fear of judgement. But when I teach, there is only joy.'

JANE
EAGLEN

ANYONE PASSING OUTSIDE Jane Eaglen's dressing room – whether at La Scala, the Metropolitan, the Chicago Lyric, the San Francisco Opera, the Paris Opéra, the Vienna State, the Bavarian State or the Seattle Opera – is likely to be regaled by sounds of rock and pop. The sounds of Whitney Houston, Meat Loaf and Bonnie Tyler emerge from Jane's famous 'warm-up tape', to which she sings along before performances of Turandot, Norma, Brünnhilde or any of the big dramatic roles for which she has become world-famous during the past few years.

'I won't go on stage until I have sung through this!' beams the British soprano who has become a particular favourite of American audiences. 'It puts me in a good mood. Then, after I have sung through it all, I begin singing some bits of opera, invariably from roles that are completely opposite to whatever I happen to be singing on the night. If it's Turandot, then it may be Donna Anna's "Non mi dir"; if it's Brünnhilde, then I'll sing some of Norma's coloratura passages; but if it's Norma, then I'll warm up with Brünnhilde's "Hojotohos". I do this in order to prove to myself that the voice can do anything I want it to, that it's under my control.'

Both the habit and the remark are typical of Jane Eaglen, as a person and as an artist: they point to her down-to-earth, no-nonsense approach to 'the whole palaver of being a diva'; and they reveal the obsession with vocal control that is the mainstay of both her technique and her artistic credo.

Eaglen, whose voice has been described as 'tough as steel, thrillingly direct, forceful, agile, seamless through its entire range', is lucky enough to possess an unflappable nature and plenty of self-confidence. 'I'm very, very calm and sort of laid back about what I do,' she confides. 'I don't get nervous or anything like that. I come from a very normal, working class family and feel that, although what I do is wonderful, it's my job. I mean you have to learn to deal with this side of things.' She is equally matter-of-fact about her weight, a subject which is something of an issue in this director-dominated age that expects opera singers to look like Hollywood stars, not to say fashion models. 'You know, my weight is so unimportant to me. If someone doesn't want to hire me because of my size, that is their prerogative. How I live my life is mine.'

Eaglen was born in Lincolnshire to a completely non-musical family, and learnt to play the piano at an early age at the suggestion of a neighbour. She always had 'a sort of pure, choirboy-type voice that was totally unsuited for pop music'. When she was about sixteen, her piano teacher suggested she might also start having singing lessons. Until then, she had no idea that one needed lessons in order to sing. 'I thought, well, can't you just open your mouth and sing? Boy, was I wrong!' She was delighted to be told that, as a beginner, she should practise no more than fifteen minutes a day – as opposed to the hours on end that she put into her piano practice!

At the age of eighteen, she was accepted at the Royal Northern College of Music in Manchester, where she met her teacher, Joseph Ward, a tenor who had sung in some early performances of Britten operas. He remains her teacher to this day and she trusts him implicitly. 'I owe him my whole vocal development. Having that continuity has made a very big difference to me, instead of chopping and changing, which is what so many singers seem to do. When I first went to him, I was very young and had a totally immature voice. But he immediately recognized a dramatic voice lurking somewhere inside and knew just how to teach it.

'His basic method of teaching is bel canto. Bel canto literally means beautiful singing, but it also describes a particular singing style. But he thinks, as I now do, that *all* singing is bel canto.' (This is a view with which Placido Domingo, for one, is known to agree wholeheartedly.) 'I sing Wagner exactly as I sing Norma. There is no difference. A technique is a technique and you shouldn't change it according to what music you are singing. There is *supposed* to be an Italian and a German way of singing but I don't believe that's true. I think there's just singing, full stop. You must sing whatever you happen to be singing as beautifully as you can. Wagner, for instance, is known to have admired Bellini. He wrote: "What enchanted us in Bellini was the pure melody, the nobility and beauty of song. Surely it cannot be a sin to assert and believe that. Perhaps it's not even a sin if, before retiring to rest, one offers Heaven a prayer that some day it may occur to German composers to write such melodies and to acquire such a manner of treating song. Song, song, and again, song."'

Eaglen found it interesting that when she sang Wagner in Italy, people went up to her afterwards and said that it wasn't 'as horrible as we thought it was.' 'Of course Germans are taught slightly differently and think that this is their heritage and, as such, sacrosanct, while Italians think of their music as *their* heritage, and equally sacrosanct. Few Italian singers have had an international career in Wagner, and few Germans in Italian opera. I mean, no Italian singer will *touch* Wagner, although there are some voices there who could sing it extremely well.[1] But we English singers are very lucky. We don't have an operatic heritage of our own to compel us to sing this or that repertoire.

[1] Barbara Frittoli expresses the desire to sing Elsa in her chapter.

'Although there is no difference in the technique, there *is* a difference in the style of singing and I believe that the Italian way, which is to say bel canto, is the right way of singing for *all* music. It's safer, more beautiful and technically better for the voice. Why? Because the voice is never slammed, there are no sudden jolts, there is a long legato style with very long phrases, and if you sing that properly, you'll never do yourself any harm. But if you sing Wagner and start slamming the voice – which is different from pushing – and thinking you have to hit a note in a certain way, then you will damage your voice because the chords were not made to be slammed around but to be *caressed* gently. So, if you approach those notes in the same way as you would in the Italian repertoire [as Domingo does, to such wondrous effect, in Wagner], then it is much healthier for the voice . . .'

Of course, Eaglen acknowledges that people are taught in many different ways and that there are equally many ways of conveying the same aims. She considers teaching singing to be very different from teaching a pianist, where the teacher can suggest where the pupil should place his hands. When faced with a singing student, a teacher can probably tell if a problem is due to the breathing, or to tension in the throat. 'But there is a lot going on inside a singer's body, to say nothing of mental blocks, that a teacher cannot see. So, it's *vital* to find a teacher who understands you and is on the same wavelength. But although there may be many different ways of singing, a good technique is the be-all and end-all. It's what allows the voice to do what you want it to, whether it's a *pianissimo*, a high B flat *pianissimo* or whatever. It should be so secure that you don't even have to think about it. It's also your only refuge on those nights when you are ill and below par.'

Ward began by teaching Eaglen to sing parts of 'Casta diva' and Brünnhilde. He told her: 'This is the repertoire you will eventually sing, so you might as well start learning the style right away. This way, when the high notes come, you will be ready.' So they did bits of Norma, minus high notes, which she didn't yet possess instead of 'wasting my time learning Susanna'. The high notes were the last thing to come, 'which I suppose is as it should be for a dramatic soprano, who has first to develop a very solid middle. But simply by waiting, they finally did come. It was when I was in my late twenties, about ten years after starting to work with my teacher, and at least six years after I started singing professionally at the age of twenty-two. It's not that I didn't have the notes before – I did. But they didn't sound like the rest of my voice. There was never a question that I was going to *miss* them, but rather of making the voice all-of-a-piece throughout the range. Yet the voice was not yet ready to do it. So, rather than push it, which is what some of the young big voices do – because having a big middle voice they think they should sound the same at the top – I decided to trust my teacher. He was convinced that my physical strength would carry the middle voice upwards and make it seamless. It was just a question of being patient. So we waited, and worked and worked and worked.'

Eaglen began her professional career in 1984 as Lady Ella in Gilbert and Sullivan's *Patience*, having left the RNCM a year before the end of her postgraduate course to join the ENO as a company member. She remained with the company for six years, singing Elizabeth I in *Mary Stuart* (the English version of Donizetti's opera, Sinaïde in Rossini's *Moses*, Leonora in *Il trovatore*, Santuzza and Donna Elvira. In 1991 she returned to sing Donna Anna and in 1994 the title role in *Ariadne auf Naxos*.

It was while performing Tosca at Perth that Eaglen sang her first high C that sounded like the rest of her voice. 'I thought, oh my God, what's that? Of course, this didn't then happen every time I had to sing a high C, but it did more and more often. To be honest, making the voice seamless throughout its entire range takes a lot of physical strength. Not stamina, but sheer physical strength. The strength to use your muscles, and the diaphragm and the rest of the body in the right way – never the throat. There must never be an inkling of tension in the throat. I very much use all my body to sing. I use my legs, bottom, everything. So the whole body was ready by then: the cords were ready, the voice was ready and the muscles were ready. A voice should always be like that – seamless, like a column of sound. But this just took time. It came through Joe's teaching and my being patient.'

Meanwhile, in addition to her ENO roles, Eaglen was performing Fiordiligi and the title role in *Madama Butterfly* in Australia, as well as many other roles which helped her find out what suited her. 'I think it's good to start off with a wide range of roles and gradually file it down to a handful that fit you like a glove, abandoning the ones that don't.'

Very important for her vocal development was Elizabeth I in *Mary Stuart* at the ENO in 1986, which obliged her to work hard on her coloratura, something that did not come naturally to her. When her teacher had asked her to sing a Handel aria back at the RNCM she had looked at it and exclaimed, 'I can't do *that*!' He calmly replied that she *had* to learn it. 'So, quite literally, I locked myself in a practice room for two weeks and learnt how to sing coloratura! It's as simple as that. The aria in question was a quite nice but obscure piece with not too much coloratura, just enough for you to have to work at it. Now, there are some light lyric voices which are naturally suited to coloratura. But most of us are not, we have to work at it. *Any* voice can develop coloratura. In fact *any* voice should be able to do *anything*. I firmly believe this. Obviously, you wouldn't like to hear me sing Susanna or a lighter voice singing Turandot. But all of us should be able to sing the notes, in our way, with our own voice, without pushing or forcing. So, coloratura is something any voice can learn to do. People who tell you otherwise are talking rubbish! All you have to do, as my teacher said, is lock yourself in a room, throw away the key, keep at it and, sure enough, it will come. There's no secret. Just start with it very slowly and gradually increase the speed.

'A key factor in coloratura is placement. You have to keep the line in one place. So you find a level in a phrase and then everything – the ornamentation – comes either above or below that level, which never changes. I have no idea how singers can sing coloratura when they're moving their mouth all the time, but it works for them. Cecilia Bartoli is a wonderful singer and her coloratura is really *exciting*. But I really don't know how she does it. So the bottom line must be that everybody does it differently, and if it works for her, and it certainly *does*, it's fine.'

Eaglen was fully aware that it was much too early for her to tackle a role such as Elizabeth I, but although it was her first bel canto part, she had a very good experience with it. She explains that this is to some extent true of all the roles a singer tackles for the first time. 'There is something very nice about the naïveté of doing something for the first time. You can bring a freshness to it that you don't get later on. That's true of all the things I sang at that time.'

Leonora in *Il trovatore* also taught her a very important lesson: that she would never have to worry about stamina because she possesses a seemingly unlimited reservoir of both physical and mental energy. 'I remember thinking before the opening night that I would have to sing "Tacea la notte placida" near the beginning of the opera and "D'amore sull 'ali rosee", nearly two and a half hours later, and that I should try to make sure I didn't run out of stamina. So I told myself to take it relatively easy at the beginning so as not to be too tired at the end. Well, I needn't have worried. When I got to the end of the opera, I felt I could start all over again! So stamina was clearly not a problem for me. And that's something you cannot learn through rehearsals. You've got to *do* it. It was a very good lesson to learn so young because one of the things people always worry about in Wagner, for instance, is the length and how to make it to the end.'

From the dramatic point of view, she didn't particularly enjoy portraying Leonora. She finds most Verdi heroines 'a bit weak', and so chooses not to do them. 'Leonora taking poison from her ring because she cannot face giving herself to Luna, for instance. I mean, I wouldn't do that sort of thing. That's not to say an actress or singer shouldn't do things on stage that she wouldn't do in real life. I wouldn't kill my children, either. Yet I can establish an imaginative link with Norma that I cannot with Leonora, or with most Verdi heroines. They don't go particularly well with my voice, my dramatic and even my physical personality.'

Eaglen, who ceased to be a member of the ENO in 1990, is now lucky enough to be able to choose what she wants to sing. 'I think that if you're in that position, it's nice to choose something that fits you like a glove vocally, dramatically and physically. Then everything can come together in a way that makes you feel you have an intrinsic link with the character. And this is the kind of role I am interested in singing from now on: Norma, Turandot, the three Brünnhildes and, coming soon, my first Gioconda and Isolde.[1] The only role from my earlier repertoire that I will retain is Donna Anna.'

'Is Mozart very good for the voice? Yes, but you have to be in total control. Intonation, purity of sound, everything has to be perfect in Mozart, and in this sense I don't think he is particularly good for young singers because he demands a little bit too much. He demands accuracy in *everything*. Mind you, I think everything should be sung with total accuracy. When you listen to a lot of Wagnerian singing, you often hear singing that is *really* out of tune. So what it boils down to is finding the right style for every composer, which doesn't come until you've worked at the music for a while and explored it. If you do what's on the page and sing as the composer has written, the style comes through. But it's very hard either to define or teach it. Of course, your understanding deepens as you get more experienced.'

For instance, she points out that Wagner wrote trills for Brünnhilde in all three *Ring* operas. Although one seldom hears them, she considers that if Wagner wrote trills, 'it means that he expected the kind of voice that can do this – a voice that can move fast. I feel very strongly that if you have the ability to sing coloratura, then you are in control of your voice rather than your voice being in control of you. And if you have this control, then you can sing Wagner as he wanted you to sing his music, so that it is not all relentlessly loud. If there's a

[1] Eaglen sang her first Isolde in Seattle in August 1998.

pianissimo written you can do it and if there is a trill, you can manage that too. Yet I was once stopped outside the theatre in Chicago after a performance of *Siegfried* by someone who said: "Excuse me, I have a question for you. Why did you put a trill into Brünnhilde's music?" I replied: "I didn't, Wagner did!" And he said he had never heard of this before and didn't believe me. But I happened to have my score with me, so I was able to show him.'

It was at Scottish Opera that Eaglen had her first opportunity to sing Wagner, as Brünnhilde in Richard Jones's production of *Die Walküre*. The company originally asked if she would cover the part, although they hadn't yet hired a soprano. Eaglen asked her teacher's advice, and he replied that he thought she was ready to *sing* the part, not just cover it. So she reported her teacher's opinion to the company, which agreed to take her. As the company couldn't afford a wig, and she had long hair at the time, she had to die her hair red!

Eaglen felt right away that Wagner fitted her perfectly: 'His characters suit not only my voice, but also my musicianship and personality. When singing Wagner, I consciously feel it's a privilege to do so. It's just *right* for me, and if something's right, you just *know* it. Right now, there is no character I'd rather sing than Brünnhilde. Of course, learning it for the first time was difficult, because it is difficult music, with all those intervals.'

Eaglen sang her first complete *Ring* cycle at the Lyric Opera of Chicago in 1996; she sang it again in Vienna a year later, and is booked to sing it at the Metropolitan in 2000. She is fascinated by the 'staggering' growth that Brünnhilde undergoes during the three operas. She matures from a carefree teenage goddess to a woman who samples the entire gamut of emotion, from love's ecstasy to deepest despair, betrayal and humiliation, and who finally achieves an understanding of the world and of her own role.

Vocally, the easiest is *Die Walküre* which, apart from the initial 'Hojotohos', lies in the middle of the voice. 'In fact it's quite low. We first encounter Brünnhilde as a very happy, young, carefree and naive girl riding into battle and bringing back heroes to her daddy, whose favourite she is, and life is bliss. But then it all comes crashing down on her. She is intelligent and listens to everything very carefully and draws her own conclusions, learning as she goes along. In Act II, she hears all that's happening in the world from Wotan's monologue and is intelligent enough to intuit what he wants. And when she comes face to face with Siegmund and he refuses to ride to Valhalla with her, she finds his reaction surprising. But she understands and learns from this, too. I particularly enjoy playing this scene, which I find very interesting, because it's possible to vary it from performance to performance – the sure mark of a great piece.

'*Siegfried* [which she first sang in 1995 in Chicago] is basically a long duet. Again, it's a learning experience, but of a different kind because Brünnhilde has to learn how to be a mortal woman. At the beginning this feels very strange – "I don't know that I like this, you'd better go you'd better go" – a bit like Turandot. I always think that the *Siegfried* Brünnhilde and Turandot are very similar characters, because I don't think Turandot is really nasty, just a misguided young girl who's scared. And the *Siegfried* Brünnhilde is the same. Vocally this Brünnhilde is certainly not easy. It is very, very high, and requires a lot of control as well as a radiant sound. Actually the worst thing about it is having to lie there on your rock for a good ten minutes before you have to sing. I remember a rehearsal at the Vienna State Opera when I actually fell asleep! It was such a comfortable set that I really nodded off and then suddenly heard the tenor singing "Dass ist kein Mann" and thought "My God!" and woke up with a start!'

'*Götterdämmerung* is definitely the most satisfying of them all, it's where the whole *Ring* comes together. And it gets more and more dramatic as it goes on. Act II is quite a big sing, but at the same time, it's wonderful to sing. Brünnhilde is vengeful, like Norma, and with equally good reason. She sees what has been, and is, happening and realizes that it's up to her to put everything right. There is a moment in *Die Walküre* when Wotan asks, "Where is the hero who is going to save everything", thinking it will be Siegmund or Siegfried. But, at the Immolation Scene, Brünnhilde understands that now things have come full circle. She's the only one who can do what must be done, what her father talked about all those years ago. It's really extraordinary. I know it sounds an awful thing to say, but I don't find it at all difficult, not any of it. I find *other* things difficult, I find Norma difficult, but not Brünnhilde.

'What *is* challenging is to communicate the essence of what's going on in Brünnhilde's mind at the Immolation Scene, the first half of which is very introspective. She's going over everything that's happened in the past, realizing her own part in it and what she has to do. And this is how I play it up to this point, very quietly and introspectively. I know that some reviewers have commented that, apart from the last quarter, my interpretation of the Immolation Scene is boring, while others wrote that for the first time they understood what this scene is really about. This is something about which I have thought long and hard, and have concluded that you have to put across every thought racing through Brünnhilde's mind. But in order to express them vocally, you have to be very clear about them in your own mind. I am not consciously trying to make the audience understand them, but to make *myself*, as Brünnhilde, understand them. Because if I do, then it will come out right. But although *Götterdämmerung* is definitely the most challenging of the *Ring* operas, it's really an incredibly satisfying thing to sing, such fun! I *love* it. But it is a very long evening – you are already in make-up by two o'clock in the afternoon and you finish at about eleven-thirty at night. *Siegfried* is nothing in comparison! I remember that when I sang it at La Scala I had dinner with the understudies at seven o'clock, usually some pasta, went home, had a shower, warmed up and turned up again at the theatre at ten, full of beans and ready to go!'

Eaglen points out that when she sang her first complete *Ring* in Chicago, she was also singing her first ever *Götterdämmerung*, a daunting experience. 'There's just so *much* of it – would I remember it all?' She had one stage rehearsal with a staff producer and one orchestral rehearsal! The only way to come through was by finding that thin dividing line between abandon and control, a subject on which Eaglen has very strong views.

'I don't believe a singer should *ever* give one hundred per cent of their voice. I never have. I think it's safer to hold something in reserve, rather than push yourself to your limits. I also think it's more exciting for the audience not to feel shortchanged, but rather confident that the singer is firmly in control of what they're doing, that they're not giving themselves over to the role to such an extent that they can't control what's going to happen next, vocally.[1] But if they feel the singer is in control and could give even more, now that's exciting. It's not a question of holding back emotionally but of being in control technically. And if you give one hundred per cent you're not. You're on the edge, and that's not a place I want to be, vocally. I want to feel that if someone were to say "I could kill you if you didn't make more noise", I probably *could*. That's the position I like to be in at *any* performance of *any* role.' The only danger in having too much control at the expense of abandon is that performances sometimes risk being devoid of a certain ecstatic dimension. I can recall a performance of Eaglen's in the Verdi *Requiem* with the Philharmonia in 1995, for instance, which although vocally impeccable nevertheless lacked mystery and awe.

Although Eaglen doesn't fret about her voice, she knows just how precious it is. A few years ago she had a very dangerous operation to remove a tumour from her thyroid, which was tricky as the two nerves linked to the vocal cords lie very close. She was not supposed to talk or produce any sound at all for several days after the operation. Yet, so fine-tuned is she to the *sensation* of her voice, that she instantly knew it felt right and scribbled 'it's fine' on a piece of paper for the doctor. All the more reason to treasure it and to hold to her decision never to tackle any role until she feels absolutely ready.

By 1993, Eaglen felt ready to sing Norma, at Scottish Opera in a

---

[1] Dame Josephine Barstow expressed an identical view in *Diva I*.

production by Ian Judge, one of the most gifted and imaginative direc-
tors in opera today and one of the few who have made the leap from
straight theatre so successfully. She had already covered the role at
Covent Garden in 1989, when Margaret Price sang it. But although
Dame Margaret cancelled one performance, the conductor, John
Pritchard, was reluctant to put her on because he thought she would
'freak out' at the prospect of singing her first Norma at Covent
Garden. 'Little did he know me! I would have *relished* the experience.
As, I already explained, I don't ever suffer from nerves. Being a typical
Aries, I tend to thrive on challenges. I also love playing anger,
vengeance and such emotions on stage.

  'Norma is a classic role for that, and a terribly interesting character: a woman who is not seen by her people very often. So there are
two distinct sides of her, the public and the private. There is the
"Casta diva" side, the hieratic side, when she is performing the sacred
rites and leading her people to war. Then there is the private side, the
woman at home, who has found out that the father of her children is
having an affair with another priestess. Ian Judge and I had a long
time to prepare my first Norma and we really found the Norma that
was right for me: 'a very, very strong woman who has the sort of
vengeful nature which, in the circumstances, I can fully understand. If
someone's done you wrong, you want to pay them back. She is also a
very noble and dignified woman. What makes her really great is that
in the end she can't go through with her revenge – unlike Medea, who
goes the whole way. Norma examines who she really is, admits her
own weakness and is willing to sacrifice herself. Of course, she does
get a vengeance of sorts, because by the end everybody knows what
she has been through. What it must have been like to hide her children
for six years and carry on with her public role as High Priestess –
having to live a lie – and how she has been wronged. But she did that
for the sake of her people, who were used to looking to her for leadership and whom she didn't want to let down. Parallel to this noble
side, there is the ferocious side, that we see at the end of Act I.'

After the success of her Norma at Scottish Opera, in 1994 Eaglen was asked to sing and record the role live (for EMI) right in the lion's den: the Ravenna Festival in Italy, where *Norma* is regarded with the sort of awe reserved by the British for *Hamlet*. In fact the opera has been performed very seldom since the death of Maria Callas, Norma's supreme and unforgettable interpreter. One of the few times was under Muti at the Maggio Musicale Fiorentino in the late 1970s with Renata Scotto. So even Eaglen, despite her proverbial cool, admits to finding the experience nerve-racking and a real challenge: 'But I thought, heck, I'll do it *my* way and people will either like it or hate it. That's fine by me.'

She also found it amusing to observe people's 'holier-than-thou' attitudes at rehearsals: 'If I moved across the stage fast because at that point I was angry with Adalgisa for having it off with my lover, they would say: "Oh, you can't do that! This is Norma. You have to be very dignified!" But I replied: "This is Norma *in her own home*, and really angry, as she has every right to be." At which point Muti walked into the rehearsal and said, "This is great, I like this tigress character!"'

'From the vocal point of view, the most difficult thing is "Casta diva" because, like Radames's "Celeste Aida", it comes right at the very beginning of the opera, virtually the moment you walk on stage. It is also so well known and loved that you have to sing it perfectly, or else . . . It would be difficult for your performance to survive an in-adequately sung "Casta diva". The only thing you have to warm up with is the recitative that immediately precedes it, but that's very brief. You move on to the cavatina very quickly, and this is so still, serene and just plain beautiful it can make you feel unworthy of singing it. Every note needs to be perfect. When I first started learning it, I told my teacher that I simply couldn't get to grips with it. He said this was nonsense and of course he was right: feeling this way about it simply won't do. You just have to sing the notes. And when you relax and do just that, you find that (a), it finally becomes quite easy and (b), it sounds like it's supposed to sound. When all is said and done, it *is* just notes and so beautifully written that if you sing what Bellini wrote it comes out the way he wanted it to sound, anyway. And that's true of all great composers. If you do what they ask for, you're fine. It's when you start playing around with it that you run into trouble.'

Eaglen sang Norma again at the Paris Opéra in April 1998, after singing the role in Scotland, Ravenna, La Scala (again with Muti), Vienna, Los Angeles, Seattle and at Carnegie Hall in 1995, when the *New York Times* wrote: 'Hers was a Norma whose vocal weight and power would have been unimaginable to Bellini and yet a Norma whose sinuous control and musical wisdom might have impressed him.'

Interestingly, the only other singer to attempt to sing both Bellini and Wagner was Callas. In the 1940s, she sang a lot of Wagner in Italian, alongside her bel canto repertoire. Callas eventually dropped Wagner to concentrate on the Italian repertoire. Whether the day will come when Eaglen – who in her mid-30s is one of the youngest Brünnhildes around – decides that she too has to choose remains to be seen. In such an eventuality, one suspects her choice will be Wagner.

In 2000 Eaglen will make her Covent Garden début in the title role of *Turandot*, a part she sang with great success opposite Pavarotti's Calaf at the Metropolitan Opera in 1997.[1] As far as future repertoire is concerned, Eaglen would like to take on another big bel canto part, probably the title role in *Medea*. She also has her eyes on Gluck's *Alceste* and Leonora in *Fidelio*. But before that, two more big parts are planned for the 1998–9 season: the title role in Ponchielli's *La Gioconda* at the Lyric Opera of Chicago after her first Isolde, at the Seattle Opera in August 1998 with Ben Heppner with whom (being computer mad and never without her laptop) she has been in contact for months. She will then sing Isolde at the Lyric Opera of Chicago. In 2002, she will sing

[1] When Eaglen's whole family attended *Turandot* at the Met, she thought she would try the three riddles on them the night before. Her mother's answer to the second – 'What burns like a flame but is not a flame – has already earned its place in any thesaurus of operatic anecdotes: 'Is it mustard?'

Isolde again at the Metropolitan in a new production mounted especially for her.

Eaglen's success in America is fortunate in more ways than one. She adores the country and everything about it, including the fact that 'they really love and know how to treat their singers there'. Soon she hopes to buy a flat in New York – at present home is a terraced house in St Albans – where she can indulge in her passion for watching American wrestling, 'a real stress buster', at Madison Square Garden. She finds wrestling 'a little bit like opera: it's extremely colourful, over the top and full of outrageous characters!'

RENÉE
FLEMING

'I'M IN THE middle of a French phase right now. I adore French music, I adore being in France and singing here in Paris', declares the delectable American soprano Renée Fleming, currently one of the hottest properties in opera. And with good reason. She possesses one of the most beautiful, sensuous lyric voices of our day: rich and creamy, with an easy bloom at the top and an unusually opulent middle. Its velvety texture and honeyed timbre have caused some critics to compare her to Dame Kiri Te Kanawa, while the 'smoky' colours she can conjure up remind others of Leontyne Price. In fact, the timbre and colour of Fleming's voice are as unique and personal as her choice of repertoire, which is varied enough to defy obvious classifications.

While largely centred on Mozart (the Countess, Fiordiligi, Donna Anna and Donna Elvira) and Strauss (the Marschallin, Arabella, with *Capriccio* and *Daphne* on the way), her repertoire also includes an increasing number of French parts: Marguerite in Gounod's *Faust*, three Massenet heroines (Salomé in *Hérodiade* and the title roles in *Thaïs* and *Manon*) and Charpentier's *Louise*. One of her calling cards is the title role of Dvořák's *Rusalka*, and she has also ventured into the Wagnerian repertoire with Eva in *Die Meistersinger*. A vigorous champion of contemporary American operas, she has performed Rosina in John Corigliano's *The Ghosts of Versailles*, Madame de Tourvel in Conrad Susa's *Dangerous Liaisons*, the title role in Carlisle Floyd's *Susannah* and Blanche Dubois in André Previn's setting of the famous Tennessee Williams play *A Streetcar Named Desire*. As her choice of repertoire indicates, Fleming enjoys being stretched. But she is totally lucid about what is good for her and what *she* is good for. She knows that, apart from plangent heroines such as Amelia Grimaldi and Desdemona, there are practically no Verdi roles for her and no *verismo*, either[1]. 'Obviously the colour of the voice is as relevant to one's choice of repertoire as its range,' she says. 'I could, technically, sing Mimì without any problems. But I don't have the right colour for the role. The real Italian sound has a "ping" to it that's missing from my voice.' There is, however, plenty of scope for her in bel canto – as her recording and highly successful performances of Rossini's *Armida* at Pesaro and Carnegie Hall indicate. At the time of our encounter she was looking forward to singing the title role in Donizetti's *Lucrezia Borgia* at La Scala in July 1998, and another famous coloratura part, Handel's Alcina, in Paris under William Christie.

Paris was where, shortly before Christmas 1997, I met and talked to Renée Fleming. The pressure on her time is such that the only possible opportunity was immediately after a performance at the Opéra Bastille of *Der Rosenkavalier* (a production also referred to in the chapters on Barbara Bonney and Susan Graham). With (metaphorically speaking) the Marschallin still in her body, she quickly changed out of her costume and we settled down on the shocking pink sofa of her 'star' dressing room. Her power to concentrate on the task at hand and switch off anything extraneous is impressive. She struck me as a charming, intelligent and, I think, a deeply *good* woman, with a profound, reflective nature. As far as the profession is concerned, a hard worker and, fortunately, a very quick learner!

[1] Interestingly, as this book went to press it was announced that Fleming was to replace Angela Gheorghiu as Violetta at the Met.

She explains that the Marschallin (which she first sang in 1995 at the Houston Grand Opera under Christoph Eschenbach) is a very comfortable role. 'Vocally, it lies very much in the middle. It's not stressful, it's not virtuosic, in fact it's not really about singing. It's much more about acting, character and interpretation. The only vocal challenge lies precisely in the fact that, lying as it does in the middle, it sometimes makes it difficult to project the voice over the dense orchestration. High notes are always easier to project.

'The role is also comfortable from the dramatic point of view because she is so rich, so complex. She is a realistic woman, a very modern woman and a timeless character in the sense that all the things she talks about are timeless. That's why people love her so much, I think. She expresses the human condition from a particularly female perspective, as well as any character in opera. It's fascinating that these two men, Hofmannsthal and Strauss, knew so much about the female psyche and its concerns – worrying about the passage of time and so on. I find it very interesting to play her now, when I'm close to her real age – I'm thirty-eight and she's supposed to be thirty-two. But I could just as well have sung the part a decade ago because in today's culture, both European and American, her kind of problems begin to worry women as early as their late twenties! We are such youth worshippers, we worship young women. But on the other hand, women now live longer and stay younger longer than ever before. So I hope that this trend will change and that we'll begin to celebrate the fact that women in their forties, fifties and beyond can be wonderful . . . The other marvellous thing about this role is that, as far as characterization is concerned, I don't have to make anything up. It's all there in the score, and all I need to do is follow it.'

While discussing the Marschallin dramatically, it is worth mentioning an important detail which was missing from this production. It is clearly indicated in the score and it is a crucial help to the singer in understanding the reason for the Marschallin's change of mood in the second half of Act I. Herbert von Karajan always explained to his

Marschallins that the change lies in the moment Ochs shows her a miniature of Sophie, his bride-to-be, when he asks her to find a rose bearer. At that moment, Karajan insisted, 'something in the music is crying', and that's when the tragedy begins. The Marschallin, a highly intuitive woman, senses the threat from a young girl and *that's* why she begins to feel old and ugly – not because the hairdresser makes a mistake with her coiffure.

Fleming, who had not been shown the miniature in the Houston production either – in fact it was Barbara Bonney who first told her that she should be shown one at that moment – feels that this is, indeed, the key to the second half of the act: 'I always wondered what triggers off this mood swing and her reactions for the rest of the act. But I had to work it out for myself. For there *has* to be a transition as the opera begins so lightheartedly. And the clue was there, all the time . . . 'But however clearly the Marschallin may be delineated in the score and libretto, she is still such a rich and varied character that one can play her in many different ways. I'm sure that, ten years from now, my Marschallin will be different, because *I'll* be different. More than any other operatic heroine, she really does reflect the person singing her. This is why sopranos love singing her throughout their careers. One can never get bored with her. I look forward to singing her for a long time to come and to digging deeper each time.'

Before moving on to other operatic characters, it seemed worthwhile to dwell on a vocal point Fleming raised earlier: the fact that roles such as this, which lie largely in the middle of the voice, are always more comfortable for her, even though, as anyone who has seen her perform or listened to her recordings knows, she has effortless, ringing high notes.

'Parts with a tessitura hovering around the middle are always more comfortable for me. High notes are no problem, but the *overall* tessitura is the key to how comfortable a part is. If I'm dealing with a role that is consistently high, then I won't find it comfortable. The three Massenet ladies I have sung – Salomé in *Hérodiade*, Thaïs and Manon – all have plenty of high notes. But overall, they are middle-weight voices. So I find them very comfortable. The voice can sit on that solid middle and climb up to the high notes in a relaxed way that doesn't leave you breathless. Rossini's Armida is another good example. Like all the roles he wrote for his wife, Isabella Colbran, it has a very low, almost mezzo-soprano tessitura. But because it's so florid, again like all the roles he wrote for her, it never feels heavy or weighs down the voice, which it would if it were not florid. You see, singing well boils down to two factors: knowing, *really* knowing your voice, and having a technique that enables you to be in control of it.'

Fleming discovered her voice very early. In fact, as both her parents were high school music teachers in their home town of Rochester, New York, she had little choice in the matter. 'For the first two years of my life I sat in a playpen next to my mother as she gave voice lessons. You can't imagine what that does for a child's musical ear, brain, everything. When I got older, my parents discussed singing every night over the dinner table . . . I had a tremendous musical education,' she recalls. Her mother, she says, had 'all the characteristics of a traditional stage mother', and was determined that her daughter should fulfil her vocal potential. Much to the child's resentment, she was pushed into performing at school and local functions with reluctant acquiescence – and precious little joy. 'It was like cleaning my room. It was a chore. I hated it,' she said in an interview in *Opera Now*. She was a sullen and withdrawn kid whom everybody called 'stone face' because she never let on that she enjoyed anything. 'And I didn't. I spent my entire childhood wanting not to be me. I envied the free spirits who were popular, smoked in the bathroom, wore nylons and fought for what they wanted.' Her only solace was her books, in which she could bury herself for hours on end. 'I just read, read all the time and sort of lived in a fantasy world. But I think this turned out to my advantage in the end because in acting the most important quality is imagination, the ability to recognize immediately what the characters are experiencing.'

It wasn't until she was on a graduate course in performance at the

Eastman School of Music, having first obtained a degree in musical education from the State University of New York at Potsdam, that she came into her own. She just woke up one day and realized that, so far, she had never made any decisions for herself. 'I didn't know why I was there. I didn't even know what I wanted for lunch.' This realization jolted her into a determination to take control of her life, 'seize the moment and set my own goals. For the first time I became ambitious for myself,' and she threw herself into her training. 'Eastman School was a wonderful academic school which gave me more integrity as a musician than most conservatoires do. I felt better prepared to do the kind of research which I think is important. 'It's not just singing, it's total performance,' she told *Opera News*. After graduating from Eastman School she won a place at the American Opera Center at the Juilliard, where she met her future husband, actor Rick Ross, and the voice teacher Beverley Johnson. She still studies with Johnson, and credits her teacher with helping her unleash her full potential.

She feels that being married to an actor is a great help because it makes her 'live and breathe' theatre. She usually visits the theatre two or three times a week when her schedule permits. Another lasting passion she discovered and developed at this time was jazz. 'I just loved jazz singing and sang with a trio or a band almost every weekend and even recorded.' She still listens to a lot of jazz – in fact apart from the operatic recordings she listens to for the purpose of learning roles, she listens *only* to jazz. She feels that the ability to improvise that she learnt and practised as a jazz singer has proved extremely useful to her in opera, especially in the bel canto repertoire where embellishing is part of the art of the genre.

After a year at the Juilliard she won a Fulbright Scholarship for a year's study in Germany, where she mostly had a marvellous time, studying with the late Arleen Auger and with Helmut Holl. She also attended a 'discouraging' masterclass given by Elisabeth Schwarzkopf which had a negative effect on her self-esteem. She still doesn't like to talk about the experience, limiting herself to a recommendation that it is better for young singers to watch, rather than participate, in famous singers' masterclasses. While still in Europe, she made an unsuccessful début as Constanze at the Landestheater in Salzburg in 1986. 'Basically it taught me that I didn't know how to sing. Mind you, Constanze would do that to any beginner.'

So she headed for home and spent a frustrating, dispiriting year when nothing seemed to go right. She still had vocal problems, and after the combined debacles of the Schwarzkopf masterclass and her Salzburg début, her self-confidence was so shattered that she even imagined problems she didn't have. Consequently she didn't audition well and thus failed to get into the sort of programmes that can provide young singers with experience and serve as useful stepping-stones to better things.

Beverley Johnson, with whom Fleming resumed her studies, realized that before this pupil could begin to fulfil her musical potential, she would have to sort out her psychological problems. She therefore recommended a lady therapist who dealt with 'self-esteem issues', the kind of complexes that underlay Fleming's stage-fright. The therapist pointed out that Fleming was visualizing audiences and judges as negative, and managed to convince her that 'even in an audition, people don't want you to fail. They want to hear someone great'. The gradual improvement in Fleming's outlook bore fruit. A year later, in 1988, she won the Metropolitan Opera's national auditions and the George London Prize in the same week, and was soon hired as a company member by the Houston Opera. The fact that she had demons to exorcise adds depth and understanding to her interpretations.

Shortly after joining the Houston Opera, Fleming had her first big professional break when she replaced a sick colleague as the Countess in a production of *Le nozze di Figaro*. So great was her success that the part soon became her calling card: she was asked to sing the role in no less than six productions in one year. The fact that her Houston début came at the time that international opera houses were planning their productions for the 1991 Mozart Bicentennial was providential! She made her début as the Countess at San Francisco (1991), the Metropolitan (1991), the Vienna State Opera (1993), Geneva (1993) and the Glyndebourne Festival Opera, for the opening of the new theatre in 1994. Yet, she hastens to add, this was purely 'circumstantial', and that left to her own devices she would never choose the Countess as a 'signature role'.

'In fact, it is quite a difficult role for me. Both her arias are a challenge. They are not as graceful as Donna Anna's are in *Don Giovanni*. To begin with, they are lower. You don't get to go up to any real high notes. Secondly, they are very exposed, especially "Dove sono" with its cadenza, which lies right on the passaggio, a very difficult part of my voice. And it goes on for so long without a break that one yearns for it to be over! "Porgi, Amor" is not quite as exposed. Many of its phrases are broken up by orchestral passages, and there is no sustained signing on the passaggio.

Yet Fleming, who nevertheless included both these arias in her solo album, was looking forward to singing the Countess again at the Lyric Opera of Chicago in February 1998 under Zubin Mehta. 'I suspect I may find myself in a whole new situation, because what I was really doing in those first years was wanting to sing Susanna, and even to *be* Susanna, if you if you know what I mean. Now I'm a little older and more mature and have my own children. I have a feeling that I'm going to feel perfectly at home with the Countess and her particular brand of poise and serenity, which I used to find disappointing. I suspect I will enjoy it much more now.' In the event, her performances turned out to be of vintage quality. 'Fleming conveys nothing less than the moral centre of the characters she plays. In her despairing aria, "Dove sono", the Countess was not simply mourning her husband's infidelities. Singing Mozart's slow, sad melody in hushed tones, she seemed to be talking to herself, exploring her soul in order to calm her grief,' wrote the Chicago *Sun-Times*.

Fiordiligi however, which one might imagine to be a far more challenging role, Fleming doesn't find as hard as the Countess. 'On the contrary! I find it much easier. In fact, I adore singing Fiordiligi. What I love most about her is the contrast between the ensemble singing, which is very high and relatively light, and the two arias which are lower but very, very florid – which, as I mentioned a propos of Armida, stops them from pulling the voice down – and great fun. It is challenging part *physically* from the point of view of stamina, because it's very long. But vocally it never frightens me. Dramatically, I find the whole plot of *Così* – the entire masquerade and the fact that they don't recognize their original lovers – very hard to swallow. But this is a case where one has to suspend disbelief and let the music, so intriguingly ambiguous, tell the story.'

In 1994, Fleming sang Fiordiligi in a concert performance at the Festival Hall in London under Sir Georg Solti, which was recorded live. The recording, released in 1996, and the subsequent artistic collaboration with Solti on several projects changed the course of her career, propelling it into top gear. Yet, as is often the case with events that become turning points in people's lives, it happened more or less by chance. Fleming was a last-minute replacement for another soprano and Solti didn't know her at all. But, after being given a tape of Fleming's Metropolitan Opera performances as the Countess, he professed himself flabbergasted. Fleming, who arrived at rehearsals straight off the plane, 'jet-lagged and feeling a wreck', was extremely nervous. But the two hit it off at once and she soon became Solti's 'last musical romance', according to Lady Solti. Under Solti's influence, Fleming signed an exclusive contract with Decca, for whom he himself recorded, and he took the unusual step of accompanying her solo album, *Great Opera Scenes* – an honour very seldom bestowed on a singer by a conductor of his stature.

Fleming's London appearances as Fiordiligi consolidated her reputation in Britain, already established earlier that year by her appearance at Glyndebourne and, a year before that, as Amelia Grimaldi at Covent Garden. Her London début, in 1990 in Covent Garden's dismal production of Cherubini's *Médée*, had been a non-occasion, and her subsequent portrayal of the Contessa di Foleville in their inane staging of Rossini's *Il viaggio a Reims* was equally lacklustre.

Solti chose Fleming to be his Donna Anna in a gala concert performance of *Don Giovanni* for the reopening of the Palais Garnier in 1996, a very big event for the French capital. In autumn 1996 they performed it again at the London's Festival Hall, where it was recorded live. To anyone who has heard Fleming's superb portrayal of Donna Anna, it will come as no surprise to learn that it is her favourite Mozart role. 'Donna Anna is the Mozart role I want to go on singing the most because she is very interesting. The enigma of her situation fascinates me. I know the whole of *Don Giovanni* well because I sang Zerlina in my student days and I still sing Donna Elvira. It is an opera that can be staged in many different ways because Don Giovanni himself is not a particular person. He is a myth onto which people project their own fantasies, which is why any production of this opera is totally governed by the charisma of the person singing the Don. It doesn't matter how well he *sings* it. If he doesn't have that, it doesn't work. It's not even about looks as such, but about real charisma, something more intangible and visceral.'

She finds Donna Anna rewarding to sing and intriguing to portray. 'When you examine her recitatives they are so full of *passion* and the music is so dramatic, especially in the accompanied recit before "Or sai chi l'onore", which is amazing, the real tour de force of the role, in fact. When I sing Donna Elvira, who is supposed to be an extrovert, I don't find her music as rich as Donna Anna's.' As she has not yet performed Donna Anna on stage, her view of the character is entirely based on her response to the music.

'The interpretation that makes sense to me, from a modern perspective, is that here is a woman who is strong and intelligent — qualities which were not useful in her day. Obviously she has a very strong relationship with her father, whom I think she truly loves. I would guess that her mother died when she was very young and so she and her father are very close. And when he asks her to marry Don

Ottavio – an arranged marriage – she agrees, although she has no strong feelings for him. My guess is that she probably met Don Giovanni at a masked ball and may even, in a weak moment, have invited him to her apartments. There is very strong attraction indicated in their music. As described in it, these two people have a lot in common. You can actually *hear* it. There is something very dangerous there, I think. I also feel that in the middle of their erotic encounter, Donna Anna probably got cold feet and thought "oh, I must be a nice girl", and tried to throw him out. She is, after all, a very highly born lady with a very strong attachment to the values of the society she lives in. And I think that when it came to the crunch, she said no. When he insisted, she began to resist. But because she really wanted him and because she doesn't want Don Ottavio, she is overwhelmed by guilt. I used to wonder why she keeps whining throughout the opera, why she doesn't even want to shake off her grief. And the answer is guilt. She feels she is the cause of her father's death.

'To my mind, what gives this away is the recitative I mentioned before, and particularly the part where she says very meekly to Don Ottavio "and I thought it was you". This is too feeble an excuse to fool anyone. So, here is a passionate woman who is constrained by society and wracked by guilt. Don Giovanni is her one passion – but he caused her father's death. When one listens carefully to her aria "Non mir dir", one realizes that there is something about it that doesn't connect with Don Ottavio. It connects much more to Don Giovanni. It is clearly him she is thinking about during all those coloraturas. I now look forward to singing the role on stage in 2000, when the Met will revive the Salzburg production.'

Meanwhile, Fleming will get a chance to expand her beloved French repertoire when she sings Louise at the San Francisco Opera and the Châtelet in Paris in 2000, for the theatre's centenary. She is experiencing a profound spiritual and aesthetic fascination with all things French and has made a long-term commitment to sing French and other roles in Paris – a commitment serious enough for her to enrol her small daughters in bilingual schools both in the United States and in Paris, so they can switch when she performs there. She even enjoys singing in French, not the easiest of languages to sing in. When told how astonishing it seems that so many American singers, such as Samuel Ramey and Susan Graham, share this liking for singing in French, she replies that it is not as surprising as it might appear, because 'there is a great tradition of French singing in America'.

'When I was a kid, singers like Beverly Sills, Anna Moffo and Victoria de los Angeles were regularly performing French operas such as *Thaïs* and *Louise* at the Met *phenomenally* well. However, what I was used to hearing was a much more *romantic* view of French opera than I would wish to hear today. After singing Marguerite and Manon in Paris I discovered that the style of interpretation in France is much more *classical*. So I had to learn that, too, along with the language.

The person who helped Fleming acquire her knowledge of the French style was Janine Reiss, the best coach in the world for this and also for the Mozartian repertoire. Fleming worked with her for five months before her Paris Manons, during which time 'Janine taught me some of the characteristics and secrets of French singing'. Reiss considers the main features of the French style to be 'clarity and measure'. In vocal terms, this implies avoiding portamenti (sliding from one note to another), strict observance of rhythm and the absence of *coronas* (lingering on particular notes and thus distorting the flow of the text). Fleming adds that for anglophone singers working on the pronunciation is also very important. 'Singing well in French is an enormous challenge and takes a long time. One has to understand the style of how the language is actually spoken, without stress. We Anglo-Saxons speak a language which is completely stressed, and which has very strong consonants. So I have gradually had to absorb all these factors that make up the French style of singing.'

Fleming's first French role was Marguerite in *Faust*, which she first sang in Chicago, Paris and at the Metropolitan Opera in the 1996–7 season. She points out that the French found her interpretation a little too 'romantic'. This was due to the fact that, as she explained earlier, this is the way French roles are usually sung in America. Indeed, John Nelson, who conducted the Chicago performances, not only allowed but even asked for portamenti, and at the time Fleming found this wonderful. 'But when I eventually sang the role at the Met, I took heed of the criticisms of my Paris performances and simplified my interpretation. I tried to make my Marguerite lighter and more luminous. And this, which was being true to the French style, automatically made her sound younger.

'From the purely vocal point of view, Marguerite is a very deceptive role. You may think it's not too demanding, but Act II is a real killer. It's very long and gets very heavy towards the end. The duet is heavy and so is her little solo. And the final trio, where she is ascending to heaven, really kills me. It's too stressful, too heavy, you have the two men singing along with you and the power of their combined singing is such that, unconsciously, you give out more than you should. It was by no means obvious that I was having trouble with it, but it wasn't as easy as I would have liked. In fact, I shouldn't be doing it anymore. Why should I, with so many other wonderful French roles beckoning?'

Her next French parts were all Massenet heroines: Salomé in *Hérodiade* in San Francisco, (which she recorded with Domingo and Dolora Zajick) and the title role of *Thaïs*, which is also being recorded with Thomas Hampson as Athanaël. She considers *Thaïs* a perfect opera for concert performance. 'It's lovely music and I'd love to do it. But the problem is that I have no time anymore for anything until after 2002.'

But it was Manon, her favourite French role, that turned her into a star in Paris. *Le Monde* hailed 'her vocal technique, her timbre, her style, reminiscent of the triumphs personified by Schwarzkopf, the beautiful bel canto art of the young Caballé and the emotional sensuality of Leontyne Price.'

Fleming states that after singing Manon, 'I understood why so many mezzos want to become sopranos. It's a gorgeous part.' Yet her love affair with the role got off to a slow start. At the beginning she didn't like the character at all. In fact she disliked Manon so much that she wondered how on earth she was ever going to bring herself to portray this woman: 'I just hated her. I hated her rudeness. My dislike was based mainly on her behaviour in Act IV, where she makes her love for Des Grieux conditional on his agreeing to gamble in order to assuage her greed. Then Beverly Sills made a comment that I found helpful. She said that at the beginning Manon has to be very innocent, really naïve. It must be made clear that she gets sucked into this mess by the men who are manipulating her, and that she herself is not the manipulator. But it was only after singing her that I really understood her. I began to understand that she is a modern woman, in the sense that she wants it all. She wants her man, she wants to live well. I thought, "really, what's so horrible about that?" And of course, the audience loves her.'

Fleming herself appears to be making a valiant and fairly successful effort to 'have it all', in the sense that she is trying to combine her career at the top with a rewarding family life. With her husband Rick Ross she has two small daughters, aged six and three. At the moment the children travel everywhere with her – and have done since they were a month old – together with their nanny. Rick meanwhile lives in New York, where he pursues his acting career, and from where he flies to all of Fleming's opening nights, usually staying with her and the children for a week or more afterwards. The family home is in Connecticut, and Fleming will try to ensure that she spends more time there after her eldest daughter reaches school age this season. Last season a fortnight was all the time she could manage to spend there.

She made a pact with her husband, who is 'the kind of supportive husband every diva needs', about the childrens' upbringing. 'We agreed that if he let them travel with me when they were young, he could then take care of them in school in one place when they get older. But I'm trying to sing more at the Met and to do more concerts and recitals, rather than too much opera, so that I can be home with them more. As the girls approach school age I really can't afford to be away from home that much, and I don't think it's right to expect them to travel with me then. But right now, while they still can, I'm in the best place in my personal life.'[1] It was interesting to discover that, unlike most singers, Fleming had no difficulty performing during her pregnancies, and kept working until two weeks before her first daughter was born. 'I felt fantastic,' she told the *Tribune* critic John von Rhein. 'The baby offers a very natural support for a singer. If anything, singing is easier while you're pregnant: it's like taking a physical vacation because the baby, does most of the work for you just by being there. But it's much harder to perform after the birth than while pregnant because then your muscles have really had it. You feel very weak for a long time. After my pregnancies, I didn't regain my full energy for six months.'

Yet amazingly enough, Fleming was back on the Met stage only two weeks after the birth of her second daughter – and for no less a role than Desdemona. Motherhood, according to those who know her well, brought a mellower, more womanly quality to her voice and psyche. If her children's happiness was at stake, she wouldn't hesitate to sacrifice her career. By 1997 she was one of the hottest properties on the operatic map, time therefore to decide exactly what sort of future she wanted and to make important choices as far as repertoire was concerned.

Despite her success as Eva in *Die Meistersinger* at the 1996 Bayreuth Festival, she had already made up her mind not to expand further into the Wagnerian repertoire. Nonetheless, she enjoyed the experience tremendously: 'I loved singing Eva, being in Bayreuth and working with Wolfgang Wagner. It was a complete luxury for me, a total immersion into the music, cult and history of Wagner, and I had a fantastic time. The experience was very interesting, and the whole place was very interesting, it's just unique. I mean, there's no other place on earth where you can work with the grandson of a great composer. That in itself is unique. Hearing Wolfgang Wagner talk about

---

[1] As this book was going to Press, Fleming and her husband decided on a trial separation. Having it all is not easy for any woman.

his experiences as a child was really fascinating and exciting. And having studied for a year in Germany as a graduate student means that I'm very comfortable with the language.

'Eva is not a typical Wagnerian role in the usual sense of the word, and this is why it is often sung by people who are not real Wagnerian singers. The problem with her, though, is not that it is a Wagnerian role, but that it's very low. And when I sang Donna Anna immediately afterwards – which has a totally different range – I didn't like the way it felt. It was uncomfortable because Eva had pulled the voice down. In fact, Donna Anna seemed considerably more difficult immediately after my Bayreuth Evas than it had the previous March. So I decided not to go back to Bayreuth the following summer and not to sing any more Wagner for the time being – despite the favourable reception. I don't know exactly what ruins voices and I don't think that anybody really does. It's a mystery. But I decided that rather than take the risk, it was better not to repeat a role that had the effect of pulling the voice down.'

So, she plans to concentrate on her existing areas of repertoire, and to expand further into bel canto. One of her 'talisman roles', is Rusalka, which she will go on performing throughout her career. Early on she won many auditions with her rendition of the Moon Song, and anyone who had heard her interpretation at once sensuous and lunar, in her solo album with Sir Georg Solti, can understand why no judge could fail to pass such a singer. She brought the house down when she sang it again at the Met in autumn 1997. 'The soprano's beautiful, creamy voice seemed to be pervaded by a yearning, hopeless love that came right from the core of her being', wrote *Opera Now*. Maybe her family's Czech origins have also something to do with her whole-hearted identification with this tragic water sprite . . . If she had to name the roles she loves and identifies with most, they would be Rusalka, Manon, the Marschallin and Desdemona.'

Fleming first sang Desdemona at the Metropolitan Opera in 1995 opposite Placido Domingo, just a few weeks after the birth of her second daughter. She was in the second cast and had not taken part in the rehearsals. Yet she did have to rehearse Act III, with its very dramatic duet where Otello hits Desdemona and hurls her to the floor. 'So, Placido Domingo came up, slapped my face and whispered: "Hello, I'm Placido Domingo, nice to meet you!" And after the rehearsal I found I could hardly walk! I literally had to hold on to the rails to climb up a pair of steps because my legs were shaking. He was so terrifying in that scene, so powerfully real, that he produced an equally real reaction in me. I had never experienced anything like that on stage before, and it was incredibly exciting. He also helped me enormously during the performance and brought things out of me that I didn't know I had. He made me *dare* more and do better than I otherwise would have done. This is what happens when there is a really collaborative exchange on stage with great artists — and it also happens when working with a great conductor.'

She feels that Desdemona is an ideal role vocally, 'so well written that there is nothing uncomfortable about it. By the time Verdi wrote *Otello* he was vastly experienced and understood the voice perfectly.' According to James Levine, Fleming's Desdemona 'ranks with the greatest'. Yet the only other Verdi heroine she things might be right for her one day — but definitely not yet — is Elena in *I vespri siciliani*, a work she adores. I suspect the key to whether she has sufficient 'ping' for it will lie in how all the bel canto singing she plans to do in the coming years affects her voice and in how she acquits herself as Violetta in November 1998.

She had already sung bel canto — 'quite a few roles people don't know about' — in New York with Eve Queler before her big break at Houston, especially Bellini heroines such as Imogene in *Il pirata* and the title roles in *La straniera* and *La sonnambula*. She has also recorded Donizetti's *Rosmonda d'Inghilterra*. But her only bel canto part in recent years has been Rossini's Armida, at Pesaro and later at Carnegie Hall.

'I loved my Pesaro Armidas, and working with Luca Ronconi. The whole production was a blast because I had to play a sorceress, something completely off the beaten track as far as my operatic heroines are concerned. And Ronconi really let himself go and did something so fanciful and wild that I loved every minute of the production. It was great fun. I also had to work with a choreographer who devised such quaint movements that there was practically nothing of myself left. There were masks which we all had to wear, and when Ildebrando d'Arcangelo walked in wearing his, my husband thought it was me! There are murmurings about reviving this production, but nothing definite so far.' Fleming's superb recording for Sony, which displays *breathtaking* coloratura singing, is certainly enough to whet the appetite.

The thing she loves most about the bel canto repertoire is its virtuosity. 'These operas are real technique testers. But more than that, they are the most liberally expressive pieces in the soprano repertoire. There's more freedom for the singer in this repertoire than any other kind of opera. In this sense you could say that bel canto is a bit like jazz: you have a stable accompaniment which provides a rhythmic base and you have improvisation, you have cadenzas which you can embellish. You also have a lot of rhythmic freedom in terms of rubato and a lot of scope for your musical imagination. In fact, probably because of my experience of jazz, whenever I hear a reprise or da capo section in opera my ear immediately begins to imagine variations. Conductors often forbid me to indulge and embellish the basic line, but the temptation is very hard to resist.

'Bel canto is the most purely vocal repertoire, and I adore the opportunity to perform it. It's much more of a vocal tester than Mozart. People are always saying that to keep your voice healthy you should sing Mozart. Well, for a soprano this is not very useful because there are no high notes in Mozart. And that is very important, maybe not for everybody, but certainly for me. Ideally I would like to sing one bel canto role each year, to keep everything in good working order.'

Of course, the real challenge is to turn these operas into something more than just a virtuosic display of vocal fireworks and invest them with dramatic meaning, the way only Callas managed to do. People always complain about the flimsiness of the libretti, yet this didn't stop *her* from extracting every ounce of dramatic truth from the often far-fetched stories. Fleming agrees that the rudimentary libretti of bel canto operas need not be an obstacle to the expression of true emotion. 'If something about the story captures my imagination, I find it really wonderful to dig into the emotion behind it. Amina's "Ah! non credea mirarti" in *La sonnambula*, for instance, is a most breathtaking aria. The way the inner tension builds up is thrilling. But you have to love this repertoire in order to do it well. If you don't, then it's not going to speak to you. Because superficially, they *are* rather fluffy stories and flimsy characters, some of them. Bel canto heroines depend on you, the singer, to bring them to life and invest them with flesh and blood, much more so than the characters in any other area of the operatic repertoire.'

Fleming's performances of the title role in *Lucrezia Borgia* at La Scala in summer 1998 will reveal whether she can make as much of a mark in bel canto as she has in Mozart, Strauss and the French repertoire. She is convinced she can perform this repertoire much, much better now than at the beginning of her career ten years ago. In the same way that when she sang Manon, she was 'shocked' by how easy it was, vocally. 'It has taken me a long time to learn how to sing, to be able to do anything with my voice that I imagine. That's what I've been striving for all those years, and finally it's in sight.'

BARBARA
FRITTOLI

'BARBARA FRITTOLI IS not a diva. She is an *artist*, which is to say that
she is more than a good singer and a good actress: a great *soul*
which would have found expression is some artistic form even if she
had not been born with a glorious voice,' said Graham Vick after
directing the thirty-one-year-old Italian lyric soprano for his 1998
Glyndebourne Festival production of *Così fan tutte*. 'She doesn't do
anything that doesn't spring from within. That makes her one of a
very rare breed.'

By nature of their work, which is to create a reality on stage by
drawing from the raw material and human ingredients within each
member of their cast as much as from their purely artistic equipment,
directors tend to probe and know the people they work with more
deeply than most. Others who have worked with Frittoli, such as conductors and managers, have also formed a high opinion of her, albeit on
a less profound level. 'She has the quality of voice and all other qualities
needed for a great career,' says Peter Katona, Artistic Administrator of
the Royal Opera, Covent Garden. 'She is a very musicianly singer, an
accomplished actress with a marked talent for comedy and also a very
pleasant, straightforward person.'

Frittoli's musicianly qualities impressed Sir Charles Mackerras at a preliminary rehearsal for *Le nozze di Figaro*, which he was to conduct at the 1998 Salzburg Festival. 'Without wishing to appear racist, one doesn't expect Italian singers to be musically sophisticated and probing! But I was forced to revise this opinion after my first working session with Frittoli. For here was a very nice young lady who also happened to be extremely intelligent and thoroughly well informed about the music she interprets.'

Frittoli, a tall, good-looking, discreetly elegant brunette, points out that 'having a beautiful voice and just singing are no longer enough. You can't ignore musical culture any longer. It's the motor of everything, part of being a true professional. And being professional – punctual, well-prepared and precise – is the norm among my generation of singers. It's what all the theatres and conductors expect.' But she agrees that despite some progress in this direction – 'nowadays it would be inconceivable to come across an Italian singer who can't read music' – her compatriots still lag behind their international counterparts in this respect: 'A glance at the billboards outside any major international opera house is enough to prove this.'

It took Frittoli less than a decade to rise to the front line of today's lyric sopranos, from her début in 1989 until 1996, by which time she was singing at every major theatre and festival. Her voice is both pure and full and has a sensuous sheen, even if the timbre itself is not instantly recognizable. But hers has been a steady, well-planned ascent to the top rather than a meteoric rise.

She was born in Milan to a family whose occupation was commerce and who were interested in classical music, though not opera. Frittoli started piano lessons very young and by the age of ten was accepted at the Verdi Conservatoire, Italy's most famous musical academy.

One of several obligatory classes she had to attend was choral singing. By the time she was twelve, the choirmaster could already single out her voice from the other six hundred in the choir. 'So he asked me to come and sit in the front row. Singing was so far from being important in my mind that my initial reaction was that he did it in order to stop me chatting to my neighbours during practice!' From then on he would ring up her parents at regular intervals to try to persuade them that she should study singing rather than the piano. 'But to my mind, being a pianist was far superior to being a singer. I had absorbed the common prejudice against singers and thought, never!' For years she evaded the choirmaster's attempts to persuade her until, finally, she decided to do the exam for the singing class, feeling certain she would be rejected and thus 'rid of his badgering'. But she was accepted.

She was then eighteen, and spent her first year with a teacher who classified her as a contralto. The result was that by the end of that year she was completely voiceless, able only to croak. For although Frittoli's voice has a certain dark colour – as do many heavier lyric voices such as Leontyne Price's and Angela Gheorghiu's – it seems inconceivable to classify her not even as a high mezzo but as a contralto. Fortunately, she realized something was seriously wrong and began to look for another teacher. Otherwise the damage could have been permanent.

Her search led her first to Bruno Pola, one of Pavarotti's former teachers in Modena. During these trips she was always accompanied by her father. 'This profession is rather singular in most respects and I wanted to project a serious and professional image. So my poor papa was dragged along from teacher to teacher.' Pola was emphatic that she had real potential and offered to take her on as a pupil if she would move to Modena. But this she did not have the means to do.

Finally, back in Milan, she struck gold in Giovanna Canetti, who taught at her conservatoire and who now heads the school at La Scala. Frittoli was almost twenty by then, and within two years Canetti had her ready for her professional début. But the work involved was long, arduous and exhausting. 'During the first month, I couldn't utter a sound. I had no idea where I should place my voice. But slowly, through exercises of all kinds, I began to recover and discover my real voice, which she channelled and placed properly. Until I acquired a technique we went very much a step at a time. I wanted to sing big, dramatic things but she made

me sing stupid little arias such as "Le violette graziose", a sweety-sweety
horror I used to loathe and still do! Naturally all this time we were working on diaphragmatic breathing. This amounts to eighty per cent of all
singing. Then comes the rest and last comes interpretation.'

Frittoli explains that it can be difficult for singers to develop their
own interpretation of everything they sing. They are so bombarded
with recordings and videos that it is all too easy to absorb somebody
else's interpretation, almost unconsciously. 'But it is essential and at the
same time very difficult to develop your own interpretation, one that's
really yours and nobody else's. The only way to achieve this is through
a long, long study of the score, when you are alone at home.'

After two year's study with Canetti at the conservatoire, Frittoli was
awarded her diploma in singing, something which in itself she considers useless. What was valuable, though, was the thorough musical
preparation she underwent there, as singers had to attend classes in
subjects such as orchestration, for which Frittoli retains a fascination.
As Domingo often points out, a musical singer will unconsciously want
to imitate the sound of whichever instrument is prominent in a given
phrase and to colour their voice accordingly. Like Domingo, the instrument Frittoli most enjoys imitating is the cello.

Shortly after her graduation, Frittoli made her début in 1989 at the
Teatro Comunale in Florence in a little known opera by Bucchi,
Il giuoco del barone. Over the next three years she sang a succession of
small roles in Italian provincial theatres and festivals, including the
Teatro Carlo Felice in Genoa, the Donizetti Festival in Bergamo and the
Maggio Musicale Fiorentino, where she sang Ines in *Il trovatore* with
Pavarotti as Manrico. In 1992 she made her début at La Scala, again in
a small role, Agnese in Bellini's *Beatrice di Tenda*, which she had to
learn in four days. 'When one is young one is very bold! One believes
one can do anything!'

Her real début, in a major role, was at the Teatro San Carlo
in Naples as Mimì. Indeed during these early years she was much
associated with this role: it was as Mimì that she made her débuts in

London in a concert performance with the LSO at the Barbican in 1994 and at the Metropolitan Opera in 1995.

Frittoli says that although she sang Mimì 'with great enthusiasm' at the time, she does not particularly care for the character, whom she considers 'too passive and not the sort of woman I can easily identify with.' She adds that she has a love-hate relationship with Puccini, permeated by both respect and fear. Mimì may be a stupendous and beautifully written part that allows you to play with human feelings and vocal colours, but it is nevertheless very dangerous. I was too young and too ignorant to realize this at the time.'

She explains that Puccini, although he often wrote a quadruple or quintuple *pianissimo* in his scores, is now perceived as a typically veristic composer, which means that conductors usually feel entitled to unleash their orchestras with unbridled ferocity. 'Needless to say, this can spell ruin for young singers who cannot hope to be heard above such mayhem without pushing their voice. This is particularly true of Act II of *La bohème* where everybody seems to shout, shout, shout. Why should they shout? We are in a theatre, not an arena. Act III is also very dramatic and risks becoming vulgar unless handled with care and delicacy.'

Frittoli remembers that when she sang Mimì for Jonathan Miller's production at the Maggio Musicale Fiorentino the stage manager in fact told her: 'You have to sing louder at this spot or you won't be heard'. Her reply was, 'I'll sing exactly as I'm singing. The orchestra will have to play softer'. For this reason she has decided not to sing this role again. 'After all, it's up to us to protect ourselves by saying no to anything that goes against our better judgement.' Frittoli, who has a reputation for being ultra-cautious and discriminating in her choice of repertoire, says that sometimes she feels she has 'made a career out of saying no'.

Frittoli's success as Mimì at the Vienna State Opera was followed there the same year by Micaëla in a revival of *Carmen*. 'Micaëla should have a certain "weight", both vocal and dramatic,' says Frittoli. She is not the milksop she is often portrayed to be, but a strong woman who knows what she wants and, as such, is a real rival for Carmen. A girl who crosses the length and breadth of Spain, from Navarra to Seville, hoping to find her "fiancé", and who later braves the smugglers' mountain is no ninny. She is a little frightened, of course. But a girl who is really frightened stays at home. So the real difficulty is dramatic rather than vocal: how to put across a real, flesh-and-blood character who *means* something in the plot of the opera. The vocal side is easy. But the danger of her appearing like a silly, colourless ninny increases when she is sung by light lyric rather than full lyric sopranos. Then you long for Carmen to appear and Micaëla to *dis*appear. Otherwise, it's a purely lyrical part with only one aria and a duet, which, makes it ideal for young lyric voices.' After Frittoli's Viennese début one critic wrote: 'At last a Micaëla who doesn't seem like an idiot'. The verdict of Frittoli's husband, bass-baritone Natale de Carolis was more picturesque: 'He said that from the moment I entered I looked like a falcon disguised as a dove!' After singing Micaëla at Covent Garden with Domingo as Don José, Frittoli abandoned the part in favour of bigger roles.

The year 1994 was a milestone for Frittoli. She sang her first Desdemona at the Théâtre de la Monnaie in Brussels under Antonio Pappano, made her London début and had her first contact with Mozart, now the mainstay of her repertoire, in four major roles: Donna Elvira, Sifare, the Countess and Fiordiligi. She also began a lasting and fruitful collaboration with Italy's two top conductors, Claudio Abbado and Riccardo Muti.

Both conductors are demanding and expect their singers to be attentive and well prepared but both, accordingly to Frittoli, are 'very simpatico' and wonderful to work with. Yet it would be hard to imagine two conductors more different in temperament, in their music-making, way of working, attitude and approach to singers. 'Muti has very clear-cut ideas, tries to transmit specific cultural points and works with singers at the piano in a very detailed way. He is very strict with tenors, less so with us sopranos. Abbado is looser and prefers not to give too many specifications before the rehearsals. Even then, he doesn't actually say very much but indicates what he wants through his conducting, through the kind of sound he elicits and through his phrasing. Otherwise he limits himself to remarks such as "slow down a bit here" or "try to bring out a different colour there!"'

Frittoli sang her first Mozart role, the Countess, with Abbado in Ferrara in a transfer of Jonathan Miller's vintage Vienna Festival production of *Figaro*. It is not an easy role: 'I don't feel the Countess should be portrayed as being too young. She is not the Rosina of *Barbiere*, but she is not the Marschallin of *Der Rosenkavalier* either. She is somewhere in between, still young enough to indulge in the whole rigmarole with Susanna even though she realizes how irregular it is for her to stoop to ask her maid for help. I try to make her very active, agile and energetic. Although she is married to a nobleman and knows she has to carry herself with a certain aplomb, she nevertheless abandons this and dresses in servants' clothes in order to trap her husband. A woman who is willing to do this must be a very particular sort of person, cunning in a way reminiscent of Rosina in *Barbiere* with her "cento trapole" – a Rosina mellowed by the years and by Mozart's being an Austrian rather than an Italian composer.'

'Vocally, it's a role that requires you to use your head. In her first aria "Porgi, amor", which you have to sing "cold" the moment you walk on stage, you have to establish a character out of nothing. You have an aria that sounds like heaven on earth but which has to explain what this woman is about, that nostalgia for lost happiness which is the real cause of her misery. That is what kills her, much more than the Count's momentary infatuation with Susanna. "Dove sono" is equally difficult but at least it comes in Act II, when the voice has had a chance to warm up and when the character of the Countess is already established.

Frittoli was looking forward to singing the role again in the 1998 Salzburg Festival with Sir Charles Mackerras. Apart from, in his own words, 'spreading the gospel of ornamentation and appoggiaturas in

Mozart to Salzburg', Mackerras plans to reverse the Countess's and Susanna's vocal line at the finale of Act I. 'Susanna will be singing my line and I'll be singing hers, which means that I will be singing a third above her. Sir Charles explained that at this particular moment the Countess is the important character around whom everything revolves, the one calling all the shots. We discussed it and I must say that his view, based on sound argument, convinced me to try it his way. It poses no vocal problems for me and my only proviso was that the singer singing Susanna should also agree. It will be interesting for me to find out if this production helps me form as definitive a view of the Countess as I now have of Fiordiligi.'

Frittoli first sang Fiordiligi, her favourite Mozart role, with Riccardo Muti in Vienna in a production by Roberto de Simone. She has since performed it in Jonathan Miller's famous modern day production at Covent Garden in spring 1998 and in Graham Vick's controversial production at the 1998 Glyndebourne Festival. It is a role that fits her perfectly, both vocally and dramatically, because she possesses the rich yet pure and agile lyric voice that the role demands. And, in Graham Vick's words, 'it brings out the extremely convincing comedian in her. What makes her so convincing is that she has a real understanding of the absurdity of human behaviour and is not scared of making a fool of herself on stage.'

Indeed, Frittoli's first comment about Fiordiligi was that she is a very funny character: 'Tortured – she and Ferrando are the opera's two tortured characters – but ultimately very funny because although she makes such a song and dance about moral rectitude and resists the "Albanians" longer than Dorabella, when she eventually gives in she becomes much more passionate and committed than Dorabella, who surrenders only for fun. Fiordiligi surrenders with her *heart*, because that's the way she is, the way she functions. This creates many problems for her. One of them is the fact that when she comes out of her rigid attachment to convention and almost Victorian set of values (unlike Dorabella, who is much more open), she really falls in love with this

"Albanian". Of course this means that she is much more *truly* unfaithful to her original fiancé than Dorabella. She and Ferrando are romantics, idealists, whereas Dorabella and Guglielmo are sensualists. That's why all four feel so good with their new partners. But maybe it's better the other way, having two complementary rather than two similar characters.'

Vocally she considers Fiordiligi 'the most complete Mozart heroine' she has sung to date. 'It has everything that characterizes Mozart as an operatic composer, both in terms of range and in the demands it makes on the soprano. It has exciting recitatives, it has coloratura, it has both lyrical and dramatic singing. It's also absolutely exhausting.' Frittoli says that none of her other roles leave her feeling so tired at the end. Indeed, when I saw her backstage after the Jonathan Miller production at Covent Garden she had a lost, glazed look about her and didn't seem to take in anything anyone was saying to her.

'The exhaustion is both vocal and dramatic. Dramatically, all evening you are carrying this very tense and *in*tense character inside you; and vocally, there comes a moment near the end where I almost run out of stamina, where I feel I cannot go on any longer. It is at the duet with Ferrando, where he sings "Volgi a me". At that point I am so overcome by sheer fatigue that I barely feel able to continue. Fortunately, it's followed by a brief respite, during which I can rest for a couple of minutes and recover my strength for the finale, the Wedding Scene, where Fiordiligi's "È nel tuo, nel mio bicchiero" has to sound blissful and lyrical.' The only other role in her repertoire that comes close in terms of sheer exhaustion is Sifare in *Mitridate*, which she sang at the Teatro Reggio in Turin in 1994 in Graham Vick's spectacular staging. She will sing this role again at Le Chatelet in Paris in 1999–2000 season.

Frittoli considers Graham Vick's production of *Così* at Glyndebourne, along with Roberto de Simone's in Vienna, to be the most interesting in her career. She stresses that the two are polar opposites. 'De Simone's was a very classic, traditional eighteenth-century production, with very beautiful Empire costumes, but also peppered by a deep understanding of the work's dramatic rhythm and by very meticulous probing of the recitatives. De Simone is an immensely cultured Neapolitan [he is also one of Cecilia Bartoli's favourite directors], who knows and understands everything about eighteenth-century style. Vick is an extremely musical director, a man of the theatre par excellence. Both have one thing in common: they pay meticulous attention to the recitatives, which they rightly perceive as the Alpha and Omega of *Così*, or indeed of any Mozart opera, where the real drama takes place.'

At first she found Vick's Glyndebourne production very perplexing. 'He staged the work as a rehearsal for *Così* by a company of contemporary singers, with no costumes and with stage hands moving furniture about. At the beginning it must have been as disconcerting for the audience as it was for us. But, again like us, they seem to end up liking it very much. Vick's aim was to explore the essence of *Così*, and to this end he stripped it of all its trimmings. Some moments, such as "Come scoglio", *are* treated in an eighteenth-century way because the music demands it. At that particular moment, Fiordiligi is indulging her blinkered, eighteenth-century morality. But in her other aria, "Per pietà", we see a woman face to face with herself, baring her soul and discovering she is not the person she thought she was. We in the cast were placed in exactly the same position: face to face with ourselves, with no filter between us and the audience. At the beginning all of us were stunned. No one expected anything like this. There was even a kind of revolt among us. When he first told me I would have to wear jeans I could have killed him! But gradually I came to love this production and to feel that Vick had brought me closer to the character than I'd ever been before. Throughout the rehearsal period he was taking photographs of each of us to see what we wore every day. And that – in my case jeans – is what we were asked to wear in the production itself.

'This means that we, too, were stripped naked. We had to look deep inside ourselves and find out who we really are. This goes against the whole grain of the theatrical and operatic professions. One of the wonderful things about working in the theatre is the very opportunity it provides to live so many different lives and be so many different characters: we can be traitors, heroines, romantic, vindictive, vicious, whatever. But Vick was after something different, and something very difficult. Because being yourself on stage *is* very difficult. Yet I found working with him enormously stimulating. He is one of the very few directors from whom you can learn something. In this case he taught me how to look inside myself.'

There is talk that Frittoli might sing Donna Anna in Vick's Glyndebourne production of *Don Giovanni* in 2000. She has sung Donna Elvira before (in 1994 in Naples), but never Donna Anna. 'Graham Vick says that having seen how I am inside he thinks Donna Anna will suit me better, and I trust him implicitly.' When asked to explain this decision Vick said that he found in Frittoli 'an inner nobility of soul which Donna Anna has but Donna Elvira doesn't. And to my mind, a successful production of *Don Giovanni* absolutely requires a Donna Anna of great fire and nobility.' (Jonathan Miller has also singled out Frittoli's 'lurking inner fire'.) 'It can survive a Donna Elvira who is not all that special,' continues Vick, 'because ultimately Donna Elvira doesn't know who she is, and cannot find out, either. She can only live through someone else and when she loses Don Giovanni she turns to God. We never find out who she is and where she came from, whereas Donna Anna is explored more deeply, both as a daughter and fiancée.'

If the assignment is confirmed, this production will feature Frittoli's husband Natale de Carolis in the title role, which should be interesting indeed. Both he and Frittoli are generally averse to the idea of a joint husband and wife career. They operate very discreetly as a couple within the profession. 'We don't do a lover's act. Each has his own career.'

Frittoli is well aware that the success of any production of *Don Giovanni* starts with the Don himself. 'Whichever way one looks at Don Giovanni and whatever one says about him, he is one of the most interesting operatic characters ever conceived, and it is he who colours all the other characters. Of course he is a man's dream.' Not a woman's? 'Not every woman's. When she is young, yes. Then, after an inter-mediary stage, yes again. If I were a man I'd love to sing him. The role needs very strong, magnetic, electrifying personalities. The whole situation around the Don and all these women is also very interesting.

'Donna Elvira is his curse, his nemesis, who appears whenever he is about to lay his paws on a woman, to ruin it all for him. In this sense alone, Donna Elvira can be said to be very funny. But, like the Countess in *Figaro*, I don't feel she can be a very young woman. She must be, as the French so aptly describe, "a lady of a certain age". She is a noble-woman but not very young. And this is what makes her so difficult to portray. She wants this man so desperately, and there is something about this obsession that suggests it is not a young, fresh obsession. There is a mature sensuality about it that suggests that although Don Giovanni was probably the first man to fulfil her sexually he was by no means the first man she had known. Then there is the fact that she travelling alone with her maid all over Spain. If she were young, there would surely be a father or a brother around to prevent this. So she must be either a widow or an unmarried woman of a certain age. This partly explains the degree of her despair. There must always be a hint of this despair at the passing of time behind her romantic and passion-ate outbursts, the sensation that she has jumped off a departing train and is desperately trying to get back on.

'Vocally it is not a very difficult role. Her music is very lively because most of the time she is in a very agitated state. But dramatically she is very difficult. She fascinates me much more than Donna Anna, whose music is absolutely fabulous and much more difficult, but whom I don't find a very interesting woman. Apart from her first entry, she is very rigid and collected.' Perhaps Vick will be able to change Frittoli's mind about Donna Anna if the two come together for the Glyndebourne production in 2001. Frittoli will be singing Donna Elvira in Lisbon, at the Paris Opéra at Vienna and at the Salzburg Festival before this first Donna Anna.

In 1994 Frittoli sang her first major Verdi role, Desdemona, at the Théâtre de la Monnaie in Brussels under the baton of Antonio Pappano. Like Fiordiligi, it is a role to which she brings both character and nobility. Indeed this is her avowed aim because she thinks that the main challenge in Desdemona is dramatic rather than vocal. She felt ready for the part, 'both vocally and dramatically' and confident enough to trust her own responses to the score and to Shakespeare's play which, of course, she read as part of her preparation.

'What struck me was how different Shakespeare's Desdemona is from Verdi's. Shakespeare's text is very strong, almost rude at times and very far removed from Verdi's "angel". This gave me food for thought. Although, of course, it is Verdi's Desdemona that I have to interpret, I nevertheless tried to keep something of Shakespeare's heroine at the back of my mind, as a guideline. My main concern was to create a character who, despite her gorgeous, truly angelic-sounding music, is not just an angelic, passive, tender and naive woman, but also very courageous and strong. Desdemona had the guts to cross the Rubicon and marry a man from an alien culture. In so doing, she burned her boats with her own class and society, in which the couple are tolerated only because Otello is a great general. Having eloped and presented her family with a *fait accompli*, she must now live with her choice which *must* be a choice for life. She places her entire life in the hands of this man and has an unshakeable faith in him and their relationship. She cannot conceive being betrayed by him, not only literally but also in his mind. This is what explains her "insensitivity" as a wife and her poor "husband management" in the scene where she presses Otello to pardon Cassio. To her it's nothing of the sort because she cannot imagine anything ever being wrong between Otello and herself.'

Another important concern of Frittoli's was not to elicit too much pity at the finale, because she feels that Desdemona is by then so disillusioned that she sees her fate as punishment for turning her back on the values of her society. This is why she does not blame Otello but herself. 'Her music, of course, is heavenly. What I find most difficult about the Willow Song and her Prayer is to show the hope in this broken, disillusioned woman, because he who prays still hopes.' Frittoli greatly enjoyed singing Desdemona both in Brussels and at the 1996 Salzburg Easter Festival, in a production by Paolo Olmi conducted by Claudio Abbado with Placido Domingo and Ruggero Raimondi.

After her success as Desdemona Frittoli, who in the same year also sang Medora in *Il corsaro* in Turin, was asked by Muti to consider Leonora in *La forza del destino*. This is a full *lirico spinto* role, which she instinctively felt disposed to decline. But 'because you don't say no to a conductor like Muti just like that', she agreed to look at it before making up her mind, and even tried it out with him before he accepted her decision to refuse. Instead, he proposed Leonora in *Il trovatore*, which she accepted initially for 1997 but pushed back to 2000, the centenary of Verdi's death.

This was a role she could accept with impunity because the orchestration, as in most early Verdi operas, is thinner and therefore does not require the singer to push in order to be heard. Frittoli points out that the only tricky spot is the 'Miserere' in Act IV, which is 'very low, very heavy and very dramatic'. Indeed, the ease with which the singer will manage the rest of the opera depends on how well she has fared with the 'Miserere', and Muti himself has urged Frittoli to prepare this moment with extra care. The other key to *Il trovatore* is pacing. As Frittoli observes, 'Verdi is not an enemy of the voice. But he *is* an enemy as far as fatigue and sheer stamina are concerned. So one should not risk giving one's all from the beginning only to find oneself out of breath at the spot where Leonora sings her beautiful, lyrical aria "D'amor sull'ali rosee", which should sound ethereal and floaty. [Jane Eaglen made the same point about Leonora.] Of course, Muti will open up all the cuts so I will also have "Tu vedrai che amore" to contend with.'

'As it is, I cannot pretend to understand the plot of *Il trovatore*.' Here Frittoli is not alone. Most people don't understand *Il trovatore*. Even Karajan, who often conducted the opera and twice recorded it, found the plot 'incomprehensible', even though he considered the work 'very satisfying, like a hamburger, because it has all the human passions: love, hate, jealousy, revenge'. The only notable exceptions are Dolora Zajick, who gives a gripping analysis of the opera in her chapter, and the brilliant and highly musical Italian director Piero Faggioni (who works a great deal less than he should because of his unfortunate tendency to quarrel with operatic managements). Faggioni sees *Il trovatore* as an opera whose real protagonist is fire, in which each of the four characters is consumed by the fire of their own passions.

As she prepares for her millennium production of *Il trovatore*, she is looking after her voice by singing mostly Mozart and the easier Verdi roles such as Alice Ford in *Falstaff*, which she first sang in 1997 in Bolgona under Daniele Gatti and will repeat for the reopening of Covent Garden in 2000. After 2000, though, she would like to attempt the title roles in *Luisa Miller* and *Aida* and, later still, Elisabeth de Valois in *Don Carlos*. She has already had offers to sing both, but needless to say has turned them down ('I told you I made my career out of saying no,' she jests). She would sing Aida right now were it not for one dangerous moment: the duet with Amonasro in Act III. 'It's rather heavy and requires a certain physical maturity, in the shape of muscular strength which I don't yet have, to support and sustain it. This is even more true of Elisabeth de Valois, both in terms of vocal extension and of tessitura, which most of the time is low, hovering around and even below the passaggio. There are a couple of high notes, but the overall tessitura is central. I will eventually come to sing roles such as this, but only occasionally and only when I can ensure they are followed by something smoother that allows the voice to shed that hardness that comes from singing too much around the passaggio and to recover its softness and sheen.'

She learnt this important lesson the hard way. In October 1997 she sang four concerts of Verdi's *Requiem*, two with Muti and two with Abbado. Immediately afterwards she had to sing *Le nozze di Figaro* and, to her horror, found that for three weeks she couldn't do the recitatives the way they should be done. 'This taught me that although Verdi is not dangerous for the voice, he does demand a lot of extra strength in the way you have to *lean* on the diaphragm to support the line. Mozart doesn't – he demands a lightness of touch and agility which doesn't put so much pressure on the diaphragm. As you can imagine, this experience really made me think! Of course I'm not going to stop singing the Verdi *Requiem*, but of all the offers I get every year I will only accept a couple. And never before Mozart!'

As far as Mozart is concerned, there are a few more parts she would love to tackle: Vitellia in *La clemenza di tito* and Elettra in *Idomeneo*. 'Vitellia is the Mozartian Lady Macbeth, a very interesting character, and Elettra is even crazier and more dramatic. I will only sing her after I have sung Vitellia. Generally I adore playing nasty characters on stage, but I never seem to find any within my vocal possibilities. My dream, which is doomed to remain unfulfilled forever, would be to sing Lady Macbeth. But my voice has neither the steel nor the right "ping" for it. Callas, for whom I have a passion, ruined the profession for us all in this sense because *she* could do everything.'

Callas's career may have been short, but Frittoli considers that decade as a beacon of light, which 'endures to this day and inspires all of us. When you listen to Callas, you actually begin to "see" whatever character she is singing before your eyes. Who cares if the odd high note is shrill or not quite perfect when there is a *fire* in her singing, a fire that makes the characters *live*. I infinitely prefer the odd shrill or wrong note in an interpretation permeated by that sacred fire of hers to someone who may sing every note perfectly, but transmits nothing and merely skims the surface of the music. In bel canto particularly I cannot bear listening to anyone but her.'

She strongly feels that Callas's amazing and uncategorizable versatility was responsible for the loss of direction experienced by so many singers of the generation immediately preceding her own: the sad phenomenon of lyric sopranos tackling dramatic parts, of Germanic voices singing Italian bel canto, of mezzos trying to be sopranos. This tendency is now almost extinct, probably because of the number of vocal casualties along the way. 'My generation seems to be more sensible and has greater self-knowledge. For example, there are many roles I would like to sing, such as Lady Macbeth which I already mentioned and Wagner parts, but which I know I can't. The only Wagner part I could and would like to try one day is Elsa in *Lohengrin*. I know it's rare for Italians to want to sing Wagner, but I really want to try one day in the right circumstances.'

In fact Jane Eaglen, who is establishing herself as one of the leading Wagnerian singers of our day, made precisely this point in her chapter, stating that she rather likes the idea of Italian voices singing Wagner: 'It could be very beautiful. They could bring to Wagnerian singing that element of bel canto which Wagner himself desired but which is totally absent from the singing of most German singers.' Of course, first of all Frittoli would have to work on the language. She does speak a little German but she is aware that she will have to do a lot better than that before she sings a Wagnerian role. She would also need the time to delve into the score in the way she likes to work, letting it gradually sink in. 'So we're talking eight, nine years from now before I'm ready for Elsa. Meanwhile, I'm starting to sing a lot of German music in concert, Mahler and Strauss, some of it with piano for the time being. A role which I would also love to sing someday is the Marschallin because I adore *Der Rosenkavalier*. When I want to relax, that's what I listen to. It is a different world and I love it.'

Frittoli acknowledges that being married to a fellow singer, with whom she can discuss every aspect of her work – even if 'often from opposite points of view' – is a great advantage. Natale de Carolis is ten years older than she, and has ten years' more professional experience. 'The fact that he belongs to the same world, means that he knows its problems and singularities and has experienced them all before me. This enormous plus offsets the sadness of working away from each other for long periods. Of course, we also discuss and argue about roles ad infinitum.' The two were together for a long time before they finally got married last year, and now have a baby daughter of eighteen months. Frittoli feels that as well as having a successful career it is also essential for her to fulfil herself 'as a person and as a woman, to have a husband, to experience the warmth of a family and the satisfaction of being a mother'. She is already dreading the thought of the separations when her daughter reaches school age, but meanwhile her mother and mother-in-law take turns at babysitting. Home is an apartment in Monte Carlo and a house on Lake Maggiore, although she says, 'it's hard to say *where* we live. Opera singers are doomed to be nomads. Luxury nomads, but still nomads.'

ANGELA
GHEORGHIU

'WHEN AUDITIONING SINGERS you sometimes come across someone in whom everything is spot on, and there is no doubt in your mind that you are in the presence of a very major talent,' says Peter Katona, Artistic Administrator of the Royal Opera, Covent Garden, the man responsible for the discovery and launch of Angela Gheorghiu, one of the most beautiful soprano voices of the century. 'This was the case with Angela, whom I auditioned in 1991, shortly after her graduation from the Bucharest Music Academy. It was instantly clear to me that here was a voice ready for a career right away: a voice of exceptional beauty, and a singer with exceptional control over her voice, despite her young age – only twenty-six at the time – with charm and everything just right: every note, nuance, accent and colour absolutely *perfect*.

'If I had to describe it, I would say her voice is like a violin, totally even and seamless throughout its range. There are no rough edges, but there is plenty of colour and character. It's an almost impeccable instrument. I mean no singer sings *totally* impeccably, it would be almost superhuman, but Angela's voice comes as close to perfection as possible, and that on almost every occasion I have heard her.'

With no hesitation – for on this occasion he didn't need a conductor's approval or anything that might have delayed his decision – Katona offered her Mimì in Covent Garden's revival of John Copley's production of *La bohème* in summer 1992 in which, incidentally, the young French-Sicilian tenor Roberto Alagna was also due to make his London début. The rest is operatic history.

With her first Violetta in a production of *La traviata* at Covent Garden in November 1994, Gheorghiu made the all-important transition to superstardom (with Cecilia Bartoli, the only female singer of our day to do so). In a portrayal to treasure forever, she vowed public and critics alike. *The Spectator* called her 'a precious jewel', *The Times* 'a remarkable new talent', while the *Financial Times* declared that 'there's no other way of putting it, a star was born'. The *Evening Standard* went even further, stating that 'she is also believable as a woman so sexy that men would kill for her or die for her'. This is a reference to the fact that Gheorghiu also happens to be one of the most beautiful women on the operatic stage, with flashing brown eyes, cascading black hair, a perfect oval face and a shapely, curvaceous figure that has caused her to be compared to the young Gina Lollobrigida. Such was the excitement that, in an unprecedented move, BBC2 quickly cleared its schedules to broadcast live one of the remaining performances to an audience of one and a half million: a star had, indeed, been born.

Yet, contrary to general assumption, this did not happen overnight. Gheorghiu had, in fact, sung a string of roles with distinction both in London and elsewhere in the preceding two years: Zerlina, Mimì, Liù, Nina (in Massenet's *Chérubin*) and Micaëla at Covent Garden, Adina for her equally successful début at the Vienna State Opera in 1992 (where she returned for Mimì and Nannetta), and Mimì at the Metropolitan Opera in 1993. This is worth mentioning because, combined with the superb training she received in her native Romania, it demonstrates that Gheorghiu's career rests on very secure foundations. This in turn may well account for her unusual poise and self-confidence.

At the same time that she hit the headlines with her Violetta, Gheorghiu also began her relationship with Roberto Alagna, whom she married in 1996. Their fairytale romance captured the public imagination and aroused hysteria in the press, including the tabloids, normally totally indifferent to operatic matters. In fact, the tabloids had not shown so much interest in opera singers since Callas's much publicized affair with Onassis. Alagna and Gheorghiu soon became household names and their popularity equalled that of the Three Tenors. Part of the appeal, as American *Vogue* put it, lay in the fact that 'every time those two appear together they are enacting, for our voyeuristic satisfaction, a love they genuinely feel'. Gheorghiu confirms that 'singing love duets with someone you love is *magnifique*'. When asked what dreams she has for herself in ten years time, both as a singer and a woman, she replied: 'that everything continues to be as it is today!'

Gheorghiu stresses that long before the two became an 'item', 'theatres were instinctively casting us together, probably because we are of the same generation and look well as a stage couple. So destiny had a hand in bringing us together. In fact, apart from that first *La bohème* at Covent Garden, the production of *Roméo et Juliette* which we sang at the Metropolitan Opera recently [spring 1998] had already been planned before we got together'.

The couple now divide their time between Paris and Geneva. In fact, shrugs Gheorghiu, 'it's difficult to say *where* we live. Mostly out of a suitcase, but I don't really mind. I'm used to it because I left my parents' home in Moldavia at the age of fourteen to go to the special school for gifted children in Bucharest', the Liceu de Arta.

Gheorghiu, whose maiden name was Burlacu[1] was the eldest of two sisters who were 'inseparable, like twins'. They were born within a year of each other to a poor but music loving family in Adjud, a small town in Romania's northern province of Moldavia. Her father was a

---

[1] Gheorghiu is the name of her first husband, whom she married about the time she graduated from the Conservatoire.

train driver, who liked to relax by listening to classical music and opera on radio and television. 'Every Saturday, there was one hour of classical music or opera on television, and my sister, who also had a good voice and became a singer, and I would immediately try to imitate what we saw and play at being opera singers.'

Then as now, Gheorghiu listened to music all the time. 'When I listen to music is when I truly live', she has said. (In fact she and Alagna are known for singing or humming their way through corridors, streets and taxi queues). 'One of the most important factors in my early musical education was Leonard Bernstein's TV series, *The Joy of Music*, a very important music lesson that formed the basis of my musical education up to the time I left for the Liceu de Arta in Bucharest.' This very special high school was to prove the real foundation of Gheorghiu's formidable musical education.

Both sisters were sent to this remarkable school, Gheorghiu says, which was 'lucky for my mother, as she could make the journey to the same place with clothes and food for both of us. Life was difficult. We did not have much money. But, thanks to the state system of education of all Socialist countries at the time, we did not have to pay fees to the Liceu or later, to the Music Academy.' Gheorghiu thoroughly enjoyed her years at this school, which was full of gifted young pupils from every field in the arts: 'Apart from my sister and myself, the other girls in our dormitory were a harpist, a pianist and a ballet dancer.' 'I wish for everybody in the world to have my kind of training. We had everything in this school. We had to fulfil the normal secondary school curriculum – sciences, philosophy, languages and the arts. We also had to study acting, ballet and a second instrument – mine was the piano – before I could get to singing. The idea was for young talents to be exposed to a variety of disciplines and thus really chose the profession we wanted.'

Gheorghiu was lucky enough to be singled out for private voice lessons three times a week. Here she met the teacher who was to prove the main formative influence on her voice and artistic development,

Mia Barbu. Barbu 'understood and didn't try to push my voice. We did exercises, *arie antiche*, Pergolesi to Mozart, full stop. She knew just how I should use my voice and body while I was still so young. She taught me all the important things for a singer, and gave me ideas about everything, not merely singing: for example, *how* to listen, comportment, everything. I still rely on the advice she gave me.

'We also read a lot, Beaumarchais, for instance, and all the background to the music we were learning. I didn't particularly *like* doing it. But Mia Barbu told me that, even though at the time I might think she was too demanding, giving me all that extra work, I would be grateful to her one day. Because in some other cases, I didn't feel that certain teachers of mine were demanding *enough*. I was very conscientious by nature, because I knew that I was here in Bucharest, and my parents were making sacrifices helping me, just in order to study. As a train driver, my father was well paid by the standards of the time, and the main part of my education was free. But my private lessons had to be paid for and so did food and clothing. So I owed it to my parents to do well. But even with my conscientious character, at times I still had to be pushed.'

After graduating from the Liceu de Arta with flying colours, Gheorghiu was chosen to continue her studies at the Music Academy where, in terms of singing, she says she learnt less than she had with Barbu. At the regime's insistence, she had to prove she had some other profession or employment in order to enter the Academy. There was a very famous madrigal choir in Romania at the time, affiliated to the Academy, founded by Constantin Marin, the father of the conductor Ion Marin. He 'engaged' Gheorghiu to satisfy this requirement 'without my ever having to set foot in the choir. So I always seem to have had a guardian angel in life.'

The curriculum at the Academy was very thorough and well thought-out, and included classes in opera, Lied, harmony, languages and ballet. 'The first year we covered the period from Monteverdi to Mozart,' Gheorghiu recalls. 'The second year was devoted entirely to

Mozart; the third to bel canto; the fourth to Verdi and *verismo*. I was assigned to the vocal teacher Arta Lorescu who always took on the best students, and who was clever enough to realize that I didn't need any lessons in technique as such after my work with Mia Barbu. I used to arrive for our lessons prepared as if for a concert and she would make comments or not, as she saw fit.'

The students had to go through a monthly examination, 'to show what progress we were making'. They had to sing an aria and a song to a panel of professors in an empty hall, which always made them very nervous, because 'all they were interested in was pointing out what you did wrong! This aspect of our training made us very tense but was, nevertheless, very conducive to learning. It also helped us learn to control our nerves, and I am very grateful for this now. In fact the longer I sing, the less nervous I become.' Gheorghiu is indeed one of the coolest singers in this respect, and her self-possession is the envy of many of her colleagues. It was therefore interesting to discover that this, too, is something an artist can actually *learn* to acquire.

In December 1989, shortly before her graduation, the revolution that toppled Ceaucescu broke out. Gheorghiu vividly recalls those terrifying days: 'We had demonstrations all day and shooting right through the night,' she shudders. 'Even in bed, you were kept awake by shooting all night long.' Yet the timing of the Communist regime's downfall was ideal for Gheorghiu's career. Having benefited from the excellent state education system could, like many of her Eastern Bloc colleagues, travel freely and have an international career.

For her graduation she had to sing her first complete opera, *La bohème* (a work which was later to prove so important in her life and career) in an Academy production in Romanian, a language which 'fortunately greatly resembles Italian'. She was the singled out to sing in a televised concert by Romanian singers in Amsterdam, 'one of the most ecstatic moments in my career', where her aria was Violetta's 'Addio, del passato'. She was spotted by the German-based agent Luisa Lasser Petrov, who had connections with Romania, and has also helped several other Romanian singers, who organized Gheorghiu's Covent Garden audition with Peter Katona.

Not surprisingly, Gheorghiu recalls the occasion as vividly as Katona: 'I had just come out of Bucharest and I had to make my way to the stage door of Covent Garden from my nearby hotel. My only words in English at the time were "Excuse me, sir, where is the stage door of the Opera House, please?" written on a piece of paper. So I duly asked a tall, slim dark gentleman. "Right here," he replied, pointing to a door about five metres away. I went in and was shown into the chorus rehearsal room, which is where all the auditions took place. Suddenly, in walked Peter Katona who turned out to be none other than the gentleman I had just asked for directions! He seemed equally amused . . . I sang my audition repertoire, which consisted of Susanna's, Louise's and Mimì's arias, and he seemed to like me.' This was the same repertoire with which she auditioned for the Vienna State Opera and the Metropolitan Opera, both of which likewise hired her on the spot.

Katona immediately offered her *La bohème*, and would also have liked to offer her Zerlina in Johannes Schaaf's forthcoming production of *Don Giovanni*, but Schaaf disagreed. 'He wanted someone more mature and experienced, not only as a singer but also as the character of Zerlina: a more mature lady who would herself be able to seduce Don Giovanni was his idea – not that Angela couldn't have done this, anyway', recalls Katona. All he could do, while privately disagreeing with Schaaf, was to suggest that she cover the production and sing the last performance.

'This was a very useful experience,' she explains, 'because although I only sang the last performance, I was also covering all the others and therefore had to follow all the rehearsals. For somebody who, like me, had only sung one single performance of a complete opera in my life – *La bohème* for my graduation in Romania – it was a godsend.'

'But I don't think Zerlina is an ideal role for me. It's too low and too short. I last sang it when this production was revived. But I love *Don*

Giovanni: it's one of the most genius-charged operas ever written. Every note and every word is spot on. There is nothing superfluous. Let's face it, there are moments in certain operas where, frankly, you feel bored because you feel that the words are merely an excuse for some beautiful singing. But in *Don Giovanni* – as in *Lucia di Lammermoor*, *Rigoletto* and *La traviata* – everything is essential.

'Do I like or dislike Don Giovanni himself as a character? From a woman's point of view, he is very hard to judge. Every woman sees him differently, while he shows a different side of himself to every woman.' Gheorghiu's views are uncannily similar to those of one of the role's greatest living interpreters, Ruggero Raimondi, who stated that Don Giovanni is 'a black hole into which everyone projects their own most intimate fantasies and longings'.[1] 'He knows whom he can conquer and whom he cannot,' continues Gheorghiu. 'Even a man of his character and super-self-confidence knows where his seduction will work and when it won't. This is a very special talent indeed. Do I, personally, *like* Don Giovanni? In another age, I might have. But not today. I am a very honest and faithful sort of woman. And if someone expects sincerity and honesty from me, then they, too, must be sincere and honest with me.'

Gheorghiu adds that she would like to sing both Donna Anna and Donna Elvira one day, having sung both at the Bucharest Music Academy during her student years. She says that of the two, the most difficult, surprisingly, is Donna Elvira. 'The reason is that like Desdemona and Gilda, poor women, she is a victim. Composers seemed to love creating suffering women. Verdi in particular has a great penchant for victims, possibly because he suffered so much himself.'

By general admission – including Katona's – Zerlina was not the sort of role that showed Gheorghiu to her best advantage: 'That special quality of hers wasn't there. But it certainly was in her Mimì in the historic revival of *La bohème* in June 1992, which also marked Roberto

[1] *Bravo: Today's Tenors, Baritones and Basses Discuss their Roles*, H. Matheopoulos.

Alagna's début here.' This is how Gheorghiu recalls her first encounter with the tenor:

'Roberto was late arriving at rehearsals, so I started Mimì's first aria. Unbeknown to me, he was listening from the wings. Never having seen me before, he wondered what this soprano who sounded so good would actually look like. I remember that I was dressed in a complete Scottish get-up: mini-kilt, white blouse with jabot, tartan scarf, sporran, the works. He walked on in the middle of my aria, and seemed to be pleasantly surprised. Next day, we started rehearsing the beginning of Act II, where we have to come on stage holding hands. I shall never forget that moment. Mamma mia! It was as if an electric current shot right through both of us. From then on we did everything we could to be together, like having dinner, going to the theatre or the movies. We just wanted to *be* together. Nothing more at that stage. Both of us were still married at the time. At the end of the run we went our separate ways, and didn't see each other for two years.'

Gheorghiu has very definite views about Mimì as a character: 'I don't think of Mimì as timid and passive. It's obvious that she was after Rodolfo from the start. She lives next door and, of course, she has seen and fancied him. In Act I she realizes the others have just gone out, and that he is in alone, so decides to take her chances. Puccini based her on a real person, as he did many of his heroines. Of course, dying on stage is always difficult, because you have to do it beautifully, whereas in reality death is never beautiful. Many people wrote to say, "Oh, how beautifully you died on stage", without realizing how much this takes out of you . . .'

To anyone who saw that *La bohème*, both Gheorghiu's and Alagna's performances will remain unforgettable. There was little doubt in anybody's mind that this was casting truly made in heaven: Both vocally and dramatically, they were ideally matched. Gheorghiu claims that vocally, Mimì is 'a piece of cake. But then, anything is after Violetta, the most difficult of all my roles to date.'

After her enormous success as Mimì, she was invited back to Covent

Garden to sing Liù in a revival of Andrei Serban's colourful and popular production of *Turandot*, and walked off with the show. Next came
the charming new production of Massenet's *Chérubin*, in which she
sang Nina opposite the delectable Susan Graham, who was making her
Covent Garden début in the title role. A few months later, in spring
1994, she sang Micaëla in an important revival of *Carmen* that also featured Placido Domingo, who has been an active champion of
Gheorghiu and who has sung several concerts with her worldwide.

Following the great success of these roles at Covent Garden, Katona
proposed Gheorghiu for the part of Violetta to Sir Georg Solti who was
planning, amazingly, the first production and recording of *La traviata* of
his career. 'He went to see her in several auditions, and although he
basically liked her, he still needed a little prodding,' remembers
Katona. 'He was taking things a step at a time. Then, he finally made
up his mind and announced: "Right, I'll take her." From that moment
on, he took to her in a very big way and went so far as to ring his
recording company, Decca, and announce that, contrary to his initial
intention to record the opera at its next revival, he wanted to do it
now.' Solti confessed at the time that 'watching Gheorghiu rehearse, I
could not speak. I was absolutely in tears. I had to go out. This girl is
wonderful. She can do anything. The music dictates her emotions, and
that's something I've seen very rarely.'

Despite such enthusiastic championing, Gheorghiu was not at all
pushy in those early years, according to Katona. 'She never said "oh, I
want to do this or that". She wasn't rushing things or doing too much.
Rather she tended to consider the offers that came her way carefully
and decide whether she was ready for the role or not.' ('My dreams are
logical, real,' she explains. 'I like to feel safe.') But, as Katona stresses,
in the case of *La traviata* she seemed absolutely determined. This was
the first time I had heard her be so adamant about anything. The next
step was for Richard Eyre, the director, to see her. He went to hear her
Mimì in Vienna and also fell for her in a big way. They had dinner afterwards and he was totally enchanted by her personality and

determination about what she wanted to achieve, and was immediately on her side. So that was that. And I must say that Angela rose to the challenge magnificently. She showed enormous professional confidence and nerves of steel.'

Gheorghiu found the fact that everybody concerned – herself, the conductor and the director – was tackling this work for the first time very helpful. Solti was an extremely accommodating accompanist, and although it was suggested at the time that this was not his usual way of working with singers, I beg to differ. Solti was always an unusually sympathetic 'singers' conductor'. As he himself explained: 'singing is a terrifying profession. Waking up in the morning and worrying about the merest hint of a croak in one's throat must make you a nervous wreck. This is why singers are often volatile and highly strung. My sister had been a singer, so I can sympathize with their problems.'[1] Both Dame Kiri Te Kanawa and Lucia Popp have stated that he was one of the most sensitive and accommodating conductors they had ever worked with, and his attitude to Gheorghiu confirms this.

At the première Gheorghiu sang almost faultlessly – barring a few understandably nervous slips of intonation at the beginning of Act I. In fact, as she and all interpreters of the role confirm, Act I is the most vocally challenging part of the entire opera. 'Violetta's first aria is really long and full of coloraturas, which have to be perfect. But the most difficult thing for me is the *character*. It *costs* me a lot to perform this role, to live it. Because finding the mysterious dividing line between abandon and control is very difficult, especially when you are young and especially when you are singing a role for the first time. Another important thing, is to be so secure technically that you can use the voice to respond to the music and make the drama live. In the case of *La traviata* it helps if you can remember what it's like to fall in love for the first time.'

[1] *Maestro: Encounters with Conductors Today*, H Matheopoulos.

This can't have been too difficult for her because, as already mentioned, those first Covent Garden performances coincided with the
beginning of Gheorghiu's passionate romance with Roberto Alagna.
He was recently widowed, his wife having died from a brain tumour,
leaving him with a three-year-old daughter, Ornella. This time it was
love the whole way. Since then the two have been inseparable, and are
obviously deliriously happy ('Oh la la, we are so *complete* now'). After
Gheorghiu's divorce, they married in 1996 in New York, during a run
of *La bohème*, the opera that had first brought them together.

Naturally Gheorghiu and Alagna want to sing together as much as
possible and in many cases this is artistically viable, as there is a lot of
repertoire suitable for both their voices. However there lurks a danger
that they might eventually hamper each other from developing as fully
as possible artistically. Gheorghiu, with her cool, objective intelligence, is acutely aware of this. She acknowledges that, shortly after
the two got together, everybody – themselves included – wanted
them to sing together all the time. 'But this has calmed down now.
One thing is very clear, though. Our artistic paths were already well
developed by the time we got together. So now we are basically three
artists: Angela Gheorghiu, full stop; Roberto Alagna, full stop; and
Angela Gheorghiu and Roberto Alagna together. We are not Siamese
twins. There are lots of roles we can, and will, sing alone, without the
other.'

One opera in which they did both sing together was Puccini's
La rondine, in a concert at the Albert Hall in May 1998 by the Royal
Opera during the rebuilding of Covent Garden. The role of Magda fits
Gheorghiu like a glove and she sang it as gloriously as one could ever
hope to hear it sung. Not even their marvellous EMI recording (which
was named Recording of the Year in 1997) had prepared one for this
real 'Sternstunde'. Gheorghiu says she is ready to sing this role on
stage 'tomorrow'. She loves the character of Magda, and says she 'tried
to express something with this fantastic music. It's not heavy like Tosca
but it's not operetta-ish, either, despite what some people say. With

music as gorgeous as this, it's crucial to *interpret* and not just to sing it. That would be a great pity . . . But as we mentioned operetta a minute ago, I would like to stress that the lighter the music, the more perfect your interpretation must be.'

At the time of our conversation (January 1998), Gheorghiu was preparing the role of Nedda in *Pagliacci* – an opera about jealousy! – which she was due to sing, at the 1998 Ravenna Festival in a production by Liliana Cavani conducted by Riccardo Muti, with Alagna as Canio.[1] Other roles in the pipeline are Suzel in *L'amico Fritz* and the title role in *Francesca da Rimini*, both in Monte Carlo. She would also like to sing the title roles in *Manon*, *Lucrezia Borgia* and *Adriana Lecouvreur*, 'because I love declaiming and speaking on stage! I adore it! I don't know why. Probably because it makes me feel like an actress! I watch film and stage actors and actresses a great deal and learn a lot from them about deportment: how to stand, how to walk, how to pronounce foreign languages. But before we do it on stage we plan a recording with Thomas Hampson. I would also love to sing the title role in *Lucia di Lammermoor*, but only on record. Among bel canto characters I do like the heroines in *Maria Stuarda* and *Anna Bolena*, which I might sing in 2000, they are more flesh and blood characters. Gilda in *Rigoletto*, on the other hand, which I was asked to record and sing immediately after my first Violettas, again with Solti, I find very dull. I prefer something meatier. But I suppose I *must* do it sometime because the music is so fabulous.

'As far as composers are concerned, I cannot say I have a favourite. I love them all. How can you compare paintings by Van Gogh, Rembrandt and Picasso, for instance. They all belong to different centuries, different countries, different cultures. All are geniuses. The same is true of operatic composers. I feel as if I am a palette of colours, from which I draw the right shades of colour for every composer. I

[1] As this book went to press, the production was cancelled after a rift with Muti during rehearsals – a rift, according to most present, that was not her fault.

learnt this from my teacher, Mia Barbu. She urged me to study and understand the background, the Zeitgeist, cultural and political, of every composer and know what kind of books or paintings Monteverdi, Mozart or Verdi might have read and seen, in order to know why they composed the way they did.'

According to Alagna, his way of working and learning roles is quite different from Gheorghiu's: 'I'm much more instinctive and like a wild animal but Angela is totally organized and planning everything she does.' Gheorghiu adds, 'people are always saying I am cool but I feel a mixture of contradictions inside me. I can be very cerebral or I can abandon myself to my instincts. On stage I must have a measure of mind control over what I do so as to arrive at a sort of economy between passion, emotion and technical control. This sort of economy is impossible without the brain. They say of some artists that they are instinctive and of others that they are cerebral. I think all of us are a mixture of both. It depends. Some have more of the one or the other. But everyone needs the capacity to understand where they are in a performance and what there is still to do.'

The audience is very important to her in this sense, as it helps draw the passion and emotion out of her. 'I want to be able to see the faces in the audience. This gives me strength, and somehow *compels* me to give. It *pulls* something out of me. I never feel alone up there, or feel that what I do is for myself alone. I feel a strength, a force coming to me from somewhere, from the public. This energy and electricity in turn feeds me with *more* power.'

Gheorghiu now stands at that wonderful turning point in an artist's career where the freshness and élan of youth are fusing with the mellowness and bloom of womanhood. This is reflected in the wonderfully sensuous darker hue in her voice which entranced her audience in the recent concert performance of *La rondine*. 'Gheorghiu's soprano has begun to mellow, taking on darker colourings in the most famous number, *Doretta's Dream*. But she still floats those exquisitely clean high notes, as in the Act II duet . . . First cool, then curious and vulnerable

and finally resigned, Gheorghiu was majestic', wrote John Higgins in
The Times.

Gheorghiu's challenge now is to preserve the freshness and spontaneity in her interpretation of roles she has sung, and will sing, many
times in her career, without becoming too absorbed either in herself or
in the lovers' bliss she is enjoying with Alagna. There was something
akin to this in her performances of *La traviata* at Covent Garden in
summer 1996.

Indeed, as Peter Katona confirms, 'the pitfalls for stunningly beautiful voices such as hers can be that they come to rely too much on their
beauty and perfection and don't bring enough emotion into their
singing. Angela was never like that in the early days. When she first
came over she had to fight for something, and she *did* fight and she *did*
give everything and the results were overwhelming. But as singers
become more famous and successful they realize that they cannot be
thrown out so easily and so they tend to start giving a little less, which
can be a bit unsatisfactory at times. This is something Angela must
ensure never happens to her.'

Gheorghiu acknowledges that the way opera houses are organized
sometimes makes it difficult for artists not to get bored with their
own performances: 'I've read the schedules of some of the great
singers of the past – one week they sang two performances of Manon,
next week they sang Violetta, and the week after that Mimì. This way
they didn't get bored, and they also kept their voices longer. Nowadays
we have to rehearse for four weeks even for roles we have been singing
for years and know backwards.

Equally wearing can be some of the senselessly eccentric productions many directors indulge in. Gheorghiu makes it clear that she
does not object to any new ideas or transpositions of the setting of an
opera, as long as it does not go against the music or call for her to do
'anti-vocal' things that make it impossible for her to concentrate on
vocal production at moments where this is imperative. 'At the
Salzburg production of *La traviata*, for instance, I was asked to take off

my ballgown and change into a nightie (why, I asked myself) in Act I just before I have to sing those coloraturas and have to think *technically* about precision. So, I refused.'

Many, wrongly in my opinion, would interpret this as diva-like behaviour, just as they did her cancellation of *La bohème* at Covent Garden in autumn 1996. That year Gheorghiu and Alagna's popularity seemed to plummet, not for artistic reasons, but rather because of dissatisfaction with their behaviour in certain quarters, or possibly because of envy at a couple for whom everything seemed to be going so well. This backlash culminated in a vicious article titled 'The Bonnie and Clyde of Opera' published in a British broadsheet. Fortunately, their sheer artistic worth helped them to survive such isolated attacks and re-emerge triumphant.

The real reason for those Covent Garden cancellations was the sudden death, in an accident, of Gheorghiu's beloved sister Elena – a shattering blow. As soon as I heard the news I remembered Gheorghiu's words to me at a dinner two years before: 'You should meet my sister sometime. She is more beautiful than I and sings even better!' – 'She was more than a sister to me,' she now reflects. 'As I said, she was only a year younger. We were inseparable almost like twins, although she was blonde and green-eyed. She was another me. But, of course, it's worse for my mother. She is really very badly hit.'

Jonathan Miller, who directed Gheorghiu in a new production of *La traviata* at the Paris Opéra in January 1998, was surprised at how easy she was to work with, how unlike a diva[1]: 'I had been led to believe she would be nothing but trouble with a capital T. In fact, she turned out to be very sweetly cooperative, extremely attentive, courteous, on time for every rehearsal and altogether charming. On

---

[1] Interestingly, when asked to define a diva, Gheorghiu had this to say: 'Everybody thinks a diva means somebody nasty and capricious and negative in every way. But on the contrary, a diva has to be *more* careful, *more* professional, *more* considerate than any of her colleagues.'

stage she was a fantastically powerful dramatic presence. At first, she objected to my concept of having Violetta die in hospital, surrounded by other moribund people. But she listened to my explanation attentively and became quite committed to the staging.'

Although it is true that Gheorghiu liked Jonathan Miller and behaved impeccably in Paris, she did not actually like the staging and tried her best to persuade him to change some aspects, especially that ending, 'especially in Paris where the public tends to be traditional and would not take to such innovations, particularly in cases such as this where the staging blatantly went against the libretto. Anyway I failed to convince him . . .' In the event, the première was a triumph for Gheorghiu and a disaster for the production.

In cases where she has to ride through an unsympathetic production, or when she is simply bored from over-rehearsing, she relies on varying her performance slightly to keep herself interested. 'In any case this happens automatically because it is impossible to do things exactly the same way at every performance. You are not a machine or a robot. You get carried away by the élan of the moment. But, with works I have done many times, I try to do this *consciously*, in order not to bore myself.'

One thing that never seems to bore Gheorghiu is recording. She is as choosy and as much of a perfectionist in this as she is about her stage appearances. According to James Lock, Chief Engineer at Decca (Gheorghiu's company until early 1998, when she moved to Alagna's company EMI), she is blessed with a voice that records impeccably: 'It's a very pure, very clean voice with excellent enunciation and accurate intonation, which makes it very easy to record. It doesn't have any of those awkward peaks that can send the metres flying over. All her notes are very clean and sound just as gorgeous on record as they do live!'

Gheorghiu is grateful to be living in an electronic age and totally disagrees with Celibidache's views on recording. 'We, the interpreters, have to do with a very transient art form. You may be hugely successful in your lifetime, you may be a genius even, yet you can end up forgotten. Because when a performance is over, it's over. Even I myself can't remember what I did last week in Vienna or Munich. So I believe in recordings *passionately*. They give us interpreters the opportunity to leave behind a tiny piece of ourselves. We have no creative talent, we are not writers, painters, or composers, all of whom are survived by their creations. The only thing we have to give, we give in our performances. And it's only thanks to recordings and television that now we, too, have a chance to leave something behind.'

GALINA
GORCHAKOVA

THE FRISSON OF one's first exposure to a great voice is quite unforgettable. One such occasion was the evening in spring 1992
when the Russian soprano Galina Gorchakova made her Covent
Garden début as Renata, the vocally fiendish role of the crazed and
obsessive heroine of Prokofiev's *The Fiery Angel*. Six years later I can still
vividly recapture the exhilaration of hearing that heavy *lirico spinto*
voice unfold with blazing power, unleashing wave upon wave of luminous, *gleaming* sound, rich in nuance and colour throughout the range.
Singing this expressively at that volume and register, hour after hour, is
a rare phenomenon characteristic only of very special singers.

The critics were equally bowled over. 'She knocked us all sideways', wrote *The Times*, while the *Financial Times* commented that she
'burst upon London audiences with tidal-wave force'. The same newspaper was equally effusive after Gorchakova's La Scala début in this
role two years later. As La Scala is a much larger theatre than Covent
Garden, it is more telling of Gorchakova's achievement to single out
this review: 'I am as obsessed with Gorchakova as Ruprecht is with
Renata in the opera,' wrote Alistair Macauley. 'Her voice is huge,
dark, heroic; and as she wields it in marvellously sweeping phrases, it

makes an incomparable effect in a large opera house. I use the word "incomparable" advisedly. Never in live performance have I heard a voice that has so excited me. I hope that La Scala soon can hear her in other Russian roles.'

Indeed the general consensus at the interval of both performances was that most of us had not heard a voice of such quality since the retirement of the great, and still irreplaceable, Leontyne Price. Vocal considerations apart, there is an extra thrill, an added emotional dimension to hearing Russian singers perform at their best and it has to do, I think, with *generosity*. There is a conscious act of *giving* that takes place on stage, which surpasses the level of what one is accustomed to, and which draws audiences not only into the character being portrayed but also into the core of the artist's own soul. Few Western artists are prepared to bare their soul to such an extent and to risk losing technical control, as they themselves eloquently and persuasively explain throughout their chapters. Yet this element of going to the brink of what is theatrically safe is what makes Russian singers so emotionally uplifting. Added to this is the unique, yet elusive quality of the Russian soul itself.

'We Russians are mysterious and sometimes difficult to understand,' confirms Gorchakova. 'We tend to be over-sensitive and inclined to introspection. We also love wallowing in our own and in other people's suffering. And as a people we have suffered so much throughout history that this reality of pain and endurance has come to be reflected in our culture, including our music. It's no accident that there should be so few merry Russian folk songs: most are soulful, melancholy and tend to express tears and sorrow. Opera, of course, is perfectly suited to the expression of such emotions, which is why we have such a rich Russian operatic heritage, and why Russian singers – of which there have always been a great many of the highest quality – have this natural gift for transmitting emotion and moving the public with the expression of their Russian soul.'

Gorchakova was one of the first of the current generation of Russian singers to emerge from the former Soviet Union. Like Olga Borodina, Larissa Diadkova, Maria Guleghina and others, she could easily have been doomed to isolation within her own country had she not been lucky enough to grow up at the right time. By 1990, when she finally reached St Petersburg from her native Siberia, the Soviet Union was fast opening up and its people, at last, were free to travel.

Gorchakova, whose ancestors were Cossacks from the northern Caucasus, was born in the small town of Novokuznetsk in southern Siberia. Her parents were both singers and her mother, who completed her musical studies when Galina was six, was hired by the opera house of Novosibirsk, a Siberian industrial city of 3,000,000. The theatre became Gorchakova's second home, her 'nursery school': 'I was left there for hours, day and night, with the children of other singers, and got to know most of the standard repertoire by heart.' But even before this, she had begun to imbibe and absorb music and singing from her mother, almost by osmosis. She remembers often locking herself in the bathroom and not emerging until she had sung every song and aria she knew. (Cecilia Bartoli, who grew up in a similar environment at the Rome Opera, explains the benefits to be derived from such an early and total immersion into the world of opera in her chapter.) Gorchakova's favourite opera at the time was Tchaikovsky's *The Queen of Spades*, with which she became obsessed 'in the same way that a child of today would be by a thriller or science fiction film'.

As soon as she could read music, she began to study the piano reductions of this opera and other favourite roles, which she used to sing while accompanying herself on the piano. Some western recordings were available in the old Soviet Union, and she remembers listening to those of Caruso and two of her favourite sopranos, Rosa Ponselle and Renata Tebaldi, especially in *Adriana Lecouvreur*, which she says, 'bowled me over. I absorbed every note.' She had started learning the piano at the age of seven, and as soon as the family arrived in Novosibirsk, she was singled out and sent to a special school for musically gifted children, where she continued her piano lessons and from

where she emerged with a diploma in the art of being a chorus master!
She then went to the Novosibirsk Conservatoire to study singing. (The
Soviet system of singling out gifted children and educating them without expense to their families was probably Communism's only positive
contribution to culture. It was interesting to find out from Angela
Gheorghiu that it also operated along similar lines in Soviet satellite
countries such as Romania.)

Naturally, the Russian repertoire took the lion's share at the singing
class of the Novosibirsk Conservatoire. But unlike Olga Borodina (who
states in her chapter that the teaching at her Conservatoire was useless
for anything except Russian opera), Gorchakova maintains that there
was also a tradition of Italian singing in Russia, instigated at the conservatoires by Glinka after his return from one of his Italian trips. She
feels she had therefore absorbed some of the basic elements of Italian
singing before she came to the West. But as far as the Russian style is
concerned, she says, 'every Russian student, even first year student,
knows everything about it, because we grow up with *Eugene Onegin* and
The Queen of Spades, just as an Italian grows up with *La traviata* and
Rigoletto. In the West everybody knows everything about the Italian and
especially the Verdi style of singing, but very few know anything about
the Russian style, which is very, very special. Russian music has to be
sung with very great precision, especially Tchaikovsky, who is akin to
Verdi in the absence of portamenti that should characterize the singing
of his music. Few non-Russian singers are aware of this, and do portamenti when singing Tchaikovsky, which is absolutely wrong.
Tchaikovsky is very exact, and every note he wrote must be sung
exactly as he wrote it. If you deviate from the score for even a single
note, the whole thing falls apart the same way that it does in Mozart.'
For this reason, and also because of the special pronunciation and projection needed for Russian consonants which so often eludes
non-Russian singers, Gorchakova recommends that they study their
roles with Russian pianists and coaches.

Of course the same is true, with a vengeance, for Russian singers attempting Italian roles. Gorchakova is mercifully free from both the typically Russian vibrato which sounds so unidiomatic in Italian singing, and the specifically Russian way of projecting the vowels by pushing the sound backwards and sideways to the resonators in the cheeks, thus widening its focus, rather than narrowing it and projecting it forward as one should in Italian singing. Nonetheless she has some way to go before she perfects her singing of some Italian roles.

But in the Russian repertoire, one could hardly hope to hear singing more evocative or rousing than Gorchakova's in her great roles: Tatyana in *Eugene Onegin*, Lisa in *The Queen of Spades*, Yaroslavna in *Prince Igor*, Fevroniya in *The Legend of the Invisible City of Kitezh*, or the title roles of *Ruslan and Lyudmila* and *The Enchantress*.

At the Novosibirsk Conservatoire Gorchakova met her husband, the singing teacher Nicolai Mikhalski, who is now her coach and artistic advisor and often travels with her and their ten-year-old son Andrei (who is looked after by Gorchakova's mother in St Petersburg for the rest of the time). After graduating Gorchakova won prizes at both the Glinka and Musorgsky competitions, and in 1988 was hired by the opera company at Sverdlovsk (now Yekaterinburg), where the Tsar and his family were murdered and which is also Boris Yeltsin's birthplace. She stayed there for two years and sang most of her Russian roles for the first time, as well as her first Italian roles: Liù in *Turandot*, Santuzza in *Cavalleria rusticana* and the title role in *Madama Butterfly*. (One shudders at the very idea of so young a voice being exposed such heavy dramatic parts as these last two.) She was probably saved from irreparable damage by the fact that the theatre already had eight star sopranos competing for leading roles, and so as a young twenty-five year-old newcomer, Gorchakova never had to sing more than once or at most twice a month – much to her frustration! Her background in the theatre meant that she never felt prone to stage-fright.

Her first Russian role there was Tatyana in *Eugene Onegin*, which remains her favourite part to this day. 'It's a bit like one's first love – it always remains special. And the fact that it's a wonderful love story by

Pushkin which all of us in Russia are brought up with as part of our heritage, means that it occupies a very special place in our heart. Vocally it's gorgeous and not too difficult to sing; it's easier than Lisa in *The Queen of Spades*, which I sang shortly afterwards. The important thing is to put across a young girl who is very strong and steadfast. She is loyal to her ideals and, in a different way, loyal both to the man she loves and to the man she marries. She has great integrity, which means that she is profoundly unhappy in a very typically Russian, soul-searching way. In fact Tatyana is so typically Russian that you could almost say that she is a personification of the collective Russian female psyche. The kind of passion portrayed in both *Onegin* and *The Queen of Spades* is totally different from anything one finds in Italian opera. It's a very northern and specifically Russian kind of passion. The difference between the two is that in Italian opera a man in despair would shoot somebody else, whereas in a Russian opera he would shoot himself. There is always something masochistic and self-destructive about Russian heroes and heroines.' Gorchakova obviously conveyed this particular quality in her 1993 Covent Garden performance of Tatyana, which prompted Hugh Canning to write in the *Sunday Times*: 'Here, in a classical Russian role where lyricism is at a premium, Gorchakova sang with breathtaking inwardness and a melancholic Russian soul, to stop the heart.'

Gorchakova remained in Sverdlovsk (the worst kind of backwater in terms of being cut off from the centres of Russian musical life) for two years. The most important event there was her singing of Clara in a production of Prokofiev's *Betrothal in a Monastery* directed by Yury Alexandrov, who was a permanent member of the Kirov Company in Leningrad (neither the theatre nor the city had as yet reverted to their pre-Revolution names of Mariinsky and St Petersburg). He urged her to audition for the dynamic new head of the Kirov, the conductor Valery Gergiev. Gorchakova did so and was turned down twice – 'I've had my share of tears and disappointments' – before finally being admitted in 1990.

Moving to either Moscow or Leningrad was essential for any Soviet singer who wanted to get on. It was only in these two centres that great careers could be forged both nationally, and on the limited international scale allowed under the Communist system. But while Moscow was the most important centre during the Soviet era, with the Bolshoi holding pride of place over every theatre in the land, as soon as the old system collapsed St Petersburg, with its Mariinsky theatre under the leadership of Gergiev, became *the* place to be. Gorchakova, who could not afford the price of even the smallest apartment, moved to a hotel room with her husband and young son.

She relished every moment in the city, with its fabled theatre (where Verdi's *La forza del destino* had its world première) and its rich cultural life. 'St Petersburg is a strange and magical city, the city where the events in *The Queen of Spades* actually took place . . .' It is also Russia's 'window to the West', and became increasingly so after Gergiev's appointment. Gergiev not only nurtured an entire generation of younger Russian singers but also transformed the Mariinsky into an important force in the international operatic scene, initially by relentless foreign tours to familiarize Western audiences and managements with the treasures of the Russian repertoire and with its magnificent new crop of singers.

'Gergiev is not only a conductor of genius,' says Gorchakova, 'but also an incomparable organizer and manager. It's a very rare combination in an artist. He is demonically intelligent with seemingly endless reserves of energy. Imagine what it took, and what it still takes, to assemble such a company in the chaos prevailing in our country and to succeed in maintaining it to such a high standard, year after year! It's clear that only an extraordinary individual could do such a thing, and he does it by sheer force of personality and willpower. It's true that he is a hard taskmaster and drives us all very very hard, but he transmits his energy almost by magic and works at a vertiginous pace. I always think of him as practically extra-terrestrial.'

The only thing with which one could reproach this remarkable

conductor and manager is indeed the fact that he does drive his
singers so very, very hard – much too hard for their vocal good. (This
could account for some of the vocal difficulties Gorchakova has been
experiencing of late.) During the Kirov's visit to the Edinburgh
Festival in 1995, Gorchakova's schedule was murderous: she had to
perform the title role in *Ruslan and Lyudmila* on a Thursday, the ferociously long and taxing part of Fevroniya in Rimsky Korsakov's
delightful *The Legend of the Invisible City of Kitezh* on the next day,
appear in *Sadko* the day after that while at the same time preparing the
title role in Tchaikovsky's *Iolanta* for the following Friday! Any
Western singer exposed to such a workload who did not refuse it at
a glance would be a guaranteed hospital case. In the event, despite her
formidable Russian constitution (shared by Olga Borodina),
Gorchakova had to cancel *Sadko*.

One of Gorchakova's first roles at the Kirov was Renata in
December 1991 in an astonishingly powerful production by David
Freeman, the same production that launched Gorchakova as a major
international singer at Covent Garden the following year. She found
the role totally and profoundly wearing, both physically and psychologically: 'The range of both its vocal and emotional extremes is
immense and, as Renata practically never leaves the stage, it is also
very demanding from the point of view of stamina. The part after the
duel in Act III is the most exhausting. The overall tessitura is also very
demanding. This role takes so much out of you, on so many levels, and
Renata as a character is so weird, manic and possessed that at times I
feared for my own mental sanity. In portraying such a character, especially if you give yourself to roles the way that I do, you really risk
becoming a bit unhinged yourself, because I don't like anything on
stage to be phoney. So I need to feel and penetrate deeply into the
souls of the heroines I portray.' After thrilling audiences at La Scala,
New York, San Francisco and Hamburg just as she had bewitched the
London public, Gorchakova decided to drop Renata from her repertoire, because of the role's psychological and vocal demands.

Gorchakova realized from the beginning that although Russian roles could form a very important part of her repertoire, she could not forge a truly international career with them alone. In 1995, shortly after making her New York début with the Kirov at the Brooklyn Academy of Music, she made her début at the Metropolitan Opera in the title role in *Madama Butterfly*. Butterfly, along with the title role in *Manon Lescaut* (which Gorchakova will sing in autumn 1998 in Holland with Gergiev), is the most taxing Puccini role after Turandot. It is relentlessly long, with very few places for the soprano to relax and catch her breath. Of course, it also demands phenomenal breath control, as the voice has to *lean* on the diaphragm in a very specific way in order to project over the loud, dense orchestration. I have not seen Gorchakova in the role, in which she scored big successes both in New York and Japan, nevertheless I fear that it might exact a heavy toll if she is tempted to sing it often. Gorchakova herself is acutely aware of the dangers:

'Butterfly is difficult not only vocally but also dramatically, because of the way you have to move on stage – almost with semi-bended knees – and because you have to think yourself small and dainty, which is not easy for a healthy Russian girl like me. I took special lessons with a Japanese teacher to learn how to act and walk in a delicate way, like a real geisha. And I was gratified when, after singing it in Japan, some critics wrote that I did it better than real geishas! Vocally, it's long and just relentless. In *Tosca*, for instance, you have gaps where you are off stage and can recover your breath. In *Butterfly* you don't. Acts II and III are exhausting. Tosca, which I love singing, and feel I almost don't need to act – so completely do I identify with her – is vocally much easier.' (Gorchakova's Tosca was well enough received when she sang the part at Covent Garden, but the general consensus was that her 'Vissi d'arte' was not yet that of a great Tosca.)

Gorchakova has now sung Tosca in most big international houses, and will sing the part again at the Teatro Colón in autumn 1998, shortly after her first Manon Lescaut in Holland. She finds Puccini ladies stimulating to portray because, she says, 'they are disposed to take their fate in their own hands, whereas Verdi heroines tend to surrender themselves to it. Of course, in Puccini's day the emancipation of women was beginning, and this made a huge difference to the way women came to be perceived. Their world is poles apart from that of Verdi's heroines, who tend to be either victims or ferocious political animals such as Odabella, Lady Macbeth, Abigaille or Elena in *I vespri Siciliani*.' Yet Gorchakova knows that her Puccini repertoire will never include Turandot for the same reason that it will never include Wagner, much though she loves *Tristan und Isolde* and *Parsifal*: 'I am besotted by them. There is something heavenly in that music. When I listen to it I feel as if I'm transformed, uplifted. I fly somewhere with it, and the experience is very difficult for me to describe in words . . . But I know I can never sing the roles in them, or any Wagner roles for that matter. My voice is much too soft-grained for that kid of sound. Although it's a *lirico spinto*, almost dramatic, it is not a full-blown dramatic voice and doesn't have that steely edge that can penetrate through this kind of orchestration.'

Gorchakova's attempts to sing Verdi have, so far, been less successful than her portrayals of Puccini heroines. Even fervent admirers among critics, including Alistair Macauley who raved over her Renata at La Scala, noticed some technical problems probably related to her breathing technique or simply to wear and tear from doing too much. This culminated in the cancellation of her concert performance of *Don Carlos* under Bernard Haitink, at an Albert Hall Prom, after recording sessions reportedly fraught with problems. The recording, in which she sings the beautiful but difficult role of Elisabeth de Valois is not one of her best (unlike the magnificent series of recordings for Philips of all her great Russian roles). But many great singers go through patches when they are below their best, and Gorchakova's is such a fabulous vocal instrument that, as she proved through her sensational portrayal of Kuma in Tchaikovsky's *The Enchantress* at the Festival Hall in winter 1998, it can recover to its stunning best. The role of Kuma is

Barbara Bonney as Sophie in Der Rosenkavalier *at Covent Garden: 'As a character, I find her a spoilt little brat, a dreadful, dreadful person! In fact I can't stand myself as Sophie!'*

Karita Mattila as Elsa in Elijah Moshinsky's Covent Garden production of Lohengrin *with (left) Gösta Winbergh in the title role: 'Her reactions are logical, human and real . . . I, too, could feel and act this way in the circumstances. And I don't think these emotions change, regardless of the setting in which the director chooses to place the action.'*

Jane Eaglen as Brünnhilde at the Chicago Lyric Opera: 'Brünnhilde is my Number One favourite character. She's such fun!'

BELOW

Angela Gheorghiu and Roberto Alagna in La Traviata at Covent Garden: 'Every time they appear together they are enacting, for our voyeuristic satisfaction, a love they genuinely feel.' (Vogue)

Galina Gorchakova, the overnight sensation in David Freeman's Covent Garden staging of Prokofiev's The Fiery Angel: 'A totally, profoundly wearing role, both physically and psychologically, that sometimes made me fear for my own sanity.'

Carol Vaness as Donna Anna in
Don Giovanni *at Covent
Garden: 'There are more
questions about this character
than any other that Mozart ever
wrote and you are always
searching for the answers.'*

*Elena Kelessidi as Violetta
in the Covent Garden
production of* La Traviata
*that launched her
international career: 'There
are two sides to Violetta,
the sophisticated courtesan
and the woman so pure
inside that I liken her to the
Virgin Mary.'*

Ruth Ann Swenson as Gilda in the Metropolitan Opera's production of Rigoletto: *'I love singing her. I love her music and the fact that she's such a heroine, so brave and so giving.'*

Deborah Polaski as Brünnhilde in Die Walküre *at the Berlin State Opera: 'Brünnhilde starts off being exuberant and confident. She's Daddy's favourite girl and absorbs every word her volatile father utters.'*

Carol Vaness as Delilah in Handel's Samson *at Covent Garden:* 'Nerves have made and ruined careers. If you are the kind of person who can handle it then you'll last as long as your vocal technique allows you to.'

BELOW

Olga Borodina in her Covent Garden debut in Elijah Moshinsky's production of Samson et Dalila: *'She is a political lady, but very erotic, very sexy, and the music is also very sexy.'*

Veronica Villarroel as Nedda in the Washington Opera's production of I Pagliacci, *'where, carried away by the very active expressionistic acting, the voice wants to run ahead like a wild horse'.*

BELOW
Susan Graham in the title role in Alexander Goehr's reworking of Monteverdi's Arianna: *'A towering achievement in which she was note perfect from A to Z'.*

Jennifer Larmore in her Covent Garden debut as Rosina: 'I don't think you should think of Rosina as a diva role because Barbiere *is really an ensemble piece.'*

Denyce Graves in the title role in Samson et Dalila *at the Metropolitan Opera: 'You use your voice in a sinuous, cantabile way that feels good while you're doing it.'*

Catherine Malfitano as Tosca in Nikolaus Lehnhoff's stunning production at the Netherlands Opera: 'A woman who, as a diva, has always had plenty of control in her life but who is caught in a real-life drama unlike anything she's ever acted on stage.'

Dolora Zajick as Amneris in Aida, 'the most difficult of the three great Verdi mezzo roles in an opera about wanting to make somebody love you who doesn't love you and doesn't want to. Of course, it's impossible!'

LEFT

Vesselina Kasarova as Charlotte in Werther at the Zurich Opera: 'Charlotte is a character imprisoned in her situation from which there is no escape. The part weighs on me psychologically because her fate touches me deeply.'

atrociously difficult, with an uncomfortable, uneven tessitura consisting of rapid leaps from low to high singing and vice versa. 'In this sense she is reminiscent of Lisa in *The Queen of Spades*, whose singing in the Canal Scene also has this sort of uneven tessitura,' comments Gorchakova. One therefore looks forward to her Manon Lescaut as much as to her Lisa, which she will sing again in productions of *The Queen of Spades* in Amsterdam and Hong Kong in autumn and winter 1998 and at the Metropolitan at the Vienna State Opera in spring and early summer 1999. Her Leonora in *La forza del destino* in Munich in November 1999 should also be a performance to relish.

'Leonora is a very interesting and vocally comfortable role for me,' says Gorchakova; indeed, when she is in top form, this should certainly be so. In fact most of the *lirico spinto* Verdi roles should theoretically fit her voice, once she gets rid of the intermittent technical hiccups that have tended to make her unreliable on occasion. (It was rumoured that this unreliability was one of the reasons why the Royal Opera's planned co-production of this opera with the Mariinsky has been shelved for the time being.) Of course, *Forza* is notorious in the operatic profession as an opera which is jinxed. Something goes wrong with almost every production, ranging from singer's cancellations to tragedy. (The eminent American baritone Leonard Warren dropped dead just after singing Carlo's aria 'Urna fatale del mio destino' at the Metropolitan Opera in 1960.) On an optimistic note, there is talk of mounting this production at Covent Garden for Gorchakova at some future date. It is to be hoped for fervently, because nothing could give greater satisfaction to her many fans than to see this great voice, 'a voice of wonderful sensual beauty' as Peter Katona puts it, fulfil its promise fully in *all* her repertoire, not just the Russian.

Elijah Moshinsky who directed *Forza* at the Mariinsky Theatre in June '98 thought 'she was in excellent vocal condition and the part suits her. In the middle of this company who has no sense of the outside world, here was somebody with a sense of Italian style. It's a very emotional role and she took it to extremes that no one, not even

Italians, could dare. Unlike American singers, she didn't "save". She wanted to squeeze all the juice out of the part. This is what Russian singers are all about: creating that dramatic effect, for which they are prepared to go to any lengths, vocally. So her portrayal was most convincing. To my mind, what distinguishes Russian singers from all others is this intensity.'

Gorchakova stresses that Verdi is a very difficult composer for everyone, not just for Russian singers. 'Vocally he demands everything that a soprano voice can do, as well as the same exactitude as Tchaikovsky. You cannot just get by with theatricality, as you sometimes can in Puccini. For example, Aida, a role that basically suits my voice and presents no problems in the arias, is very difficult in the ensembles, such as the Triumph Scene, when she has to be heard above the mayhem. This is utterly exhausting.' This proves the point that Gorchakova's is a heavy lyric voice, and not a *dramatic* soprano.

Gorchakova's career is and will remain two-pronged: firstly, performing at the Mariinsky Theatre or on tour as part of the company, and secondly pursuing an independent international career in the great Western theatres and festivals. She has reduced her appearances in St Petersburg itself because the theatre still operates on a repertory system, rather than the 'stagione' system prevailing in the West at such theatres as Covent Garden, the Paris Opéra, La Scala and the Metropolitan Opera. In practical terms this means that at the Mariinsky she ends up having to sing 'Tatyana today, Lisa tomorrow, *Mazeppa* on the day after that and *Betrothal in a Monastery* on the day after *that*. I find that very difficult and draining on all levels.'

But, perhaps perversely, she *enjoys* the rather chaotic hurly-burly back at the Mariinsky more than the super-efficient way in which most Western theatres work. As she confided to her countryman Victor Borovsky in *Music Magazine*, 'I would say that in Western theatres the ethos is more businesslike, cooler and more cerebral, more of a production approach. There is great discipline, everything is done on time, everyone knows what their job is and they do it with discipline.

At the Mariinsky there isn't such order. But the Western theatre is more soulless. I don't mean in the relationship between colleagues; it's something to do with the punctuality, the regimentation, the serious-ness of purpose – somehow it kills spontaneity. I don't wish to diminish the quality of Western opera houses; everything there is done to the highest specifications and is admirable. Everything is thorough and that is what we should learn from them. In Italian theatres, things are a little more happy-go-lucky and spontaneous. But in England, the States and Germany they are more disciplined. But I need these two very com-plementary experiences and ways of working: feeling myself a company member at the Mariinsky and working abroad as an individ-ual artist.'

She feels profoundly thankful to be living in the Russia of today rather than that of the recent past. Firstly because of the religious free-dom: Gorchakova appears to be a believer, and was wearing a Russian Orthodox cross around her neck at our meeting. Her profound faith is reflected in the frequent references she made during our conversation to God and 'fate'. Secondly, because of the artistic freedom to travel and to perform works – such as *The Fiery Angel* which were previously banned or frowned upon. She also approves of the current liberation from the previous regime's stultifying over-attachment to cultural 'tradition' in the negative sense that used to plague both the Bolshoi and the Kirov, crushing new ideas and causing stagnation. Now things are different except for one thing – as true of Russia as it is of every Western country: 'The power of the conductor in an opera house is like Stalin's!'

Unlike some of her colleagues, Gorchakova has no desire to settle in the West. Home is still St Petersburg, where her mother looks after her ten-year-old son Andrei during her absences abroad. As she declared in *Opera News*, 'the only reason we would ever remain in the West would be if the Communists returned to power in Russia.'

MARIA
GULEGHINA

'WHAT, THEY HAVE better voices than yours?' exclaimed Maria Guleghina's father one day when she came home tearful because her teacher had refused to let her sing a solo in her school choir, an incident she remembers as one of the biggest disappointments not just of her childhood, but in her life. 'Yes, or at least my teacher thinks so', she replied sobbing. 'Don't worry. You *will* sing one day,' answered her father. 'Everyone at the clinic where you were born foretold you would have a singing voice because they had never heard a baby cry so loudly!' For added consolation he reminded her that absolutely everyone in his family – his father, brothers and grandfather – had beautiful singing voices, although none of them sang professionally. 'They were serious people with serious professions – doctors and so on', explains Guleghina.

Guleghina's father was Armenian, and her mother Ukrainian. The family lived in Odessa, and she remembers with bitterness that 'being Armenian in Russia at the time was not very pleasant. Even at school I was made to feel an outsider, a second-class citizen.' Guleghina's dark, striking Mediterranean good looks must have made her seem like an exotic creature from another world. This sense of alienation probably explains why, as soon as she was professionally and financially able (after her 1987 début at La Scala in *Un ballo in maschera*, followed by *I due Foscari* in 1988, and a triumphant *Tosca* there in 1989), she bade good-bye to Russia and settled permanently in Hamburg with her husband, former baritone Mark Guleghin, whom she had married during her student days at the Odessa Conservatoire. She does not appear to harbour any sentimental attachment to her native country, and there is nothing remotely 'Slavic' in her artistic make-up, vocal or emotional. She is a dramatic soprano born for the Italian repertoire.

Guleghina's huge dramatic coloratura voice is unique in our day: unlike some dramatic voices of both the distant and recent past it is totally free of vibrato. Her sound is radiant and has infinite power and thrust yet is devoid of that relentlessly steely shrillness that can render even the most exciting dramatic voices unpleasant to the ear. There is nobody alive – and not many voices from the past either – that I would rather hear in the big dramatic Verdi roles such as Abigaille in *Nabucco*, Odabella in *Attila*, Elvira in *Ernani* and the title role in *Lady Macbeth*. She is also a distinguished singer of *verismo*, whose Tosca, wearing Callas's *own dress*, is the only one I have seen that did not make me yearn for my great compatriot.

Not surprisingly, with attributes such as these, and with her good looks and commanding stage presence, Guleghina rose to the top quickly. Her début at La Scala, at the age of twenty-three, was soon followed by German débuts in Hamburg as Tosca and in Munich as Amelia (*Un ballo in maschera*), both in 1990, and in Berlin as Tosca in 1991. The following year she made her début at the Vienna State Opera as Tosca, returning for Maddalena de Coigny in *Andrea Chénier* and Lisa in *The Queen of Spades*, a role she also sang at the Metropolitan with the Kirov Opera under Valery Gergiev. During the 1993–4 season she made her début at the Lyric Opera of Chicago as Tosca, sang the role with both Domingo and Pavarotti and made her London début at the

Barbican in a concert performance of *Ernani*. In 1995 she made her Rome Opera début as Lady Macbeth and her Paris Opéra debut as Abigaille; she also opened the Metropolitan Opera season as Maddalena de Coigny and toured Japan with the Met as Tosca and Santuzza under James Levine. In 1996 she made her début at the Verona Arena as Abigaille and her Covent Garden début in the title role in *Fedora*, and in 1997–8 she opened the season at La Scala as Lady Macbeth.

Guleghina wanted to be on the stage as far back as she can remember. She was stage-struck the moment her mother first took her to a special eurythmics school and the flames were fanned by weekly visits to the opera or ballet. Eventually she was judged good enough for serious professional training as a ballerina, but her father would not countenance her 'raising a leg in public'. She also learned the piano and, on top of her normal school and ballet school, also attended a special music school that specialized in training conductors. At the age of fifteen, she was taken by her mother to a preparatory music school where she was accepted for a conducting class in which she was taught by students. Her voice was very odd at the time, she admits: 'Only two parts of it were developed – very low and very high. I had no middle and used to leap between the two extremes in a sort of vocal acrobatics.' She stayed at this school for a year and a half and graduated two months before her seventeenth birthday.

Her aim now was to study at the Conservatoire. But she was considered too young, 'a baby', and told to go to college first and come back in four years. There and then she suddenly realized how important singing was to her: 'It was all that mattered. Maybe it was in my blood and my soul, but I *knew* then that this was the only thing I wanted to do in life. And, having been shy and polite throughout my audition, I shouted, "I'll study here anyway" and banged the door.'

After one year at this college, her voice began to get higher. She had originally been classified as a contralto, then became a mezzo and finally a soprano. The most useful things she learnt at this college were diction, movement, acting and every aspect of stagecraft. After graduating, she finally enrolled at the Conservatoire, where during her first year she had quite a good teacher with whose help her real voice began to emerge. She then seemed to get stuck. The teacher she really wanted to study with was her pianist's husband, the renowned Professor Evgeny Ivanov, who had taught many of Russia's most famous basses and baritones. Yet the matter was delicate because her current teacher was also a friend of her pianist, making any attempt to change awkward. But then fate took a hand. One day, Ivanov happened to be at home when Guleghina was working with her pianist, preparing for a competition. After hearing a few phrases, Ivanov remarked: 'This is very bad. Your voice is at a very dangerous point right now. If you continue along these lines, you'll be ruined.' Horrified, she asked him to explain what he meant. So he explained what she was doing wrong, which boiled down to her trying to sing with a bigger voice than she had. He then showed her how it should sound, and gave her some useful exercises. She begged him to take her on as his pupil. He replied that given his wife's friendship with her present teacher, it would be too embarrassing. But she insisted, pointing out that for her, as an aspiring singer, this was a matter of life and death. Gradually he relented and said he would try. 'If you are intelligent, you will understand. But you must remember everything I say because I won't ever say anything twice,' he warned. 'So I concentrated as hard as I could, and only made the same mistake once. All he said then was "I've already told you that!" It did not happen again. Nowadays I'm amused when conductors tell me that my mind is like a computer. It's true I can remember everything – unless, of course, I don't want to!'

While studying with Professor Ivanov, in 1985 Guleghina was hired by the opera house at Minsk in Belarus where she began by singing small roles such as Countess Ceprano in *Rigoletto*, occasionally taking on more demanding parts such as the title role in Tchaikovsky's *Iolanta*. At the same time she won first prize at the Glinka Competition and third prize at the Tchaikovsky Competition.[1] The theatre sat up and started taking more notice, giving her such parts as Elisabeth de Valois in *Don Carlos* and Rosina in *Le barbiere di Siviglia*.

Meanwhile, her lucky stars were again at work. Two or three years earlier, the Georgian bass Paata Burchuladze had come to Odessa to study with Guleghina's professor after his return from the school of La Scala, and had heard Guleghina in one of her lessons. He had subsequently made his triumphant début at La Scala, where the General Manager, Cesare Mazzonis, asked if he knew any singer in the Soviet Union capable of singing Abigaille. Burchuladze replied that he knew a girl who was very young but who could sing *anything*! So when Mazzonis planned a talent-scouting trip to Moscow, he sent for Guleghina.

'One day, the director of the Minsk Opera called me into his office and told me, in a very formal manner, that the director of La Scala was in Moscow and wished me to audition for him. I felt this must be a nasty joke and as I was particularly low at the time – Mark and I had no money and my salary was so low that we lived in separate rooms in a youth hostel – I was not amused. But he assured me it was no joke and handed me two train tickets for Moscow, for my pianist and myself.'

So the next day Guleghina and her pianist set off for Moscow, her first ever visit to the Russian capital. 'It was a great adventure. We were total strangers, but as my pianist knew a lady there, we went to her apartment to change and freshen up for the audition, as no provision had been made for any hotel or place where we could relax for a moment and catch our breath. As it was, we arrived at the audition half an hour late. Luckily it didn't matter because almost every young singer in Moscow who had heard that the director of La Scala was in town was queueing up for an audition.'

---

[1] It became a joke in Russia that the prize to go for in this competition was the third, won by both Dolora Zajick and Guleghina.

Guleghina was the last in line and sang 'Pace, pace mio Dio' from *La forza del destino* and 'Una voce poco fa' from *Barbiere*. Mazzonis asked if she knew anything more dramatic. 'La Gioconda' she replied. 'For goodness' sake not until you're forty,' he exclaimed, horrified. He then asked if she would be interested in singing at La Scala. 'What a question! I was wondering whether he had a small role in mind or even a place in the chorus. Then he asked if I could sing Abigaille! I was so stunned that all I could manage to answer was that I would ask my professor. He appeared to like this attitude. So I went home and rang my professor. "This is your chance," he said. "Either you'll sink or you'll swim".'

Guleghina, even at that young age, knew that Abigaille was hardly a role for a beginner. But on the other hand, she could not afford to close the door on an opportunity such as this. Fortunately, the mind-boggling inefficiency of the old Soviet bureaucracy came to her aid. Gosconcert, the official Soviet agency through which all artist's contracts with foreign theatres had to pass, managed, incredibly, to lose her contract. Undaunted, La Scala came back with another contract, for Amelia in *Un ballo in maschera*, which she would cover and then sing at the last performance. This time, Gosconcert did not lose the contract. But they did add their unmistakable touch by managing to send her to Milan twenty-five days late, three days before the dress rehearsal!

Normally, La Scala would have kicked out any artist arriving this late for rehearsals. But Mazzonis knew how the Soviet system worked and had been impressed enough by Guleghina to want to try her out at all cost, so he bent the rules. Also in the cast was Pavarotti as Riccardo, Nucci as Renato, and Cossotto as Ulrica; the conductor was Gianandrea Gavazzeni. 'Imagine what it felt like coming out of the USSR for the first time and being on stage at La Scala with these people! From the day I arrived, the coaches were drilling me like a parrot, teaching me how to pronounce a double 't' and double 's' the Italian way, where I should and where I should not double them, until

I was dreaming of this at night. And, because both the soprano who sang the première *and* the soprano who was second cast were booed, I ended up singing three performances instead of one . . . and I was a success. They applauded. I couldn't believe my ears. Frankly I didn't understand why because I didn't think the other two ladies had been any worse. So audiences, or this audience at least, struck me as being very mysterious . . .'

Mazzonis was so pleased with Guleghina that he invited her back for *I due Foscari* the following year and for a new production of *Tosca* in 1989 directed by Piero Faggioni, a brilliant operatic director who, Guleghina says, taught her almost everything she knows about stagecraft.

Their first encounter is amusing for anyone who knows the operatic profession because it shows Piero Faggioni — whose only drawback is a propensity to quarrel – in the role of peacemaker. 'I was in the middle of a music rehearsal and asked the conductor to please adjust his tempo at a certain passage. To my amazement, he said no. I replied that in that case I, too, say no, and would not sing it at this tempo. So he said he would go up to Mazzonis to inform him that I would not be singing Tosca. At that moment, Piero Faggioni appeared like a *deus ex machina*, beaming and in a very good mood: "Hello, let me introduce myself, I am Piero Faggioni, the director. What's happening? Can you sing for me?" I said we had just finished and the conductor also refused. But Piero, who looked me over in a penetrating way, calmed him down and we began. He told me later that from the moment he looks at some-body he understands their personality, and that he was sure I would make a good Tosca. When we reached the point where we had dis-agreed, Piero, unprompted, asked the conductor to do exactly what I had asked. And from that moment on, we worked as one spirit. It was quite wonderful. This was the first time I understood what it means to be an opera singer, a singing actress. He drew out everything I had to give. Having studied ballet for years, I knew how to move, and of course I knew how to sing. What I didn't know was how to coordinate the two. He kept asking me what every phrase I was singing meant, so that I could coordinate it with just the right glance, expression, gesture or movement. He also showed how to walk in those marvellous Empire-line dresses.

'Unbeknownst to me, Faggioni had got hold of Callas's dress from Covent Garden for Act I. Can you imagine my emotion? Then he also produced two selections of costume jewellery, one very shiny and very obviously paste and another, very dirty, and sort of blackened by time. I chose the second, and when everyone wondered why I said that maybe Callas had touched that jewellery and maybe it was a benediction.'

Maybe it was, for Guleghina scored a huge success and made her international reputation as a result. As I mentioned earlier, she is the only Tosca since Callas to convince me totally, vocally, physically and dramatically. She exudes an authentic Tosca *aura*. But that, she explains, is because she does not just sing or perform Tosca: 'I *am* Tosca. I am very like her in character. I too am very jealous by nature, although my husband doesn't give me any reason to be. But if I see a girl just look at him, I feel like killing her. Because for me he's not only a husband, he is a *friend*, a father, an adviser, he's everything. I have seen many people separate even after being together for many years, but I am sure this won't happen to us and I'm not afraid to tempt fate by saying so. So I'm jealous. And what I can't show in real life I show as Tosca. I love every word I sing and every movement I make in this role. I find it very easy, and I love Puccini's way of demanding two or three different vocal colours within a single phrase. Vocally, the most difficult spots are in Act II where she calls Scarpia an "assassino" and where she tells him "non m'avrai stasera giuro" ["I swear you won't have me tonight"], because both these words have to be *spat* from the chest, with full power, in a way reminiscent of Santuzza, which is to say very dangerous.'

Two details of Guleghina's portrayal are still so vivid in my memory that they are worth describing, to illustrate why her Tosca was so authentic. The moment in Act II, after she has given away Angelotti's hideout to Scarpia, she showed such regret, such awareness of the horror of what she had just done to stop her lover's torture. It was a look of shame such as I have never seen in another Tosca, and it is a powerful indication of how she sees the woman. The other moment was in Act I, when Scarpia has succeeded in rousing her to a frenzy of jealousy and ironically remarks, 'in chiesa?' ['in church?'], to which Tosca replies 'Dio mi perdona. Egli vede ch'io piango' ['God will forgive me. He can see I am weeping']. Guleghina cried in a most convincing and affecting way, rather than in the usual, cheap theatrical manner one often sees.

After her success at La Scala, Guleghina was invited to perform Tosca in Hamburg (1990), Berlin (1991), San Francisco (1992) and the Lyric Opera of Chicago (1993–4), and has since sung the part all over the world. In the 1993–4 season she also made her London début in a new role, Elvira in *Ernani* at the Barbican with the London Symphony Orchestra. She so wanted to sing this role, which she rightly felt was tailor-made for her, that she instructed her agent to accept this single engagement rather than a more lucrative string of performances elsewhere at the same time. I was lucky enough to be present at this outstanding début, and wrote then that Guleghina was 'one of the most exciting and interesting voices to emerge out of Russia, with a timbre that creates an instant, visceral, authentically Verdian atmosphere. She has the coloratura, she has the colour palette, she has the volume and amplitude, in fact she has the lot, and I can't *wait* to hear her as Elena in *I vespri siciliani*, where she would also be mind-boggling dramatically, with her dark, mysterious beauty and striking stage presence. The only thing still needed is a little refinement here and there before her huge instrument can be said to be completely under her control.'

Guleghina had almost achieved this total control – which comes more slowly to very big voices than those of smaller size – by the 1994–5 season when she sang another rivetting early Verdi heroine, Odabella in *Attila* at the Houston Grand Opera. She was a last-minute-replacement for Jane Eaglen, but had in fact already learnt and sung the role, in concert, because she likes the part and knew it would fit her voice. Like a true 'animal di palco', she had very strong ideas about the character and about how the opera should be staged: 'Odabella is a warrior, like some of the Palestinian women today. She is an Italian patriot, and her appeal to her countrymen should sound *meaningful*. The music is so rousing that it gives you everything and tells you everything about the character. You should simply do what the music makes you feel you should do. Imagine my amazement when I walked on stage for the rehearsal and they wanted me to wear high heels! I said "No way! Give me boots!" They suggested flat shoes instead, but I insisted it had to be boots. And I also asked for a belt from which I could hang my sword. Odabella should walk on stage brandishing her sword, and she should have the sort of costume that makes it possible for her to walk as a warrior would. They were all stunned, but I felt this is how the music suggests Odabella should be. Musically I loved it – it's ideal for my voice with a lot of coloratura, which I like, and I did the E flat at the beginning of my aria every night, to the conductor's evident astonishment. He thought I was crazy.' The Houston *Attila* was a result of that *Ernani* concert performance in London, which Guleghina *knew* would open doors for her in the repertoire that she wanted. It did, with a vengeance.

The Rome Opera House got in touch almost immediately with an offer of Lady Macbeth, in 1995. Guleghina jumped at it: 'Lady Macbeth is an enormous challenge for any singer in both the vocal and the dramatic sense. Vocally it demands at least three kinds of voice, because you need a different colour for each of her arias. So it's very difficult to establish exactly what kind of voice Verdi had in mind, except that it has to be a voice able to express excitement and lust. The first area is definitely for dramatic soprano; "La luce langue" is definitely for a mezzo; the Brindisi is for a light voice with coloratura. So I sing the first aria with my real voice and in the Brindisi I try to sound as Lady Macbeth would have others perceive her: as a nice, affable hostess. So I use a voice a little bit like Gilda's, sweet, beguiling, with portamenti, and *false*, because she's pretending to be someone she's not. But the second verse of the Brindisi, after Macbeth's hallucination, should sound a bit lost and mystified. That's why the ideal place to do *Macbeth* is in a small theatre, where you can make it more like straight theatre and where people can see the different expressions on your face.

'I know this may sound strange, but I don't see her as wholly bad. She's terribly ambitious. To her mind killing a few people on the way to getting what she wants – to be queen – is not that wrong. She just loves her husband and herself more than anybody. And I don't think that, in her first aria and first duet with Macbeth, either of them realize what killing really means or where it leads to. But in the second duet, where she wants to kill everybody, they do. At the Sleepwalking Scene – which drove me so crazy while I was learning it that I would wake up at night and sit on the floor, rubbing my hands – she tries to remove the spot. But, unlike Abigaille, she doesn't repent of her actions. In this sense, psychologically, she is more difficult than Abigaille.' Guleghina next sang Lady Macbeth in Monte Carlo and the opening of the 1996–season at La Scala, under Riccardo Muti.

It was also with Muti that she sang Abigaille at La Scala, in 1995. It is a role she says she was 'dying to do' because she wanted to show how it should be done. 'I *wanted* to be compared to all the other singers doing it because I felt I would win. Compared to parts like Santuzza and Aida, Abigaille is not difficult vocally. All these early Verdi roles are not difficult, they're *exciting*, really exciting! Abigaille is also a very interesting character, much more human and fragile than she is usually portrayed to be. She starts off thinking she is a king's daughter, but she's not and she finds this out in the most brutal manner. The shock hits her like a thunderbolt. Were it not for this, she would probably have been a normal person. Of course she is jealous of Fenena when she discovers Fenena is loved by Ismaele. This is the main reason why she turns into a warrior. It is the first rejection. To begin with, she sings horrible things to him to make him cringe.

Then her music changes and the *real* person, a woman who longs to be loved, comes out. At this point at La Scala I convinced them to let me remove my heavy helmet-like head dress and let this wig of cascading hair tumble down, as the music softens and the real Abigaille is revealed. This longing to be loved is a crucial point. Only when she realizes she is not loved by anybody does she freeze inside and want to kill everybody. But first she kills her own soul, the person she was up to then. Only a short while ago she was telling Ismaele that he would be freed and his people also if he would only love her. But he refuses. Everything she says in her aria "Abigaille e schiava" is understandable. By the end of it she becomes an animal, but an animal in pain. And the fascinating thing about this aria is that its tessitura is not that of a dramatic soprano but of a mezzo. It's Fenena's tessitura, and in this aria Abigaille also uses some of Fenena's language. I asked myself why Verdi wrote it like this? I think it's because as she is hit by everybody's lack of affection for her, she yearns, she tries, to be like Fenena, thinking that maybe this way she too might win their love. Then when she can't, she really turns murderous. But it's very important that she should sound like Fenena at this point, and for this reason I always listen very carefully to the mezzo singing Fenena to pick up her particular sound, be it Violetta Urmana or Elena Zaremba. And the lower the mezzo the better, because the contrast between my singing in this aria and my natural voice becomes greater. Here, Abigaille tells Nabucco, "But you also have another daughter" and his brutal reply is, "But you're not my daughter, you're a slave". The point I'm making is that Abigaille always tries to elicit a little bit of love, and she's always rejected. It's crucial to show this fragile side, too, otherwise her last lines, where she prays to be forgiven, wouldn't make sense. I find her a very interesting girl.'

She singles out her performances at La Scala with Muti as the most exciting she has sung to date. 'They were fantastic, positively electric, even though there were some high notes I had sung in Paris which he wouldn't let me sing. He also showed me how to inject energy into my singing in long sustained *piano* passages or even when singing *mezzo forte*, which is easy when you feel waves of it coming up to you from the orchestra. This was Muti's tenth anniversary at La Scala and we had a big success and a wonderful response from the public.

In her discussion of Abigaille, Guleghina made the astonishing statement that it was not as difficult for her as Aida – surely the hardest of all her Verdi roles. From someone who sings all his dramatic heroines with their vertiginous coloratura, a statement like this calls for an explanation. Of course, Aida is not written for a dramatic soprano but for a *lirico spinto*, or even a heavy lyric soprano such as the inimitable Leontyne Price. As such it calls for much sustained *pianissimo* singing and delicate shading which does not come naturally to a dramatic soprano. But Guleghina starts with a big advantage in the Triumph Scene, effortlessly soaring above everybody else in the ensembles and even the chorus, whereas most lyric sopranos struggle to be heard at this point (as her compatriot Galina Gorchakova candidly admits in her chapter).

Guleghina's first Aida was at the Hamburg State Opera, and she says she worked on it non-stop for two years with her husband, who as a baritone is perfectly capable of coaching her and who, she says, is 'the only one who really understands my voice, and voices in general, with uncanny accuracy.'

Guleghina had started off convinced that this was not really her kind of role, and recalls that when she first sang it in Hamburg it was a disaster, because she had not yet learned how to pace herself. 'Being still a stupid young soprano I gave it my all in Acts I and II and duly soared in the Triumph Scene, only to be left voiceless for Acts III and IV. Pacing and balancing the vocal and dramatic requirements of every role is essential. When I came to sing it in Verona in summer 1996 I had learnt this lesson and my Aida was a great success.' She is due to sing it again at Verona in summer 1998 and later that year in Munich, and at the Metropolitan Opera in the 1988–9 season with Placido Domingo conducting.

Needless to say, Guleghina's Aida is neither a victim nor passive, but 'a very strong woman like Tosca, only braver. Because it takes much more courage to choose to die as she does, buried alive and watching the man she loves die, maybe before she does, than to jump off the Castel Sant'Angelo. Only a very strong, quietly courageous person could do that. And as for her arias, which I used to think of as rather soppy, I came to understand them for what they are: "Ritorna vincitor" is permeated by nostalgia for something lost forever and "O patria mia" by the plight of a princess who, despite her present situation, cannot forget who she is or the suffering of her people and her responsibility to them. It was a big challenge for me, both vocally and psychologically. I did the E flat that Callas used to do in the Triumph Scene which I think is very important for people to hear because this point is a psychological climax for everyone. There is always a reason for very high notes. Composers didn't put them there just for sopranos to show off.'

There are, of course, two kinds of Verdi heroines, warriors and victims, and Guleghina tends to sing more of the former. Yet she feels that even the so-called victims, of which Aida is one, should never be played as wishy-washy, passive girls. 'Even Gilda is far from passive. She is a strong girl who chooses to sacrifice herself, knowing that the man she's doing it for is not worth it. Her ideal of love is worth it, and I don't think that shows a weak character. I always try to find something real, some "balls" to use your word, in the heroines I interpret. Because I don't like women with no balls. Even "Caro nome" should sound exciting and *sexy*, because Gilda is a girl who has just been awakened sexually. I am also opposed to Violetta [in *La traviata*] being sung by light lyric voices – I think Verdi would have preferred a darker voice, even in Act I. "Sempre libera" should not be sung with a sort of fluttering butterfly sound. It should sound more powerful because it's about *dishonour*, about a woman who may be dreaming like Cinderella one minute but who knows who and what she is and realizes this dream is impossible – "What? Me? Forget it!" And this moment where she sings "Follie" should sound dramatic, expressive with a tinge of hysteria. I can do a *piano* but I don't think this is the moment for it. At the finale, I think the dark colour of a dramatic voice would make it sound much more genuinely ill in the scene where she reads Germont Père's letter.' Guleghina would love to sing Violetta some day and it will be interesting to see where or whether she will get this chance.

Guleghina is well qualified to pinpoint the difference between Verdi's and Puccini's heroines. In musical and vocal terms, the difference, she says, boils down to the fact that 'if you sing Verdi with heart and emotion, the truth about the character comes out. He paints with a very wide brush. Puccini needs more artifice, more attention to detail. *He* paints with a very *fine* brush. Sometimes a very short phrase consisting of two or three notes may require a different colour; and sometimes he has phrases that come quite close to the spoken word, to straight theatre.' The only other Puccini heroine Guleghina sings is Manon Lescaut, which she was preparing to sing at La Scala in June 1998.

Her other *verismo* heroines include Maddalena de Coigny (*Andrea Chénier*) as well as the title role of *Fedora*. Maddalena she finds very interesting: 'You have to show the change in her in Act I after Chénier sings the Improvviso. She opens up like a flower through the action, from a sheltered girl to the courageous woman who chooses to die with Chénier. Fedora on the other hand I initially found very difficult not so much to sing, but to *live* as a character. It's so over-melodramatic. When I first looked at it I began to laugh, it was so stupid! In fact I only did it because Placido asked me to, and I promised myself I never would again. Yet after I sang it I did begin to understand this woman. She is in love with one man, Vladimir, but then when she meets another man, Loris, she feels a strange attraction for him because he's a dangerous person and some women are attracted by dangerous men. And once you get enmeshed with a man like that the mutual danger brings you closer because you feel you're in the same game. I always *try* to understand the characters I sing and, having made a tenuous link with Fedora, I *might* sing it again.' Another *verismo* role she sings only sparingly is Santuzza.

Guleghina's future plans, apart from those mentioned already, include her first staged *Ernani* at the Vienna State Opera in June 1999, a new production of *Tosca* by Franco Zeffirelli in Rome to celebrate the opera's centenary, new productions of *Macbeth* in Paris, *Un ballo in maschera* in Tokyo, two new productions at La Scala during the Verdi Centenary of 2000–01 and participation in their Japanese tour of that year and her first Norma in Seville. She is dying to sing Norma and is sensibly trying it out first in a reasonably small, secluded theatre. Instead of Norma, though, she is always being asked to sing Turandot. 'They say "you have such a powerful, penetrating voice and you have the high Cs." I reply, "Yes, but I don't want to lose them!"' When asked if she has any hobbies, Guleghina replied 'Yes, singing! Because, joking apart, my work takes up all of my time. People seldom realize that being a diva is very hard work: training, training, training, like a horse.' Yet she loves her profession passionately – I am sure it is obvious by now that Guleghina does everything she does with passion – and, unless she is feeling ill, she longs to go on and sing. She very seldom suffers from nerves – a rare case was when she had to sing Aida in Verona with only one dress rehearsal – but even then, 'the moment the music begins, I lose myself. The music unleashes everything I have inside. I couldn't sing without passion. I know some singers who do, who can sing in a cold, detached manner and I hate them for it. When I sing it's as if I have a speedometer of passion. And every time I have to go past its limits.'

After a performance it's always straight back home with Mark. The two are constantly together, going for walks, riding horses or jogging, and constantly talk about music. 'It's as if we were born together,' she recently told an Italian magazine. 'Because you cannot live a life like ours [a diva's] without love. From the beginning my husband and I decided to be together all the time. He gave up his career to be with me. I have not been much of a mother to my daughter, Natalia, who has been looked after by my mother, at home in Hamburg[1]. (Her mother also looks after Guleghina's beloved poodle, Floria Tosca, and four other new dogs prevented from joining her in Britain by our absurd, outdated quarantine laws.) 'In fact,' she added, quite realistically, 'Mark is only free when I sleep!'

[1] Guleghina is currently preparing to move to Luxembourg.

$E\,L\,E\,N\,A$
$K\,E\,L\,E\,S\,S\,I\,D\,I$

I<small>T's NOT OFTEN</small> that one can participate in and contribute to the making of a new operatic star. Yet this is what I was privileged to have the opportunity to do for Elena Kelessidi, the Greek soprano whose triumph in *La traviata* at Covent Garden in 1996 set her on the road to an international career. In the summer of 1998 she sang Violetta again at the Covent Garden season at the Albert Hall and at Baden-Baden under the baton of Placido Domingo, and sang Rossini's Desdemona at the Vienna Festival. As my involvement in launching her career was both extensive and decisive, this chapter is written in a more personal vein than I normally allow myself to indulge.

I first heard Elena Kelessidi, who was born in Kazakhstan of Greek parentage and emigrated to Greece in 1992, at the Athens Megaron. This sensational concert hall, inaugurated in 1991 is generally considered along with Tokyo's Suntory Hall to be one of the best modern concert halls in the world. The Megaron's large auditorium has a multi-purpose stage that allows it to mount several operatic productions a year. As its Artistic Adviser and United Kingdom representative from 1991 until 1996 (when I joined the Philharmonia as Special Consultant for Vocal Projects), I was actively involved in the casting of some of those productions, and in helping bring great artists for solo recitals. After Ruggero Raimondi's electrifying solo evening in October 1992, the Megaron asked him to return for an opera, preferably *Don Giovanni*. He replied that he would be interested, but as a director rather than as the star, and added that he would prefer to direct a cast of young, inexperienced singers. Therefore why didn't we organize an international singing competition aimed at finding new singers for all the roles in the opera? Who knows, this might produce the definitive Don Giovanni of the future. So we did, with a project titled 'The Quest for Don Giovanni'. Sadly, we did not find the Don Giovanni of the future.[1] But we did find Elena Kelessidi, who was to prove one of the most moving Violettas in living memory.

The competition took place in three stages between September and November 1994. We held two preliminary rounds, one in Athens for Greek and East European singers and one in Paris for Americans and Western Europeans. The winners for each role in these two rounds were then invited to Athens for the finals. The jury at Athens consisted of the sopranos Wilma Lipp and Jeanette Pilou as well as myself; in the Paris jury were Dr Claus Helmut Drese, the former director of the Zürich Opera and the Vienna State Opera, the soprano Graziella Sciutti and myself. The jury at the finals was chaired by Ruggero Raimondi and included all the above, with the addition of Maestro Nicos Tsouchlos, Director of Artistic Programming at the Megaron.

So, one day in September 1994, I found myself sitting in the darkened Dimitri Mitropoulos Hall (the smaller of the Megaron's two auditoriums), auditioning candidates for the role of Donna Anna. We had already heard a few disappointing candidates, and one promising one. Then out stepped an attractive brunette with wistful eyes, in a

---

[1] But Sorin Coliban, a very promising young Romanian bass having a good career, may develop into a great Don in the future.

long black dress. Something about those eyes bespoke an artist (as Placido Domingo also noticed, without having ever heard her, when I introduced them at the canteen of Covent Garden two years later). And something about her air predisposed you (or me, at least) in her favour – I remember wanting her to be good, wanting her to win. She began with 'Non mi dir'. I was instantly struck by the distinctive timbre and colour of her voice, and most of all by its expressiveness and innate communicative gift. This girl seems to have everything that cannot be taught, I thought to myself. (Interestingly, Elena's agent, Alan Green of Columbia Artists, thought the very same thing when he auditioned her quite some time later.) She obviously *felt* everything she was singing, and experienced the music with every nerve and fibre of her being. Once into the music she even forgot to be nervous, and really *became* the character. Her Italian was atrocious – in fact it was barely recognizable as such – and her Mozartian style needed polishing. But these things can be learnt. I was determined to pass her through to the finals, and knew Raimondi would like her. After much discussion with my fellow jurors, during which Wilma Lipp voiced doubts about her style and Jeanette Pilou about her Italian – we decided to pass her. I went backstage and told her what she needed to work on in the intervening two months. With the help of her first-rate coach and pianist Medea Iasonidou, an inspired musician now embarked on a singing career, she did. And fast. She had to. At the finals the improvement was immediately audible. She had all the attributes that had transfixed me before, as well as intelligible Italian and an authentic Mozart style. Obviously a quick learner, I noted.

This competition proved the making of her career. For Peter Katona, Artistic Administrator at Covent Garden (and solely responsible for the magnificent casting for close on fifteen years), was also transfixed. 'You weren't conscious of any deliberate effort to achieve something, vocally or dramatically, and either achieving it or failing to do so. The character seemed to burst out of her, totally naturally. You weren't tempted to compare it with other singers' portrayals or say oh, it's too this or too that. It was totally natural and compelling. This is what struck me about her.'

Having now heard her in several productions of *La traviata* and also as Cleopatra in *Giulio Cesare*, Katona feels that this characteristic remains the most striking thing about her. 'She is very fresh, instinctive and spontaneous, and that includes any flaws she might have. You don't have the impression that she is acting, or phrasing consciously, or indeed making any calculated effort. It comes across as if the character in the role is speaking directly to you, with absolute immediacy, and the music also sounds totally fresh – you feel you have never heard it before. It's like meeting a new person in real life, who speaks to you very immediately, and you fall under their spell. Only in this case it's an operatic character, such as Violetta, who speaks to you in this very immediate way.'

After being so struck by her at this competition, Peter Katona asked if I could arrange for him to hear Kelessidi in a full performance of *anything*, to see to what extent she could carry through an entire evening. The only thing she was scheduled to sing was Constanze at the Athens State Opera five months later in March 1995, for which we flew out together. Even with the odds against her – a revival mounted with minimum rehearsal – she came through and sang very respectably, scoring a good success with the public. A private audition had already been arranged for the following afternoon, which coincided with a big bank holiday weekend in Greece. But the Megaron obligingly made arrangements for its large auditorium to remain open for us.

She walked onto the empty stage and began a selection of arias, from Gilda's 'Tutte le feste al tempio' and 'Caro nome' to bel canto – *Lucia*, *I puritani* and *La sonnambula* – each more beautifully sung than the last. When it came to Amina's 'Ah, non credea mirarti', Katona and I were both practically in tears. I can honestly say I have never heard it better sung in my life (having not seen Callas in this role). We looked at each other in amazement and Katona whispered in my ear that he would revive *I puritani* just for her, though this was a long way off.

'Meanwhile,' he asked, 'shall I take the biggest risk of my career and give her *La traviata*?' I stared at him in disbelief. Violetta at Covent Garden to a *beginner*, who had sung three small roles in Kazakhstan and one at the Athens National Opera? Angela Gheorghiu, who had triumphed in the role the previous November, had sung it only after five other, much easier roles at Covent Garden (Zerlina, Micaëla, Liù, Nina and Mimì), with considerable career experience behind her. Well, this would make or break Elena Kelessidi. At a stroke. With all this flashing through my mind, I swallowed hard and whispered back, 'Why not?'

Peter Katona, being the kind of person who puts his money where his mouth is (see for instance the chapter on Angela Gheorghiu), and realizing that this was a special case with very particular needs, arranged for Kelessidi to spend two separate fortnights in London. Here she was to receive intensive coaching from the expert Royal Opera staff, which included Tina Ruta, its Italian language coach, and Mark Packwood. During those periods she stayed with me, and I was able to follow her development every step of the way. It was refreshing to see someone so keen to succeed and do well, and to whom everything about the profession was totally new. She did not know the ropes, who was who or what an international career means.

Before moving on to the première of *La traviata* in London that proved the making of Elena Kelessidi, I have to say that her performances as Donna Anna in the production of *Don Giovanni* at the Megaron in March 1996 were disappointing. She came to the rehearsals unprepared, behaved childishly throughout and did not seem to respond to direction with the quickness one might expect. (Only later did it become apparent that in fact she understood almost nothing of what was said to her.) Both Katona and I began to have misgivings about whether she would be able to cope with the stress and challenge of a Covent Garden *Traviata*. But before we come to that landmark in her life, it is high time to let Elena Kelessidi tell her own story.

Her grandparents, Greeks from Constantinople, had fled from

Turkey to Georgia during the persecution and massacre of Greeks in
1922, part of nearly two million people who fled north to Russia
(another one and a half million fled west to Greece). During Stalin's
rule, many Georgia-based Greeks were forcibly moved to Central
Asia, in an attempt to counterbalance the Muslim populations. Her
mother, then a child, recalls living in a tent for three years before her
family was properly housed. Elena's father was an engineer by profession, but at the same time immensely musical, with a good tenor voice.
'He played three instruments and had a lovely dramatic tenor voice,'
says Kelessidi. 'As soon as he realized I could sing he made me start
piano lessons, and often asked me to sing along with him. I remember
him putting me on a chair and singing songs and duets together, both
at home and in the houses of friends.' The child was obviously gifted
and musical but lazy, and concentrating over protracted periods was
not easy for her. 'But, whenever I neglected my piano practice,' she
continued, 'my father would beat me. So I didn't do that very often. I
suppose it's thanks to his insistence that I am what I am now.'

Her home town was Chimkent, Kazakhstan's third largest city, with
about 600,000 inhabitants. After attending the local music high school,
she was accepted by the conservatory at Alma Ata, the state capital,
where she studied singing for four years, the first Greek ever to study
there. She did not much care for her singing teacher and was frustrated
by the fact that nothing was ever sung in Italian. Nonetheless, the fact
that she has a very good vocal technique means that the training must
have been sound. She soon became known as 'the Golden Voice' of the
Conservatoire. What she really enjoyed were the acting classes: 'The
teacher, Professor Pavlov, had been a pupil of Stanislavsky and detected
a natural acting instinct in me. He thought I was the best student in the
class and taught me the difference between straight acting and operatic
acting: how to move and walk on stage, plus a few gestures. He pointed
out that in opera you cannot make the same naturalistic gestures that
you make in straight theatre, because you have to move in rhythm
with the music. "Forget about real life," he said. "In real life you don't

get to sing high notes! Another thing you should remember is that on stage you should always die beautifully, even though in real life death is never beautiful. This is theatre, this is opera." And, of course, this is what I love about it.'

While still a student she married Andrei Monitz, a forestry student, and had a baby daughter, Veronica. 'In that part of the world if you weren't married by the age of twenty, you were considered to be on the shelf. I was married with much love and we were so happy!' Meanwhile, before graduating from the Conservatoire, she also sang a few roles at the local opera house – Leïla in *Les pêcheurs de perles*, Zerline in *Fra Diavolo* and Serafina in Donizetti's little known *Il campenello di notte*. She also took the part of Marfa in *The Tsar's Bride* in the Bolshoi Theatre Company when it visited Alma Ata.

After graduation she was offered a place at the opera house. But it was then 1991, the old Soviet Union had broken up, Kazakhstan had become an autonomous republic and nationalism was on the rise. 'All traces of the Russian language were swept away, from street names and admission desks in hospitals to the opera house. My contract stipulated that I should sing all roles in Kazakh!' Her father was dead by then, and her mother pointed out that there was no future for them in Kazakhstan, either for Elena or for her little daughter. Best to join the tide of Greeks pouring out of the newly opened Russian frontiers to Greece. 'Fortunately we had enough money to bribe the right officials and get our exit visas quickly.'

So the whole family, none of whom spoke any Greek (Stalin had forbidden minorities to be educated in their own languages), arrived in Greece. Elena was the only member of the family to have visited the country before, in 1990 while she was still a student. 'With two other Pontian-Greek opera singer friends – soprano Elena Panaki and mezzo Inga Balabanova – I got a job on a cruise ship going from Georgia to Greece. Our job was to sing over dinner. I shall never forget my first sight of Greece. One morning we woke up, and there was blue water, a blue I'd never seen before, and that magical light all around me. In the distance I could see a city, towards which we appeared to be heading. I asked its name and was told it was Salonica. My heart began to beat so loudly and as we approached it nearly stopped. You cannot *imagine* the emotion of seeing your country for the first time when you have been brought up in exile in a foreign land. For while I loved Russia and was happy there, there was never any doubt in my mind that I was a Greek. Greece was omnipresent in our home – as indeed it was in the homes of most Greeks in exile. It was full of pictures of its landscapes, its ancient ruins and Byzantine churches, books about its history and archaeology and cassettes of Greek music, brought back by the lucky few who could travel there. My brother and I were mad about Greek music, we listened to it with passion, and we managed to learn the songs and words by heart phonetically.' (Years later she met the composer of many of those songs, George Hadzinassios, in Athens.) When the ship docked in Athens, she went to see its unprepossessing opera house (a converted cinema) out of curiosity and also met its highly able director, George Sinodinos.

When she finally arrived in Greece for good, however, many of her romantic views about the country were dispelled with a bang. Life was very hard for all new settlers at first, until they could be housed and settled in jobs. The worst shock was being referred to as 'Pontians' ('Black Sea Greeks') or even worse, 'Russo-Pontians'. 'Can you imagine the hurt? All those years generations of Greeks in Russia had endured untold hardships, sustained by their knowledge and pride in being Greek. The Russians called us Greek. But, the Greeks didn't.'[1]

Elena applied for an audition at the National Opera right away, helped by Medea Iasonidou, who accompanied her on the piano and acted as interpreter. 'I sang Gilda's two arias and Juliette's "Je veux vivre". I was accepted there and then and offered the role of Madame

[1] Some refugees were called 'Pontians' to distinguish them from those from Ionia, the shores of Asia Minor; and the term 'Russo-Pontians' in turn distinguished the new settlers from Russia from previous groups from Turkey.

Herz in Mozart's *Der Schauspieldirektor* and another small role for the 1993–4 season. Then there was a long strike at the theatre, which meant that I never got to sing either.' Desperate to make ends meet, she took a job singing in a Russian restaurant in a smart Athens suburb and in the choir of the Russian Church, where she made many friends some of whom helped the family cope financially.

When the theatre reopened she was immediately re-engaged, this time as Constanze in two runs of *Entführung* , as second cast in autumn 1994 and as first cast in spring 1995 (when Peter Katona and I came over to hear her). In summer 1994 she heard about the Megaron's *Don Giovanni* competition, and right away decided to apply. 'My pianist thought I was mad,' she remembered. She said I didn't have the right voice for Donna Anna, nor for Donna Elvira nor Zerlina. So what was the point? But I saw it as a chance to show my voice to a panel of international people. I didn't expect to win anything. But I wanted someone to know I existed. This is the sort of risk you *must* be prepared to take if you want to succeed. And this is where you came in. I remember every detail of that day when I stepped out on the stage of the Dimitri Mitropoulos Hall at the Megaron, and seeing three ladies sitting in the stalls, two in the front row, and you a few rows back, on your own. I even remember what you wore.

'It must have been obvious how nervous I was, because after the first aria you asked if I would like a glass of water. So I had one, and felt a little better. At that point I began to feel a sort of benevolence, something positive coming at me from you, and I sang "Non mi dir" better. I remember you shouted "Bravo".'

She admits that when it came to the production of *Don Giovanni* she made 'a bit of a mess of things. I had been overwhelmed by Covent Garden's invitation for *Traviata*, and thought I had already arrived! So maybe I didn't prepare myself as seriously as I should have. I understood nothing about the profession as yet. On top of which I had a giant complex about my inability to speak any language other than Russian. Everyone around me spoke at least two foreign languages – Greeks are good linguists, as you know – and I didn't even speak Greek properly, or worse, understand it. And I was too ashamed to admit it. So when the conductor, Gustav Kuhn or Ruggero said something to me – which already had to be translated into Greek – I didn't dare say I could not understand even that. So I pretended I did. Now, of course, I would ask for a Russian interpreter. But back then, I was no-one.'

She was acutely aware of the disappointment she caused Raimondi, the Megaron and myself. It was not that she sang all that badly but that scenically she was completely wooden (surprising in view of the fact that she is a natural actress), and did not seem to have absorbed any of the fascinating things about the character that Raimondi had painstakingly tried to teach her. At the last minute she was moved to second cast, an experience which really stunned her. But it taught her a lesson: she determined that nothing like that would happen at Covent Garden.

'I read everything there was to read (in Russian, naturally) about *Traviata* and the Dumas story, and tried to see every film version of *The Lady of the Camellias*. Even now, having done it twice in London, twice in Munich and once in Baden-Baden, I still try to read something more each time I do it. And each time, I find something new in the role. The work is never over. A role develops along with you and each time, if you let the music speak to you, you notice some new detail, something you hadn't noticed or thought of before. I think that whatever talent I'm meant to have consists mainly of being able to *feel* the music very deeply and respond to it. This instinct I do have. Others may be quicker in learning things by heart or more brilliant in other ways. *My* gift lies in feeling and experiencing the music very deeply and very intensely. This also helps me quell my nerves because as soon as I start singing I'm not nervous anymore, because I'm no longer Elena but Violetta, Gilda, Cleopatra or whoever I happen to be singing.'

This quality is what gave Katona the confidence to offer her *Traviata*. As he explains: 'It's not the voice – although it's a beautiful lyric instrument of great sweetness with a light, fast vibrato, now firmly under control, that can be very appealing – or the looks or the acting. It's the total thing, the person creating a role up there for you, creating a character that speaks directly to you. It's not someone in a costume and wig doing their job terribly well, and that's what's so touching. Because this is what you ideally want from a performance, especially with those pieces you hear every five minutes. With her you feel there is only *this* Traviata. And in performances like this, you discover things that you have never heard before, or at least not consciously. Of course, they are there all the time, but certain artists have the gift of drawing attention to lights and shades in the score that make it seem new to you. This is true of all great artists, pianists and conductors as well as singers.'

In July 1996, after a fraught rehearsal period when for a moment it looked as if she might be thrown out of the production – she had not yet grasped the role fully and again there was the language barrier – Kelessidi pulled herself together and sang a triumphant dress rehearsal. The première went even better, and she was cheered and cheered. I sat there during the prelude, crossed myself the Greek way and prayed that our faith in her, and all those months of hard work, during which she was helped by some generous Greek friends, would come to fruition. By the end of Act I, I knew there was nothing to worry about. I even forgot I was watching a friend on whose behalf I was anxious, and was totally drawn into Violetta's story. She had won. At Bertorelli's restaurant opposite the stage door at Covent Garden, the diners burst into applause when Kelessidi entered and several people came to the table to ask for her autograph.

Next morning, the reviews were excellent: 'On Wednesday night the operatic world may have found another darling,' wrote *The Times*. 'She is Elena Kelessidi, born not much more than twenty [actually thirty] years ago of Greek parents in Kazakhstan, where she made her début in 1991. She then moved to Athens where she now lives and sings; as of now, that is. Tomorrow, the world. The voice is not huge, but it projects easily. The sweet vibrancy of its tone is reminiscent of Pilar Lorengar and there are fascinating undertones giving the sound a sense of depth that makes up for her, as yet, limited colour. She has all the notes evenly placed up to an (unwritten) E flat. She is also pretty as paint, tiny and with great big dark eyes. Her Violetta was fragile, doomed and quite heart-rending in the last act.'

With this Covent Garden début Kelessidi's career moved to a new level overnight. Invitations began to pour in, and agents fought to represent her (during the year and a half up to this début it was I who helped her correspond with the theatres and request auditions). It was now time for her to get the best possible manager that she could find. She chose Alan Green at Columbia Artists, who is passionately committed to opera and to his artists.

'This is when I began to realize just how big a step my Covent Garden début was,' she says. 'I had arrived at rehearsals as if this were a normal assignment. Only afterwards did I comprehend what it meant and what it implied. In retrospect, although I know how lucky I was and how unusual, not to say unique, my instantaneous access to the top was, I think it's better for things to happen a bit more gradually. This way you learn, understand and get used to all aspects of the profession. I landed at the top, but without knowing anything – even things that everyone takes for granted – about what such a career means, until later.'

'Yet I also realize how blessed I was to be given the chance to start my international career in *La traviata*, a truly fabulous opera. Even within Verdi's own output it's special and occupies a place of its own. It doesn't *sound* like typical Verdi most of the time. If you hear even a few bars of *Rigoletto*, *Il trovatore*, *Ballo*, *Forza*, *Aida*, *Nabucco*, *Attila* or *Ernani* you instantly *know* it's Verdi. With *Traviata*, if you didn't know it was by him, you might not guess it. Maybe that's why it was a flop when it first opened. Or maybe it was because the soprano who sang Violetta was fat. This is one role where you just can't have a fat soprano!'

As far as the interpretation of Violetta is concerned the crucial thing, in her view, is to show Violetta's two sides: 'One side of her is the courtesan: a very sophisticated, high-class courtesan whom I liken in my mind to the ancient Greek 'hetaire' – brilliant, well-educated women of many accomplishments such as music, languages, a knowledge of politics, and possessing great style and elegance, light-years ahead of the wives of the period.

'On the other hand you have a woman so pure that in my mind I equate her with the Virgin Mary. A woman with a big, generous heart and soul that could love a young man who had nothing. And love him to the point of self-sacrifice. I find it so moving that she had all these men but stayed pure enough inside to be able to love truly. She could accept all these gifts from so many men but she could also give, both materially – as she does to keep Alfredo and herself at her country home – and emotionally, of herself. Even though she knew that the sacrifice of giving up Alfredo would kill her, and very quickly, too, she still did it. I think that what makes her love him is the fact that he doesn't care about her having been with so many men, that he's the first to love her – no-one had ever *loved* her before. I think she's a very special woman. When I read the story I cried hard.

'To express all of this your acting must be esoteric, from inside. And you should sing as expressively as you can, colouring and shading your phrases with a very fine brush to bring out these two sides. Basically, it needs three voices, as Verdi wrote. In Act I, I don't feel the coloratura should be *brilliant*, as it would be in say, Handel, Constanze or in bel canto. It should be *dramatic* and sort of *hysterical* (Carol Vaness makes the same point in her chapter). "Gioir, gioir!" should sound hysterical because here Violetta is fighting with herself. In one breath, she melts when she hears Alfredo singing "L'amor è palpito"; then she tries to fight herself by singing "Follie, follie". So "Gioir, gioir" shouldn't sound like a bel canto coloratura.'

Kelessidi was gratified to discover that the late Sir Georg Solti, who liked her and was going to conduct Covent Garden's performances in Baden-Baden in June 1998, had the same feelings about the coloratura at the end of Act I. In the event he was replaced by Placido Domingo.

'I remember going to his house to audition for him when I was preparing for my Covent Garden Cleopatra in *Giulio Cesare*. Feeling very nervous, I started singing the Act I finale and he listened to me with his eyes closed, beating the rhythm. Then when I sang the E flat, he picked up the score and said: "Do you see an E flat here? Verdi didn't write an E flat. Why not? Tell me." I said nothing, except that Callas had sung it and to me that was enough, it amounted almost to the voice of God! But he replied: "Can you understand why he didn't write it? Because this is a tragic moment. Violetta is a tragic personality, and here she's hysterical. This is not bel canto, and she is not a canary. It's a different style, a different kind of opera." He said that twice – "with me you'll *never* sing that E flat!" So I said OK. I said that not only because I could hardly say anything else, but because I understood that he was right.

'Then he asked me how old I was and I replied, "How old do you think I am?" He said, "Somewhere between eighteen and eighty!" I said, "That's exactly how I feel." Sometimes I feel eighteen and at times when life crushes you and makes you feel bogged down, eighty.' Solti was very impressed with Kelessidi and told everyone concerned how much he was looking forward to working with her. (He even told the tenor Marcelo Alvarez four times that he would be working with a soprano who was fantastic and very beautiful.)

'I would say that each act is difficult in a different way,' continues Kelessidi. 'Act I requires great stamina to get to the finale, where you have this great aria, which is really very, very difficult. You need legato singing at the beginning, then a very dramatic recitative which says everything Violetta wants to say, all the doubts that she sings about immediately afterwards. Then you have the gorgeous aria "Di quell'amor" which you have to sing *pianissimo*, pouring all the expressiveness you're capable of into each phrase and each word, and colouring the word "misterioso" to convey the very mystery she's thinking about. Then you have a big cadenza and then the "Sempre libera". After the fourth performance the conductor Simone Young told me I was like a tigress on stage at this point; and a friend in the audience said I was like a panther!

'The duet with Germont in Act II is very dramatic, and requires a very special way of breathing. Then you get a few moments rest, before a sudden legato and *pianissimo*. Then "Morrò, morrò," which is a very dramatic moment.' At this point in the staging she banged the table with her fist at Germont, which some, myself included, found unattractive (the only unattractive gesture in the entire production). But the director, Richard Eyre, was absolutely sure he wanted her to do this. 'The only other thing he said was to make sure I did the pause before "Addio" – "Siete felice (pause) addio",' she explains. 'Then at "Amami, Alfredo" I felt so overwhelmed that in one performance I hugged Alfredo (Alvarez) so realistically that he guessed I was "in character" to such an extent that I didn't realize I was not in a position to sing the following phrases. So he pushed me up and placed me in the right position, from where I could sing.

'So, control, control, control. It's something one must always learn to think about. But it's difficult.' (Vesselina Kasarova, another natural actress who throws herself into her roles with great nervous energy and intensity, makes the same point in her chapter.) 'Vladimir Chernov, who was singing Germont with me at the Albert Hall, says I give two hundred percent. He says I mustn't, and that I should think of a long career . . .' At the second Albert Hall performance, Kelessidi's 'Amami, Alfredo' was simply *perfect*, and more moving than I've ever heard it. Violetta's realization that she has limited time seemed to hang in the air and permeate the whole atmosphere – as indeed it should but seldom does. Other magic moments were an exquisite *pianissimo* beginning to 'Dite alla giovine' and the way she pronounced and stressed every word of this aria showed a real artist's soul. At her entrance in Act III, I've never seen a Violetta look quite as forlorn as she did, *oozing* unhappiness from every pore: a great, unforgettable performance.

Act III is even more difficult vocally, and especially emotionally. 'You should start off with a very faint voice. She asks Annina for water; she is without hope. In "Addio, del passato" we opened all the cuts, which means that during the very dramatic second verse, where she sings that no-one will come to her grave, you should immediately change colour. You should do so again when Alfredo comes and Violetta becomes momentarily stronger and *wants* to live. Then, for the crucial phrase "Gran Dio! morir sì giovane" you should colour the middle voice. Placido Domingo, who conducted the Baden-Baden performances, told me he got goose-pimples at that moment and that, as a singer, he knew how I felt.'

From the sheerly vocal point of view, Katona has noticed a marked development since Kelessidi's Traviatas of 1996: 'Two years ago, I was a bit worried about her having too much vibrato. This time I didn't even notice it. So she is obviously picking up things and learning all the time. She has a lot of work now, and that training and stage experience will help stabilize a lot of things and maybe even help with her nerves – although at the end of the day, that's part of the person.' (Richard Eyre told her that he loves the fact that she is nervous on stage and nervous off it!)

In summer 1995, while Kelessidi was in London for her first period of coaching at Covent Garden, I had written to Peter Jonas, the Intendant of the Bavarian State Opera in Munich, asking if he would audition her. He did, and offered her some performances of *La traviata* in autumn 1996. She scored such a big success that they immediately offered her a further run of performances for the following season. There are rumours of some very exciting projects there in the future.

Shortly after her début at Covent Garden, the House had also offered her further projects, the first of which was Cleopatra in *Giulio Cesare* in September 1997 (the Royal Opera's first production 'in exile', away from its own theatre). Though she did not much care for the production, especially the sets and costumes, she loved the role. 'Musically Cleopatra was very, very difficult to learn – there are seven or eight very ornate arias with da capo sections. But once I'd learnt it, I found that it wasn't actually all that difficult to sing. Of course you have to sing every aria, and especially every verse differently, as this is part of the baroque style. But it has to sound joyful and effortless. I would love to sing more Handel. His music is like an aspirin for the voice.'

'Her Cleopatra was colourful and charming in a way that you don't necessarily associate with an "academic" Handel performance,' says Peter Katona. 'She managed to instill so much colour into the music. Cleopatra is a wonderful character and when performed like this, with every aria sounding completely different, it throws a different light on the character. When people think of Handel, they usually think, "Oh my God, there's about thirty-five arias, one very much like the other." But good Handel performers – both conductors and singers – make every aria sound absolutely different, and the moment they do that, each aria sounds fabulous. I think Elena achieved just that.'

The summer of 1998 had two major new challenges in store for Elena Kelessidi: at the end of July and beginning of August Desdemona in Rossini's *Otello* at the Wiener Festwochen under Lord Menuhin. Rossini's *Otello* is seldom performed, probably because it requires no less than three tenors, and was 'a beautiful discovery' for her. 'I had never sung Rossini before, and it was a new world for me. The music is *gorgeous*, poised somewhere between the baroque and bel canto. This is Rossini *serio*, so it's a much *softer* role, softer music than the brilliance we're used to in the comedies. It's also very dramatic music, and because the character is Desdemona, who's going to die, you have to be able to act the role. Musically there are some breathtakingly beautiful moments, such as Desdemona's famous Willow Song, accompanied by a harp, a beautiful bel canto aria sung by many famous sopranos from Caballé to June Anderson, which is *fantastic*. There isn't very much coloratura singing, and what there is is in tempo, baroque style. There is also a very dramatic aria and a very dramatic duet before Desdemona dies.'

Much more difficult than this Desdemona is the title role in Verdi's *Luisa Miller* which she will sing in London in June 1999. 'I am fully aware of its difficulties, yet I loved learning it. It's heavenly music, especially in Acts II and III. Not having heard the opera before, the beauty of the music came as a wonderful, joyous surprise. Of course, Luisa is a title role with two arias, each with cabaletta, and like Violetta she is on stage from beginning to end. From the vocal point of view it's typically Verdian: you have those wonderful, virile rhythms and the trills. Depending on the staging, it can also be quite interesting from the acting point of view. Paolo Gavanelli, who was my Germont in some of the Munich *Traviatas*, will be Miller and Franco Farina will sing Rodolfo. How difficult is it compared to Violetta? Well, nothing can ever be as difficult as Violetta [as all sopranos who sing the role, including Angela Gheorghiu and Carol Vaness, agree]. 'I would place it somewhere between Violetta and Gilda, which is easier and which I'm greatly looking forward to singing – I love not only her music, but the whole opera, Rigoletto's music, the Duke's music and that fabulous quartet.'

Although she is ecstatic at the way her career is going, Elena is also discovering how gruelling this profession is and how great the sacrifices it demands. In a way, she thinks it is easier for single people,[1] because they do not have to cope with the agony of being separated from their families, and especially their children, for long periods of time. Good marriages, she considers, are rare in the profession. Her own foundered just as her international career was taking off. So is it worth it? 'If you love, really love music, yes.'

Elena Kelessidi has more than vindicated the high hopes so many of us placed in her. 'What I admire is that, considering the difficult background, the lack of any high-class experience of operatic life, coming from nowhere to the top, speaking no languages, lacking all the *tools* for making a career, she still did it. She was suddenly thrown in right at the deep end, which scared me no end before it happened. But somehow, despite her nervous disposition and insecurity in many ways, she got out there and managed to stand up rather than fall flat on her face. She

---

[1] The few single people in the profession do not agree: they find the loneliness of hotel rooms hard to bear.

always makes everybody in the House mad and sick with worry, with her disorganization, scattiness, tendency to drop and lose and forget things at every corner and corridor. She lacks that professional poise and assurance of her American colleagues – with them you can always be sure they know exactly what to do at each turn, and you can rely on the knowledge that the result will never fall below a certain standard. You don't need to worry. With her, you're totally confused and don't know what to expect. And then, as if by magic, a miracle happens.' says Peter Katona.

CATHERINE
MALFITANO

'MY WORK IS my spiritual world, my place of worship. When I ask myself why I do what I do, it's clear that it's because I'm constantly searching for something. This something is certainly not just the most perfect vocal technique. That in itself doesn't interest me. The only important thing about technique is that it should be near-perfect enough to set me free to find the things I'm searching for. What I find fascinating in my search is that we are all bound together: the fact that I'm the conduit, the mirror that shows people how we all experience those extraordinary passions and feelings described in the operas I interpret. I feel deeply grateful that I've been given the chance to do it, because it's this communal aspect, this sharing that moves me most in this work, the giving and the taking. But mostly the giving. It's what inspires and sustains us during the long rehearsal periods, when you learn a lot and become a wonderful family together.

'But for me the mystery, the true mystery, is the performance: what happens between the audience and a performer. I don't think it can be explained. Why, for example, audiences connect with one performer and not with another; why certain performances have that magic dimension and others don't. It's all a mystery. Because you can sit in your dressing room before the performance and not know what kind of performance it's going to be. But I like mysteries . . . And to me the most meaningful aspect of my work is this opportunity to connect with and move people.'

Catherine Malfitano does this with a vengeance. At a recent revival of Elijah Moshinsky's production of *The Makropulos Affair* at the Metropolitan Opera the director reports that he had never seen a comparable audience reaction in all his life in the theatre: 'It was as if the Met *exploded*. What was even more amazing was the fact that it happened in a show that no-one was expecting anything much from, as it had not been particularly successful when first mounted. But by sheer force of character, Catherine was able to make this opera have an extraordinary effect on the audience. It was a personal triumph. So much so, that the management have added an extra week to the Met's 2000–01 season just in order to bring back this opera, with her.'

This is not altogether surprising to those who have followed Malfitano's career and know her ability to rouse audiences to the edge of their seats. For there is a fearlessness about her – vocal, physical and emotional – that engages the public at a very deep level, and which has also enabled her to develop a very rich and versatile career. She has never been afraid of taking risks, but being both highly intelligent and extremely analytical, those risks have always been calculated, and hence very successful. This trait means that she has the ability to *think* her way around the characters she portrays before abandoning herself to their passion. 'She's as careful as an instrumentalist in executing her part', says Donald Palumbo, chorus master at the Lyric Opera of Chicago, who has worked with Malfitano on many operas over the years.

Malfitano attributes the control she brings to her passionate nature to an admonition given to her years ago by the great bass George London, who told her to watch out for that temperament of hers. 'He affirmed that a strong vocal technique had to be the basis for that passion. Without it, I would burn out. It was only later on, when I began to feel all this temperament and personality I had to give, that I realized how important his advice was.'

The same logic and control has gone into the planning of her career. At first glance it may appear unclassifiable, for very few singers, if any, have ever sung the particular combination of roles in which Malfitano excels. Yet, as has been pointed out by Epstein, now Artistic Director designate of the Lyric Opera of Chicago and for many years Malfitano's agent and friend, it can be divided into three distinct periods, according to the vocal *weight* of the roles she was tackling.

At the beginning of her career, from 1972 until the end of the decade, she concentrated on some of the lighter lyric parts such as Susanna, Nannetta, Pamina and Manon in Henze's *Boulevard Solitude*; the next phase, up to the mid-1980s, saw her expanding into bigger lyric roles that also require agility, such as Constanze, Massenet's Manon and Violetta, these last two with particular success. Then came a crucial year of transformation, 1986 (which she discusses at length later in the chapter), during which she retrained her voice in preparation for the heavier parts for which she is now famous: Butterfly, Salome, Tosca and Lady Macbeth among others. The new millennium will see her take on even more dramatic roles: Renata in Prokofiev's *The Fiery Angel* and the title role in Shostakovich's *Lady Macbeth of Mtsensk*, as well as her first Wagnerian heroines, Kundry in *Parsifal* and Senta in *Der fliegende Holländer*. 'She is the kind of diversified artist who will lead us into the twenty-first century', said the late Ardis Krainik, former Managing Director of the Lyric Opera of Chicago.

Malfitano attributes her versatility to the fact that she was brought up in a world of great diversity. 'My life has been full of-it from the beginning,' she remembers. Her mother, Maria Maslova, half Irish, half Russian, was an actress and dancer; her father, who had Sicilian blood, was a violinist in the Metropolitan Opera Orchestra[1] and also played as a soloist. He was always practising the violin at home. 'So,

[1] She describes the strange experience of performing Violetta in 1983 at the Met, when her father was still in the orchestra there, and looking up from her deathbed and seeing his face in the pit!

from an early age I was accustomed to various musical languages,' says Malfitano, 'from baroque to contemporary. So it's not strange that I developed an appetite for diversity.' Indeed, her own repertoire extends from Monteverdi's Poppea to William Bolcom's *McTeague*.

It was an interesting, stimulating childhood for Catherine in a house full of Siamese cats. (The foundation for her lasting passion for these creatures!) She was the eldest of three children. Her brother is now a film and television editor, while her sister is also involved in singing – 'We were a very theatrical family'. She got her first taste of performing at the age of six, when she was asked to sing a song in school. Without knowing why, she hopped onto a table, and to this day she can clearly recall the elation she experienced – 'that incredible adrenaline rush from opening up and exposing myself'. Her first singing teacher was her father, from whom she learnt about vocal technique and professional discipline, while from her mother she learnt about acting and movement. The basis for Malfitano's ability to blend all the elements that make up operatic performance – singing, acting and movement – was inherent in her background and upbringing.

It was clear to everyone, herself included, that Catherine was going to do something in show business, although she was not as yet decided on being an opera singer. But her teachers at the Manhattan High School of Music and Art (which her daughter Daphne will also attend in a couple of years), saw the pleasure she took in singing in the choir, correctly assessed her voice and steered her in that direction. She had further opportunity to absorb the operatic profession, by osmosis, when she hung out backstage at the Met during her father's rehearsals. (Her daughter Daphne, who would like to be an actress and a film and opera director does much the same thing now. She attends all rehearsals and performances, sometimes playing cards with the cast and sharpening her critical faculty.)

Yet when it was time to enroll at a music college, Malfitano was in for a deep disappointment: she was turned down by the Juilliard. And not simply turned down, but also told that she could forget about ever having a career as a singer! But her parents' experience in 'showbiz' resilience came up trumps. Instead of allowing her to become demoralized, they simply told her to forget it and try elsewhere. This she did, at the Manhattan School of Music (often mentioned in these pages as one of the top places of study for American singers today). During her years there she got her first reviews in the *New York Times* and *Opera* magazine, when she sang Suzel in the school's production of *L'amico Fritz* ('a voice of power as well as sweetness' was Arthur Jacobs's prophetic judgment).

After graduating, Malfitano worked for a year as an usherette at Carnegie Hall, and across the street at Patelson's music store. (Even there she did something original, she organized a section devoted to black American composers.) And meanwhile, she was auditioning everywhere.

She made her professional début as Nannetta in Central City, Colorado in 1972, shortly before joining the Minnesota Opera Company for a year, during which she performed a variety of roles including many in operas by contemporary American composers. In 1973 she joined the New York City Opera, where she remained until 1979, the year of her Metropolitan Opera début as Gretel in *Hänsel and Gretel*. In the intervening years she had made a string of important débuts, many of them as Susanna: at the Holland Festival in 1974, at the Lyric Opera of Chicago in 1975 and at Covent Garden in 1976, the year in which she also made her début at the Salzburg Festival as Servilia in *La clemenza di Tito*. In 1980 she sang Antonia in Florence in *Les contes d'Hoffmann* and all three roles in this opera in Salzburg in 1981. In 1982 she made her début at the Paris Opéra as Nedda and the Vienna State Opera as Violetta.

In 1977 she had met and married Stephen Holowid, an actor, singer and musician who worked in the NYCO administration. Holowid, whom she calls her 'life-support system and rock', is an attractive, erudite man, knowledgeable about the profession and deeply involved in her career. His presence at her side provides the right balance for her inner wildness, and also helped her absorb and overcome one of the most traumatic experiences of her career: being booed at the Paris Opéra in 1989 as Constanze in *Die Entführung aus dem Serail*.

'It was an extraordinary experience, highly enlightening in a spiritual way. It taught me what tremendous reserves of courage, strength and belief I possessed. But at that actual moment, it was *so* difficult. It would have been even more so without Stephen. He helped a lot. What is it like to be booed? It felt like a terrorist attack out of the blue, like a *bomb* coming at me. Of course, it wasn't coming from the whole audience, just a few individuals and orchestrated by a claque of supporters of Christiane Eda-Pierre, the Paris Opéra's established Mozart soprano. The odd thing is that I didn't run off the stage, I just stood there, listened and took it all in. I thought, that's an interesting sound, I've never heard that before. Now I'm hearing it, I'm feeling it, it's happening. So I just smiled, opened myself even more to the experience and accepted it. I remember Kathy Battle, who sang Blonde in the production, being stunned. She said she couldn't understand how I managed it, how I handled the emotional side of being booed and added that, had it been her, she would have run. But I said I couldn't do that, I just had to accept it. Fortunately, Stephen was taping every performance and when we went home I listened to the tape. I heard some things I didn't like – no more than a couple of notes, a couple of phrases here and there – so I kept working at it, kept on improving. At times like this it's important to keep your equilibrium and to see things in perspective. Otherwise you might be tempted to think. "Am I singing *that* badly?"'

A month later Malfitano sang Constanze at the Met, and scored a big success in the part. Having used the Paris experience to grow musically, vocally and emotionally, the performance was indeed better. 'I had to pull myself together and create this improvement,' she says. 'Again, Kathy Battle, who went to the performance, was incredulous. She said, "I can't believe this. You got booed last month and it's just gotten better!"' Next season Malfitano returned to the Paris Opéra, where she scored a big success as Manon.

Most singers would be hesitant to mention booing incidents in interviews to the press, let alone for a book. But both Malfitano and her husband feel that some of the most interesting things singers can talk about are their *problems*, their difficulties, both technical and emotional, how they overcame them, and 'how they got through their depressing periods'.

In 1986, in mid-career, Malfitano took an enormous step that held the key to her future development: she took a year off and retrained her voice for a heavier repertoire. 'It was clear both to me and to other people that there was a voice in there, wanting to break out of this strictly lyric repertoire and encompass some of the *lirico spinto* and dramatic qualities. My temperament and dramatic ability also wanted to go in a different direction.'

At that point Matthew Epstein recommended the conductor Henry Lewis. As Epstein recalls: 'I always felt that Catherine's voice had two issues: one was lightness and flexibility; the other a strong, *weighty* quality. It was always clear that this side would need further development, and that if it *did* have further development, it would lead her towards another repertoire. I remember telling her that as she was about to have a child, this was the ideal time to work on this side because when you have a child your muscles have to be restructured. And that's exactly what she did. She took a little time off. After having her daughter, in 1986, she started studying with Henry Lewis. She was never somebody who needed a teacher as such, but rather an expert musician and coach. And Henry, having been the principal builder of Marilyn Horne's voice, knew all about the areas that Catherine needed to learn about: breath support, the amount of weight one can put on the various registers of the voice and how to balance the voice in a different way. It worked very well and the result was her ability to sing Butterfly, and later Salome and Tosca.'

Malfitano adds that she put herself in Lewis's hands so completely that she felt like a beginner or a student. 'This was not an easy thing to do in the middle of one's career. In a sense, it was also a spiritual quest. I wanted to find out more about myself, to open myself up more and, in many ways, to become more humble again. Which, I repeat, was not easy to do after you'd already proved yourself and had big successes. I remember that when Matthew told me that he thought I should study again and encouraged me to go to Henry Lewis at first it was not an easy thing for me to accept. But I'm glad I listened to him, because this decision was the key to everything that has happened since.'

Malfitano worked with Henry Lewis for nearly ten years, up until his death in 1995 – not all the time, of course, but regularly, between engagements. He had very specific ideas about what constituted good singing. 'Good singing for him was on the breath, which is to say a very *honest*, supported way of singing throughout the range, for every role. He also taught me how to use the depth and breadth of my voice more fully. How to use the resonators in certain ways for certain registers. How to place vowels in different way; how to rely on certain sensations we singers have, which are very difficult to explain in words but which can tell you when things are as they should be; and how to make certain modifications in the passaggio. We didn't start with any specific goals other than to prepare for my first Butterfly, at the Deutsche Oper in Berlin in 1987. But we also re-studied Manon, which was even more difficult. Unlearning something you had learnt earlier and trying to apply new methods of singing to it is very difficult. At times I felt like a complete idiot, very slow, and doubting that I was ever going to get it right. It was extraordinary to experience those student reactions again. But Henry was so infinitely encouraging and patient, never tiring of repeating himself, because this, he said, was part of the learning process. And because he never lost patience with me, I didn't lose patience with myself.'

The real test was seeing whether she could apply what she was learning and re-learning to the stage, during this period of readjustment. 'Applying these readjustments, taking what you're learning in the laboratory to the stage takes awhile. Because under the watchful

eye of your guide or guru you take baby steps, you're led in the right
direction. But when you're on stage, you're alone. And until you finally
catch up with yourself through repetition and in-depth understanding,
you fall back a few steps. But going through this whole process gave me
courage for the future. It taught me that you can always start again,
over and over again, and renew yourself. And as you get older, it
becomes even more important to renew yourself. You've got to be *constantly* transcending, transforming and reinventing yourself. But that's
a life's work. It takes a long time to learn this . . .'

One of the most interesting, immediate results of this transformation was a concert Malfitano gave with Alfredo Kraus at the Met,
where she had to sing Antonia from *Les contes d'Hoffmann*. They had not
sung together since they had recorded *Roméo et Juliette* in 1983 and
Kraus, as astute and pernickety a judge of singing as any, was impressed
enough to remark: 'Catherine, you sound more beautiful than I
remember you sounding before. Most singers tend to sound less, not
more beautiful with time. What have you been *doing*?' When she
replied that she had been studying he was even more surprised, and
added that that was something very few singers did.[1] 'And coming
from someone like Kraus, this meant a lot'.

The first full opera Malfitano sang after her year of study with
Henry Lewis was *Madama Butterfly* at the Deutsche Oper in Berlin in
May/June 1987. She says that no amount of vocal study alone would
have contributed to a portrayal as powerful as the one she delivered if
she had not recently become a mother. Both she and her husband
dote on their daughter, Daphne Rose, with a passion and depth of
understanding both moving and rare. Malfitano has gone so far as to
call giving birth to Daphne her 'greatest achievement', and adds that
'she has enabled me to go even beyond my wildest imaginings'.
Daphne appears to be an unusually well-balanced and insightful

---

[1] An encouraging sign in this decade is that more and more singers are in fact
studying throughout their careers, as numerous of them testify in these pages.

twelve-year-old, light-years away from the neglected and clingy type of child one comes across in the operatic profession. (For most of whom the word that springs to mind is 'casualties'.)

The choice of name came to both of them when Malfitano was six weeks pregnant. One night, they both had very similar dreams: 'Stephen dreamt of a little girl running, and heard the voice of a woman, calling "Daphne, Daphne, come here". Whereas my dream was that I was walking in a country landscape; suddenly there was a big firework display and the name "Daphne" was spelt out in blazing letters in the firework display. Then, as the fireworks dissolved, the letters spelling her name fell all over me and they turned out to be rose petals. Later, when we found out from the amnio that the baby was a girl, there and then we decided to name her Daphne Rose. So, with both Daphne and Butterfly on the way, you can say that 1986 was a great year of transformation for me.'

Butterfly is now the role Malfitano has sung more than any other, yet she remains deeply attached to it spiritually. 'I look for this dimension in all my roles,' says Malfitano. 'But Butterfly is *extraordinary*. The motherly part of her is something I adore. I feel blessed that I'd just become a mother myself when I first sang her. Even though I'd often been asked to sing the role before, I'm glad I never did. I think the opera itself is about transformation, the transforming story of a butterfly emerging from a cocoon. And it's heart-rending. Yet when I'm actually playing it, I don't feel the tragedy of it or any sadness, because she has this tremendous belief and strength and purpose and devotion. She has this wish to give something worthwhile, something of beauty to her child. Her sacrifice is not about "I have to kill myself, poor me," but rather "I can't offer you anything, but *this* I *can* offer you: something that's going to allow you to have a better life than you ever, *ever* would here, in this country and society of which I'm no longer a member." I think it's quite beautiful that she can do that . . .

'Act I is already heart-rending. 'Cio-Cio-San is a prototype of a very modern, contemporary woman who has visions of what life could be, of what *her* life could be. To me this is extraordinary. Because, as a woman from a culture like that, she's *choosing* to embrace another religion, she's choosing a vision of being taken away from this society, which is what she really wants. The only snag about it is that she chooses the wrong man. Of course, she doesn't know this, she's very naive. But then, we all were at fifteen or sixteen – how could she judge? What she does have, and what I love most about her, is the *spirit* to want to excel and better her life and have more. It's very modern and, in the context, extremely daring. This is why I disagree with those who see her as a victim. She's not a victim at all, she *chooses* her destiny. It's a very strong choice, and the way things turn out there is unfortunately no escape for her. And we can all identify with that, especially when Pinkerton is played by Ricky Leech. When, I look up at him, as Butterfly it's *gorgeous*!'

Malfitano has now sung the role more than a hundred times with immense success all over the world, including Covent Garden and La Scala for her début in 1990 and at the Metropolitan Opera in 1994 and 1998. Yet she still rates that first Berlin production under Sinopoli as the best. With characteristic candour, she describes her reaction when she first heard the tapes from Berlin. 'I thought God, how come I had such success with it? I barely got through Act II! When I got to that Flower Duet in Act II, I thought I was going to die – and I still had the whole of Act III to get through! I hadn't yet learnt to pace myself, you see. Yet the audience absolutely adored it and the reviews were incredible! And, listening to the tapes, I thought there were moments in it that were really wonderful and others where it was clear that I had to learn to pace myself, and that vocally there was still a long way to go.'

One of the ways was to build up her stamina through an intense regime of physical exercises: weight-lifting, jogging, cardiovascular training – even mountain climbing. 'I wish the outdoors were more part of my life. I wish we lived somewhere where I could walk in the country all the time and climb mountains. When we rented a house outside Salzburg for many years I used to climb two or three times a week. I like this kind of thing, it's a combination of mental and physical meditation. Nature, and sometimes being in slightly dangerous circumstances, focusses your mind very much on exactly what you're doing. There is something very purifying in that, something that also connects to what I do in my work: learning how to focus, how to get on the track and stick with it, and being mindful, learning to be mindful of the moment.' Meditation had come into her life in the late 1960s and early 70s, before the beginning of her career, when she also became a vegetarian. 'That's the time when body-mindfulness and spiritual mindfulness came together. It went through phases until I realized through it all that the career was being fed from it. Since then I don't meditate as I used to. I meditate all the time – when walking, exercising, climbing. It's a state of being that permeates my whole life.'

Expressing and transmitting these states is never easy. Suffice it to say that they are reflected in the 'wholeness' of her portrayals – and also in the fact that she has preserved her own childlike dimension in a profession that tries very hard to take it away from you.

Interestingly enough, this was the aspect that most struck Sir Charles Mackerras, even before they collaborated on the Metropolitan Opera production of *The Makropulos Affair* mentioned earlier. Very shortly before they began rehearsing, Malfitano finished her run of performances of *Madama Butterfly* (her second at the Met). Mackerras says he was amazed at how she eased into being 307 years old from having just been fifteen: 'Her Butterfly was quite, quite wonderful. What was so marvellous was the way she managed to really be a *child*. Because the difficult thing about Butterfly is that it has to be childlike and yet demands this huge voice. Well, Catherine had both these things. She is a great singer. Her Salome – which I consider one of the greatest things I've ever seen on the operatic stage – is a bit similar in this sense, so childlike and pure.'

Malfitano admits to being 'an eternal child' and to loving characters who are on the brink of realizing their sensual and sexual capacity, something that came to her at sixteen: 'Rediscovering this feeling over and over again through characters like Butterfly, Salome and the young Elina Makropulos, is my work.'

She considers this woman–child factor to be crucial in Salome, which she first sang in Berlin in 1990, and then in a landmark production by Luc Bondy at the Salzburg Festival in 1992 and at Covent Garden in 1995. It rates, along with Butterfly and Emilia Marty, among the towering achievements of her career. Yet when she was first asked to sing it she asked herself whether she really wanted to portray this woman. Then, after delving into the story and realizing the horrific family background – in Wilde's play Salome's father had been kept prisoner in the same cell as the Baptist for twelve years, before being killed by Herod at her mother's instigation – she came to view Salome as 'a classic case of child abuse' and to ask herself, 'how could you *not* love this character?'

'Another question I keep asking myself is: so what if the Baptist had let her kiss him? What harm would there be in it? She didn't ask him to let her make love to him. Only to let her kiss him, to touch what he represents – an image of purity light-years away from Herod's depraved court. Maybe that would have been the end of it all.' Hildegard Behrens, the other great Salome of the last quarter century, stated that she was convinced that 'had it been Jesus instead of the Baptist, he would have seen through her, understood her need and transformed her, the way he did Mary Magdalene. But we are still in the harsh, unforgiving world of the Old Testament.'[1] Malfitano adds that she thinks it was the Baptist's fear of his *own* sexuality that dictated his reaction: 'This was powerfully suggested in the Bondy production and Bryn [Terfel] did it quite beautifully. He could play, really *play* the part. It's not often you get an equal partnership on stage. But Bryn's an interesting character, and can also be a very *dangerous* one on stage.'

The production – which she explains was the result of a real collaboration between the director, the choreographer and herself –

[1] Divas: *Great Sopranos and Mezzos Discuss their Art*, H. Matheopoulos.

culminated in one of the most erotic renditions of the Dance of the Seven Veils anyone has ever seen. Far from being a striptease, it was not only arousing but also managed to tell the story of what was going on in Salome's heart and mind as well as her body. Both audiences and critics went wild.

'Malfitano is small and athletic – and sexier in the Dance than the bare-all Maria Ewing without removing a stitch of her clothing – and her voice is close to the ideal soprano Strauss imagined: a girlish timbre with a penetrating, silvery top and the stamina to stay the course for more than an hour and a half over a thick orchestration . . . only rarely does she have to force her essentially lyric voice. Her transition from sexually inquisitive woman-child into bloodsucking maenad is terrifying. Malfitano is surely the great Salome of our time. The first-night audience seemed to think so and she was overcome with emotion at her rapturous reception,' wrote the *Sunday Times*.

A personal triumph in every sense. For as Christoph von Dohnányi, who conducted the production, rightly points out, the Dance is usually the weakest point in *Salome*: 'In any case it was composed by Strauss afterwards as a kind of filler, and presents both singers and directors with a problem: how to invent something seductive which doesn't exhaust the singer for the final scene. Usually it's danced for the audience rather than for Herod. But in our production it was danced for Herod, and Catherine's impact was overwhelming. She was terrific throughout the role. What is outstanding about her is the fact that, being deeply musical, her only wish is to be as faithful and near-perfect in her interpretation of the score as possible, and to combine stage personality without losing voice quality. That is very, very rare. Singers usually have either a vocal or a dramatic approach. Usually people with great voices don't care much about the drama and vice versa. But Catherine has the ideal combination: she sings near-perfectly and is a terrifically strong personality on stage. Another thing I particularly like about her voice is the fact that it is also a very well-trained *character* voice. Where needed, it has that *bite*.'

Indeed Malfitano never tires of stressing that singing should be expressive as well as beautiful. She has proved how the two can be combined in a masterly way through her portrayal of Lulu, which she sang in Chicago and, quite superbly, in Munich in 1985. 'To irritate people, I said that I sang it in a bel canto way. What I meant was that *Lulu* is beautiful music which needs to be *sung* and not just declaimed, which is what most people tend to do both with this piece and with *Wozzeck*. The Italian language is the basis, the jumping-off point of operatic singing. Even when I sing in other languages, I still think of the Italianate way of phrasing and articulating the language. Bel canto means beautiful singing but – and this is a big but – I don't interpret this in a slavish way. I don't think everything has to sound merely beautiful. I think bel canto music also happens to be some of the most expressive music, highly emotional and exciting. At times in the expression of the emotion or, as in *Makropulos* in the articulation of the language, you have to put *bite* in the way you sing some of the words.' (Exactly the point made by Dohnányi.)

Two years after her first *Salome*, Malfitano decided to accept another mammoth challenge: singing Tosca in a filmed version, televised live and shot in Rome at the locations and at the times of day specified in the plot! This meant that it was filmed over nearly twenty-four hours: Act I in the church of Sant'Andrea della Valle in the morning on day one, Act II at the Palazzo Farnese that night and Act III at the Castel Sant'Angelo at dawn the following morning. Malfitano and her co-stars – Placido Domingo as Cavaradossi and Ruggero Raimondi as Scarpia – were sleepless for nearly two days. And it was her first Tosca!

What fascinates her most about this opera – apart from the fact that as a singer she identifies with Tosca ('which I'm sure every singer who portrays her does') – is the interplay of life and art, and the circumstances of life imitating art in which Tosca finds herself. 'Both she and Cavaradossi are thrust into a world of politics which neither of them is capable of handling. This is most true of Tosca, who is pitched against a satanic political figure in Scarpia. The situation becomes really eerie. It's as if she's stepped into a play that's gone wrong and come to life! She could be in any opera like the ones she performs all the time – but in this case it's happening for real. She's a woman who's always had plenty of control in her life – as a diva, a woman of great consequence in her career, she's used to controlling everything, including Cavaradossi (as she shows in Act I where she virtually commands him to her villa that night). Yet she gradually realizes that she is losing control by the minute: caught in the middle of a drama unlike anything she's ever acted on stage. She doesn't know the outcome, she doesn't even know what the next lines are. It's *fascinating*. Every step of the way she thinks she can recapture control, and every time it recedes from her until – against her principles and character, but also through a sense of abandonment and conviction that God will help her – she commits the murder. That's her naïveté, which I find lovable. She's *so* human, *so* lovable and has so much *passion* . . . To me, the whole situation springs from the fact that Cavaradossi didn't trust her enough, for whatever reason, to reveal that he was hiding Angelotti in Act I. And I feel a whole set of circumstances, that whole web they're caught in, spinning around this little flaw.'

Malfitano goes on to explain the reasons why she accepted the immense challenge of the 'live' *Tosca*, from which she emerged triumphant: 'I don't want to reach my deathbed regretting *not* having done anything. This consideration is behind all my decisions, such as doing Tosca for the first time on television, live over twenty-four hours, which was a mad, crazy thing to do. But I do these crazy things primarily because I realize my life is short, it flows on and if I didn't do it, then someone else would. And I would lose the opportunity and regret it. In a way death is a friend, because it keeps reminding me to fulfil myself. This is also the message of *The Makropulos Affair*, which is so marvellous.

'People are always asking me which among all the heroines I portray is my favourite. I reply that I'm extremely promiscuous and at the same time extremely faithful: faithful to the one I'm singing at the moment before I move on, very easily, to the next one! Yet I must say that right now Emilia Marty in *Makropulos* is very close to the top. Because the whole opera has the message I like more than any, in any opera I've sung: that life is meant to be enjoyed for what it is, and life is good because it's short. It's not meant to be extended beyond the natural lifespan. What makes it so thrilling is the thought that we're going to die. This message speaks to me because I've always had a very close attachment to death, I don't know why. But I know that when I say this to people, most think I'm being morbid.'

In the opera, the singer Emilia Marty is given an extended lifespan. She is 337 years old, not out of choice, but because the inability to die is inflicted on her. 'She begins to fear death, which is forever receding from her. Through the story of the opera, she learns to embrace it, primarily because she realizes that she doesn't *feel* anything any longer. She's tired of seeing everyone she cares for dying, and tired of having relationships with the offspring of men she knew long ago. But, because of people delving into her past, she comes to that *cathartic* moment when she is able to think again about what happened to her all those years ago: when, at the age of sixteen (again that magic number), she unwittingly caused her father's death, as Elina Makropulos, by fleeing the country armed with the formula for immortality her father had invented for Rudolf II. The king had seen her sink into unconsciousness, and did not wait long enough to see that the formula had worked. When she awoke she fled the country with the formula, and her father was imprisoned and killed. When she re-enters her past, her lost innocence, she realizes that the answer for her now is to die gracefully . . . It's the most spiritual opera I've ever been involved in, both in its message and its music, which is extraordinary.

'Vocally, much of the role is declamatory. But it ends with a wonderful, huge, old-fashioned, vocally expansive operatic aria, with great lines, like a Liebestod, in a way. It's an emotional outpouring which is so overwhelming that it hits the audience all the more for being so unexpected. Alongside this finale, the vocal writing is very exciting, challenging and modern. A lot of the time you have a sensation that you're not really singing but speaking a wonderful play, and it *is* a wonderful play. The language, for someone who is not Czech, is an enormous challenge – being able to spit out those words, full of consonants, sometimes at breakneck speeds – especially at the Met with Sir Charles Mackerras, who wanted a lot of energy and velocity and naturalness with the text.'

She impressed Mackerras, the renowned Janáček expert who conducted the revival, with the way she mastered the Czech language. 'She managed to grasp this enormously complicated role in Czech without making a single mistake and without speaking a word of the language. It was most impressive, as was her whole demeanour during rehearsals, when she contributed a great deal to the production which had not been a great success when it was first mounted. Not surprisingly, it was Malfitano herself who had added to the challenge by *asking* to sing it in Czech, having previously sung it in English at the Lyric Opera of Chicago in a production by David Alden. 'But when I started learning it I cursed myself for my foolhardiness.'

Malfitano collaborated with David Alden again for the next big challenge in her career: singing Lady Macbeth for the first time at the Houston Grand Opera, in 1997. Lady Macbeth is an enormously challenging role from every point of view and one that marries the music and the drama perfectly – which is to say a role guaranteed to appeal to Catherine Malfitano! 'There isn't a dull moment in this opera, either musically or dramatically. Vocally it's quite demanding. I put a lot of training into it for an extended period of time before I sang it. What kind of training? Hours and hours of sheer repetition! The most challenging aspect was the demand for agility – lots of coloratura singing – which is something I hadn't done since my earlier days when I sang Manon and Violetta. But the kind of agility required here is totally different from Manon's and Violetta's. It's *dramatic* agility. It was wonderful to discover I still have the capacity for that in my voice. The next step was to develop the *power* that you must inject into Lady Macbeth's coloratura singing – and of course work on the high notes. I think I can say that this role took my voice forward a great deal.

'As a character, evil though she is, I love her passion and the *manly* side of her. Above all, however, I loved the great dramatic opportunity and the great music. Alden's production was very dramatic and atmospheric. There was a spookiness about it, almost like a Hitchcock film, with the supernatural element strongly emphasized. The witches' theme was very strong, and they looked different every time they appeared. (In their first appearances they were nurses in a military hospital where the wounded were being taken, and they had red beards). The tale was taken out of its setting, with me wearing a short red wig and a black knee-length cocktail dress, but it worked. The most rivetting part was the Sleepwalking Scene, done in front of the curtain, which was pitch black. Instead of me holding a candle and groping in the dark, I, the doctor and lady-in-waiting crawled under it. A red, bloodstained hand was created by spot light against the black background symbolizing that the bloodied hand was the reality in her mind. The effect was tremendously powerful.

At the time of our encounters in Salzburg, Malfitano was preparing for Kurt Weill's *Rise and Fall of the City of Mahagonny* for the 1998 Salzburg Festival. As with Salome, she had wondered whether she wanted to portray as unsympathetic a character as Jenny, the whore who refuses to bail the lover she actually loves, when Jimmy is faced with execution over an unpaid beer. "She's a typical Brecht character, a whore interested only in survival, interested only in her own skin and running away from the fact that she loves him. Then all she's left with a dead man. And she'll realize that surviving is not what it's all about. Yet this surviving is all she'll ever be able to do. This is what we're trying to bring out in this production: the exhaustion and emptiness of her life.'

Malfitano feels that it is from this dimension of exhaustion that Jenny is escaping through Jimmy and his wonderful fantasy. 'He offers her some wonderful moments of escape. We are including the Cranes

Duet (but placing it in Act II), a very poetic, very beautiful duet, quite unlike anything else in the opera, written in a kind of Baroque musical style. This scene is typical of what I've just said: Jimmy and Jenny are watching two cranes flying in the sky. And nobody knew this, but Jerry Hadley (who is singing Jimmy) did some research and found out that cranes mate in the air. They have a very unusual, beautiful mating ritual. But immediately afterwards they part and go their own ways — the exact opposite of swans, who stay together forever. Their mating and coming together is heavenly but shortlived. In this production this moment is staged like a scene from *Romeo and Juliet* or *West Side Story*. Everything stops. The stage is very crowded, with people eating, making love or boxing, and suddenly you have this magical moment when the world stops . . .'

Vocally, she says that Jenny is 'something of a vacation' from the more exhausting heroines in her repertoire. This is just as well, because as mentioned earlier, her repertoire will soon include such demanding parts as Renata (*The Fiery Angel*) and the title role in Shostakovich's *Lady Macbeth of Mtsensk*.

In the new millennium Malfitano will also sing her first Wagnerian heroines, Kundry and Senta. Senta fascinates her psychologically because, she says, she 'likes possessed, obsessional women': 'I love them — women to whose obsessive dreams reality can never compare. Senta, which is written mostly around the passaggio, is the most vocally challenging of the two, probably because Wagner was still young and inexperienced when he wrote it. So it's going to require much more preparation and negotiating on my part.' Kundry, which she will sing first in San Francisco in 2000 and later in Chicago, will not present so many problems. 'When I first listened to it very carefully at Bayreuth, I realized that the orchestration in her scenes is not very big. There is an intimacy throughout the Seduction Scene. The music revs up and gets more dramatic when the voice gets higher, at the point where Parsifal rejects her. Then I listened to it again in Berlin and didn't hear anything in it that I was afraid of. As a character, Kundry takes on board all the seductresses I have ever played, from Poppea and Thaïs to Manon and Cleopatra.'

She had already been offered both parts shortly after her first Salome in 1990, both in high profile places and with very interesting conductors. 'But vocally, it took me a while to decide if this was something I wanted to do,' she says.

Matthew Epstein thinks that Malfitano is now reaching a stage when she can sing absolutely anything that interests her: 'I wouldn't think she can lighten up [her voice] and go backward into the roles in her past but she can certainly sing more dramatically. I think the idea of singing Kundry is very interesting, as is that of singing Renata in *The Fiery Angel*. I don't think she's going to harm herself as long as she goes back to Butterfly and Tosca in between for the line, to keep the voice fluid. The legato singing that those pieces require will mean that she doesn't put pressure on the voice constantly. Vocal health is always a matter of balance.'

So, as she points out, 'there are plenty of wild ladies coming up!' She once confided in *Opera* that 'one of the fortunate things about being an artist is that you're permitted to be a child for the rest of your life and get into the worlds of other characters.' ('And get paid for it', adds her husband.) 'I love being other people – I'd hate it if I were just Catherine Malfitano all the time.'

So, who is Catherine Malfitano?

'That's a hard question to answer! Because one of the reasons why I do what I do is that I find bits of myself in all my roles, and this helps me to understand who I am, over the years. But I think that deep inside, there is a very spiritual person, constantly wanting to forgive and have compassion for the human condition. Because while on one hand the human condition is extraordinary and uplifting, on the other it's extremely perplexing and difficult to understand. Sometimes we choose to ignore the latter part, of accepting our lives and ourselves and having compassion. Somehow I've always wanted to understand what is most difficult in human beings to understand.

'In this sense I feel like I'm a closet priest, because in my work I draw constantly on compassion from myself for the characters I portray, and try to draw it from the public, too. I suppose it has to do with healing, I feel we all need to be healed in life, and in performing I also want to heal people. This is an admission I've never made before – I've always said I wanted to reach out and communicate with people. I feel there is a circle of communication between the audience and myself which is deeply spiritual, but for me there is also a depth of healing involved in my wish to perform. I value the idea of entertainment as part of performing, but I don't think I can accept that as being the end of my mission in life. I'm not saying that this in itself is not glorious, because entertainment is also a healing thing.

'I hate putting these things into words, because it takes away a little bit of the mystery of the communion that takes place between myself and the audience. But if pushed to it, I'd say there is some quality of healing that takes place in the act of performing. In this sense, yes, it is my mission in life.'

KARITA

MATTILA

'GORGEOUS TO BEHOLD, wondrous to hear', wrote the *Sunday Times* after Karita Mattila's heart-rending portrayal of Elisabeth de Valois in Luc Bondy's deeply probing production of *Don Carlos* at Covent Garden. It's a spot-on description of the sublime Finnish soprano, who during the past three years has risen to the pinnacle of the profession through a series of roles in which she has no equal in the world today: Chrysothemis in *Elektra* (at the 1995 Salzburg Easter Festival, under Claudio Abbado); Eva in *Die Meistersinger von Nürnberg* (at the Metropolitan Opera under James Levine, also in 1995); Elisabeth de Valois (at Covent Garden, and the Théâtre du Chatelet in Paris in 1996, in the same production); and Elsa in *Lohengrin* (in San Francisco, Paris and Covent Garden in 1997).

'I am fascinated by female characters who are vocally challenging and right for my voice,' Mattila declared during our recent meeting in London. 'Equally important is the dramatic side, their story. This intrigues me enormously because I love *theatre*, I love *drama*; and I think it can be put together with the musical side in a way that makes the whole thing work and become *real*. It doesn't always happen. But I have had some moments in my career which have been like dreams come true. And this is what one strives for.' Mattila is, indeed, an 'animal di palco', born for the stage. Her performances display a scorching intensity that renders them utterly convincing. 'When we worked together on *The Queen of Spades* at the Met,' the director Elijah Moshinsky recalls, 'I stressed that we should approach the character of Lisa in a Dostoyevskian manner, as a character swallowed by melancholy to the point of suicide. She has this searing aria before she throws herself into the Neva and Mattila carried the character to amazing extremes. It was a completely logical performance as convincing as any actress's, say, Helen Mirren's would be. The contrast between this scene and her cool, Grace Kelly-like demeanour in Act I was very affecting. She is the best embodiment of the new breed of opera singers who act the parts they sing as convincingly as film stars. Mattila is also devoid of any of the traditional "stuffiness" of a Diva: Just terribly good at what she does.'

Mattila has also achieved total control of her powerful lyric-dramatic voice, a glorious instrument with a lustrous patina and characteristic 'blonde' colour (Hugh Canning's word aptly evokes its luminosity). This vocal growth and control came gradually – in earlier years Mattila had occasional problems with intonation – though hard work with her excellent singing teacher and through a judicious choice of roles, each of which took the voice a stage further in the right direction.

'I need at least one new role each season to renew myself and keep busy', says Mattila. She points out that by the millennium her repertoire – which also includes the Countess, Fiordiligi, Pamina, Ilia, Donna Anna, Donna Elvira, Amelia (*Simon Boccanegra*) Tatyana, Lisa, Hanna Glawari, Rosalinde, Agathe, Reiza (*Oberon*), Musetta and the title role in *Jenůfa* – will have expanded to twenty-one roles. She will add the title roles in *Manon Lescaut* (which she will sing in 1998–9 in Finland and San Francisco) and *Arabella* (at the Chatelet in 2002).

I first met Karita Mattila, then twenty-six, shortly after her Covent Garden début as Fiordiligi in 1986. Fresh, wide-eyed and instantly likeable, she radiated health, *joie de vivre* and that magical and elusive quality of charm (which Callas, who also found it as hard to define as to resist, called 'grace of the soul'). It was the morning after the last performance of a hectic season, and she was ecstatic at the prospect of wallowing in a sauna and splashing in the Finnish archipelago that same evening. 'I'll be rowing, I'll be swimming, I'll be singing in the sauna – oh, this is going to be a long evening in Finland!' By the time we met again in spring 1998, Mattila was a poised, sophisticated diva with the operatic world at her feet: glamorous and stunningly dressed (*the* best-dressed singer along with Denyce Graves off stage), yet just as radiant and equally likeable. As will be seen later, this conversation would also end on a Finnish theme . . .

Mattila was born on a farm in a rural community called Perniö, near the charming historic town of Turku. Her family had no musical back-ground. Her parents were farmers, but sang in choirs. Her father, who cannot read a note of music, plays both the piano and the guitar by ear. So there was a lot of singing in the home, and this led to singing in the local choir – almost the only amusement in a community which Mattila says was over-conservative and in which 'almost everything seemed to be forbidden'. (One senses that her upbringing may have been restrictive.) She learnt to play the piano at the age of nine and began taking singing lessons at fifteen. As soon as she left school she enrolled at the Sibelius Academy in Helsinki. Her first Professor of Singing at the Sibelius Academy was Liisa Linko-Malmio, who from Mattila's description was a warm, nurturing personality who guided her first steps, both as singer and human being, with tenderness and perspicacity. (As we shall see, Mattila was to prove blessedly fortunate in her teachers – a sure sign, to my mind, that a singer has luck on her side.)

Mattila loved every minute of her studies at the Academy, the place where her voyage of self-discovery really began. Everything was new to her. Coming straight from her parents' farm, 'it was like being Alice in Wonderland', as she confided in *Opera*. She threw herself into her studies of music history, theory and harmony with gusto and alacrity.

At that time she did not have much confidence in herself as a singer. But her teacher had enough confidence for both of them, and tried to instill some of it into her promising pupil. She encouraged her to enter Finland's top vocal contest, the Lappeenranta Singing Competition, which Mattila, to her amazement, proceeded to win. Her teacher however was not surprised.

1983 was a milestone year for Mattila. While still a student at the Sibelius Academy she was named the first ever Cardiff Singer of the World. This prestigious competition, which is televised live on the BBC, always brims with journalists, agents and talent scouts from most important theatres and managements, and affords the winners much wider exposure than most other singing competitions, however distinguished. Mattila also found it 'a very good dress rehearsal' for a career, because it enables young singers to take their own measure at this very early stage: 'You test your stage presence, your nerves, your own limitations'. In short, as Mattila explained in *Opera*, you learn how to cope.

This was just as well, because within a year of being named Singer of the World Mattila's international career began in earnest. But first, having sung the Countess in *De nozze di Figaro* at the National Opera House in Helsinki shortly after her graduation, she moved to London. Here Mattila found her second teacher, Vera Rozsa, a wonderful Hungarian with whom she works to this day. Rozsa was also the guiding spirit behind Kiri Te Kanawa's career, and has taught some of the world's greatest singers including Lucia Popp and Ileana Cotrubas. She has been instrumental in overseeing Mattila's vocal development, and has also proved a tower of strength as a human being. 'I simply wouldn't be where I am now without her,' stresses Mattila. 'Not only does she know my voice almost better than I do myself, but she is also an exceptional person, fizzing with energy and an infectious *joie de vivre*. "Darlink, you must enjoy life, enjoy what you do and not push yourself too hard", she keeps telling me in her wonderful Hungarian accent.'

Vera Rozsa stresses that a good teacher-pupil relationship is based on mutual understanding. On the teacher's side, this understanding should extend to the singer's character as much as to their voice. 'Karita is a very sensitive, almost hyper-sensitive person, I should say, very genuinely modest and unaffected by all the success, recognition, or even by her ravishing good looks. And so considerate that in all the fourteen years we have been working together, I have never known her be even a few minutes late. She is a tremendously hard worker who has worked for every inch of her accomplishment, and she is also very conscious of and grateful for the gift of her voice and appearance. She has always been willing to listen to advice and to wait until she was vocally ready for each of the parts for which she is now famous. Another thing that has always struck me is her spiritual generosity – I have never *ever* heard a derogatory word from her about a colleague. And as I'm sure you well know, this is not the norm among female singers!'

Within a year of graduating from the Sibelius Academy, Mattila began string of international débuts: at the Théâtre de la Monnaie in Brussels as the Countess, at Scottish Opera as Donna Elvira in a production of *Don Giovanni* directed by Graham Vick and in Washington, also as Donna Elvira, all in 1985. A year later came her Paris and Covent Garden débuts as Fiordiligi, which she first sang in Strasbourg. She was immediately invited back to Covent Garden for Pamina later that year and for the Countess in 1987, in Johannes Schaaf's production of *Figaro*. This was the first opera in an ongoing Mozart cycle in which Mattila was to appear again on two occasions, as Donna Elvira in 1992 and Donna Anna in 1993. Meanwhile she had also sung Agathe in Covent Garden's new production of *Der Freischütz* in 1989–90, and Musetta in 1993.

Throughout the first decade of her career Mattila tended to be known primarily as a Mozart singer, although she had made forays into both the Italian and the German lyric repertoire. She sang Amelia in *Simon Boccanegra* first in 1987 in Helsinki and later in Geneva and at the Teatro Colón. But her triumphant appearances as Eva in *Die Meistersinger* in

Brussels in 1985 and at the Munich Festival in 1986 offered a glimpse of another, bigger voice lurking within and biding its time.

'I started off with Mozart. But even during the time when I was singing mostly Mozart, I was already developing into something else,' says Mattila. 'But I didn't quit Mozart until ten years after my first Eva. I quit him at the right time, although I still sing donna Anna and Fiordiligi to maintain the flexibility in my voice amidst all the bigger roles.'

Donna Anna, which Mattila will sing again at the 1999 Salzburg Festival, was the most challenging of all her Mozart roles, even though it is not nearly as long as Fiordiligi. 'The reason is that Donna Anna has a consistently high tessitura that doesn't come down at all to allow the voice to relax. Fiordiligi is more flexible and allows you to use the whole register, thus keeping the voice open throughout. Donna Anna is also very demanding as far as dynamics are concerned: in Act I you have several big *fortes* in "Or sai chi l'onore", while in Act II you have to rein yourself in in order to sing "Non mi dir", which has a high *pianissimo* right at the top of the register as well as dramatic coloratura. So you need almost two voices for Donna Anna. This is why, for a very long time, I felt safer singing Donna Elvira.' (Mattila has also sung this role in Japan, at Hamburg, the Vienna State Opera and at the Lyric Opera of Chicago.)

Mattila's first Wagnerian role, Eva in *Die Meistersinger*, was in a production at the Théâtre de la Monnaie in Brussels in 1985 by Kurt Horres, featuring José Van Dam as Hans Sachs. The late Harold Rosenthal, editor and founder (with Lord Harewood) of *Opera Magazine*, described Mattila as 'the best Eva since Tiana Lemnitz in the mid-Thirties'. During our first meeting, Mattila had explained that Eva had been a very important landmark for her vocally, dramatically and psychologically: 'Although I love Mozart and his roles passionately, in Eva I found *my* role, the role I felt most comfortable in. Through her, I made the acquaintance of a completely new me, somebody I didn't know was there. I grew a lot because of Eva. She gave me the courage to be myself, and to have confidence in myself. There was something about this character that somehow *forced* the real me to come out, to try and be like her. At the time [Mattila was then twenty-six] I saw her as someone younger than me because she is always being treated as someone very young, a wonderful young girl just ripening into womanhood. But I think she's far from being either naive or the pure young thing she pretends to be in front of her father. She is very determined, with a strong will of her own. I like this sort of character. Some of Wagner's heroines are really weird. But Eva is a wonderful, *healthy* character experiencing all those marvellous emotions that young people go through: being in love, having this 'Liebeskummer', and surrounded by men, with all of whom she seems to have wonderful relationships – her father, Walther and Sachs. It's thrilling. I think she must also be quite intelligent because she manages to get her way without upsetting her father. I also admire her serenity and peace of mind amidst all the mayhem and her freshness, honesty and optimistic outlook on life.'

According to Mattila, the most interesting aspect of the role is Eva's relationship with Hans Sachs – a relationship which might have evolved quite differently if the action were taking place in our own day. 'The two know each other very well and Eva loves, trusts, respects and feels very secure with Sachs, with whom she also seems to communicate more openly than with her father. It's to him she runs whenever she has a problem or wants to find out anything about Walther. Of course, it's Walther she falls in love with. But there is something in her deep feeling for Sachs which she doesn't quite understand. It hovers on the borderline where trust, respect and affection end and something else begins. This something is what Eva spends a couple of sleepless nights trying to figure out, and whatever it is, it's very powerful. Of course, in our own day, Sachs would probably have made a move. But in the opera he has a complex about his age, and takes the attitude that a bond between a young girl and a middle-aged man is impossible. But in our society we don't believe that age makes a man less attractive. I think a modern-day Sachs might have made it more difficult for Eva to choose. I don't think he would have fought in a straightforward, out-and-out way. He would have fought with his brain, with savoir-faire – unlike Walther, who would have fought with his sword – and tried to influence her in a way that would have made her come to him instead.'

Mattila considers herself lucky to have sung her first Eva for a very good director, Kurt Horres, who created a 'stunning' production and worked with every member of the cast in a very personal way. 'This is very rare among directors. For someone like me who was new to the role, it was wonderful. It was he who helped me discover this Eva who could have been me. This is why, in 1985, I was able to fly to the Munich Festival at such short notice, two weeks, and replace Lucia Popp. I could never have scored the success I did if I hadn't been so thoroughly prepared in such a good production.'

Mattila's first experience with Wagner back in 1985 brought home to her the fact that Wagner is radically different from Mozart, both vocally and in terms of stamina. 'Although Eva is not a long role it is so *heavy* that it takes much more out of you than even the longest Mozart role. Act III in particular is so heavy and so low – yet the voice must remain girlish-sounding throughout – that it showed me that, for the moment at least, this was my limit with Wagner. It was as far as I could go. The combination of the orchestral and vocal writing – the way the voice lies – is so different from what I was used to that it took an awful lot of physical as well as vocal strength to pull through. And this called for stamina and made it a tremendous effort physically.'

Mattila felt there was 'a big physiological lesson' to be learnt from this experience: 'It made me realize the all-important physiological connection between the voice and the rest of the body. That's when I began exercising and working out on a regular basis – five times a week – both on an exercise bike and with the help of fitness videos. I concentrate on a programme designed for my back and abdominal muscles. This is excellent both for building up stamina and keeping my weight down. I have a huge appetite and a tendency to put on weight immediately. Without my exercise programme I would need to be on a constant diet. But this way I can eat what I like *and* build up my reserves of strength and stamina, so crucial in the bigger roles. Because you *have* to be in good physical shape for this profession.' (This is where my first conversation with Mattila in 1986 had left off, and it is exactly where it picked up twelve years later).

'The last time I did Eva at the Metropolitan Opera with Jimmy Levine [1995], I was in such good shape – as was also the case when I sang Elisabeth de Valois for the first time in Paris a year later – that I surprised myself with what I could do on stage, both vocally and dramatically. Eva now felt so comfortable that I've decided to keep coming back to it and to try to bring something special to it every time. Although Eva is very young in years, vocally it's a very mature part. I don't think a young singer, as I was when I first sang it, could sing the role on a regular basis without taking a very big risk: the part is so heavy and so low that it risks pulling the voice downwards.'

In the same year that she sang Eva at the Met, Mattila took on the big, demanding role of Chrysothemis in *Elektra*. She was convinced she was ready for it by Claudio Abbado, who holds her in very high esteem. She had already worked with Abbado on several important projects, including Luc Bondy's fascinating and controversial production of *Don Giovanni* at the 1989 Vienna Festival. 'Had it been any other conductor, I would have refused outright. But as it turned out, his instinct was right. I remember one particular scene in this Salzburg production which I think of as symbolic of my subsequent artistic development: Chrysothemis was supposed to be in a cage, with some animals. And when Klytemnestra is killed, she is supposed to burst out of it. So when that moment came, I burst out and sang my heart out. I was in ecstasy. I always get an ecstatic feeling when singing with Claudio, but this was something special. It was as if I, too, was bursting out of my vocal and dramatic cocoon, bursting beyond what I had thought of as my limits. I learnt an enormous amount about my voice from Chrysothemis, notably that my voice suits Strauss. Both vocally and dramatically I gave so much out at each performance that when we finished the run I rushed to London to Vera to see if I had damaged my voice for *Don Carlos*. But she said I was in fantastic form.' The public and critical response was enthusiastic, as it was also when Mattila sang the role again in 1997 at Covent Garden, in a vocally vintage production featuring Deborah Polaski in the title role.

Chrysothemis was the turning point in Mattila's transition to a heavier repertoire. A year later, in 1996, she sang Elisabeth de Valois in the French, five-act version of *Don Carlos* in Luc Bondy's production, first at the Chatelet, where it was conducted by Antonio Pappano, and then at Covent Garden with Bernard Haitink. (Both conductors delivered different, but superlative readings of the score.) Right from the start Vera Rozsa told Mattila that she was lucky to be singing this demanding role in French because she felt it would suit both her voice and personality better than the Italian version. Indeed, the spirit and emotions of *Don Carlos* – centred on the constant call for duty and self-sacrifice as well as the loneliness endemic in the royal condition – are more 'French' than Italian. So too is the poise, dignity and overall *elegance* characteristic of Elisabeth's actions and comportment. The role seemed tailor-made for Mattila and singing it for the first time with such success in French, in France, was a great moment in her career.

Mattila is convinced that regardless of whether this opera is sung in French or Italian, it must always be performed in the five-act version which includes the Fontainebleau Scene. If this is omitted, she rightly feels that the opera does not make sense dramatically or, in Elisabeth's case vocally. 'Elisabeth needs the Fontainebleau Scene. She *needs* this music, which returns again in Act V when she is thinking about the past, about what might have been. From the dramatic point of view, this is also where she establishes her character and when her story begins. We have the opportunity to see who she really is: a young woman in love, excited and rapturous and behaving like all young people do when they're in love, whether they happen to be princesses or farmers' daughters. It's important to show the contrast between this radiant princess in love and the sombre, restrained queen of the following three acts, before we meet the real Elisabeth again in Act V, where she reflects on the past.

'I remember going to see the four-act version of *Don Carlos* at Savonlinna as a young girl. Not knowing the story, I failed to understand what that lady in black was really doing there, standing like a statue, wearing those gorgeous clothes and occasionally singing the most sublime music. I didn't know what she was about. In those days I was a farmer's daughter with no musical background. But when I went to the theatre I wanted to understand the story unfolding before my eyes without having to do any homework. And I now like to feel that *my* audience doesn't need to do this either, in order to understand the story of an opera. If they *want* to know more, they can read it up, of course. But they shouldn't *have* to.'

They certainly do not have to in the five-act version of *Don Carlos*, which, Mattila says, establishes Elisabeth from the very beginning as a character so patriotic that she puts duty to her country above personal considerations. 'This sense of self-sacrifice and obligation towards her people is in her blood. It's part of her character, part of the upbringing she received from her father, the King of France.[1] This is why she is so incensed when King Philip doubts her fidelity in Act IV. Doing so implies questioning the very foundations on which her life is based, and for which she gave up marrying Don Carlos. Having controlled her emotions and personal feelings so rigorously since then, she falls into a state of shock when her royal husband presumes to doubt her. For although she never loved him, the two must have shared some comfortable moments together and she does expect his implicit trust, trust in her acceptance of this sacred sense of duty on which kings and

---

[1] Interestingly, King Juan Carlos of Spain recently referred to this specific point by saying: 'Before I was old enough to understand this sacred principle of duty and self-sacrifice consciously, I had already assimilated it by osmosis.'

queens base their lives . . . It's a wonderful story, with many moments you can choose to enhance or bring out. In Luc Bondy's production we saw Elisabeth at this point in Act IV actually lose control of herself and have an outburst, which is written in the music.

Elisabeth de Valois is also very challenging vocally, especially for somebody like Mattila who came from a background of Mozart rather than Verdi. 'In Verdi you have to learn to let go much more than you do in Mozart. This is why Chrysothemis – where I did let go so much – was such an important station on the road to Elisabeth. The most difficult thing, of course, is the Act IV Quartet and the last aria, which is to die for, but which is written in a way that doesn't give you anywhere to breathe, not even a single bar. It's a *killer*. But I imagine that the more I sing the role, the easier it will become.'

Although this production had a star-studded cast that included Roberto Alagna in the title role, Thomas Hampson as Rodrigo and José Van Dam as King Philip, all in top form, the *Sunday Times* wrote after the London première that 'The evening's star, however, was the ravishingly lovely Elisabeth of Mattila, who sang not one unlovely note nor made one untruthful gesture throughout a long evening. This shining lyric soprano, Cardiff Singer of the World in 1983, is in her prime.' (The review ended with this chapter's opening words.)

Mattila proved beyond doubt that she really was in her prime during the following season, when she took on Elsa in *Lohengrin*, first in San Francisco, then in Paris in an iconoclastic production by Robert Carsen and finally at Covent Garden, in Elijah Moshinsky's spare, atmospheric staging. She stresses that going from Eva (*Die Meistersinger*) to Elsa was a very big step: 'Elsa is a very long part and I realized immediately that I *needed* to have these performances of Chrysothemis and Elisabeth already under my belt before I sang it. Because without the experience of those long roles behind me, I could easily have run out of stamina. From the vocal point of view, Elsa doesn't get really high until Act III. I particularly love and look forward to this act – I love the emotions and the way they are expressed musically, with Elsa showing so much of her human side. Her reactions are logical, human and *real*. What's happening to her at this point could happen to anybody, anytime. I, too, could feel and act this way in the circumstances. And I don't think these emotions change, regardless of the setting in which the director chooses to place the action. The time could change, the place could change, but the emotions wouldn't.'

Mattila explains that she is particularly fascinated by relationships and emotions that transcend time and place, and relishes portraying them on stage. As part of her course at the Sibelius Academy she had studied straight acting with two professional actors. 'They passionately believed that a good story can unfold and put across its message in any setting. If you have got the human relationships right, if you know who you are as a character and if you know what your story is and where you come from, then you have good enough reason to be on stage. I am deeply grateful to my actor friends for teaching me this basic truth about dramatic reality. Although I love glamorous productions with beautiful costumes, I can function and make my characters live just as easily in any setting, as long as I have a strong, convincing director.'

Indeed, the production of *Lohengrin* in which Mattila most enjoyed portraying Elsa was Robert Carsen's Paris staging, which lifted the opera out of its medieval setting and placed it in postwar Germany. The French critics hated it and, admits Mattila, at first so did she. 'But all it took was one session with Carsen for me to be totally convinced by his concept. I found his idea that out of all this ugliness – the costumes were so drab as to be almost rags – comes something as beautiful, vital and *new* as Lohengrin very moving and convincing. Of course, first you have to establish an imaginary link with what Lohengrin stands for – the idea that miracles *can* happen, even if only in people's minds and hopes. I loved this concept, as well as the stark contrast between the drab, ugly setting and the beautiful music, especially in terms of the human emotions it conjures up. Carsen's way of seeing *Lohengrin* was lovely, and I came out of the experience infinitely richer.' Elijah Moshinsky who directed the Covent Garden performances found to his delight that 'Mattila is so confident about her stage craft that she deliberately left some parts of her performance open to improvisation. She and Gösta Winbergh were so good at this that there were certain moments where, although we all knew where they should be heading, I left them free to improvise the steps by which we got there. This was something very new and psychologically very unusual to have in a German opera which usually demands rigour and planning.'

Elsa also enriched Mattila vocally, in the way that the right roles at the right time will always take the voice a stage further towards the ful-filment of its potential. She had previously turned down many proposals to sing Elsa, knowing that there are special vocal dangers involved in singing Wagnerian roles: 'One of the main difficulties is that the orchestration is very heavy, so you need to give out plenty of volume. But the volume should come in such a *natural* way that you don't need to force. If you did, if you tried for more weight than you have, you would risk losing your colour. My natural way to Elsa was via the roles I sang before – I needed them all. From now on, my Elsa can only get better, and I look forward to singing it again this autumn at the Metropolitan Opera with Jimmy Levine.'

According to Matthew Epstein, formerly Director of the Welsh National Opera and now Artistic Director Designate of the Lyric Opera of Chicago, Mattila's gradual development of her repertoire is not only impressive but also a guarantee of her continuing vocal health: 'She started off with roles of medium weight, made sure those fitted and felt comfortable, and only then did she move on to heavier parts such as Chrysothemis, Elisabeth de Valois and Elsa. She will be forty by the end of the century and is now looking at Leonore in *Fidelio*, Sieglinde and possibly Salome and thinking that in two or three years' time she may do them. This attitude is very healthy. Anyone who, like Mattila, has waited until fifteen years into their career before tackling this sort of repertoire is on the right track and has made the right choice. This way her voice will continue to develop naturally, and eventually she may well turn out to be the "hochdramatisch" soprano we've all been waiting for, the new Salome, Sieglinde, Senta and who knows what else. In addition, she is also keeping the lightness and flexibility in her voice by continuing to sing Donna Anna and Amelia in *Boccanegra*. That's a very good sign that her voice will go the distance.'

The reason why Mattila is so careful about accepting Wagner roles is precisely because of the risk of losing the lightness and flexibility in her voice. 'The danger of singing too much Wagner is that most of his female characters are not very high – they are written mostly around the middle voice. And if you sing them month after month and are not sufficiently alert, you will find that your way of singing will change. I don't mean that you would necessarily start pressing and pushing the voice, but that you will try for a heavier sound. You would get so used to expecting the orchestra to be dense, heavy and stormy that – unless you sing something in between to lighten your voice – you would be tempted to give out full *power*, even when you're not giving out full volume.'

Mattila safeguarded against this by interspersing her Elsas with some recitals, to preserve the lightness and legato of her voice. Richard Strauss, on the other hand, does not pose the same threat to the voice. 'Strauss and Wagner are totally different in their vocal writing. Strauss writes very high, while Wagner writes for the middle section of the voice. But the moment you overtax the middle voice, you lose your support. If you do have a good middle and lower extension though, Wagner roles are wonderful because, as a soprano, it's good to be given the occasional chance to use that part of voice too. It's only when you stay down there on a regular basis that you run the risk I mentioned. That's why after being asked to sing Sieglinde for years, I finally accepted an invitation to sing one concert performance of *Die Walküre*, in Paris in December 1998 with Placido Domingo as Siegmund. That alone is good enough reason for me to learn it! I know some people who ended up with huge vocal problems after Sieglinde, but maybe they weren't careful enough about what they sang immediately afterwards.' Mattila is guaranteed to bring to Sieglinde that radiant spiritual quality one has not seen since Behrens.

One of Mattila's two new roles last season was as different from Elsa as one could imagine: Hanna Glawari in *Die lustige Witwe*, which she sang at the Paris Opéra in December 1997. She had been looking forward to this for a long time, but the production proved a vast disappointment. 'It was a missed opportunity. And what an opportunity! What a cast! I had the most gorgeous Danilo imaginable, Bo Skovhus, whom I love being on stage with. We look so alike that he could be my middle brother, and he is a great colleague, a great singer and actor. So everything was right. But we had this unsatisfactory director who was supposed to stage German dialogue though he didn't even speak the language. I'd love to have the chance to sing Hanna again because I adored being able to dance, act and have fun! Vocally it's perfect for my kind of voice because it's fairly low with only one or two high notes. In fact it's rather easy. The challenge is to move well, dance well and be *elegant*. I was very proud of the fact that I managed to dance throughout my aria, which took my mind off the high notes I had to sing in a few minutes. I also enjoyed the *laughter* in this part and the fact that, in the end, I get the man I love! Such a change from many of my heroines who, like Elsa, Elisabeth and Jenůfa, are mostly tragic.' Jonathan Miller, who worked with Mattila on a production of *Così fan tutte* confirms she has a great gift for comedy. 'She was a slow start, but when she caught on, she was an extremely natural comic actress. Looking at her, you would think of her much more as a *dramatic* kind of singing actress. But actually, she's very funny, with a subversive sense of comedy.'

Jenůfa was another new role for Mattila in 1998. In April she sang it in Czech at the Hamburg State Opera, and she will eventually sing it again at the Metropolitan Opera and the Salzburg Festival. 'I love this variety and the self-renewal I experience through singing such varied characters. Many singers make a career out of singing two or three major roles. But as I said earlier, I need at least one, or two, new parts a year to keep myself busy.' She is fascinated by the Slavic repertoire which, she rightly feels, suits the colour of her voice. She would like to add more Janáček heroines in due course, perhaps Kát'a Kabanová, and she has already performed the two great Tchaikovsky heroines, Tatyana in *Eugene Onegin* (in Hamburg and Madrid) and Lisa in *The Queen of Spades* (at the Metropolitan Opera in 1995).

In the 1998–9 season her big new part will be the title role in *Manon Lescaut*, which she will sing first in Finland and then in San Francisco in 2002. Her only Puccini role so far is Musetta, which she sang enchantingly at Covent Garden in 1993 and later at the Metropolitan Opera. So *Manon Lescaut* will be a very big event for her. 'I really enjoy singing in Italian. I know some people speculate that I am a Germanic type and so on. I am aware of their misgivings but I ignore them. I just do my job and leave speculation to others! In any case, it's good to have one or two Italian roles in your repertoire for the reasons I explained earlier. Another part I would love to sing sometime is Desdemona.' Like Elisabeth de Valois, Desdemona would suit Mattila perfectly, both vocally and dramatically.

Looking back on her meticulously planned career, Mattila is thankful that as well as being lucky in her teachers, she was also fortunate enough to find the ideal agent right away in Diana Mulgan. In those days Mulgan was with Lies Askonas, but she eventually moved to IMG to be with her husband, Tom Graham. Graham, who also happens to be deeply knowledgeable about the voice, has been looking after Mattila since Mulgan's illness. Mattila very much liked and respected Diana for her deceptively laid back manner, wonderful wit and firm belief that singers should not be pushed into doing more than they want to do.

'This is the kind of support young singers need, and I'll mention an important incident that will help you understand exactly what I mean. When I made my début in Washington as Elvira, back in 1985, I was asked by my American agent at Columbia Artists to audition for James Levine at the Met. I didn't want to, but my American agent felt I

should, because the only way I would ever sing at the Met was by auditioning for James Levine, "like everybody else". I begged to differ.
Maybe because I am a farmer's daughter from a small country, I always
thought of the Metropolitan Opera and Carnegie Hall as almost sacred
places. I only wanted to sing there after being *invited*. I wanted to
come in through the front rather than the back door. I suppose it was
a courageous attitude, considering I was no-one at the time. But my
American agent tried to push me. Desperately unhappy, I rang Diana in
London to ask for her and her partner's opinion. She said, "Look, *we*
think you will sign at the Met one day *anyway*. So, it's up to you to
decide when." I was *so* relieved! In the event I was invited, and made my
début there as Donna Elvira in 1990. The same thing happened with
Carnegie Hall. An organization once asked me to sing there for some
charitable or business function. Again, I said no, I would wait until I
was invited. And after the last revival of *Meistersinger* at the Met in
1995, I was. I'll be making my début there in a recital in February
1999.'

This recital will contain Finnish music, including the *Poem,
Rynopolku*, by the important contemporary composer Jouni Kaipainen,
which Mattila will first sing in France. Not surprisingly, she feels she
has a 'special relationship' both with Finnish music and Finnish audiences. 'I want to sing something in Finland every year, even if it's only
a concert. I have a *fantastic*, supportive audience there and even *thinking* about them, let alone singing for them, moves me.' Mattila's
husband – tall, handsome and blond like her – is also a Finn and gave
up his job as a car salesman to travel with her. Their base is London.

Mattila's relationship to Finnish music is deep and passionate. 'I've
often wondered why such a small country has produced and continues
to produce so many wonderful composers. It could have something to
do with our wondrous, vast, empty, silent landscapes which incline us
to be hermits, and encourage composition. At Carnegie Hall I will
present both established (Sibelius) and contemporary Finnish music. I
think it's essential for well known and successful singers to perform

good contemporary works that they personally like. This is what the famous singers of the past did with our "classics", who were then contemporary. Because it's not fair for today's composers to have their music performed only by so-called specialists – which, I'm afraid, tends to mean singers who have no opportunities to sing anything else. The way to do justice to modern composers is for singers like myself who can make their living in the standard repertoire to start performing their music. I feel very strongly about this. And when I give that recital at Carnegie Hall next February, it won't be just another feather in my cap. I will be feeling *proud* to be in New York, in one of the greatest concert halls in the world, and singing Finnish music. Because if I didn't, who would?'

DEBORAH
POLASKI

'I LOVE CHALLENGING productions that take a lot out of you, *if* they have a consistent idea and *if* this idea serves the text. Why go and noodle out something you've done before? It's important to do something new, something that makes you *think* and work physically.' This is the view of Deborah Polaski, who is about to sing Marie in a concert performance of *Wozzeck* at London's Festival Hall with the Philharmonia Orchestra under Christoph von Donányi.

As a supreme example of what she means, she cited Peter Stein's riveting Salzburg Easter Festival production of *Wozzeck* conducted by Claudio Abbado, at which the public went on applauding even after the final curtain. 'It was hard work, but at the end of the day you knew why you were tired. It was so sparse, so threadbare – an exact reflection of Berg's way of writing: incredibly clear patterns, clear rings you can see through. This is the way the piece is composed and in order to make it work emotionally you have to keep that. You can't pad it with nice things to make you feel good – it's not that sort of piece. It's a piece after which – an hour and three quarters later – you are devastated . . . The public reaction was amazing. I've never seen such a public reaction before. That's the kind of inspired input from a director intent only on realizing the piece.

'Conversely, there's nothing worse than a director who comes to a production unprepared and uninterested in the work at hand, intent only on making his own way. It's devastating – and it happens all the time. Because, in operatic terms, our age is definitely the Age of the Director. Is he a saviour or a scourge? Depends on what his name is! The great directors I've worked with – Harry Kupfer, Peter Stein, Dieter Dorn, Ruth Berghaus, Nikolaus Lehnhoff – know that you have to serve the piece. That's all you have to do. Then everything works *and* you serve yourself in the process.'

Polaski is one of the world's leading 'hochdramatisch' sopranos, whose voice is richly shaded in both colour and dynamics. Its luminosity and sheen, according to her teacher Irmgard Hartmann, reflect her inner world, 'because the timbre of a voice is an expression of a singer's soul.' Polaski brings to her characters, especially her Wagnerian heroines, not only an ideal voice and physique, but also a spiritual dimension and radiance without which these parts can easily degenerate into athletic feats centred merely on decibels and stamina.

This inner spiritual dimension has also helped sustain Polaski through a road to the top that was unusually long and arduous, as well as through a crisis involving a voluntary eight-month withdrawal from the stage in 1988–9. It was present in her life right from the beginning. Born in Wisconsin, she came from a wonderful home: 'We were extremely poor, but not poor in love or in emotion, which is the most important thing: that stays with you always. We always sang.' Polaski's father was a minister in an evangelical church in Hill Creek, a small Wisconsin community. It was one of his first churches and he had no salary. 'He did it all for the love of God and out of commitment to his church. We depended entirely on what went into the collection box. Some people gave money, while others brought eggs or produce from their farms or gardens.' The expression on Polaski's face as she remembers this indicates that her childhood was a happy one. Her maternal grandfather was also a minister of the church. 'We always sang, both at home and in church, and my grandfather in particular had a beautiful tenor voice.'

Polaski's decision to become a singer came relatively late, at around the age of twenty-three. Her first degree, from Marion College, Indiana was in musical education, and she was lucky enough to find a teaching job in an elementary school in Indiana immediately upon graduation. 'It was a huge challenge. I had to take the music classes for every age group, which was mind-boggling. There's no other way to describe it except to say that I had no idea where to start and where to end! By the end of the academic year I had learnt an awful lot from those kids and got terribly attached to them. Teaching is very emotional.'

Yet the experience made her realize that teaching was not her life's work. She returned to study singing full time at College Conservatory in Cincinnati, Ohio. Everyone in her class seemed to be preparing for the all-important Metropolitan Opera auditions which, in her case, came to nothing. But at the same time a very good music summer school in Graz was also holding auditions, and was sufficiently impressed by her voice to invite her to Graz for two successive summers in 1975 and 1976. The most important part of these summer courses were the masterclasses given by George London, the renowned American bass-baritone, which were an invaluable experience for a young singer.

'He was the most important influence in my life so far. He'd been there and done it all. Mind you, he could be awful, too. But if he felt you were well prepared and really keen to get things right, he was prepared to work and work and work with you. We worked on my first Senta. He pointed out useful tips such as: "I have heard so many sopranos die at this spot, and you must absolutely do it this way if you don't want this to happen to you as well." The problem is that much of Senta lives in the passaggio. It's a real "specialist" part because Wagner was still very inexperienced when he wrote it, and his way of composition did not have the maturity of his later life.'

Senta in *Der fliegende Holländer* was the role in which Polaski made her professional début in 1976 at Gelsenkirchen, where she was engaged for one season. Senta is an incredible challenge for a young singer to begin her career with – even seasoned Wagnerian sopranos are wary of it, as it mostly lies in the passaggio. But it taught Polaski the valuable lesson of pacing ('especially in the Act II duet'), crucial in any long role, and especially so in the Wagnerian repertoire. 'Senta was part of a process, a walk through to this Wagnerian life. I sang it quite often at the time but don't any longer. I guess I don't have the call for it and by now my voice has taken a different direction. It's got larger and *ampler*, and I'm not sure I would wish to scale it down to fit Senta.'

After two years at Gelsenkirchen under the Greek conductor Spiro Argyris, Polaski moved to Karlsruhe. After two seasons, 1977–9, she was abruptly fired. She spent one year freelancing, and then went to Ulm in 1980–81 (the very theatre where Karajan had spent seven formative years), and thence to Hannover (1981–3), Freiburg (1983–5), Mannheim (1985–7) and Stuttgart (1987–9). During 1988 she made her début at Bayreuth in the *Ring*, her first really important break. By contemporary standards, hers was a slow, step-by-step progress: thirteen years from her arrival in Europe to a world-class international stage.

But these were hectic years, during which she learnt much repertoire, including all the heavy roles in which she now excels. 'I used to have to learn five or six roles a year at a time, and I well remember learning Elektra and Leonore sitting cross-legged on my bed, with my hair in curlers under the hairdryer, studying the score while waiting for my hair to dry! It was the only way I could do it at the time. Then later, when you do a role again and again, you get to the subtleties, the pearls that make all the difference, sometimes unconsciously. Then, when you begin to analyse it, it's like a flower opening up and divulging all its secrets to you . . .'

Elektra, which Polaski first sang in 1984 at Darmstadt, is now her absolutely favourite role, draining yet rewarding. 'She's such a *tortured* character, there so much *emotion* in her. One knows she loved and adored her father and there's this ferocious disgust for her mother which is incredible, yet she's still blood. And that's something you can't forget, the fact that there's a blood bond there. Then there's Chrysothemis, the sister whom she just uses without having any real feeling for her. But she adores her brother, or rather the memory of him . . . And when he returns and she finally recognizes him she can let go of all the feelings she's kept bottled up inside herself all this time. Vocally it's incredibly demanding. You have to have a top, a bottom and a middle, you have to have a good supported *piano*, you have to have volume, you have to have ecstasy, in short, you have to have everything. The only thing it doesn't have is a real love scene.'

Polaski has now sung Elektra in most big international theatres: in Berlin, Vienna, at the Paris Opéra, the Salzburg Festival and Covent Garden. Her portrayal is emotionally overwhelming and quite exquisitely sung, with subtle shades of colour and dynamics. 'Deborah Polaski's first London Elektra was sensationally good,' wrote *The Times* in May 1997. 'Indeed, you would have to go back many years to find such secure, radiant singing in this role. She has the necessary big guns (ringing top Cs) but she has much, much more: the ability to float soft, high notes with ravishing sensitivity and to mould Strauss's long lines into seamless, wonderfully expressive entities. Her solo in the Recognition Scene was sung gently, softly, with piercing beauty. It's musicianship that marks great Strauss singing, not noise.' The *Sunday Times* wrote that she was 'the most moving, beautiful-toned and inexhaustible [Elektra] at Covent Garden, perhaps the greatest Elektra of the post-war period.'

At the opposite end of the spectrum is Leonore in *Fidelio*, 'one of the most technically difficult roles in the repertoire,' according to Polaski. She considers that this role, which she first sang in 1983 at Freiburg, demands a classical discipline. 'It's not a question of whether it's written well for the voice or not. It's not written for the voice *at all*! It's written for an instrument and has to be sung instrumentally, which is to say that you should treat your voice as an instrument and just sing it properly. Discipline, discipline, discipline is the keyword. You just can't let go. It's frustrating because you can't allow the emotions in the piece to get hold of you. If you do, then you'll pay for it. So you have to be extremely picky about where you allow yourself to show emotion and how much. When you do, you have to rein yourself in immediately.

'As a character I like Leonore; she is almost obsessional in terms of what she thinks is right in trying to find her husband. It's a total, all-absorbing kind of dedication. She's prepared to lay down her life for him, so it's the ultimate love. But musically, it's not composed in an extremist way. That's why singing it properly means singing it instru-mentally: singing very clean, controlled notes, strung like a string of beads. Most of the time it's not sung properly, in the right style. I greatly look forward to going back to it now that my voice has grown and my technique developed.'

It was during Polaski's hectic period at different German opera houses in the early 1980s that she first sang Brünnhilde in the three *Ring* operas that feature this role. The first was *Siegfried* at Oxburg in 1981 followed by *Die Walküre* at Rouen in 1983 and finally *Götterdämmerung* in 1986 at Mannheim. She auditioned for Bayreuth and was invited for two complete *Ring* cycles in 1988, directed by Harry Kupfer. It was after her first *Ring* with Kupfer that her ideas about Brünnhilde began to crystallize. 'In *Die Walküre* she starts off being very exuberant and confident. She's daddy's favourite girl, and absorbs every word her volatile father utters. Then begins a growth process, through human life, pain and humiliation, that ends at the finale of *Götterdämmerung*, where she throws her wisdom back at her father. Through her own wisdom she has learnt how to let go of all the hurt, make her peace with her father, make her peace with Siegfried and her final peace with her horse. This is where she ties up all the loose ends in the *Ring*.

'In every sense, vocal and dramatic, *Götterdämmerung* is the most difficult because it's the longest. Act I is about two hours long, as long as a complete opera! It's also the most dramatically and emotionally demanding. In Act II, you have that duet, you have the vengeance trio, it's incredible how much you have to give. And if you have a conductor who's over-emotional, you've had it. At the end you're totally spent, but happily spent . . . But to reach the finale with your voice intact for the Immolation Scene, you have to be very wise as far as pacing is concerned and very secure technically.'

Polaski had not yet reached technical security in those early years leading up to her first Bayreuth *Ring* cycles. She was singing those mammoth, ultra-demanding roles so technically unprepared that, according to her teacher Irmgard Hartmann, 'only the fact that her voice is basically very healthy prevented any lasting damage. Also the fact that she had the instinctive sense to sing only with the power, weight and volume she had instead of trying for more.' Yet while she managed fine in some performances there was the odd occasion at Bayreuth when she was booed.

This experience, combined with working at breakneck speed and intensity for so many years, singing those big roles for the first time, often in far from ideal circumstances and in many different houses, took its toll. After the 1988 Bayreuth Festival, Polaski decided to quit the profession. There was speculation in the German press that she was going into a monastery or had joined a Christian sect. None of this was true, although religious reasons – 'private reasons', as she puts it – had a lot to do with her decision. 'Having a God-given voice, I feel I have to serve God first and my career second. I felt at the time that my career had become my god, and that I needed to get my priorities right again.'

After approximately eighteen months, she had made some deep inner readjustments to her priorities, and felt free to return to her career. Since then, it has gone from strength to strength. She found in Irmgard Hartmann the right teacher, and with her developed a technique that has enabled her to reach her full vocal potential. It is important to know that great singers also encounter difficulties and crises of confidence, and that these crises *can* be overcome with the right attitude.

Matthew Epstein, Artistic Director Designate of the Lyric Opera of Chicago and someone who has known Polaski since those days, remembers that hers was 'a big crisis, both vocal and emotional, a kind of fear. I think the stress she had put on herself during those years was such that she got into difficulties. But she realized she was in a crisis and did something about it. She understood there was something that needed fixing, both technically and emotionally, and she fixed it. And she emerged the better for it, and is now singing splendidly.'

Indeed, by the summer of 1991 Polaski was back at Bayreuth with her problems safely behind her. Polaski is terribly grateful to Irmgard Hartmann, who made this possible on the technical side. 'She taught me a technique that's continuing to develop. This is important, because you never stop working.' (Other great singers, such as Renée Fleming, Karita Mattila and Dolora Zajick, are also adamant about this point, of which all promising young singers should take note.) 'She said that the most important thing was to develop a technique that would enable me to sing even when I don't feel well because I have a lot of problems with barometric pressure, especially low pressure. We have now been working regularly since 1990.' Since that time Polaski has been based mainly in Berlin.

Hartmann considers that confidence, 'the single most important thing' for any singer, was also the key to Polaski's vocal rehabilitation: 'When a singer is insecure, I try to find out why. In Deborah's case, I discovered that her technique was not developed enough for her to feel free: the resonators were tight, there were problems with some of her vowels and her breath support was too high, by which I mean that it was not spread widely enough around the body. Good breath support does not rely only on the diaphragm. Then we worked on diction, because only when your diction is right, when all your vowels are right, can you go for a really deep breath support. So we started off finding out which vowels were right and which were not and tried to make them all even. That opens the throat and frees the breath, enabling it to flow freely. Of course, we had to go step by step. She was busy performing all the time, so we could not change everything at once.'

Hartmann points out that singing Wagner without a good breathing technique is very dangerous. 'You should also be in very good physical and mental shape, and you also need an excellent high *pianissimo*. This is very important for preserving your voice because it enables you to mark during rehearsals. The *balance* of the voice is also vital, the ability to mix all the registers by taking the head voice down and the chest voice up. You should start by taking the head voice down, rather than vice versa, but gently and gradually, never abruptly. One should also try for agility in all the registers.

'The most important thing about teaching, however, is to under-stand each individual singer and their voice. Luck plays a very great part in bringing the right teacher together with the right pupil.' Hartmann stresses that Polaski understands what she tries to explain to her, and that she in turn understands Polaski's voice and what she can do for her. 'There are all kinds of singers and all kinds of problems. You, as a teacher, have to find out where and why there is a blockage. Deborah was always very open, very disciplined and never too tired to work. This is a great gift, for it takes great patience and willpower for someone to go on fine-honing, with great precision, long after they have acquired a basic technique.'

After 1991, when Polaski returned to Bayreuth, fully in control of her voice and her artistic and spiritual goals, her international career took off. She returned to Bayreuth in the summers of 1992 and 1993 for complete *Ring* cycles, made her Metropolitan Opera début as Kundry in 1993, and sang at the Vienna State Opera. She made her Covent Garden début in 1995 in *Die Walküre* and returned in 1996 for a complete *Ring*, made her Paris début at the Chatelet as Elektra in the Berlin State Opera's production, and her Salzburg Festival début as Elektra.

Singing the *Ring* again with her new, secure vocal technique was an entirely new experience, and enabled her to *enjoy* the roles and also to reap the full benefit from them, in both artistic and spiritual enrichment. 'The vocal demands of these roles are enormous and you just *have* to be on top of them. The *Walküre* Brünnhilde is tricky. She starts off very high, with those "Hojotohos", and then comes down to the middle voice in Act II. It's important not to make it too thick down there in the middle, but to keep it as light and "heady" as you can at this point, even though it's all too easy to get thick and start sounding like a mezzo. Easy but fatal. Because the voice has to be able to blossom at the finale of Act III, Wotan's Farewell, and if you let it get thick, it's very hard to lighten it again.

'The finale of *Die Walküre* is a preparation for the *Siegfried* Brünnhilde, which is totally different. It's *extremely* high, and quite uncomfortable for almost everyone. The reason is that if you have the necessary weight and the heaviness in the middle that you need as a Wagnerian soprano, this can make singing at the very top quite difficult. For me the key to the *Siegfried* Brünnhilde is not to sing her too dramatically, but as lyrically as possible by sounding almost naive, because this is where she is waking up to human existence for the first time. If I keep this concept in my mind, it solves almost eighty per cent of the vocal difficulties, because the mind – having the right mental concept of what a role is – is the basis for everything and a great help in solving technical problems.' Irmgard Hartmann confirms that Polaski 'prepares every detail of a role in her mind and imagination. When the mental picture is right, she feels secure'.

Polaski continues her analysis of the technical demands of the *Ring* by explaining that Act I of *Götterdämmerung* begins just as *Siegfried* ends, very high and very jubilant. 'Then, when Siegfried leaves, it begins to get more dramatic and weighty. As the questions build up in Brünnhilde's mind, so the role becomes lower, darker and more dramatic. It has a very wide range that reflects the gamut of emotions she is going through: the pain, the agony and humiliation. Here I found

Richard Jones's idea for his Covent Garden production of having her wear a paper bag simply brilliant. And the end, the Immolation Scene has to be very emotional, very loving and very retrospective, because she goes through all the past in her mind. This scene has just about everything you could want to show.'

Polaski's performances in all her *Ring* operas in London drew high critical praise. The review by the veteran Wagnerite Michael Tanner in *The Spectator* was representative: 'All the women were admirable [including] the ever more inspiring Deborah Polaski. One of her numerous merits – she seems to be the most impressive Brünnhilde since Astrid Varnay – is a capacity and willingness to sing quietly, without sacrificing colour or body of tone. It makes the love duet very moving . . .'

Having now sung Brünnhilde in so many productions throughout the world, Polaski singles out two productions by Harry Kupfer – at Bayreuth the second time and in Berlin – as her favourites (though she also found some of Richard Jones's ideas for the Covent Garden production 'absolutely stellar'). She and Kupfer have developed an extremely close relationship, built over many years and many productions, not only of the *Ring* but also of *Lohengrin*, *Parsifal* and *Elektra*. 'It's almost like a family rapport,' she says. 'If I feel he's in a bad mood I leave him alone because I know it'll go away and he'll be better tomorrow. If I sense it's something more than that, something to do with the production, I can always go to him, and he'll say: "Let's talk about it. Lets fix it so that it's right for you because I *want* it to be right for you." He's that open and that approachable. But as I said, we have become such friends over the years that there are no misunderstandings between us.'

As far as directors in general are concerned, Polaski says that you have to know 'when to be a good girl and when to dig your heels in and be more assertive'. Although Polaski is typically American in her meticulous preparation and complete professionalism (the reasons, she says, why theatres everywhere are so keen to engage American singers), she is concerned as much by the degree of the director's power in opera today as she is by the level of some of the younger generation of directors.

'Their power has risen and risen until it almost surpasses even the conductor's. They make all the rules. They arrive with a team of four or five assistants, many of whom are often totally musically ignorant and sometimes even lacking in knowledge of basic stagecraft. You ask why we singers don't make an international, concerted revolt. I don't think this could ever happen. I think it's the whole system that has to change. As I'm sure you realize, I am not against new, different, even iconoclastic productions, provided they have something to say and are thoroughly thought through and prepared. What I *am* against is arrogance and ignorance, plus phoney, ill-prepared concepts. I feel that many of the newest crop of directors don't know their job and don't know how to help young singers learn how to relate to each other on stage, which is to say they don't know the basics. This is the way some of the youngest singers are also growing up not knowing, because there's no-one to teach them. This director-dominated era means that conductors are also coming to feel that if this is all there is to it, they too might as well jump on the bandwagon and play the game. So you get conductors who don't know the voice and who can't teach the singers or breathe with them. So it's a double catastrophe.

'You rightly ask why the singers of my generation sometimes compromise and agree to work with such directors. It can be for a variety of reasons: it may be that the production involves a conductor you want to work with; or it may have a cast you would like to be part of; or it may belong to a series of productions of works by a certain composer that you have already done and wish to continue. Nevertheless, if it comes to a point where I feel the piece is going to suffer, or if I can't stand behind the director's concept, then I won't get involved. Because ultimately it's I, as a singer, who have to sell it to the public.'

Polaski, a committed performer and an excellent actress who totally immerses herself in her parts, is the ideal artist to sell any production she is convinced by. Some very exciting projects are in store for her in the near future: shortly after the London *Wozzeck* in November 1998 there will be a new televised production of *Elektra* in Cologne in December; and in 1999 there will be two new productions of *Tristan und Isolde*, the first at the Salzburg Easter Festival under Claudio Abbado and the second at the Maggio Musicale Fiorentino under Zubin Mehta. These will be welcome opportunities for international audiences to see Polaski in this role, which she sang first at Freiburg in 1984 and later in Dresden.

'Isolde is less three dimensional than Brünnhilde, being a woman rather than a goddess who becomes a woman, but no less gratifying for that. In Act I you see a woman dealing with her anger and sense of betrayal at Tristan's hands. In Act II you have that ecstatic love duet, which is unbelievably glorious to sing. The difficult thing about the role up to this point is how to keep body energy high enough to sustain over the Act II and III, intermission and Tristan's Big Scene leading to the Finale. The Liebestod starts off low but spirals up and continues to do so until you reach the stratosphere. You have to remember to sing it extremely legato and stay high on the voice, so that you can let your body work for you. Instead of thinking vertically, you have to think horizontally, along a long, legato line. Is Isolde more difficult than the *Götterdämmerung* Brünnhilde? It depends on the singer. For my voice, yes.'

Kundry in *Parsifal*, which Polaski first sang at Bayreuth and at the Metropolitan Opera in 1993, is easy when compared to these two roles. 'It's a cakewalk! Generally it's middle to low, and only gets high when she gets angry. It's interesting that as the seducer, she's a mezzo. And when Parsifal rejects her and gets enraged, she becomes a soprano! That's not to say it's easy. What I meant is that it's simply *easier* than the other two.'

At her concert performance of *Parsifal* at the Festival Hall in London in spring 1998 Polaski surpassed anything she had done at Bayreuth in 1993, bringing a vast palette of seductive colours to her singing. The

Financial Times wrote of her: 'Deborah Polaski – a Kundry who can wail and shriek with the best of them, but whose transformation in Act II from tender plausibility to castrating vamp was outstanding. The seductive kiss that she nearly extracted was more authentic than any staged performance I've seen'. *The Spectator* hailed her as 'the great Kundry of our times'. Also fascinating on this occasion was the mesmerized concentration with which she watched the performances of her colleagues, notably Domingo as Parsifal and John Tomlinson as Gurnemanz. It is rare to see such rapture in a singer's face at another's performance, for in truth most singers are quite monstrously egocentric. When I mentioned this to her she replied: 'It's *very* important to enjoy your colleagues! I've been generally blessed with very good colleagues, and it's gratifying to sing with people who enjoy their work. When it also happens to be in partnership with a good conductor and director, it's a fantastic thing to be called to do.'

The most exciting challenge ahead of Polaski, however, will come in summer 2000 when she will sing both Cassandra and Didon in *Les Troyens* in Salzburg. This will be a completely new direction for her, and her first plunge into the French repertoire. 'I was looking for something outside Wagner and Strauss to expand my horizons and to excite me. You can only eat so much red meat! I felt I needed something different, vocally and spiritually.' She plans to study the roles with a good French coach such as Janine Reiss or Denise Massé as well as with her own teacher.

In the past few years Polaski also ventured into Lied, which is proving a great source of satisfaction to her. At the beginning, though, she was terrified at the prospect of singing without costumes and without the barrier of a role between herself and the public. This is a very different kind of experience, as Irmgard Hartmann points out: 'Lied is a whole new world for a singer – it opens up a new window on the soul. You must know exactly what it is that you have to give. Working on Lieder was an important new dimension for Deborah. Also a very useful one, I would say, because Lied helps preserve the lightness in the voice amidst all those heavy roles, and also helps to fine-hone your interpretation, by concentrating on detail and on precision for every word and phrase. Your nerves, your feelings, your whole body and entire mind have to be hyper-alert in Lieder. This is especially good for big voices and helps them become more expressive in their operatic work as well. Isolde, for instance, is a role which is so deep in feeling that it benefits from the kind of penetration with which you approach Lied.

After a recent recital in Bordeaux (which Polaski repeated in Paris and London), one critic wrote: 'Abandoning Wagner's world, whose heroines she normally represents, for an evening, Deborah Polaski devoted herself to the intimacy of song. She surprises in this repertory with musical intelligence and leads the lyricism of Brahms, Mahler and Strauss to absolute heights. She especially succeeds in transforming her own imagination into music and expressing it clearly. It is given only to very few artists to express music with more than just a narrative sense. Deborah Polaski's singing is born out of inner feeling, out of the search for naturalness – absolutely essential for recitals. Her interpretation was, without doubt, great enough to be on that level.'

It was one evening after just such a recital as this in Paris, accompanied by Charles Spencer, that I met Deborah Polaski for our first interview. She was tired but glowing. It had been good recital, one of those evenings that make the sacrifices involved in the profession not seem like sacrifices at all. 'When do they seem like sacrifices? When too much is happening at the same time and I catch myself wondering what day of the week it is . . . But on days like today, I feel, "What a fantastic thing this is to be called to do! Thank you, Jesus." It's wonderful to be able to do this, to use oneself as an instrument for this sublime music to flow through.'

RUTH ANN SWENSON

'NOBODY TOLD ME I had to be a singer, nobody forced me or pushed me into it. It happened naturally because my parents were both singers and in our home singing was always in the air. I was surrounded by it', explained the dazzling American coloratura soprano Ruth Ann Swenson on a wintry New York afternoon between performances as Liù in Franco Zeffirelli's spectacular production of *Turandot* at the Metropolitan Opera. She went on to explain that she learnt to play the piano and the oboe as a child, sang in local choirs and started taking singing lessons at high school. After being asked to sing Pamina in a student production of *Die Zauberflöte*, she decided that this was *it*: 'I decided I was to be a singer on stage. I didn't want to teach singing or do anything else connected with music. I just wanted to sing! and I still feel this way, despite all the boloney that surrounds the business side of the profession.

'If you want to stay sane, you have to separate yourself from all that. But it's very hard. Because singing is such a personal thing, such a private thing, such a part of you, that anyone saying anything against your voice or talent is attacking *you*. And that's very hard to handle. Because what you are as a person comes out in that voice and that performance. In fact it's in every performance and every character you do. You can't hide what kind of person you are, whether you are singing Susanna, Gilda, Lucia or Semele. You are in every role you do. It's your soul and spirit, as much as your voice and artistry, that make you special and make what you bring to your roles special.'

If one had to single out one specific quality that Swenson brings to every role she sings apart from her sweet, shiny light lyric voice and dazzling technical brilliance, it would be joy, a quality she radiates in an almost palpable sense. However difficult the music, however high the notes or vertiginous the trills and roulades, one is never aware of any strain, nor is there any question about whether she is going to pull it off. By the time of the performance, as she explains later, she has done her homework so thoroughly that the role has become second nature. Only the most solid and secure of techniques can give this freedom. Swenson acquired her technique at an early stage, and consolidated it gradually, through learning and performing the right roles at the right time. Fortunately, although her career began very early, it progressed step by step, in a relaxed and healthy way that allowed her to build her artistry on a very solid foundation.

Swenson was born in Bronxville, New York and brought up in Long Island by parents who were both singers and performed around New York State. When she was eight she saw her first opera, a production of *Aida* at the Terme di Caracalla in Rome on a family holiday. On her return she wrote in a school essay that she was going to become an opera singer. At the age of sixteen she began taking voice lessons from a local teacher who also mounted student operatic productions in her studio. The production that clinched Swenson's determination to pursue an operatic career was, as she mentioned, *Die Zauberflöte*. Her Pamina is preserved on her father's home video of the opera. Her husband, who is an accomplished vocal coach, claims that even then she was good. After high school, she joined the Philadelphia Academy of Vocal Art where, at the age of nineteen, she was one of the youngest students: 'Everybody else seemed to have music degrees from this college or that university.' On her graduation in 1981 she won a place as an apprentice at the San Francisco Opera.

As soon as she arrived in San Francisco, another great blessing came her way: the right teacher, Dickson Titus, who understood her voice, guided her to the right roles and coached her through all of them. She still studies with him to this day, between engagements. Like her colleague Renée Fleming[1] she believes that the art of singing is a life-long study. 'It's very important to continue studying, throughout your career, with a teacher you trust. I think that a lot of professional singers stop taking lessons, stop studying technically, as soon as their career takes off or hits the big time. They think, "oh, I don't need this sort of thing anymore, I have a career now." But they're wrong. The voice is something that should be constantly exercised and massaged.'

Swenson was also lucky in the fact that the director of the San Francisco Opera at the time was Terry McEwen, who brought to the job a vast experience of the voice from his previous position as head of Decca Records in the United States. He believed in Swenson's talent from the start and chose her repertoire carefully at each stage of her apprenticeship and early career. She started off with Mozart roles – Susanna, Despina and Pamina – which are 'ideal for young singers'. (At least for light lyric sopranos. Renée Fleming expresses the opposite view about the usefulness of Mozart roles for young sopranos in her chapter.) 'Mozart is vocally healthy and musically a very good discipline,' continues Swenson. 'In order to achieve the purity of sound and intonation that Mozart demands, you *have* to acquire a technique. You also have to learn to confine yourself only to what's written in the

---

[1] As the magazine *Appellation* points out, a little piece of operatic history took place when Ruth Ann sang in an all-state high school chorus: 'There was this other girl who was going up against me for the solos, and she could really sing'. Swenson later learnt that the 'other girl' was Renée Fleming, only a year older than herself. Many years later, the two sang together in the Paris Opéra's production of *Le nozze di Figaro*! This year, they will both sing their first Traviatas.

score. If you add anything, it immediately sounds wrong. Mozart is also healthy for the support and the legato line and not too taxing for young voices. You don't have huge crescendi or very high notes.'

From 1979 to 1980, Swenson was part of the Merola Program, and in 1981 became the Adler Fellow with the San Francisco Opera. During the two years between her arrival in San Francisco in 1979 and her début at the Opera house, Swenson also learnt a string of *ingénue* roles such as Norina (*Don Pasquale*), Adina (*L'elisir d'amore*), Nannetta (*Falstaff*), Sophie (*Werther*) and the title role in *Roméo and Juliette*. She got a chance to perform them, together with her Mozart roles, on tour through the Southwest, at small theatres, school halls and even, on occasion, at shopping malls. Her official début at San Francisco came in 1983, as Despina in *Così fan tutte* when she had to step in for a sick colleague. According to Alan Ulrich, critic of the *San Francisco Examiner*, this role 'fits her like a glove. These *ingénue* roles might have been written for her. Not only is her voice perfectly placed for them, but they bring out the sweetness and charm in Ruth Ann herself.' Swenson admits that 'they come naturally, because I love being playful on stage, I love to have a good time. Those little minxes, those wicked coquettes who are not really bad inside are terrific fun to do!'

Those out-of-town tours had also provided Swenson with the perfect conditions to learn Gilda, a role that was to become one of the most important in her repertoire. She remembers that when she was first given the part to understudy, she gazed at it in disbelief, 'Coming from the Mozart repertoire, I thought, "I can't do this! I can't sing all those high notes up there, I'm not a coloratura soprano!" At the time, you see, I thought of myself as a lyric, destined for Susanna, Pamina and Mimì. I never thought of myself as a high note singer. But both my teacher and Terry could diagnose my real vocal potential much better than I could at that stage. As a young singer you can only discover what kind of voice you have as you watch it grow.'

She felt particularly grateful for the chance to sing Gilda 'at least twenty-five times' on tour because this role was not only a breakthrough from her previous repertoire, but also a part which calls for 'all the technique you can muster. At the beginning I found it very difficult, mainly because it's not the sort of role that you can give your all to from the beginning. To make it work, you have to learn where to relax, where to breathe and when to open up the full voice. The first half has some very difficult coloratura singing. Then, towards the middle, it evens out and becomes more lyrical. "Tutte le feste al tempio" is already fuller and more lyrical. It obviously reflects Gilda's own growth from an innocent young girl in love to a woman who experiences betrayal and disillusionment and is willing to sacrifice herself, rather than let go of her dream of love. You have to show this growth in both your voice and your acting. And, in the finale, you must lighten the sound again for the Death Scene. And I can tell you that there's no better way to learn a role like this than the way I had the chance to do: singing it again and again, out of sight; working out the placements that are comfortable; getting the breathing right and watching it become better and better each time.'

Once Swenson had mastered the vocal technicalities, Gilda became her favourite role. Unlike some sopranos, who after singing it once declare they would not want to sing her if *Rigoletto* were the last opera on earth, Swenson finds her 'incredibly fulfilling to sing. She's got so much going for her, both vocally and dramatically. I love singing her. I love her music and the fact that she is such a heroine, so brave and so *giving*. That's what makes her so compelling. When you add up all her qualities you come up with a character I *like* better than anyone else I have performed so far.'

She adds that Gilda is also a beautifully written part in an opera which is a masterpiece. One can fully understand why *Rigoletto* remained such a firm favourite with the public ever since its première in Venice in 1851. 'All the feelings, all the emotions Verdi wanted are in the score. If you really look at what he wrote on the page – not just the notes but also the words – it tells you all you need to know. And if you get a good Rigoletto to sing with, it's a thrilling experience. In

terms of *performance*, yes, Rigoletto is more important for Gilda than
the Duke, because she has much more music to sing with him. As far
as the Duke is concerned, what you have to establish from the beginning is the depth of her feelings for him, and let that feeling carry
through everything she sings to her father. Technically, she has only one
duet to sing with the Duke, when he comes to her house in scene 2 of
Act I. But, as she explains to Giovanna just before, she is already hope-
lessly in love with him. When he comes to her and speaks the very
words she has been dreaming of – for God knows how long – it's a
dream come true for her. It's perfection. She never wants to let go of
this moment and *that's* why she's willing to sacrifice herself. She can't
give up her dream of love even though it goes against her father's
wishes. Even her love for *him*, even the evidence of his awful behaviour,
cannot change her feelings for the Duke. She stays faithful to her
dream. That's what she's about.'

Swenson's response to music and to her roles is spontaneous and
instinctive, straight from the heart, rather than intellectual. 'I take
what I feel is in the music and my response to it at the moment I
perform it, and bring these two together,' she says. 'I do this with all
my roles and with every composer. I don't sit and selfconsciously ana-
lyze the music, thinking: "Oh, this is Mozart therefore it must be sung
this way, and that's Verdi and has to be sung *that* way." I'm not the
intellectualizing kind of singer. I just interpret the music and discover
the characters through the music. This is why I am maddened by the
kind of director who keeps talking about the *play* rather than the opera
at hand – in the case of *Rigoletto* about Victor Hugo rather than Verdi,
for example – and then wonders whether we could, perhaps, cut "Caro
nome". Don't laugh, this has actually happened! So, to your question of
whether I consider the director in opera today a saviour or a scourge
my answer is: definitely a scourge!'

The enormous success of Swenson's Gilda at the San Francisco
Opera led to invitations to sing it all over the world: at the State
Operas in Berlin, Hamburg and Vienna, as well as at the Metropolitan

Opera, where she had earlier made her début, in 1991, as Zerlina in *Don Giovanni* under James Levine. Levine pronounced her 'a big-house voice', and has invited her back every season for Adina, Susanna, Rosina, Juliette, Zerbinetta and Liù, and is mounting a special production of *Lucia di Lammermoor*, for her in December 1998, directed by Nicholas Joel and conducted by Carlo Rizzi. Her début at the Lyric Opera of Chicago was as Nannetta in *Falstaff*, and she has returned for Norina, Anne Trulove in *The Rake's Progress* and for Dominick Argento's *The Voyage of Edgar Allan Poe*. Her European début was at the Grand Théâtre de Genève as Despina, and she has been invited back for Norina and her first Elvira (*I puritani*). She made her Paris Opéra début as Susanna, and has sung Konstanze at the Bavarian State Opera. She also sang *Moses und Aron* at the Salzburg Festival, the Netherlands Opera and in other European houses.

The next big landmark for Swenson's repertoire was *Lucia di Lammermoor*, which she first sang at the Washington Opera in 1994, and repeated in San Francisco and Dallas. To sing her first Lucia is an enormous challenge for any soprano, and Swenson was no exception. 'I spent a year learning it, working it into my voice and making sure everything was right. It was, as you say, a landmark for me because it demanded much more voice than anything I had done to date. On the one hand you have the coloraturas which have to be spectacular. On the other you need a lot of sound in the middle. You can't go for one and forget about the other. This role requires *all* your voice, not just parts of it. So you must have an even sound throughout. Fortunately, one of the things my teacher tried to do over the years was to make my voice seamless – without that, I couldn't have done Lucia.'

Surprisingly, the hardest part in *Lucia* for her is not, as one would expect, the Mad Scene but Lucia's duet with her brother, for both vocal and dramatic reasons. 'He's *at* her all the time. She has to explain things to him and beg him not to make her marry Arturo. So you have to colour your voice accordingly and incorporate this into your acting, because she's singing all this while he's hurling her to the floor and so on. What's so difficult is keeping a level head and keeping the voice working the way you want it while doing all these things on stage. The sextet is not that hard. Once again, pacing is the keyword. But until you're in it, until you're rehearsing it, you don't know how much you need to give and how much to save. Mind you, in a role like this it's hard to save *anything*. In any case, saving voice and energy is not something I like doing because it could appear as if I were holding something back. And I'm *never* holding back, it's not the way I am, or the way I function.'

'I knew Lucia from the recordings of Callas and Sutherland. I appreciate what Callas does for the words and the emotion, as well as her incredible vocalism. She didn't have the most beautiful voice but she could sing like nobody else could. She had an incredible technique. But she didn't' have a beautiful voice like, say, Tebaldi. I really respond to the things she did with a role like Lucia or Traviata but as a sheer vocal technician Sutherland was incredible. And she had the right size of voice, that big voice needed for this repertoire. For parts like Susanna and Mimì my idol is Freni. Caballé was another singer whose beauty of sound you can't beat. And what she did with those *pianissimi*, the stamina and the support and the breath control was quite breath taking. These are the people I admire.'

Swenson, who very much enjoys singing Lucia, says it was one of the most difficult roles to learn. 'It took tremendously hard work and study for it to become second nature. I'm not one of those singers who learn their roles on stage. Vocally it has to be second nature before I step out for the first rehearsal. Only when I'm vocally on top of the role, free from any technical problems or worries, can I begin to be an actress. Another thing I had to learn was how to go from role to role and opera to opera – going from Liù, for instance, to Adina in *L'elisir d'amore*, for which I will have to get the voice higher and more flexible. I learned what you put next to what is vital. Doing two things at a time is the most difficult part of our work. You have to try and give your voice a chance to rest and get ready to go from one role to another.'

I wondered how Swenson, whose sunny nature gives little impression of her suffering from pre-performance nerves, would spend the day leading up to a performance. 'Well, I don't talk too much. I have a good night's sleep. I eat well, usually something early in the day and again around three or four o'clock in the afternoon. I drink plenty of water and always bring some fruit, like apples, to the theatre. It's a trick I learnt from Alfredo Kraus when we did *Roméo et Juliette* together. He was always eating apples because, he said, they're good for the throat. They clean everything up. And since then I have done the same. Fruit helps get things going. It helps the stamina and keeps everything moisturized. I also drink a sports drink which comes in various flavours and is a hydrating drink. It's very important to keep your throat lubricated, what with all the heat and air conditioning going on all the time in the theatre. Having a dry throat is the worst thing that could happen to me. I can sing with a cold, I can sing with a sinus infection but if my throat dries up, I can't. Of course, when singing with a cold or when you're ill, you have to sing more carefully. But, you know, sometimes the best performances happen when you're not well because you're concentrating a little harder, you're being more careful. Maybe that's how one should always perform, but usually when I'm on form I just go out on stage, put my elbows in the air and do it. But dryness is really dangerous because the cords have to vibrate and if there's no moisture I get hoarse and things don't work.'

Swenson's next important new role was the title role of Handel's *Semele*, in which she made her Covent Garden début in 1996 to great public and critical acclaim. That season also saw big successes in San Francisco as Ophélie in Ambroise Thomas's *Hamlet* (with Thomas Hampson in the title role), as Gilda and Elvira at the Metropolitan Opera and as Gilda at the Paris Opéra. Swenson's first encounter with Handel had been as the Shepherdess in *Orlando* at the San Francisco Opera in a production directed by John Copley and conducted by the renowned Handel expert, Sir Charles Mackerras. As she rightly points out, this was by no means a minor role, because in Handel 'you have four or five arias no matter who you are.'

Sir Charles Mackerras and John Copley were also in charge of the Covent Garden *Semele*. 'I can't tell you what joy it was to work with a great Handelian who knows everything there is to know about this style. He also happens to be a conductor who understands a singer's needs, takes each singer for what he or she is and doesn't try to be inflexible! This was particularly crucial with a role as complicated as Semele, which needed to be learnt over a long period, absorbed a step at a time and which demands just about everything you can do as a singer: coloratura, flexibility, purity of tone and intonation and phenomenal breath control. When I first looked at the Mirror Aria, for example, I thought, "when is this *ever* going to end, where am I going to breathe?" Memorizing something as complicated as this was also very, very hard. Because you can't go on stage and wonder what verse or embellishment comes next. Yet remembering what comes next was one of the biggest challenges of the role. When you have a da capo every other page and a first and second section plus embellishments, it's very easy to get confused. In fact if you weren't careful, it would be easy to substitute a cadenza from *Orlando*.

'Another major challenge, as in all coloratura parts, is to try and make those coloraturas expressive, and not merely displays of vocal virtuosity – which in Handel they often are! But as in bel canto, I tried to think of the emotion the character is experiencing while singing these coloraturas. This is much harder in Handel when, as I said, you have a da capo every other page and you have to make each repeat a little different. So you have to ask yourself: "Why is she singing it a second time? What *more* is she thinking about at this point?" Mind you, you can't go too deep in this sense because incredible vocalism and fireworks *per se* were part of the style of the time. So you just show another way of expressing the same emotion – like seventeen more notes than in the section before! That's why you have to be such an incredible technician to sing Handel! But at the same time that you are thinking of what's coming next you've got to feel *joyful*: I have to think of what's coming next, but I can't just sit there and be nervous about it. If I did, I'd be a wreck!'

Despite its difficulties Swenson loved singing Semele. The British public and critics loved her singing of the role too. 'As Semele, Ruth Ann Swenson surpassed wildest expectations,' wrote *The Times*. 'Her tone in the flesh is even sweeter than on record, her technique fail-safe, her wit dazzling, the pointillist staccatos and triplet runs delivered with accuracy and both musical and dramatic point . . . All this with sensuality and pathos, too – pure perfection.'

Swenson says that people at the time asked her if she thought the character was a bitch. 'I said "what?" She's not evil, just a bit selfish. She has a sympathetic side, a side that regrets that she's asking for too much. If you played her as too hard, too mean about what she's deter- mined to do from the start, which is not really evil, you wouldn't get the audience's sympathy. So you have to play her as a little naughty, but you also have to give her that charm that will endear her to the audience and that touch of vulnerability at the end, where she knows, admits and regrets her mistake. Coming to think of it, life is full of people who never admit they're wrong. But she's a smart woman and she does. It was a high point in my career to make my début at Covent Garden in such a showpiece role.' Semele certainly whetted Swenson's appetite for further Handel roles. Sadly she pulled out of the Paris Opéra's scheduled production of *Giulio Cesare*, in which she was to sing Cleopatra (although she will soon record some arias from this role). She would welcome another chance to sing it, and also Alcina, which would seem a natural role for her.

Swenson will soon take another important step in her career with her first Manon, which she sings in Michigan, and repeats in the summer of 1998 at the Opéra Bastille in Paris. She has already scored great success in French repertoire, as Juliette, which she sang in San Francisco and, in 1996, at the Metropolitan Opera with Richard Leech as Roméo. *The New York Times* wrote of their performance: 'It's hard to think of current singers who could top this pair of star-crossed lovers. Ms Swenson may be singing at her peak right now. Her sound is radiant, full and unforced. Her cleanly executed roulades and trills always emerge as embellishments to an arching melodic line, never as interpolated acrobatics.'

Both the timbre and the weight of Swenson's voice are ideal for the French repertoire. What remains to be seen is whether she will master the style and deliver the text as idiomatically as the French public and critics will expect, as is right. Swenson is aware that she should place greater emphasis on language for her Paris performances than she might, perhaps, at home. 'I love the French language. Its main characteristic is that it's not very accented. It's a very flowing language and the music is very *clear*. Manon will also be a great challenge dramatically, because she is a very interesting woman – someone who, during the course of the evening grows from being a child into the kind of woman she becomes. I'm working at it already, and vocally it sits very well for my voice. The real challenge lies in the dramatic side, to bring out the woman she develops into. And for that you have to move from coloratura singing at the start to full-throated singing that portrays the change in her. Right now I am steeped in her. I live and breathe Manon.'

A few months after her Paris Manons Swenson will take on another all-important role in a soprano's career when she sings Violetta in *La traviata* at the Lyric Opera of Chicago in Autumn 1998. Violetta will be perhaps the biggest challenge in her career so far, especially from the dramatic point of view. It is perhaps the most complete portrayal of a woman in the entire operatic literature. The question therefore is whether Swenson, who has hitherto excelled in portraying *ingénues* and whose whole demeanour, despite her thirty-eight years, is girlish rather than womanly, will find in herself the emotional and spiritual ingredients to bring to the role. But with her first *Manon* and her first *Traviata* looming, Swenson certainly seems to have made 1998 a Year for Taking Chances. 'It will be fascinating to watch Ruth Ann tackle the

big roles she's heading into now,' says the *San Francisco Examiner* critic
Alan Ulrich, who has followed her career from the beginning. 'Not
everyone makes the transition successfully, and some that make it can't
return vocally to the younger roles they started with.' Swenson is
determined that neither of these calamities will happen to her.

Swenson felt that her current role – Liù at the Metropolitan Opera –
would help her with parts such as Manon. 'When you really have to
pull it all out. I love the character, her soul, how giving and self-sacri-
ficing she is, and I love playing her. But if you don't have a *pianissimo*,
you can forget Liù . . . Generally, I *love* singing in the low part of my
voice. I love singing Rosina, for instance, in the mezzo key. People keep
asking if I would like to do it in the soprano key but I say no. It just feels
so right in the mezzo key and I'm so comfortable in the middle voice.
That's why I would love to do Semiramide one day, in concert if no
stage productions are planned anywhere; and also Amenaide in
Tancredi, and maybe *Anna Bolena* and *Maria Stuarda*. But the orchestration in the last two is getting heavier, more Verdian, and you need that
steel in the voice to cut through it, which I don't have.

'But I'm aware that you can't do everything you want to do in this
life. I know I can't sing all the roles I want to sing. But I hope I *can* sing
the roles to which I bring something very special – not in competition
with anybody else in any given role – but because I feel I have something to bring to them.

'I feel very blessed, both in my career and my personal life. I'm now
thirty-eight and I have been married for twelve years. I met my husband, David Bernacus, two years after I arrived in San Francisco, when
I was twenty-six. He is a full-time baritone in the San Francisco Opera
Chorus and also a répétiteur and voice teacher. So we work on all my
roles together. He is very supportive, very loving and always there for
me.' (A friend who knows the couple remarks that they complement
each other very well, with Ruth Ann being spontaneous and intuitive
and David thoughtful and analytical.) Of course, being able to do the
tremendously hard work of preparing roles such as Ruth Ann's at

home, with the person one loves, is indeed a blessing and also a very great help for her as an artist.

The couple have two dogs. 'I would love to have a child someday, but I think it would be very difficult' says Swenson. 'I think that, being the person I am, I would hate to leave it at home with nannies. The result would be that I would be pulled in every direction. And it would be difficult to have a marriage that way. I mean, a singer's life is not glamorous at all, despite what people think. They think it's all flowers and applause, but it isn't. It's very hard work and demands sacrifices'. Swenson's home is in the Napa Valley in California, where 'it's friendly, it's quiet, it's beautiful, and I can go to the grocery store in jeans and a ponytail'. As her husband explains, 'jetting around to cities might sound glamorous, but we do that for work. We don't want to do it on our time off. Now, being at home is like a vacation.' Ruth Ann adds, 'I have a horse I like to ride. I love being a normal person. I *am* a normal person. I'm not a diva. What does being a diva signify to me? Well, usually the term signifies an attitude, a way of behaviour – one which is totally different from the American ethos which is about doing a job as well as you know how *and* enjoying it, and not boring everybody with moans about how difficult it all is.'

I remark that not since interviewing the unique Leontyne Price for the first volume of Diva had I come across a singer who so enjoys her voice and is so conscious of it being a blessing. 'I do and it is! Yes, there's sacrifice and hard work involved in it but that's my job. That's what I give back in return for being given this talent. It would be wrong for me not to use it. Anyway, if I didn't sing I don't know what I'd do. I feel with every fibre of my being that singing is what I was *meant* to do.'

CAROL
VANESS

'YOU ASK WHY, with singing being the kind of unpredictable thing it is, we singers are not all nervous wrecks. We *are* all nervous wrecks! If you were to spend an entire performance day with a singer, you would soon realize what I mean,' says Californian-born Carol Vaness, one of the most distinguished American sopranos in the operatic world. 'Some of us never get out of our pyjamas. Others stay in bed all day. Some are sick and some actually vomit in the mens' or ladies' room. I, too, sometimes used to throw up at the beginning of my career. I would gag up with nerves. Of course, now the nerves are different. But you still have them. They vanish only when you walk on stage because then you get involved in singing, acting and *concentrating*. It's the thinking about it *beforehand* that's so hard.

'But in the end, you're either the kind of person who can handle it or you're not. I know that nerves have made careers and ruined careers. If you are the kind of person who can handle it, then you'll last as long as your voice allows you to. But I'm here to say that the nerves never get better. What gets better is your ability to think your way through them.'

This is a heartening statement for young singers at the beginning of their careers, and all the more surprising for coming from an artist of the calibre of Carol Vaness, who rose to recognition fairly fast and who has had an eminently satisfying career. She has sung in all major international theatres and festivals and her repertoire includes some of the 'meatiest', most musically exquisite roles in the repertoire: almost all the Mozart ladies (Fiordiligi, the Countess, Donna Anna, Donna Elvira, Vitellia and Elettra), most of the interesting Verdi heroines (Violetta, Amelia in both *Simon Boccanegra* and *Un ballo in maschera*, Desdemona, Leonora in both *Il trovatore* and *La forza del destino*, Elena in *I vespri siciliani*), as well as Tosca and, at the opposite end, Handel.

Vaness's highly individual and instantly recognizable *lirico spinto* voice (it was the great Leontyne Price who confirmed that Vaness now belonged to this select group when they were singing *Dialogues des Carmélites* in 1982 at San Francisco) is ample, richly expressive, even in tone and colour throughout the range and, unless she is feeling below par, beautiful. She has a secure top which she can lighten at will (as for instance in Elettra's exquisite music in Act II of *Idomeneo*), a rich middle and full, dusky low notes. Indeed, Vaness first trained as a mezzo and, not surprisingly, enjoys this lower register the most. As a performer she is highly emotional and empathetic, charging the stage with nervous, physical and psychic energy from the moment she walks on. Yet mysteriously (and this is the crux of the mystery of the interpreter), this co-exists with acute simultaneous mental and technical control.

Yet as she was growing up in Los Angeles (where her family moved from her native San Diego), with her two younger sisters who now both work in hospitals, Vaness never wanted a career in music. Painting and drawing were her passions and whenever she was asked what she wanted to be when she grew up, her answer was, an artist. She learnt to play the piano at a young age, and when she went to California State Polytechnic she decided on a double major in English and the piano. 'I really don't know why. I was terrible at English. I enjoyed reading, but only when I wanted to, and I couldn't write well. I was terrible at the piano, couldn't play, really, but you were required to have voice lessons as part of the piano major.' Her first teacher, the baritone Charles Lindsley, classified her as a mezzo, which she says was not surprising, because 'I have a very low speaking voice and an easy middle register.'

She graduated in 1972 and Lindsley thought her good enough to recommend further study, as a graduate at California State University at Northridge. There she found the teacher who correctly diagnosed that she was a soprano and developed her technique, David Scott, who works with her to this day. After singing for him 'about fifty' of her favourite mezzo pieces including 'O don fatale', Scott amazed her by saying that he thought she was a soprano. 'Oh no I'm not', she retorted, thus offering a rare example of a mezzo not wanting to be a soprano! Instead of contradicting her directly, Scott displayed the insight of an enlightened teacher and cleverly put forward a proposition: for one year he would teach her as a soprano and if by the end of that time she still had doubts, he would then switch to teaching her as a mezzo. During her first year they studied *Tosca*, which she thought of as 'a kind of mezzo-ish role with a couple of high notes'[!] and Donna Anna. By the end of the year she had no doubts about her teacher's diagnosis. She *was* a soprano.

Vaness is one of the lucky few who found the right teacher straight away, and she is fully aware of the blessing: 'David is terrific for me. He gives me something I can take away with me,' she told *Opera News* in 1986, just as her career was reaching the top. 'He believes in the fundamentals of absolutely, completely natural singing. You take a good breath and you support. Also in the correct placement of vowels. I already had the whole range, top to bottom. What I didn't have was the same colour. I always had a pretty middle voice but though the top *could* be pretty, it sometimes wasn't. What David did over six or eight years was to help me make it more beautiful all the way through. That's why it sounds even today.'

After her graduate year, Vaness, who in 1976 won the San Francisco Opera auditions, mustered up enough courage to ring Kurt Herbert

Adler, then the inspired head of the San Francisco Opera, to ask if she could be part of their Affiliate Artists Program for young singers. This resembled the studio programmes of some European houses, but also involved performing all over California, in schools, old peoples' homes, clubs and marts. Adler said that he would first have to find a sponsor for her. Immediately he rang up the great soprano Beverly Sills, then adviser to the programme, to ask if she could procure the funds for 'a terrific young singer you don't know'. Sills called Atlantic Richfield, and by the next day they had the money. Adler called Vaness with the happy news and suggested she call Beverly Sills to thank her (Sills was to prove crucial to Vaness's career on two further occasions). 'I still can't believe I had the nerve to call Mr Adler, but I'm glad I did', she remembers.

Vaness moved to San Francisco and plunged herself into her apprenticeship with consummate enthusiasm. One of the things she most enjoyed about the programme was that the singers didn't just have to sing, but also had to give short talks to their audiences about the operas and roles they were about to perform and this created a warm sense of communication, well suited to Vaness's empathetic nature.

During her time as an Affiliate Artist something happened that could have spelled the end of her career. She had sung an outdoor performance of *Così* at Napa Valley with tonsillitis and a temperature of 101 degrees. Next morning she felt very unwell but was called to a rehearsal. She told the director she was ill, but he replied she had been ill enough times that season and had to come. She went and wasn't allowed to mark. So she sang out with an irritated larynx, a set of sick tonsils and a pair of exhausted vocal cords. 'I haemorrhaged a vocal cord and went on to the most challenging and painful time of my young career.'

She had her tonsils out and took a three-month leave of absence. Unbeknownst to her, the doctor wrote in his notes at the time that she had a paralyzed vocal cord and that he doubted she would ever sing again. But she went to her teacher every day, 'to relearn the sensation of singing'. At first her voice was smaller, lighter and higher than before. After three months' rest, it took another three years to get it back to normal. It was only later, when she went to consult her doctor about a cold, that she discovered his earlier opinion about her previous condition. 'That shows what can be done with absolutely correct technique. My technique fixed itself during those three years and no-one except my teacher knew I had a problem. I studied and worked very hard with him to get around it. It was very, very painful, but essential and absolutely worth it. It taught me a lesson I never forgot: never to misuse the voice and *never* to sing when sick.'

In the spring of 1977 Vaness made her professional début at the San Francisco Opera in a role that was to make her famous and which she has now sung all over the world: Vitellia in *La clemenza di Tito*, which she first sang in English. Right from the start she found Vitellia 'a wonderful part', and one which suited her perfectly both vocally and dramatically. 'It's short and the music is incredibly beautiful. When I was first asked to sing it I looked at it and thought this was not too hard. It was high, it was low, but my voice, which was always wide-ranging, made it possible for me to do wide sweeps in one breath. Yet if I were speaking generally rather than personally, I would say Vitellia is a very difficult role, because although mostly low, it has a very high trio. This lasts three minutes and it's three minutes of fingers crossed, on top of your technique trying to place every high note absolutely perfectly.' In fact at that point Vitellia's music sounds more like Elettra's in *Idomeneo*. Yet the overall tessitura of the role is low. Her famous aria "Non più di fiori" is almost a mezzo aria. Of course, I can't claim that it was as comfortable then as it later became, because I still needed a lot of work in the passaggio zone of my voice.'

Now, twenty years after she first sang the part, Vaness does not find Vitellia that difficult. But the trio remains very hard, very complicated. 'I hate using the word "hard" because I try to think of technical problems as something to which you know the answer — you just have to find *your* way to the answer. But even after all these years, the trio always remains a spot where you muster all your technical resources and feel that if you can sing this, you can sing anything.'

Vitellia proved a lucky role for Vaness. Indeed there are so few sopranos around who can sing this part with distinction – perhaps only Julia Varady in recent years – that when Julius Rudel at New York City Opera was looking for the right soprano, Beverly Sills rang him up and told him she had the perfect singer in mind. Sills had first heard Vaness rehearsing Amelia in *Ballo* which she was covering for another soprano in San Francisco. 'So I went up to my good friend Kurt Adler and told him he was a fool: "Why do you need anybody else when you've got yourself a star?"'

Vaness got to know Sills even better when she sang Enrichetta to her Elvira in *I puritani*, a role for which she was chosen because she was the same height as Sills and could therefore be easily mistaken for her, as the plot requires. The great diva decided there and then that she would back this young soprano all the way, and called Rudel.

So Vaness came to New York 'with a job, unlike so many other young singers who come to seek their fortune', and sang Vitellia at New York City Opera in October 1979 with great success. Since then she has sung it at Glyndebourne, the Metropolitan Opera, Covent Garden, Geneva and for her début at Salzburg Festival in 1988. Out of all these performances, she treasures those with the late Greek-American mezzo Tatiana Troyanos as Sesto. 'It was wonderful. Her intensity gave me the courage to *return* her intensity and that was the most exciting thing, both vocally and histrionically. I've never seen anything like it. I loved it. Tatiana gave 125 per cent and if for an instant she had more, she'd give it. She would never think of saving. She wasn't a saver. She would just give all she had. She was just so special. To me she's a real legend and I wish she had recorded more. I have sung with some very great mezzos – Cossotto in an *Aida* in San Francisco in which I sang the Priestess, and Suzanne Mentzez as Adalgisa to my Norma – but I have to say I've never heard anything like Tatiana's burning commitment.'

Vaness was a full company member of NYCO from 1979 to 1983 and sang in a variety of roles. Her next big role at NYCO was Donna Anna, which was to become her most famous Mozart role (she has sung it at Munich, Vienna and Covent Garden, as well as several times at the Met). But even after so many performances and despite her love of the role, she finds it frustrating dramatically: 'I always try to put as much temperament as I can into it, but the role itself has its boundaries. Because of who she is – very constricted, as if in a corset – you can only go so far. Yet there was not *ever* a single rehearsal or performance of Donna Anna *anywhere* when I felt this role was easy. Both vocally and dramatically it was and remains a challenge. For a start it's so full of questions. There are more questions about this character than for any other Mozart role, and you're always searching for answers.

'Like, for instance, what happened before the beginning of the opera? It depends on who the Don is and who you have singing Don Ottavio. Each production, and even each performance, has to be tailored around this very crucial factor. If you have an extremely strong Don Ottavio, which you sometimes do – Gösta Winbergh, for example, was amazingly strong – then you don't play the attraction to the Don. You play the outrage, the Spanish woman and her honour sort of thing. The fact that the Don as much as entered her room was a problem in Spanish society. If you have a weak Ottavio, however, you could hint strongly at Anna's attraction to the Don. I've had all sorts of Don Ottavios through the years, including studious, intellectual and learned ones. One of the most interesting was Keith Lewis in Sir Peter Hall's Glyndebourne production [1982], who was portrayed as an older man. This makes instant sense of his telling Anna immediately after her father's murder to transfer those feelings to him – "hai sposo e padre in me" ("you have both husband and father in me"). Because again, you can choose to make Anna's rejection of Ottavio into as big or as trivial an issue as you like. Basically she only rejects him a couple of times, which is no big issue. But you can *make* it into a big issue.

'The ambiguity of the character extends to its vocal make-up.

Basically it's an extremely difficult role because of the tessitura, which is very high. The comparative difficulty of the two arias, though, has changed as the years go on. At the beginning the second aria, "Non mi dir", was very easy for me. Yet when I last sang it at the Met it was a lot harder than it used to be: not the first section, the slow section, but the bits of coloratura, probably because I hadn't been singing coloratura recently. I'd been singing Elvira at the rehearsals, and then asked to switch roles when our Donna Anna withdrew, because it's easier to find Donna Elviras than Donna Annas!' Karita Mattila, who also sings both roles, states that Anna may be the more unrewarding of the two dramatically, but certainly the most challenging musically: 'Nobody really knows just how hard it is to sing it well. When I sang Donna Elvira to Carol Vaness's Anna at Covent Garden, I always gave her applause in my mind after the sextet – it's a killer!'

'But at the time,' continues Vaness, 'the aria "Or sai chi l'onore" was definitely the hardest. I would just count the notes to the end and tell myself that I knew we could make it, so let's just do it, let's just count! For good measure someone stupid saw fit to point out that there are thirteen As in Donna Anna, to which I replied, "Did you *have* to tell me about this lucky number?" But seriously, the secret in this aria is not volume but *intensity*. Psychologically, people *think* they've got to hear something loud at this point, but if you look at the score you will see that Mozart marks it *piano*. But it should be a very intense *piano*. I think you should start softly and then *expand*, making a crescendo that isn't super-loud. But the movement from *piano* into a suspended crescendo creates that intensity. That suspended crescendo on A shows just how *fanatical* Anna is. If you sang the aria just with a big, loud sound, it would be a let-down. For there is ambiguity in the air. "Or sai chi l'onore" is definitely not a kind of bombastic, bring-the-rafters-down kind of aria. In Mozart things are often not what you think they are. You have to look for the clues.'

At this particular point in the opera the ambiguity starts in the recitative that leads into 'Or sai chi l'onore', which is one of the most dramatic Mozart ever wrote. For this reason the clear understanding and articulation of the words are crucial. It was Sir Charles Mackerras, a renowned Mozart expert both as a conductor and a musicologist, who pointed out to Vaness one of the most unusual things about this recitative: 'We were discussing the E flat major chords in it and he said that E flat major is actually the key of deception. I thought, how *interesting* . . . In this light, Anna's phrase "da lui mi scolsi" ["I managed to extricate myself from him", i.e. from his embrace] becomes even *more* ambiguous: it could mean either relief or disappointment, or even a reproach to Ottavio – "and where were *you* . . ." So, the role is endlessly enigmatic and, like the whole of the opera, endlessly fascinating. I was never bored in *Don Giovanni*.' After her performances in Johannes Schaaf's controversial 'black' staging at Covent Garden in 1992, *Opera* wrote: 'Carol Vaness was in wonderful voice. Is there an Anna to touch her today?'

Yet, after 178 performances of Donna Anna to date, Vaness has now become more interested in Elvira. Of course, she stresses that she still loves this calling card role and that she has several performances of it still coming up. 'But you have to work very, very hard as Donna Anna and frankly, Elvira is more satisfying dramatically, as a character. The two roles are poles apart, both vocally and dramatically. They are night and day. I wouldn't say that Elvira is necessarily easier, just different, and wonderful to sing. Take "Mi tradì", I mean, what an aria! Then there's that exquisite Balcony Scene and the Trio. All her music is just *so* beautiful.

'The character is also very interesting. She is a very smart lady to be able to actually *find* the Don. She's the only one in the opera who has actually tasted him and followed him. In many ways, there is something of the modern woman about Elvira: she is alone, she makes love before marriage and she wants Don Giovanni back. She thinks she is married to him. So, she does what probably no woman of her class would do in those days – she goes off and finds him. I don't agree with those productions that show her as either crazy or *deliberately* funny. I think that's missing the point. Certain situations become much funnier if played "straight", in a serious vein. Then the audience is not laughing *at* her but at the situations she finds herself in, which is much more powerful.'

Vaness's first series of *Don Giovanni* at NYCO in 1981 opened the door to Glyndebourne for her, thanks to John Cox, Glyndebourne's director of productions at the time, who was impressed enough to recommend her to Bernard Haitink and Peter Hall – despite an earlier less than impressive audition.

But before she went to Glyndebourne for what became a successive string of superlative Mozart portrayals (that in turn opened all international doors to her), Vaness made an unscheduled début at Covent Garden in early 1982 as Mimì, a role she had already sung at NYCO. Her second appearance at Covent Garden, in early summer 1982, was also unscheduled. This is so typical of Vaness in every way – especially of her knack for being at the right place at the right time and delivering the goods in even the most challenging circumstances – that it is worth reporting in full. Vaness had arrived in Britain a couple of days before she was due at Glyndebourne in order to spend a little time in London, looking up friends. (Her gift for making friends everywhere she goes is also typical of her.) She went to tea with the mezzo, Ann Murray, with whom she had worked very happily in the United States, and who had also invited along the conductor Jeffrey Tate, who was then conducting *La clemenza di Tito* at Covent Garden. Vaness and Murray told him about the happy time they had had singing this opera in New York; he in turn told them about his current Vitellia, Elizabeth Connell, who as a former mezzo also had the beautiful middle voice the role requires.

Early next morning, Vaness got a call from Covent Garden. Connell was ill, and could she stand in for her that same evening? Yes, replied Vaness, without giving any thought to the fact that the version she had performed in New York, although in Italian, had not included all the recitatives. She found this out that morning at the first and only rehearsal. Tate, realizing this, plus the fact that she had not sung the part for seven months and was still jetlagged, was worried enough to go backstage and enquire if she was really sure she could do it. 'Carol must have been insulted,' he recalls, 'because she replied: "It's all right. I have nerves of steel." And she does. She sang Vitellia immaculately.' Vaness laughs at the mention. 'Sure I told him I have nerves of steel. But after I said it, I went to the bathroom and threw up!'

After this cliff-hanging experience, Vaness proceeded to Glyndebourne. Her Donna Anna there was such a success that she was invited to sing Elettra in *Idomeneo* the following summer in a new production again to be conducted by Bernard Haitink, and directed by Trevor Nunn, and to sing her first Fiordiligi in the summer after that (1984).

But before that came a traumatic experience at the NYCO in September 1982 which might have broken a lesser singer. Vaness was due to sing her first Violetta but felt distinctly unwell. As the rehearsal period had been unusually fraught, she attributed this to nerves and decided to go ahead. She did not want to let the side down, especially her mentor, Beverly Sills, by then General Director of NYCO. But while warming up she noticed that she kept having to clear her throat. Once on stage she could feel her temperature rising, to 102 degrees! She was sweating and could feel her voice going. After the chorus left, she managed to get half way through 'È strano' and realized she was just not going to make it through 'Sempre libera'. So she apologized to the conductor and the audience and said: 'Excuse me. I'm very sorry but I must stop. I'm very ill', and walked off. She was so desperate that she went out and had too much to drink before going home. Next morning she saw the doctor who announced that she had a larynx infection with high fever. She was relieved: it was not nerves! But it taught her a lesson of never going on stage when feeling unwell, and she spent the remaining week on penicillin. (Ashley Puttnam, who happened to be in the audience that night, had continued the performance.)

Vaness was scheduled to sing again on the following Saturday. A few days before, Beverly Sills sent flowers, then rang her up and told her that she would be a great Violetta when she went back. However, Sills warned that everyone would be out for her blood, and she should do herself a favour: 'Just sing it. Don't *prove* you can sing it. I know you can, you know you can. So just do it, because if you try to prove it, you'll lose.' Vaness says that she has thought of those words on every single opening night ever since.

After a successful remainder of the season at NYCO, Vaness returned to Glyndebourne in the summer of 1983 for Elettra in *Idomeneo*, a role which suits her vocally and dramatically and which she would later sing all over the world with great success. 'Vocally, it's much more difficult than Vitellia. Dramatically, although she is a very tortured character, I don't think she's totally crazy. That would be too cardboard. Coming from that highly dysfunctional family background, she's always hanging by a short thread emotionally, but it's an *emotional*, not a mental short thread. Otherwise, how can you explain her singing music of such beauty as she does in "Placido è il mar"? But as she is hanging on a tight thread, she starts off by spitting out her emotions in her first utterance, "Prence, signor, tutta la Grecia oltraggi" and the aria that follows it, "Tutte nel cor vi sento" which is sung to an impending storm with the knowledge that the Furies were chasing her brother (and to the Greeks a storm was a bad omen anyway). So she reacts by pouring out all her fears and feelings of hell. At this moment she could almost be psychic or prophetic, and I always try to add this dimension to a character that is fragmented anyway.'

Indeed, Vaness stresses that this fragmentation is one of the big problems in this part. Elettra appears within the first fifteen minutes of the opera, sings her very dramatic first aria and then is not seen again until a good forty minutes later, well into Act II. 'And having been previously seen ranting, Elettra now has to appear happy, because of everything which has gone on in the meantime. She has this aria which shows her in a completely different light. But we haven't had a chance to see what she's like normally, because these two arias, her previous one and the one she sings now, "Idol mio", followed by "Placido è il mar" represent polar opposites and two kinds of emotional extremes. There is no character *development* to put across. Each time she appears it's with a new costume, a new wig and a new emotion.

'The worst part of it is that each appearance also requires a new voice. You definitely need three voices for this part. Her Act I aria can be sung by any mezzo in the world, as its highest note is A flat. You just need a big, bright, full middle which, thank God, I have. Her second aria, "Idol mio", although not very high, nevertheless has a tricky tessitura which means that you have to be technically on your toes all the time. It also has to sound very loving. The words are very loving but also very revealing about her character: She's so in love with and obsessional about Idamante that she will have him even if he's distant and austere with her, so confident is she that he will come to love her in the end. The ensembles in this act are also very difficult, especially the trio, because they are very high.

'Then comes "Placido è il mar" which, although only two pages long, is *the* most difficult two pages I have ever had to sing in any Mozart opera. It's so beautiful, yet so high that you can't just throw yourself at it. It's not marked *piano* but it's not marked *forte*, either, it's marked *dolce*. So it must be full and rich and climb to A natural in the opening phrase and, in the end, up to B natural. But the voice must climb neither softly nor loudly, so that the audience gasps and goes "aah". It's a great musical moment because of how beautifully the chorus is singing alongside. There have been evenings when it was good and I thought, "thank you, God, for giving me this tonight"; and others when I felt, "well, we've gotten through this and I hope it sounded OK".

'Act III has a different kind of problem: unless Idamanate is sung by a tenor, which it very seldom is these days, Elettra is basically singing a mezzo line. But if Idamante *is* a tenor Elettra has the top line, which is ideal because the voice isn't allowed to drop. Also the top line suits the character better because it has more chromatics and this suits Elettra, as do the pseudo-changes of key within this quartet. After that comes her "crazy" aria "D'Oreste, d'Ajace", with its amazing recitative "O smania, o furie", in which she is being driven about as far as she can go. She can explode and she does, into this aria. This is what it's about, for me. Whatever "craziness" I do is in the recitative, which is fascinating harmonically, with those leaps and crazy changes of key and chromatics. It almost sings itself, and feels so good while you're singing it – you feel as if you're involved in an athletic endeavour. But to be honest with you, the problem is that, depending on where you're singing it, a part of the audience will have gone by the time you come to sing it. *Idomeneo* is *opera seria* and relatively long, which means it's harder work for the audience. Thankfully surtitles seem to have made a difference here in the States.' Vaness has always scored big successes as Elettra, both at Glyndebourne and at the Metropolitan Opera. She has also recorded it for Deutsche Grammophon with James Levine, a recording which illustrates all the points Vaness just made.

At the close of the 1982–3 season, before her Glyndebourne Idomeneos, Vaness ceased to be a company member of NYCO. A few months later, in February 1984, she made her début at the Metropolitan Opera as Armida in Handel's *Rinaldo*, with almost no stage rehearsals. 'It was scary', she admits, in the understatement of her career. But the concentration needed to cope with the mind-boggling technical demands of the role, as well as the fact that she was singing with Samuel Ramey, the gorgeous bass with whom she had often performed at the NCYO helped to steady her nerves.

She vividly recalls this evening, destined to propel her career into top gear: 'Armida's entrance in this production was made from the inside of a mountain. When that mountain parted, I saw the Metropolitan Opera House out there. I'd never seen so much red in my life! Yet there and then I felt I belonged. It was such a *serious* experience that it changed my whole opinion of what it was that I had to deliver. From that moment on, I was going to perform up to the standard I believe a Met singer should.'

Vaness's successful Metropolitan Opera début led to invitations to perform Vitellia and Fiordiligi in the coming 1984–5 season. The preceding summer she performed Fiordiligi, which she says is her favourite Mozart role, at Glyndebourne, again under the baton of Bernard Haitink. 'First of all, she is the most feminine of all my Mozart heroines and, as such, a joy to perform. Secondly, there is just so much to *do* in Fiordiligi. There's a challenge at every turn. Dramatically, she is a character whom you can transform during the course of the opera because she goes from being one kind of lady at the beginning to a totally different kind of lady by the end. In no other Mozart heroine is there such a huge transformation. What happens to her is so human and understandable – it could happen to any woman. Fiordiligi takes four hours to fall in love. At the finale, I never believe the girls go back to their original men. That epilogue always sounds half-hearted to me – even though I've tried to smile at the performances. You shouldn't try to make it a happy ending because it isn't. Especially for Fiordiligi and Ferrando, when you consider what they've been through before admitting that they love each other. Because Fiordiligi and Ferrando really *are* in love. "Volgi a me" is a lovely moment of love.'

Vaness finds Fiordiligi vocally quite similar to Vitellia in that it has a lot of low singing, even though the use of the chest voice, where called for, should be different: '"Per pietà", for instance, is very low. But because Fiordiligi is very feminine, you should *colour* the chest voice and make it very warm, more like your speaking voice. That apart, the most difficult things in Fiordiligi are not her arias but the ensembles, in which you are the top voice. Much though I love them, I keep wishing I could surface for breath for a second.' Her Glyndebourne performances, with their long, six-week rehearsal period at the hands of a top Mozartian conductor such as Bernard Haitink, prepared her so well that when she sang it at the Met she got rave reviews.

The Met was also the venue for the Countess in *Figaro*, in the 1985–6 season. This is a role about which she has misgivings on the dramatic side. 'It's one of those roles into which it's very hard to inject some temperament. Yet musically, it's my most favourite Mozart opera. I love her music the best, I think it's incredibly gorgeous and *so* human. But dramatically I almost have too much temperament for the role. Everyone says I should play her like Rosina in *Barbiere*, to which I reply that I would, if I had an aria like "Una voce poco fa" to sing, or something that shows her temperament. But apart from one moment at the finale of Act II when she sings "Non son rea", nothing in her music shows any temperament. Her music is that of a dignified noblewoman – you can't go charging around the stage like Donna Elvira when playing the Countess. It doesn't work, it doesn't fit the music. Can you imagine anyone stomping around and singing either "Porgi, Amor" or "Dove sono"? It's impossible! The only thing that helped a little bit, I found, was the late Jean-Pierre Ponnelle telling me that the Countess was still the young, laughing, fun-loving Rosina in her private life – we showed her giggling on the floor with Cherubino – but in public she puts on the Countess act. This way when it came to "Dove sono" the contrast between the laughing woman they'd just seen and the sadness of this aria made a far greater impact on the audience. I also learnt a lot from Ruggero Raimondi, who was singing Figaro, about savouring every syllable of every word in the recitatives. I enjoyed that Countess, but if I never play it again, that's OK with me.'

It was in the mid-1980s that Vaness's acting skills truly began to emerge. Although she was always an intensely *emotional* singer, she limited herself to expressing the feelings behind the text and the music, rather than giving the words themselves the importance due to them. By then she was technically secure enough to work every nuance of the character, the actress in Vaness began to surface in earnest.

This went hand in hand with the gradual expansion of her repertoire into Verdi roles. The first were Amelia in *Un ballo in maschera* for Australian Opera and Amelia in *Simon Boccanegra* at Glyndebourne. In 1987 she sang Desdemona in Seattle as well as Leonora in *Il trovatore* at Covent Garden, which was so successful that *Opera* magazine expressed the hope that they would be 'the first of many.'

Vaness feels that she is temperamentally most suited to Verdi. 'To sing Verdi successfully and to artistic effect you must come into it slowly, because it's big singing.' (The exact words of Placido Domingo, who told me in an interview that 'Verdi is the biggest and most serious singing you're ever called to do'.) 'At the same time,' continues Vaness, 'it must be very, very musical. I'm not one of those people who can go on stage and just *yell* myself through Verdi, whose roles require a great deal of *class*.'

During our encounter she explained that Verdi ladies are different from Mozart's not only vocally and stylistically, but also in the way audiences experience them: 'With Mozart ladies, you feel their pain, but when they're finished, it's over for you, too. You can go through Fiordiligi's pain, for instance, but because of the way the music is written, by the end of the opera you feel light, you feel cleansed. And although you're moved, you don't feel bad. With Verdi heroines you do. And again, it has a lot to do with the way the music is written. Verdi's music has a heartbeat running through it. This is something weird that you are hardly aware of, yet people who arrange sound-tracks for the movies are, and they take it into account when choosing the music. They know that your heart responds to this heartbeat unconsciously, but at a very deep level. It's more obvious in early Verdi, where it's part of the rhythm running through most of the music. In his later operas it gets to be more hidden, but it's still very much there. If you listen to the music leading up to Elisabeth de Valois's aria, "Tu, che le vanità" in *Don Carlos* for instance, you'll hear Verdi giving it to you.

'Dramatically speaking, Verdi ladies tend to be uncomplicated. But I try to make them complicated for my own interest! Take Desdemona: it's very easy to play her as a victim, but I play her as a fighter to the end, even in the Willow Song and the Prayer. I draw from the old Olivier film of the play. Of course, this requires some previous dis-cussion with the tenor singing Otello, so that he doesn't over-react. In the scene where she asks him to pardon Cassio, for example, I don't think Otello should start off being that angry from the start, because if he were Desdemona wouldn't have gone on insisting. And in Act III, the outbreak shouldn't begin until the start of the quartet. She should look worried when she comes in, but not *terrified*, otherwise we'd already be in Act IV.'

Another opera in which, according to Vaness, it's essential to liaise meticulously with one's colleagues is *Il trovatore*, and especially with the baritone playing the Count di Luna. 'You would do it differently with a baritone who isn't fiery and more obsessed with the troubadour than Leonora than you would with one who plays him almost like Scarpia. Mind you, they're all obsessional in *Il trovatore*. There's also a lot of mysticism in this work . . . But as Leonora, you are given precious little in the way of plot around which to build your portrayal. It's from yourself that you have to fill out this character with flesh and blood.'

In this sense Vaness finds Violetta the easiest of all Verdi heroines to understand dramatically. She is also the absolute favourite of *all* her roles, because Verdi has given the character so much. 'I regard Violetta as a gift to sopranos by Verdi and his librettist. You don't have to do *anything* more than Verdi wrote in the score; you don't have to fabricate. It's very human, so human that your own nature comes through. I love showing the audience who I am, showing them a real rather than a fabricated weakness. As I said, Verdi gives you everything: the breathing, the coloraturas, even the coughing – he even tells you exactly where to cough.'

She does not agree with those who maintain that Violetta needs four different voices, but rather considers that it requires four different *facets* to the same voice. 'Act I, for instance, is not full of coloratura, but *fioritura*. The "Sempre libera" is not a coloratura showpiece, because here you have a woman driven to the edge of hysteria. She sees a man she wants, but doesn't believe she can have him. So there has to be the right amount of fear and emotion and intensity. Incidentally, I don't sing the E flat, I can't anymore. But the *fioritura* comes out of this desperation, along which the cabaletta *drives* to the end. The aria is low but climbs up to a high C, because Verdi meant it to be an aria of extremes. The duet does have proper coloratura, because this is Violetta the way she wishes to appear. In Act I you seldom see the real her – only for a moment in "O tal pallor" – until "È Strano" at the end.

'In Act II, when Violetta believes herself secure, the voice acquires warmth and depth, while in Act III, where she has lost Alfredo, the moment when she sings "Alfredo, Alfredo" should reflect tremendous fragility. Act IV is all middle voice, almost a speaking voice, until Alfredo comes and she gets *energy*. Verdi *gives* you the energy in the music. I tell you he gives you everything.'

Shortly after our conversation in Vaness's West Side apartment in New York, just a stone's throw from the Met, Vaness was off to the Vienna State Opera. (She has since moved to California.) In this theatre, where she has already performed most of her famous Mozart and Verdi roles, she was to sing Elena in *I vespri siciliani*, a role which she first sang in San Francisco in the late 1980s. It is one of the most fiendishly difficult of all Verdi roles. 'Vocally Elena is a monster! The first three acts are very low, almost low enough for a mezzo – much lower than Eboli, for instance – with very few high notes. Then, in Acts IV and V, it becomes a true *lirico spinto* role. It's extremely *satisfy-ing* to sing, but terribly difficult to cast.' This is unfortunately true: apart from Vaness, only Maria Guleghina today can probably do the role justice. As a character Vaness sees Elena as 'a very militaristic, almost like Odabella in *Attila*, until she discovers that the man she loves is not a traitor. Then she changes inside, which is why I try to sing the Bolero not just as a great coloratura aria. I try to bring some lyricism to it, because in the second verse, Elena says there is enough of this bloodshed.' As it turned out, Vaness was extremely disappointed by the Vienna production of Herbert Wernicke, which she regards as 'the biggest waste of time of my career.' Imagine a director who says, as he said to me, that the words don't matter, that he doesn't *care* what the words say, that it's the picture that counts!'

In autumn 1998 Vaness will sing another big Verdi role, Elisabeth de

Valois in *Don Carlos*, at the Paris Opéra. Just as the Countess in *Figaro* is the least favourite among her Mozart roles, so is Elisabeth her least favourite in Verdi, and for the same reason: that it is hard to bring temperament into a part that doesn't allow it. 'I try to inject some character to it. Of course, first and foremost it has to be incredibly beautifully sung. Her first aria is a most gorgeous piece. But the only moment where temperament comes through, "Tu, che le vanità", comes at the very end of the evening.' Vaness considers this aria 'a series of emotional statements' that culminate in a big phrase and broad sweep of emotion. 'This definitely places the role a step up from the Countess, and close to Desdemona, which I love to sing. But in both cases your one chance to show temperament comes very late in the opera, when you have been singing a long time – for Desdemona in Act III and for Elisabeth in Act IV (or Act V in the longer version).' Of course, Vaness considers it essential for stagings of *Don Carlos* to include the Fontainebleau Scene. 'Then you have somewhere to go. There is a *reason* for her being nervous about having a letter from Don Carlos, it explains the need for secrecy. Otherwise the audience doesn't know where this woman comes from. There is no departure point because you haven't seen her make that enormous sacrifice, you haven't glimpsed the possibility of what might have been. The role then is just limited to duty, duty, duty. The music is *fantastic*, although anyone with a voice could do this part.' It will be interesting to see what Vaness will make of the role in Paris, whether they have chosen the four-act version that omits the Fontainebleau Scene.

There is one role I didn't want to leave Vaness without having discussed – the title role in *Tosca*, which she took on in the 1990s and which is her 'new favourite'. Interestingly, it was the first role she ever sang as a student. She was then twenty-two years old, and when she looked at it, she certainly thought it was difficult. 'My opinion remains the same. The hardest part is undoubtedly the "Vissi d'arte", because everyone knows and waits for it, so it has to be perfect. It's a satisfying-the-audience moment. Of course, this being Puccini, you can be a little self-indulgent and hold a note a little longer than you normally would. I learnt a great deal about it recently from maestro Nello Santi, one of the few conductors left who not only knows every phrase of every opera inside out, but also *takes time* to teach you. He helped me find an interpretation of "Vissi d'arte" which is so *individual*. Until then I thought I probably sang it OK, but as for putting my stamp on it, I wasn't so sure. But by the time he was finished with me and we had done it together, I knew that people who heard this "Vissi d'arte" would remember it.

'And this is because of what he gave me: freedom, confidence, the ability to be self-indulgent in the right way for the actual expression of the words and the line, to hold this note a bit longer at this moment. But the *reason* you're holding it is that Tosca is in extreme pain at this moment. Santi went through the whole role in this kind of detail. Every note he gave me *meant* something, even if only a very tiny thing that you had never thought of before but which made all the difference. And it was so wonderful to look down at the pit and see his beautiful smile, giving me the confidence to try something new in front of 4,000 people.'

In the mid-1980s Beverly Sills had predicted for Vaness that 'some-day there is a Tosca in her,' but stressed that at that time it was still too early and would have been dangerous. A steady diet of Toscas is dangerous at any time, though, and Vaness, who is acutely aware of this takes particular care in how she schedules the part. If, for example, I'm singing Donna Anna and somebody offers me Tosca immediately afterwards, I can consider it. If they offer it before the Donna Anna, I cannot. It's very important to know what you can mix with what, even though occasionally surprises spring up. When we toured Japan with the Met, I was offered *Tosca* with Luciano [Pavarotti] and Fiordiligi. So I thought, hmm, although it doesn't *sound* logical, it's not a bad idea when you think about it because the *range* in Tosca is the same as in Fiordiligi. Tosca is a middle-to-upper range part with a couple of high notes and a lot of low singing. And if I were to describe

Fiordiligi, I'd say that it's a middle-to-high sort of role with a couple of very high notes – a high C and a couple of B naturals – and a lot of low singing. Both roles lay in the same part of the voice, and I was able to accept. I probably sang the Toscas more like Fiordiligi, in the sense that if I had an option in performance to sing harder, I didn't. I thought I'd just let my natural voice expand into this or that note, without pushing. And because I sing Mozart – and the good thing about singing Mozart is that you learn control – I was able to control the excess and the excitement. Because Tosca is to *die* for. And her personality is so like me. It really *is* me. It works for me: her quicksilver moods, her desperations, her great love, her jealousy, the way she moves, it all fits. *And* you have to be able to wear that dress!' Interestingly enough, every soprano past or present who has performed Tosca has the same personal, intimate way and thinks she *is* Tosca, probably because Tosca herself is an opera singer.

Being an opera singer is, of course, not always the glamorous profession it appears to those who don't know, but a career that demands rigorous self-discipline and a great many personal sacrifices. 'It's so very, *very* lonely,' Vaness said of the very time when hers was reaching its peak. 'It's difficult to spend time with the friends you want to be with, if you know you have a long rehearsal the next day or a performance the next evening.' For a long time after moving to New York in 1979, she missed her family and carefree Californian lifestyle, 'going to the beach and hanging out with a couple of friends who know nothing about opera.' One imagines that her marriage a few years later helped ease the loneliness.

Yet, like all true artists, she finds her work worth every sacrifice because as she explained in *Ovation*, it *is* so very fulfilling: 'My voice fulfils me in every way: it's so attached to the soul. I enjoy the communication with the audience, the actual sensation of singing, the high that you get – because when you sing your awareness is up. You have to think on twenty different levels at the same time: how's my voice? What's the conductor doing? How's the orchestra doing? Am I in the light? Where's my colleague? And then you have to sing musically and perform the stage action, and get the language correct. And you have to make great art of it all. All these different levels are going on at once, so your body is at a very high pitch. Your face actually buzzes a bit. And the feeling that comes is very satisfying.'

Jonathan Miller, who directed Vaness as Donna Anna in a production of *Don Giovanni* in Florence, was taken aback and mesmerized by this 'high' that Vaness experiences and exudes on stage: 'She has an explosive, almost disruptive erotic energy. She needs to be guided and provoked, but when she *is* guided and provoked, she is a huge, high-explosive presence on stage. She is, of course, a beautiful woman but she also has extraordinary dramatic vitality, a vitality so intense it's almost desperate and rather frightening, it's so volcanic.'

Perhaps, as Piero Faggioni said of Placido Domingo,[1] Vaness in performance experiences a liberation, an explosion of energies from within which can be freed *only* through singing, 'like a volcano which can free itself only by erupting.'

---

[1] *Bravo: Today's Tenors, Baritones and Basses Discuss their Art*, by Helena Matheopoulos (Weidenfield, 1986; Harper & Row, 1987)

V ERONICA
V ILLARROEL

V ERONICA VILLARROEL'S CAREER is an unusual one. But then, she's an unusual lady. In the fiercely competitive, back-biting world of operatic divas (as she says, 'would you believe that some people won't say hello to me because we sing the same repertoire?'), she is the odd one out. She never wanted a career in opera. It happened by chance. She needed the money badly to help her large family – ailing father, mother and six siblings, five younger than her – so she leapt at it. She sang her first operatic role without reading music or having had a singing lesson. She was accepted at the singing department at the Juilliard without reading music. Two and a half years later, having won the Metropolitan Opera Auditions, she made her début at the Metropolitan Opera.

'The career started very fast, without me knowing if I really wanted it and what kind of life I would have to live as an opera singer. I had very mixed feelings about it, because it was this profession that took me away from my family. That was very, very painful for me; I wasn't prepared for it emotionally. I came from a very close-knit, sheltered background. So when the career found me [indeed Villarroel's story could well be titled 'A Career in Search of a Diva' rather than the other way round] half of me wanted to follow that talent that every-body saw in me, while the other half was pulling back and saying, no no, I'm afraid.'

All who love opera should rejoice that she chose to follow that talent. For she is the possessor of an expressive, sturdy lyric voice with sufficient weight to stretch to *lirico spinto* territory, plus coloratura. It's an exciting instrument, with a visceral edge that renders it ideal for early Verdi (oh, the thrill of hearing a voice like this in *Alzira*), some *verismo* and the more dramatic bel canto parts. In addition, she's an excellent actress who moves on stage with the grace of a dancer and is good-looking to boot: with a long mane of black hair, dark doe eyes and a good figure.

Villarroel, now thirty-three, was born in Santiago, Chile. Her mother was a fabric designer and her father a salesman of medical instruments. She was the second of seven children. She hardly noticed the fact that they were poor, she says, because she was so happy at the time. She was always mad about dancing, rock and roll and popular Spanish songs. It was in 1984, during her third year at college studying advertising, that a severe blow struck, which was to have far-reaching repercussions for her future. Her father had a heart attack and could no longer work, so all of the family who could began working. She gave up her studies and started working as a door-to-door salesperson of window-cleaning spray.

As she had always loved popular music and had a very good ear, she joined a local Zarzuela company (a kind of Spanish operetta) as a chorus member and rehearsed with them in the evenings, to counter-balance the boredom of her day job. Though she couldn't read music, she was judged good enough for the leading roles in two of the most popular Zarzuelas, *Luisa Fernanda* and *La verbena de la paloma*. 'I would just imitate the other singers. I had no difficulty memorizing anything by ear. But occasionally on the high notes, I felt a sudden twinge in my throat. Not having studied singing, I didn't know what was going on, and felt frightened.'

She saw a newspaper advertisement for a chorus member at the local opera house, and at the suggestion of her Zarzuela colleagues, who knew she needed the money, she applied. 'So I went and auditioned with Zarzuelas, the only thing I knew. And they took me! I was so happy because I, we, needed the money for the family. It was wonderful news for us, because we were in a very bad economic situation. Although my father had recuperated a little he was not well enough to resume his work.

'I was in the soprano section of the chorus and the first piece we had to sing was the Mozart Requiem. Of course, everybody could read music and was buried in their scores, which to me were like Chinese!' Still, the chorus master was delighted with her voice and soon recommended her to the director, Andres Rodriguez. She didn't know any arias with which to audition so a friend in the chorus (making friends and being herself a very good friend is an innate and lasting characteristic of hers) lent her a cassette of 'Ritorna vincitor' which she says she learnt 'quite easily.'

So, 'trembling with fear' she walked on stage at the Teatro Municipal and sang 'Ritorna vincitor'. 'Andres Rodriguez then rang me,' she continues, 'said he knew about me, knew that I had never taken singing lessons but would take a big risk and give me Musetta next to Renata Scotto and Giacomo Aragall! As you can imagine, I could hardly believe my ears. Again, I learnt the whole of Musetta by ear, from a cassette and with a language coach. And would you believe it, I had a wonderful success! So everyone, especially Andres Rodriguez, asked Renata Scotto (who appeared to like me very much) if she could do anything for me.' Despite the fact that Villarroel could not read music, Scotto personally arranged for her to study singing at the Juilliard as an exception, on a scholarship; she also lobbied the Chilean government for a study fund. Andres Rodriguez, who had believed in her voice from the start, also chipped in.

'So I arrived in New York in the autumn of 1986 not speaking the language, not knowing anything about what was going on at the

Juilliard or about the operatic profession. People talked to me and I didn't even know what they were talking *about*. They didn't know how to treat me, because they had never met anyone who didn't read music before. I felt like I was back at kindergarten. I didn't know why I was there, or even if I *wanted* to be there, whether I wanted a career in opera. Everyone was so competitive and knew so much that I didn't know that I felt like nothing. I missed my family atrociously, but I hid my suffering from them because I didn't want them to suffer.'

She was lucky to be assigned to an intelligent and sympathetic teacher, Ellen Faull, who guided her through the two and a half year course gently and very constructively. 'Ellen is so special to me. I knew things I'd learnt through tapes, but I didn't know what they meant. She started me off by making me lie down on the floor, the better to feel all the muscles in my body, and then explained naturally the art of singing to me.' Faull also acted as a sort of surrogate mother, helping her pupil through her bouts of homesickness and melancholia.

Indeed, a gentle melancholy has been as much a feature of Villarroel as her dancing gaiety: 'Ever since I was a child I was melancholic, and very romantic. I used to write a lot and have insights and presentiments about things. I also liked to draw and compose some very sad music for the guitar. I have always had problems with the fact that we're going to die and disappear. I just can't accept it. If I believed in an afterlife it would be different, I guess. I was also scared of some of my psychic powers, things I could do. But this went with time. I was also very gay and carefree.'

With Ellen Faull's help, these problems were kept in perspective and Villarroel made steady progress. So much so that a year and a half later she won the prestigious Metropolitan Opera Auditions *and* the Pavarotti Competition. A year after that, in 1990, just two and a half years after arriving in New York without speaking English or reading music, she made her professional début at the Teatre del Liceu in Barcelona as Fiordiligi, replacing Pilar Lorengar at five days notice!

'That's where my training at the Juilliard proved invaluable. I had studied the role there with my teacher. I like the character. She is very melodramatic because she wants to stay true to this ideal of hers, but at the same time she's captured in a situation she cannot control. Her relationship with her sister – her attempts to dictate to her, "you cannot go this way", "we must always stay together" and "we have to be faithful" – always make me think that she's probably the weakest of the two. And the way she develops and becomes much more deeply involved than her sister is interesting. You have to have the flexibility to be dramatic, melodramatic *and* comic at the same time, but without ever *trying* to be funny. If you play it dead serious then it becomes funny. But translating the emotions you find in the music into physical gestures and movements is what's so difficult about operatic acting.'

Vocally, she finds it a very comfortable role. 'It's wide-ranging, both very high and very low, with plenty of coloratura which I have. It's also very good discipline. You have to attack the notes in a very clean way. It's fantastic to have the opportunity to try these parts and find out which ones you feel good in and which ones you don't. When something seems difficult and uncomfortable, I work at it twice as hard so that it improves. Of her two arias I like "Per pietà" best because it is more true. Fiordiligi is showing us who she really is here. So you open your heart and show people who you are. But for this reason you can lose vocal control more easily here than in "Come scoglio", which is more melodramatic.' Villarroel has also sung Fiordiligi, her only Mozart role, at Aspen; and at the time of our meetings (in Washington and New York in late November and early December 1997) she was scheduled to sing it again at Oviedo.

After her success in Barcelona, her next roles were Serafina in Donizetti's *Il campanello* and Nedda in *Pagliacci* – an unusual double-bill. A year later, in 1996, came her début at the Metropolitan Opera, as Mimì. 'I love it, love it, love it,' she says of the part, 'both the music and the character. She's a very interesting lady, a very flirtatious lady, not at all modest as she's often portrayed to be. She knows exactly what she wants, and is, to put it mildly, rather forward. She has been involved with many other men before. She has this sickness that makes her recognize the beauty in life's simple things: she enjoys each touch of the sun on her face, the silk flowers she makes, or a simple smile. I just love it . . . Vocally it's not difficult. Act I used to be difficult because I was so nervous. And it's so delicate that I felt the slightest nervousness in my body would show in the singing. Now I don't have any problems with it anymore.' Indeed Villarroel was to make a string of major international débuts in the role: at the San Francisco Opera in 1993, the Hamburg State Opera in 1994 and the Deutsche Oper in 1997. She has since gone on to sing two more important roles at the Met; Violetta in *La traviata* in 1993 and 1994 and Liù in *Turandot* in 1996. She was also offered Butterfly which, for reasons she explains below, she refused.

It was in the role of Violetta that I first saw Villarroel, in a production in Bonn and conducted by Placido Domingo. I was immediately struck by the expressiveness and sincerity of her portrayal, especially in Acts II and III, where she brought a very sensitive palette of colours to the whole death scene. There was momentary, almost imperceptible strain in the coloraturas in 'Gioir', but the portrayal was moving and convincing. It's one of her most favourite characters (as it seems to be with all interpreters of the role), because as Villarroel says, Violetta 'feels everything all women feel. We want to feel free, we want to be loved, we tend to hide past hurts behind a mask of superficiality. The real inside, your centre, you keep for you alone. You don't show it to anybody. This is very important in the character of Violetta. She understands where she is and where she is going. But when she lives through this beautiful moment of love, in Act II, being so *complete* for the first time in her life, I think she forgets she's sick. She believes she's going to live.

'In Act I, in "È strano", she has obviously been touched by this guy in a different way than by the men who surround her, and she's *afraid*. She didn't *want* this to happen, "Croce e delizia", love is torture and bliss at the same time. Alfredo touches her in her secret heart, the place we all keep to ourselves. She knows she could give herself to that opportunity to have love, real love. But then she gets scared and thinks no, this is stupid. I'm going to laugh, have fun, sleep with people. But that's a lie. She cannot resist love. It's stronger than we are.

'Then there is her renunciation in Act II, because she knows that society she lives in and accepts that what Germont says is true. Do I think she would have done this if she were not sick, if she didn't know she was going to die? Yes. Because it's not just her illness that makes her what she is, but her character. For me the most challenging part is definitely Act I – how to lighten the voice and sing in a very pure way, with long breath but without losing contact with your body. Later on the role becomes much easier for my voice.' Villarroel sang the role again with the Royal Opera in the Albert Hall with consummate artistry, under less than ideal conditions. She was certainly luckier in her conductor in Bonn, where Domingo was with her every step of the way, with his usual hypersensitive accompaniment from the pit.

Villarroel had originally met Domingo at an audition, during which he had given her some very helpful advice. A month later, the director of the Santiago Opera rang her, and asked her to sing in a concert with Domingo in Chile, the first time he had visited the country in twenty-seven years. 'You can imagine how scared I was to sing with this superstar and hero! I thought I wasn't good enough, and wondered what could I do to show I was grateful for the opportunity and not let the side down. But he was wonderful. He made me feel like an artist of equal stature, like a colleague. It was unbelievable. He was very nice to me and invited me to sing many more concerts and operas with him.

'So that's how we began our professional association. I admire him enormously and his influence on me as an artist has been very impor-tant. I also admire the way he protects his personal life. I can't do that yet. I have to think where I want to go. It's very difficult. Sometimes I even wonder if it's worth it. People are afraid of us divas. They think we are emotionally volatile, up and down and all the rest of it. Sometimes, in order to get to know people, I hide who I am and what

I do. I don't want people to befriend me because I do a certain kind of job or have money or whatever. That's not the way I am. But Placido handles it all with tremendous *grace*.'

Domingo and Villarroel had worked together on a major project the year before the Bonn *Traviata*, Werner Herzog's spectacular, poetic staging of Gomes's *Il Guarany*, again in Bonn, under the dynamic management of Giancarlo del Monaco. *Il Guarany* is a rewarding, colourful score with Verdian overtones, and very singable. How did Villarroel set about learning a piece that practically no-one had ever heard? 'Believe it or not the only person who came up with something that helped was a friend from Chile who sent me a score and a cassette! Then I went to my coach. I like the piece. It's very similar to Verdi, especially the third aria. There is coloratura singing, but with *voice*. It's powerful coloratura, which is much, much easier. And, thank God, the conductor – unlike many I could name – John Neschling let me do it *my* way.'

At the time of our encounters, Villarroel was again working with Domingo, singing Nedda to his Canio in a wonderfully imaginative production of *I Pagliacci* by Franco Zeffirelli. (She had meanwhile made a sensational Covent Garden début the previous summer in a concert performance of Verdi's *Alzira* into which, she says, she poured her all, because 'there was just this *one* opportunity to sing this piece at Covent Garden. I though I'd better do my best, so I prepared it really well.')

The production of *Pagliacci* was shared with the Los Angeles Opera and was the best, most enchanting *Pagliacci* I have seen or hope to see. Nedda is a very active role, as Villarroel points out, especially so in this production. 'You can let everything out. The problem is that when you have a part like this with very active and expressionistic acting, the voice also wants to be free to run ahead like a wild horse and you have to rein it in. Nedda is not a difficult role as such. You have to be very extroverted, not very refined. It's easy to run out of breath because you have to run around a lot and sing over a big, dense orchestration. So you have to keep the lungs very full of air. At the same time you have to be feminine, because although she's not a fine lady she's not *rude*. She's earthy and very passionate but not a prostitute, rather a woman waking up to all sorts of feelings which she never experienced with her husband: *sensuality*, the smell of this guy, having this young guy to touch, to feel. Maybe Canio loves her, but he doesn't make her feel this way. But she's loyal. She won't leave Canio although she would like to. He's probably crude and abusive with her, but she's loyal if not faithful to him.

'Vocally, it's not difficult. You can hide behind the drama. But unless you're careful, if you give too much vocally, it can destroy and abuse your voice. The way the part is written, because she's a strong, earthy woman, means you have to give a lot of voice and push a little. But a little is the operative word. Do I like the lady? Yes, I do. I think she's very brave and loyal not to give away her lover's name when her life is threatened. At the same time she is also very vulnerable. There is a wonderful scene where she is dreaming, she would like to follow the birds, play with the children – you sense that she would like to be married and have children . . .'

The night I saw the production Villarroel moved with elfin grace and sang the part fantastically throughout. At one point, Domingo, as Canio, swept her into a waltz. It made for a magical moment and it was only afterwards that I found out this had been a completely spontaneous, unrehearsed impulse for this, their last performance. Domingo had severe toothache throughout and Villarroel said she hadn't slept the night before because she was packing. Yet they produced greater magic than on any of the other evenings. Such is the mystery of performance – but it takes a flexible and receptive partner to capture your mood and ride along with it.

Villarroel would like the opportunity to tackle more *verismo* parts, such as Suor Angelica and especially Butterfly. She had previously been asked to sing Butterfly and had gone so far as to schedule performances at Toulouse, Florence, Los Angeles and the Met. But she cancelled them. As she explained: 'Not necessarily because I couldn't sing Butterfly, though it was a bit heavy for me at the time, but because I couldn't have sung a *string* of Butterflies. People had even proposed Aida, Tosca and Maddalena in *Andrea Chénier*. But what I would most like to expand into is the more dramatic bel canto repertoire, such as Lucrezia Borgia, Anna Bolena, Gilda and Medora in *Il corsaro*. So I have been careful.'

Meanwhile, there are plans for further Verdi roles: Desdemona at the Teatro Colón in Buenos Aires, Elisabeth de Valois in Montreal and Elvira in *Ernani* when the Royal Opera moves to its new theatre. 'Little by little, I began to take the responsibility of managing my career instead of letting others do it. At the beginning, because the career happened so fast, I didn't bring those two – Veronica and the opera singer – together. Earlier on, I was not an ambitious person. But now I feel it's important before we die to leave something that is the best of us behind, and be remembered for that. So I would like to do many roles in many theatres, but with good colleagues and cooperative conductors, not with egos that have become too big. I think all of us should have more simplicity and more humility, be open to ideas and help rather than fight each other. I hate working in an ugly atmosphere. It depresses me and freezes everything in me, locks it inside.'

Villarroel, who has currently chosen to remain single, would nevertheless like one day to have 'an ideal love'. Marriage and commitment she has always shunned: 'I don't believe in permanent bonds. I like freedom. But I would like a love partner, because whether you are single or married, you want to *share*. Life in hotel room is terribly lonely and depressing, and it's difficult to go on alone. Being with my family and friends is the most important thing for me.' (Indeed some member of her family always travels with her.) 'I need the affection and protection to give me strength to continue living this nomadic life of going onstage and becoming someone else. It's beautiful when it goes well. But when it doesn't, that's when you need to have those you love with you in such moments, and always to remember who you are and where you came from. Sometimes I think "Why do I keep doing it?" I don't think I have found the answer to this question yet. But, like Verdi heroines, I believe that love and passion are what gives meaning to life. And that's what opera is about.'

Angela Gheorghiu in Act I of Covent Garden's production of La Traviata in which she was called 'a precious jewel'.

Angela Gheorghiu as Violetta in Richard Eyre's Covent Garden production that turned her into a star: 'It costs me a lot to perform this role, to live it. Because finding the mysterious dividing line between abandon and control is difficult, especially when you are young and singing a role for the first time.'

Susan Graham (left) and Renée Fleming (right) as Octavian and the Marschallin in Der Rosenkavalier at the Opéra Bastille. 'The end of the opening duet in Act I, when the birds start chirping and light pours into the Marschallin's bedroom and Octavian sings "Warum ist Tag" is one of the "Holy Moments" in the opera.'

Denyce Graves, the Carmen of the decade at Covent Garden: 'An unhappy woman because she fears the loss of freedom and control that goes hand in hand with falling in love.'

LEFT
Renée Fleming as the water-sprite Rusalka at the Metropolitan Opera. Rusalka is her talisman role that always opened doors for her.

Barbara Frittoli as Fiordiligi in Graham Vick's controversial Glyndebourne production, in which she was required to wear her own clothes: 'This meant that, like the characters, we too were stripped naked, with no barrier between the audience and ourselves. We had to look deep inside us and find out who we are.'

Olga Borodina as Marina in the Kirov production of Boris Godunov: 'Sometimes I do enjoy the sound of my own voice. But very seldom!'

Maria Guleghina as Abigaille in La Scala's production of Nabucco: 'When she finds out she is not a King's daughter, the shock hits her like a thunderbolt. If it weren't for this, she would probably be a normal person.'

Catherine Malfitano in the title role in Madama Butterfly at the Metropolitan Opera: 'It was marvellous the way she managed to really be a child, in this very difficult role that has to be childlike and yet demands a huge voice', according to Sir Charles Mackerras.

Vesselina Kasarova (left) and Barbara Frittoli (right) as Dorabella and Fiordiligi in the Vienna Festival's production of Così fan tutte *at the Theater an der Wien: 'Mozart conceived the two roles so that they could be sung alternately by the same singers, which is crucial to the concept of the opera. But the way Così is performed today, you would think Dorabella is a mezzo and Fiordiligi a high soprano, which is historically wrong.' (Kasarova)*

LEFT

Galina Gorchakova: As Tatyana in Eugene Onegin *at Covent Garden; 'The kind of passion in* Onegin *is a very northern and specifically Russian kind of passion. There is always something masochistic about Russian heroes and heroines.'*

OVERLEAF

Cecilia Bartoli at her Metropolitan Opera debut as Despina in Così fan tutte*: 'Although she pulls herself together, because she must, she will never be at peace with herself because she realises that she has helped ruin the lives of these four people who can only patch, but never mend, their relationships.'*

Ruth Ann Swenson in the title role of John Copley's Covent Garden production of Semele: *'You can't hide what kind of person you are whether you are singing Susanna, Gilda or Semele. You are in every role you do.'*

ABOVE
Vesselina Kasarova, 'the most electrifying "boy" onstage' according to Jonathan Miller, as Idamante in Idomeneo *at the Chicago Lyric Opera.*

Karita Mattila as Elisabeth de Valois in Luc Bondy's landmark production of Don Carlos *for the Châtelet and Covent Garden: 'A character so patriotic that she puts duty to her country above personal considerations. This sense of self-sacrifice and obligation to her people is in her blood, part of the upbringing she received from her father, the King of France.'*

Cecilia Bartoli as Angelina in La Cenerentola, *who can 'be played in many different ways: she can be passive and melancholy, or she can be the opposite: a very active girl, still very good but with her feet firmly on the ground.'*

Dolora Zajick as Azucena in Il Trovatore, *the role in which she made her professional debut and in which there is no one to touch her: 'Azucena is a very interesting character. She is the key to the whole opera. If you get a director who doesn't understand that, then the whole of* Il Trovatore *becomes a joke.'*

MEZZO-SOPRANOS

CECILIA
BARTOLI

CECILIA BARTOLI IS probably the most publicized female opera singer of our day: a superstar whose fame extends to cover stories in journals such as *Newsweek* and *Vanity Fair*, and television profiles on *The South Bank Show*. Within the musical profession itself normally hard-to-please critics vie for superlatives with which to praise her fruity mezzo voice, its dazzling agility and range of three and a half octaves and her bubbly, magnetic personality which sets the stage alight. Max Loppert in *Opera* called her 'one of the glories of our age', while William Weaver, the noted Verdi biographer and veteran critic who has been based in Italy for a quarter century, singled her out as the singer who has most excited him since Callas. Artists of the calibre of Andras Schiff have accompanied her in concert and on record. According to Decca, the company responsible for her discovery and launch, Bartoli is the best-selling classical artist in the world after Pavarotti.

The only chink in this formidable armour was, for a while, the risk that Bartoli's recordings would outnumber her live appearances, especially on the operatic stage. Combined with the extravagant (but effective) hype with which she was marketed, it gave rise to what Loppert rightly pinpointed as a measure of 'sales resistance' in certain sections of the Press. Some reviewers who had not seen her 'live', particularly in Britain where she has still to make her operatic début, began a whispering campaign of 'yes buts', claiming her voice was 'manufactured' by the recording industry and that it was too small for the theatre, especially for large houses.

Bartoli, who is both very intelligent and street-wise, realized that it was up to her to prove that she is as remarkable artistically as she is successful commercially. She set about demonstrating this with a vengeance during the past two seasons. Her début in 1996 as Despina at the Metropolitan Opera, one of the largest theatres in the world, and her triumphant appearances in the title role in *La Cenerentola* in October 1997 silenced the 'small voice' lobby once and for all. Through her portrayal of the title role in Paisiello's long-forgotten opera *Nina* in Zürich and her Euridice in Haydn's *L'anima del filosofo* in Vienna she revealed her passion for musicological research and a zeal for championing neglected works. These highlights in two fruitful, 'quality' seasons have proved beyond doubt that Bartoli is not only as good as her publicists, her recording company and throng of adoring fans claimed she was, but even better.

Now at just thirty-two, Bartoli is in complete control of her career and determined about the direction in which she wishes it to go in its second decade. (One is apt to forget that it is only eleven years since Bartoli burst onto the operatic scene.) Her appraisal of her vocal gift is realistic and accurate, and her choice of repertoire judicious. She now limits her appearances to between forty and fifty events a year. 'I felt myself at a crossroads. I couldn't go on performing just Mozart and Rossini forever. My voice was developing and *I* was developing. The choice before me was either to expand into *verismo* or stay with the eighteenth century, the Baroque and Classical composers, which seems to suit me vocally and artistically. For although I enjoy going to see *verismo* operas, I feel they are very far away from my own vocal and emotional make-up. So I've decided to plunge into the treasure trove of the eighteenth century.'

She relished her experience of performing Haydn's treatment of the Orfeo myth, *L'anima del filosofo*, with Nikolaus Harnoncourt, one of her first and lasting mentors, at the Theater an der Wien. 'It was a completely new experience for me, as I knew Haydn mainly as a symphonic composer. Apart from *La fedeltà premiata* and *Il mondo della luna*, I had no idea that he wrote such marvellous operas, especially *opere serie* such as *Armida*, which I shall be doing with Harnoncourt in Graz in July [1998] and then in Zürich. I'm also going to start exploring Handel. In December 1998 I will sing the part of Pleasure in his oratorio *Il trionfo del tempo e del disinganno*, again with Harnoncourt at the Musikverein in Vienna. A fascinating feature of my part is that it includes an aria set to the same music as "Lascia ch'io pianga" from *Rinaldo* (though the middle section and the words are different).' There are also plans for Bartoli to sing *Rinaldo* with Christopher Hogwood, though no dates have as yet been set, and to give a concert of arias from *Agrippina* and *Lucrezia* with William Christie and Les Arts Florissants at Paris and Versailles.

'Another composer for whom I have a passion is Vivaldi. I very much hope to revive his opera *La Griselda* with William Christie and Les Arts Florissants. Vivaldi is a very neglected composer, especially in Italy, which is unforgivable when one considers that he is such an important link in the Italian musical tradition. I don't see how any of us can presume to sing opera without knowing where it sprang from. And while the importance of Monteverdi, and to a lesser extent Cavalli, has been recognized, Vivaldi has yet to be fully appreciated.' Bartoli has performed Vivaldi in concert all over the world, notably with the string ensemble I Delfici (in which her much-loved brother, Gabriele Bartoli, who died of a brain tumour earlier this year, played the viola). 'I'm not sure any major singer today could have executed the technical feats Bartoli did in her Vivaldi motet, cantata and aria and do so as brilliantly,' wrote the doyen of Chicago critics, John von Rhein in the *Chicago Tribune*. 'It is not just that she sings flawlessly and gorgeously but that she connects so completely with her public in the process.

In so doing, she dissolved the distinction between song and singer: Bartoli *was* the music.'

Bartoli explains that the Baroque style of singing is something 'you acquire the moment you immerse yourself in the music. Handel himself shows you how you should use your voice. His music carries you along the way he wants you to sing it. You don't have to think, "oh, this is Handel, therefore this is where I should place the voice." What you *do* have to work on are the trills and embellishments. The ability comes in the singing of it. It's up to you, the interpreter, to open your mind, your ears and heart and *understand* what the composer wants.'

There was never a time when music was not part of Bartoli's life. She was born in Rome on June 4 1966 to parents who were both singers. Her father was a member of the Rome Opera Chorus while her mother sang in the chorus of the Accademia di Santa Cecilia. Music was therefore passed on to her with her mother's milk, so to speak.

One of her vivid childhood memories is of playing with the children of other singers backstage at the Terme di Caracalla during the Rome Opera's summer season and jumping on the stuffed lions in *Aida* while her parents were on stage. At the age of nine she made her only appearance as a child, as the Shepherd-boy in *Tosca*. Although she loved the stage and was always somehow involved in it, she never planned to be a singer. As a child she learnt to play the piano; then she studied the horn for two years. When she was thirteen she developed a real passion for flamenco, took lessons and wanted to become a flamenco dancer; she even took part in some flamenco shows. 'Basically I wasn't at all sure what I wanted to do and what road to follow.'

Then, when she was about sixteen years old, her mother began giving her singing lessons, just for fun. She was very clever about it, so as not to arouse resistance because, as Bartoli is quick to point out, teaching your own child isn't easy, either for the mother or the daughter. 'I think the key to unlocking whatever potential I had lay in the fact that there was never any notion of *imposition* about those lessons, as I didn't plan to be a singer. So I approached them in a very relaxed way. Gradually I began to realize that something there was beginning to emerge, and this intrigued me. I started feeling curious about this mysterious instrument inside me. After several months of working with my mother, day after day, we came to the conclusion that it would be a good idea to enrol in the Conservatoire of Santa Cecilia.'

There, too, coming from the sort of home she did made all the difference: 'It meant that, as music was at the centre of our life at home, I never really stopped studying. I lived and breathed music twenty-four hours a day. So, I made gigantic strides and in a short space of time managed to cover ground that it would have taken a normal pupil six years to cover.'

Nonetheless, it took a tremendous amount of hard work to bring out her voice. 'Yes, I was born with a voice. But I had no idea how to use it. Technique doesn't come naturally, believe me. It has to be acquired, worked at. If anyone tries to tell you otherwise, they are lying. I wasn't born with my voice placed in the right position. We worked step by step, my mother and I, until little by little, we began to get some results. The same is true of my range of three and a half octaves. You can bet that wasn't there, either! Nor was the ability for coloratura. There was a *predisposition* for agility, yes. But we had to work on it endlessly and painstakingly, sometimes working on a single note for days or even weeks – doing vocalises on "oo" for instance. Until slowly, with time, study, hard work and the mellowing that comes with growth, I expanded my vocal range and acquired agility. I was lucky because my mother understood both my voice and the importance of technique. This is even more important as we develop and grow older. When we are young, we hold all the cards in our hand and can draw on them at any time. But as we mature, we rely on our technique, and put it into practice, reaping all the benefits that it can bestow on our voice and career. This is what Mirella Freni does to this day and what enables her to do what she does so superbly.'

In 1985, when Bartoli was nineteen and three years into her vocal studies, she took part in Pippo Baudo's immensely popular television talent-spotting show on National Italian Television (RAI). She was noticed immediately and was invited to perform a recital of Rossini arias in Rome and to participate in a televised Callas memorial concert in Paris. Again, she made such an impression that she got telephone calls from both Daniel Barenboim and von Karajan, who asked her to audition for him in Salzburg. Karajan was so enthused that he invited her to perform Bach's *Mass in B Minor* at the 1990 Salzburg Festival. His death, in the summer of 1989, meant that this plan never materialized. Meanwhile, Bartoli was discovered by one of Decca's top recording producers, Christopher Raeburn, a man of great musical culture and experience of voices.

'It was one of those "sausage machine" auditions in Milan, where I heard forty-six singers,' he told Francis Wheen in the *Sunday Correspondent*. 'From the moment Cecilia appeared I was spellbound. She sang Isabella's aria "Cruda sorte" from *L'italiana in Algeri* and "Di tanti palpiti" from *Tancredi*. All I wrote down was "Very remarkable indeed. VVG." I had not heard such incisiveness and definition since Berganza and, before that, Callas. What is riveting to discover in this last comment is that Bartoli's exceptional flair for enunciation, gift for colouring and *energizing* every word and syllable, was already there, at the age of twenty-one. Raeburn didn't hesitate, and immediately signed her up for a recording of *Il barbiere di Siviglia* and a solo album of Rossini arias. Back in London, he set in motion the marketing and publicity machine that went into the launching of Cecilia Bartoli, Superstar. The rest is operatic history. It must be said that Bartoli's performances at every stage of her eleven-year career have vindicated his judgement and the faith his company placed in this unique young artist.

The record of *Barbiere* was released in 1989, the same year that Bartoli made her professional début in this work at the Rome Opera. (The last performance there, incidentally, in which her father performed as a chorus member.) At the time she had already developed a passion for Rossini, and considered herself a specialist in this composer, whose music she had discovered at the age of nineteen. She felt that the role of Rosina was 'ideal' for her. 'The age of the character is very important and so is the kind of voice it demands. I think Rosina *has* to be a mezzo soprano and not a soprano: a little high-class Carmen who lives in an aristocratic milieu', she said at the time. But now, as she explains later, she feels she has outgrown the role.

Almost immediately after her Rome début came her international début, as Cherubino in Jean-Pierre Ponnelle's production of *Le nozze di Figaro* at the Zürich Opera. This was her first encounter with Nikolaus Harnoncourt, who remains to this day an important figure in her artistic life. She found Cherubino 'a fabulous role', and went on to sing it all over the world. But, like Rosina, she feels she has now outgrown this part 'in every sense of the word, including physically'. (Bartoli's figure has filled out somewhat in recent years and would, indeed, not suit Cherubino any longer.) So she has given up the role, but not *Le nozze di Figaro*, which she now sees more from Susanna's point of view.

'Let's face it, I've lost some of my youthful innocence. (Some, not all – I still retain a certain measure.) And although I could still sing Cherubino, it would be a much more mature Cherubino, which is to say that he wouldn't really be Cherubino anymore. So although vocally I could still do him justice, I feel in every way that I'm now much more suited to Susanna. She's a marvellous character, a typically Italian "donna di casa", the kind of domestic servant who has to make everything work and run smoothly. Her music is sublime, that goes without saying as it's Mozart. But what I like and admire about her as a character is that she manages to have good relations with everyone. She is elastic, flexible enough to find a point of contact with everyone – and that's a very important lesson in life, one of the greatest qualities anyone can have. Susanna is friends with Cherubino. She has her bond with Figaro. She is the Countess's confidante. She also struggles to maintain a good contact with the Count: she never plays with his feelings, but simply confronts him with the fact that what he is doing is not right. She is never acquiescing, she never thinks that as he is the Count she had better accept his advances so as to have a better life. She is always very definite, very clear about where she stands. But as I said, she's also elastic and diplomatic with those around her, while always maintaining her dignity.

'Vocally, it presents no problems. The tessitura is central, and although the role is usually sung by light lyric sopranos, it can, like Zerlina, just as easily be sung by a mezzo. In any case, in Mozart's day there was no difference between a soprano and a mezzo. Mozart has marked all the female parts – the Countess, Susanna and Cherubino – "soprano". Naturally, what he had in mind was sopranos with a very different vocal colour.' At the time of our encounter (the day after the première of *Nina* in Zürich), she was preparing to sing Susanna for the first time, under Harnoncourt in Zürich in March 1998. So, as far as *Figaro* is concerned, she seems to have come full circle. (In the event, the performances were postponed until July 1998.)

To general astonishment, Bartoli chose another 'donna di casa' – Despina in *Così fan tutte* – for her début at the Metropolitan Opera in spring 1996. Perhaps, smart as she is, she did this to test her voice in that huge theatre before sailing in with a title role. In the event, the size of the house turned out to be no problem because of the fantastic acoustic. 'People were very surprised at the time,' she acknowledges. 'Because making such a big, important début in a part that is not a title role is a very unusual and, if I may say, "un-American" thing to do. But in *Così fan tutte* there *is* no title role. There are six characters, all of whom are protagonists. You cannot do this opera without all of them being of a high standard. So although the Met was aghast at the time, I said I was very happy to make my début in this role, provided it was in a good, tasteful production, which turned out to be the case [by Lesley Koenig and conducted by James Levine].'

Bartoli says that she has her own vision of *Così*: a tragic and gloomy view, because at the end all the characters are faced with a void, which to her mind is worse than death. 'Each of the four lovers will have to live in a void, a lie, a life of complete loneliness and this is why I con-sider this a very dramatic opera. As for Despina, although she pulls herself together, because she must, she will never be at peace with her-self. She realizes that she has helped ruin the lives of these four people, who can never completely mend their relationships. For this reason I find *Cosí* the most serious and saddest of all three Da Ponte–Mozart operas. It plays with people's feelings. There is nothing quite as deep or painful as that in *Don Giovanni*, for instance. What do I think of Don Giovanni? He is the most sincere person alive, which is to say that he is hated by everyone.'

Just as Bartoli planned to swap the role of Cherubino in *Figaro* for that of Susanna, she is planning also to swap Despina for Dorabella and Zerlina for Donna Elvira, again in Zürich under Harnoncourt. She doesn't consider Elvira, which can be sung by a mezzo, as necessarily too dramatic a role. In any case, Bartoli's decision to see these three operas from a new perspective is part of a process of self-renewal signalled by the end of one cycle, the end of her first decade on stage. She has set about this change in a confident and authoritative way, as someone who likes to set herself realistic challenges and is in full charge of her career.

After the enormous success of her Despina at the Met, Bartoli felt confident enough to return in October 1997 in the title role in *La Cenerentola*, an opera which had never before been performed in this house. Bartoli herself had already performed the opera in Bologna, Munich and Houston, where it was televised live (a performance now available on video). She considers *Cenerentola* to be 'a magical opera, like *The Magic Flute*. It has that spiritual, supernatural dimension. The character of Angelina is very versatile and rewarding to portray. Unlike Rosina, who is a rather limited character and who hardly develops through the course of the action, Angelina changes a great deal. Depending on your director and colleagues, she can be played in many different ways: she can be passive and melancholy, or she can be the opposite – a very active girl, still very good, but with her feet firmly on the ground, a survivor who has learnt to get by simply by reacting to whatever each day brings. She doesn't have any impossible or grandiose dreams – or rather, she does dream, but without believing anything will ever happen to her. Unlike her ugly sisters, she has a firm grip on reality. And probably *because* she doesn't expect anything, everything happens to her . . .

'It is a very long opera, three hours, and a perfect lesson in how to pace yourself so that you stay fresh for the finale, where Angelina has a great aria that everyone is waiting for which must dazzle with plenty of bravura. Pacing is something you only learn by experience, on stage, during the rehearsal period, which I consider the most beautiful and interesting part of our work. That's when you develop a character, by working together with your colleagues. I love the process of discovering my character *with* other people. That's when you really learn a role, because your colleagues' temperament and reactions on stage can modify the way you portray a character. This is particularly true of Angelina, who is so dependent on her sisters and how *they* play their parts, because she has to *react* to them.' (Bartoli caused a local scandal at the Bavarian State Opera by insisting, and getting, two weeks' rehearsal when she sang the part in Munich.) Meanwhile Bartoli also insisted on having Cesare Lievi, with whom she worked before in Zürich, stage the work at the Met. He tried very hard to reduce the stage space to compensate for the Met being in some ways too large a theatre for this work.

The reviews were ecstatic: 'No audience could have been more enthusiastic than the one that greeted the opening *Cenerentola* at the Met. The crammed House laughed and applauded from the Overture, crisply conducted by James Levine, to the final rondo, where Bartoli displayed the full measure of her pyrotechnical ability. The curtain calls went on and on . . . But Bartoli's Angelina was not just a warbling doll. Jacopo Ferretti, the Roman poet who supplied Rossini with the text in 1817, magically created a three-dimensional character, alternately wistful and wry, tart and assertive, reticent and outspoken. Bartoli was always aware of Angelina's complex nature', wrote William Weaver in a review in the *Financial Times* titled 'Bartoli Bowls over the Met'.

Bartoli will return to the Met in the autumn of 1998 to sing Susanna under James Levine, confident from experience that theatre size is no problem for singers in control of their voice. What *is* an issue, on the other hand, is a singer's choice of repertoire. For while technical problems can be solved if a singer is working with the right teacher, the problems arising from the wrong choice of repertoire cannot. For this reason, Bartoli has no plans to expand into Rossini 'serio': 'My voice is not right for the Rossini trouser roles, which are very different from Mozart's.' (Apart from Cherubino, Bartoli has sung Sesto, Idamante, Cecilio in *Lucio Silla* and Sifare in *Mitridate*.) 'They demand a much more contralto-like voice than mine, which is a high mezzo. So I could never do Malcolm in *La donna del lago* or the title role in *Tancredi*, much though I love this opera. Basically the Rossini parts suited to my voice are those he wrote for his wife, Isabella Colbran.' She does not exclude the possibility of one day singing *Carmen* provided the production is 'un-touristy'.

'Carmen is, of course, one of the operas I intend to sing at some point in my career. A lot of people ask me when and my answer is always the same. That is to say when I will find the right theatre, stage director and conductor to do it with and that we will all agree on the way it should be done. For me Bizet wrote Carmen for the Opéra Comique in Paris which is a small theatre and for a not so big orchestra as one uses nowadays. This opera to my mind was conceived in a much more intimate way that it is known today and this is how I would like to do it. If you ask me "when?" I will tell you that I will seriously start looking at doing it from the year 2,000!!! But it might take me a few years from then to fulfil my pre-conditions.'

Bartoli's aim now is to concentrate on projects that really interest her musicologically as well as purely vocally, and that involve 'the musician as well as the singer in me'. This, indeed, is the key to one of Bartoli's most remarkable characteristics as an artist. In addition to her vocal and scenic gifts, she encompasses an entire vocal civilization whose roots stretch back to the very origins of opera. This thought occurred to me as I sat, utterly spellbound, at the opening night of Paisiello's *Nina* at the Zürich Opera in march 1998.

This work, which was premièred in 1789, enjoyed huge popularity in its time and in the early decades of our own century. It has also proved to be one of the greatest tours de force of Bartoli's career. She is required to portray a temporarily 'mad' heroine while singing vertiginously difficult music for *an hour and a quarter without a break* and, after a short respite, to come back for more! Written for the famous mezzo, Celeste Coltellini, the music calls for everything a lyric mezzo can do: trills, roulades, singing long, languid lines *pianissimo* and then leaping to *fortissimo* high notes within a single phrase. All done while running around, raving, or rolling on the floor.

Bartoli's fascination with *Nina* began in 1994, when the director Roberto de Simone, with whom she had collaborated on productions of *Così fan tutte* at the Theater an der Wien with Muti, *Le cantatrici villane* in Naples and *Cenerentola* in Bologna, told her that he thought she should absolutely perform this forgotten opera by Paisiello. After hearing all about its enormous success in its own century, Bartoli became curious and began to examine its various editions. 'The version we chose to perform in Zürich is the first edition, with spoken dialogue, which was quite a new departure for me because I had never actually spoken on stage before. Recitatives are not the same thing, because they are spoken on the breath, in the singing position. But in this case, the moment I finished speaking I had to start singing, which is very, very difficult. I had to work hard to find a way of passing from speaking to singing and vice versa in a smooth way.'

This edition made it easier for her to discover the character from the dramatic point of view. She was also greatly helped by the director Cesare Lievi, who developed a 'specifically eighteenth-century psychology' for the role: '*Nina* was premièred in the year of the French Revolution and is rooted in pre-revolutionary mentality. This historical background is crucial in understanding the opera, because the crux of the work is Nina's relationship with her father, a typically eighteenth-century relationship. Everything that has happened to her before the beginning of the opera and which has caused her to feign insanity happened because of her father and what he had arranged for her, which ruined her life'. Nina's father originally agrees to allow her to marry her beloved Lindoro. But almost on the eve of the wedding, her father changes his mind and decides to accept the offer of an even richer and more highly-born suitor. The two suitors meet by chance on Nina's property and fight a duel in which Lindoro is wounded. Nina faints. When she recovers and sees Lindoro on the ground she believes him dead and lapses into madness'.

Bartoli considers that Nina's relationship with her father is the key to her 'madness', and thus to its interpretation on stage. 'Nina is not really mad. She is feigning madness and using it as an escape route to freedom, because this is the only way she can survive without either having to marry a man she doesn't love or becoming a nun, which she would automatically have been forced to do, as women were in those days. I feel this is still relevant today, because although parents no longer have the power to enforce their will on their children, many of them nevertheless still try to interfere and influence their lives.'

In addition to the dramatic challenge of portraying a character acting a part of a mad girl (who does it so well that at one point she almost does become mad), Bartoli found *Nina* a very interesting experience musically. With her director Lievi and conductor Adam Fischer she revived a tradition in keeping with the practice of Paisiello's day. They interpolated an aria 'Ah, lo previdi', by Mozart, that he had written to the text of Paisiello's *Andromeda*. 'The insertion of arias by different composers into operas was very widely practised at the time. Mozart had already written an aria for Paisiello's *Il barbiere di Siviglia* as well as for works by Piccinni, Galuppi and Hasse, while we also know that Haydn wrote and inserted his own arias into all the operas he performed at Eszterháza. We chose to interpolate this particular aria by Mozart because it had been written to the text of *Andromeda*, and it seemed interesting to revive this tradition and bring together those two composers, who were so linked in their time. Of course, at the time, Paisiello was by far the more famous and successful of the two.'

Mozart's aria was, indeed, the most difficult moment in *Nina* from the vocal point of view. 'All of this opera was difficult. But there were moments which were especially so and demanded tremendous concentration. "Ah, lo previdi" was perhaps the most difficult, because anything written by Mozart is both very difficult and a great responsibility. I always feel a sense of awe when I have to tackle a piece by Mozart. Because in Mozart, we are completely naked, completely unarmed. We cannot fake anything. And if, as I do, you consider Mozart the greatest of all geniuses, then you cannot help wondering: how can I *dare*? How can I find the courage, to sing this music? Of course, at the time of performing, you have to shake off this sense of responsibility in order to bring joy to your singing. But basically, this is how I approach Mozart and, to a lesser extent, all the composers I sing.'

To my remark that it is unusual for a singer to be so well informed musicologically, Bartoli exclaims, 'But it is my job! I love singing, but I also love historical and musicological research into the works I perform. The historical background is very important, especially for someone like me who has such a strong preference for Baroque music, which corresponds to what I can do vocally.' This is why, in performance, Bartoli never gives the impression of being in any way scared or nervous of the very difficult music she sings. The impression is always one of joy. 'Musically I'm never anxious or afraid because I have solved and mastered all the technical vocal problems before I come to rehearsals. You *have* to do this in advance, on your own. You cannot allow the vocal side to create problems in your interpretation.' She added that for *Nina*, for instance, she worked out all the technical, vocal side before beginning to work, privately, on the character with the director.

Away from the stage, Bartoli is as natural, down to earth and unspoilt as can be. Her charm and spontaneous warmth (evident in the graceful courtesy with which she greets each in her throng of fans) render her instantly likeable. 'I never wanted to be a diva,' she explains, almost apologetically. 'The career came, and I was there'. The real Bartoli is far (perhaps deliberately far) from the glossy diva image staring out of countless posters and record sleeves. She turned up for the premiére party of *Nina* on the stage of the Zürich Opera without make-up and wearing nondescript clothes. She had already explained in *You* that 'the way I look is important, but not that important. I'm not Claudia Schiffer. I don't live by looks alone. All I want from my clothes is to be comfortable. People don't expect that, of course. They imagine a diva putting on her diamonds and high heels at eight o'clock in the morning.' (A *diva* getting up at eight o'clock in the *morning*! I have yet to see this, Cecilia!)

Yet small, plumpish (what the French charmingly call 'rondelette') and effervescent, Bartoli effortlessly dominated the overcrowded premiére party. Whether she likes it or not, she *is* a diva, a real diva in the best sense of the word, which is to say that her vocal material and artistry is of top quality, her personality lights up the stage and fires the public's imagination and she delivers the goods every time. There have been only very, very rare exceptions to this, such as her lacklustre Salzburg début in an uninspired production of *Così*. Her wise decision to go for quality and underexposure, rather than the opposite, helps preserve her voice, star status and market value. Yet money is not what makes Cecilia Bartoli tick. When a journalist, amazed at the battered Fiat Topolino in which she drives herself around Rome, teased her about not having a Ferrari, she exclaimed, 'Are you kidding? I'm a mezzo soprano, not a tenor!' Last year she turned down $1,000,000 to sing in an American stadium. 'Life is too short to concentrate only on making money. Sure, I like caviar, but I'm just as happy with a plate of beans. Some people's tastes change with fame but I think I've kept my feet on the ground.'

What really makes Bartoli tick is her dynamic, almost febrile passion for what she does – not just for her own singing, but for the voyage of discovery involved in musicological research, the human and artistic camaraderie of rehearsal and of course her deep and infectious love of music. But she is acutely aware that there is a life after the end of an operatic career, a life that can be all too empty if the singer hasn't paid any attention to the 'human' side of life *during* her career and developed interests, friendships and personal relationships. She is determined that this will never happen to her.

Her own personal life appears happy and fulfilled at the moment. She has a serious attachment to a young man called Claudio, who owns a vineyard in the Veneto where they spend many happy weeks between her engagements. He also attends most of her opening nights and recording sessions. The rest of her free time is spent in the flat in Rome that she shares with her mother Silvana (now separated from her husband, with whom Cecilia remains friends) and architect sister Federica. This is where she gets her 'fix of real life': 'When you are twenty, you want to leave home. When you are thirty and travelling all over the world, you can't wait to get back there. Home is where you sleep well, eat well and where you can be yourself,' she told *You* last year.

As Claudio had just arrived to pick her up, I thought I would wind up our conversation by asking whether there was anything she wouldn't like to die without having done. 'Having a child,' was her immediate, unhesitating reply. 'Nothing seems so sad to me as to live a life without one. Yes, I know it's hard to combine motherhood with a career such as ours. But it can be done. It's also very important to have a private life and combine it with one's professional activity. In the past, singers used to neglect this side and sacrifice everything to their career. But in my generation, we want it all.'

OLGA

BORODINA

'YOU WON'T HEAR better singing than this. Anywhere. Why do tenors get all the fame and fortune? What about moody, magnificent and majestic mezzo sopranos?', wrote the *Glasgow Herald* after Olga Borodina's solo recital at the 1994 Edinburgh Festival. The point raised is fair enough, and the adjectives chosen particularly apt to describe Borodina's artistic presence and personality. Her velvety, erotic mezzo voice has earned even more extravagant yet richly deserved superlatives: 'An extraordinary instrument,' according to Peter Katona, Artistic Administrator of the Royal Opera, 'pouring out tones like molten gold' (the *Sunday Telegraph*).

Borodina is one of the shining stars of the new generation of Russian singers that began to flood into the West when the old Soviet Union started opening up. The phenomenon of so many young, good-looking singers, excellently trained musically and mostly with good vocal techniques, astounded everyone in the operatic profession even though some of the singers lacked refinement and stylistic finesse. Borodina explains that this 'phenomenon' was not really new, and that the sudden emergence of so many very good Russian singers was not sudden at all. 'There have always been plenty of great voices, including many great mezzos, in Russia. But people in the West didn't know about them. What changed everything was the fact that, suddenly, we were allowed to travel. Even Chaliapin, who had been very well known in Russia for a long time, only became internationally famous when he emigrated to the West. Personally, I was very lucky that the beginning of my career coincided with the opening up of the Soviet Union. Otherwise, it would have been impossible for me to have an international career. In a way, my generation has had the best of both worlds: freedom to travel, plus the benefit of the excellent, state-provided musical education.'

Ever since her childhood, Olga Borodina wanted to be a singer. 'I always had this drive, this longing to sing. There was never a conscious moment of choice. Singing was what I always wanted to do, the *only* thing I ever wanted to do. Nobody in my family was a musician, but my parents loved music and engaged in sing-songs whenever we had guests. But I just had this dream. I didn't even have a voice at the time. So I started working on it and developing it, by myself. I joined a children's choir and, as I had a good ear, I worked on it until it slowly started to develop.'

Towards the end of her high school years, she went for an audition at the Leningrad Conservatoire. But they wouldn't accept her. This didn't altogether surprise her because her self-taught voice was still at a stage when it was constantly changing. Instead, she enrolled at a lesser establishment, the Music School which was under the umbrella of the Conservatoire, while working at a chemical laboratory to make ends meet. After two years at this school and after her third audition, she was finally accepted at the Conservatoire, where she studied for five years. According to Borodina, the teaching of vocal technique there left a lot to be desired. 'At the time, there was a very strange, authoritarian school of thought in Russia and this extended to music. Teachers would force their own technique and way of singing on their pupils, regardless of whether this was suitable for their individual voices. I don't know how things are now, but this is how they were then. As you know, this is wrong: no teacher's method can work for everyone, although it may work for some pupils. I quickly understood that the method of my teacher, Irina Bogachova, was not quite suitable for me, so I tried to adapt her method to my own voice. I always think of myself as self taught, because I really worked out my own technique and vocal development.'

Borodina is acutely aware of the tendency of many Russian singers to sound unidiomatic in Italian, French and Mozartian singing. She is sure that this stems from the fact that 'the technique taught in Russian conservatoires is good and valid only for Russian singing. It is impossible to sing anything else, such as Italian opera, with that technique and voice placement. It sounds utterly wrong. "Style" and all it implies was totally unknown to us until we came to the West. And, of course, all the operas were always performed in Russian, even in the big theatres such as the Bolshoi and the Kirov. None of us were ever taught foreign languages, either at school or the Conservatoire. And, believe me, it is much more difficult to set about learning a foreign language when you are an adult, especially a working adult. This was a pity because the overall musical – as opposed to the purely vocal – part of our education was excellent.'

During her third year at the Conservatoire Yuri Temirkanov, the superb conductor of the Kirov (now Mariinsky) Theatre, took her on as a member of the company. 'And this is where I really started to develop. The theatre had good coaches, with whom I studied all my repertoire; and, of course, stage experience itself is a great teacher.' Her first role there was Siébel in Gounod's *Faust*, and her first important part Marfa in Musorgsky's *Khovanshchina*, which she eventually also sang abroad, both with the Kirov and other companies. It remains one of her favourite roles.

Borodina considers Marfa to be 'a very difficult role, both musically and dramatically. In both those senses, one can spend a lifetime developing it. Every time you return to it, your own attitude and relationship to her changes, and so consequently, does your interpretation. My own understanding of love, pain and spirituality has changed over the years, as I became older. Inevitably this affected my view of Marfa, who is such a rich, deep, many-sided character, a very spiritual character who reveals a new facet every time you come to sing her, sometimes in the simplest phrases. For, as often happens in life, the simplest things sometimes hold the key to insight into the most complex truths!

'Of course, Marfa is a historical character in an opera based on real events. *Khovanshchina* is set in history, and is *about* history. This already places the character within a certain dramatic context. Like most Musorgsky heroines, she is steeped in political and dramatic events. Undoubtedly, Marfa is a religious fanatic. Many consider her a witch, a madwoman who burns herself out of love, divines the future in a bowl of water, and so on. I think that, on the contrary, she is a very intelligent woman, a real politician who knows, a priori, the inevitable eventual outcome and who manipulates everyone and everything accordingly. But, unlike Marina Mniszek in *Boris Godunov*, [a role Borodina first sang in the West at the Paris Opéra in 1992, and with which she made her Metropolitan début in December 1997] whom I don't like, Marfa has very deep, genuine feelings. Musically, it's beautifully written for a low mezzo voice, and very comfortable to sing. Your vocal interpretation very much depends on whom you're singing it with, because most of the time Marfa is singing *with* someone. There are moments when she sings alone, of course, usually very simple lines, full of meaning. But most of the time, you must adapt to your partners.'

Borodina's favourite Russian opera is Rimsky-Korsakov's *The Tsar's Bride*, in which she sings Lyubasha, and which is an altogether easier, simpler work 'which goes straight to people's hearts. Even people who don't know what it's about can respond to it because the music, which is full of folk tunes and not very difficult, touches their souls. On top of this, the plot is straight out of real life: once a woman has given a man everything, all her love, he loses interest and turns to another. This strikes a universal chord that everyone can identify with.'

Shortly after Borodina's début as Marfa, the Kirov began to travel abroad. They had already sent her to an international competition in Barcelona in 1989, where the judges included Placido Domingo. He remembered her well and when, two years later, the Kirov were performing Musorgsky's first opera, *Salammbô*, at the Merida Festival, he asked her to join him for the final scene of *Carmen* in his solo concert conducted by Rostropovich. She had only a week to learn it – in French. Afterwards both tenor and conductor appeared so delighted they announced to the press that Borodina was their 'god-daughter'.

It was Domingo who launched her international career in earnest when he suggested her as his partner at the Royal Opera's revival of Elijah Moshinsky's production of *Samson et Dalila* in 1992. 'This was the first time I was singing abroad alone, away from and without my theatre. Apart from that one duet from *Carmen*, it was the first time I was singing in a foreign language. I learnt the French style, which is difficult for a Russian, with the coaches at Covent Garden.'

I was at the opening night and can testify that she was both vocally and dramatically perfect. The critics concurred. She earned an ovation as long and noisy as Domingo's. The *Sunday Telegraph* wrote that she 'sang with a tone like molten gold, supple and thrilling in the lower register, secure at the top apart from a momentary tightness', while *The Times* was equally enthusiastic: 'In an outstanding Royal Opera début, Olga Borodina didn't make any attempt to sugar the malice and religious fanaticism which motivates Dalila . . . Her voice is all of a piece throughout its compass and devoid of Slavic throb but instead a Slavic muskiness that adds credence to Saint-Saën's raven haired temptress. She took "Mon coeur s'ouvre à ta voix" with proper, caressing softness for once: a Dalila lissom in voice and limb'. This interpretation was a deliberate choice, for Borodina finds Dalila 'more romantic than many of my French and most of my Italian roles. She, too, is a political lady, but very erotic, very sexy, and the music is also very sexy. Yet there are moments in it that make it clear that she doesn't love him anymore, that she's doing this only for political ends.

Yet this is a contentious point. In certain moments I always wonder: could she be pretending one hundred per cent, especially in that gorgeous aria, "Mon Coeur s'ouvre à ta voix"? Because a woman can't pretend to such an extent, I don't think. She must have still felt some of her previous love, or infatuation for him. After all, he was a young, big, beautiful, heroic man.' Borodina is due to sing Dalila again for the opening of the Metropolitan's 1997–8 season.

After her spectacular triumph at Covent Garden, Borodina's international career took off in earnest. She was immediately invited back for *La damnation de Faust* under Colin Davis, to the Salzburg Festival for Dargomïzhsky's *The Stone Guest*, and to the Metropolitan for the Kirov production of *The Queen of Spades* and *Boris Godunov*, which she also sang in concert performance with the Berlin Philharmonic in 1993. In 1994 she returned to Covent Garden to sing the title role in *La Cenerentola*, in which she also made her début at the San Francisco Opera in 1995. Although most critics were more than satisfied, personally I didn't find Borodina totally convincing in this part, either vocally or dramatically. She had mastered both the language and the coloratura, but there was a slight impression that her voice was a little bottom-heavy for the part, and that its real centre of gravity lay a trifle lower than the tessitura of this role. Although she sparkled dramatically and looked dazzling at the finale, her presence was altogether too healthy and wholesome for this heroine, especially in Act I. I prefer to see this sublime mezzo in roles which she can sing better than anyone, and was relieved to hear that, as she explains later, she plans to drop Cinderella from her repertoire. This brought us to the question of whether she herself enjoys the sound of her own voice.

'Sometimes. But very seldom. When I feel one hundred per cent healthy and rested, yes. But the times when we, singers, feel fully healthy – when we have no allergies, no hint of a cold, no stress and no fatigue – amount to about once a year! It's very rare that I feel physically so well that I am free to do anything I like with my voice, free to interpret without fighting anything.' Borodina in fact has the constitution of a proverbial ox, which she stretches to the limits by singing concerts and recitals at schedules so tightly packed that they would certainly flatten anyone less robust. 'Can I think of an occasion when I felt really pleased with myself? Mmmm, let me think. Yes, the last time I sang a concert of duets with Hvorostovsky in London's Barbican Hall. And the last of my recent run of performances of *Carmen* at the San Francisco Opera [November 1997], where I finally sang this role for the first time. I say finally because I had been asked to sing it many times, but always refused, because I was scared. I always associated Carmen with danger, possibly because so many of the world's best mezzos have already sung it. So there was a stereotype of her in my mind. And I very much didn't want to conform to this stereotype. I wanted my Carmen to be different from everybody else's. I am rather phlegmatic by nature, so I couldn't identify with or find the energy for a scenically "busy" Carmen.

'I wanted my Carmen to be more still, more sure of her own sexuality, confident enough to know that by just sitting or standing there and emoting, she can get any man she wants. So I decided to give it a try, in a production by San Francisco Opera's general director, Lofti Mansouri. But I was right about one thing: that sense of danger I told you about a minute ago. Because two days before the dress rehearsal, my father died. So I wasn't all there in every performance. Maybe this was a good thing, because the papers wrote that Borodina's Carmen was good and quite *different*.' She adds with a twinkle that it could hardly have been otherwise because, apart from her view of the role, she was inthe first stages of her pregnancy at the time and weighed 'a hundred kilos'. 'But in the last performance, I *was* all there, and felt pleased with my performance.'

The *San Francisco Chronicle* concurred: 'From her first entrance, Borodina's Carmen projected precocious weariness, sexy earthiness and utter willpower. Hers was a young woman who had seen it all and had them all. Tragedy was foretold from the moment she set eyes on the handsome Basque officer.'

In addition to her close collaboration with Gergiev at the Mariinsky Theatre, Borodina has during the course of her career worked with some of the world's greatest conductors. To her great sadness Solti died a week before they were due to perform two concerts, in September 1997. She has also worked with such outstanding directors as Harry Kupfer, for Covent Garden's *La damnation de Faust* and Elijah Moshinsky for *Samson et Dalila*. 'I've been very lucky only to work with very good directors who have something to say, or in revivals, such as Ponnelle's *La Cenerentola*. Because it's so rare to see a really interesting production today – most are so boring. Mainly one comes across directors who know and understand nothing about music or opera, and have even weirder designers. Sometimes the works get so dreadfully distorted that your hair stands on end. And it's not always a question of transposing the work out of its period. I sang in a very modern but very interesting production of *Khovanshchina* in Hamburg, for instance. The important thing is to have ideas and to want these ideas to serve, to illuminate the work at hand, rather than just to capture the headlines with yet another "scandal".'

Looking to the future, Borodina points out that for a mezzo voice like hers, there are not all that many 'big, interesting roles' available. The trouser roles are obviously out, but an exciting possibility would be Didon in *Les Troyens*, for which she would be ideal. She has already sung Eboli spectacularly well at a Royal Opera Promenade Concert at the Albert Hall, and has also recorded the role. 'But whatever you like to say about the part or my performance, Eboli is a very short, secondary role with only one big aria. The Veil Song, which is sung in the garden, is not "in character", but a song sung simply to entertain the court. It is not even written in a typically Verdian style, but is more in the style of Rossini, with a lot of coloratura. The tricky thing about it is that it is light and requires agility, while Eboli's big Act IV aria, "O don fatale" is very, very dramatic. So you practically need two voices for the part.' However lukewarm Borodina's own response to the role may be, it is fervently hoped that she will go on singing it for years, for it suits her voice. 'Borodina's rich mezzo brought the house down in her fourth act aria; just as impressive was her playful seductiveness in that most psychologically telling of operatic serenades, the Veil Song', wrote the *Daily Telegraph* after the Albert Hall Prom in July 1997.

Another Verdi role beckoning is Amneris in *Aida*, which she will sing at the Vienna State Opera with Placido Domingo conducting – an all Russian *Aida* with Maria Guleghina in the title role and Vladimir Bogachov as Radames. Because she is now taking on these heavier roles she is thinking of abandoning Rossini, at least to a very large extent, because the two styles are not compatible. 'Although it would be good to sing Rossini occasionally to preserve the freshness and agility in my voice – maybe Isabella in *L'italiana in Algeri* one day.' This, one feels sure, is indeed the right way for Borodina to go. Vocally, physically and temperamentally, she is far better suited to womanly rather than girlish roles, and she is sure to prove as outstanding a Didon and Amneris as she is an Eboli and Dalila. Charlotte in *Werther* is another role that might suit her, though she did not mention the part in our interview. In the Verdian repertoire, there is little else she could try. 'Ulrica is a contralto and Azucena is for, let's say, mezzos of a certain age. While I'm still capable of singing big roles, I don't want to throw myself away for small change.'

For this reason Borodina now devotes over half her time to concerts and recitals. 'The song literature is vast, and full of beautiful music for the mezzo voice. Although I have always thought of myself as an opera singer, I must say that I derive enormous satisfaction from recitals, especially in small, intimate halls such as the Wigmore Hall in London, where I can really see the faces of my audience. But recitals are very difficult things. The composition of a song recital usually consists of several different styles and languages and composers within a span of under two hours, and this makes them very difficult to sing. I always study and coach extra hard before recitals and write the exact translation of every word in my score, so that I know what I'm singing at every second. This is essential for colouring the words appropriately.

You say that I give the impression of being a calm person who is not easily nervous before performances. Well, in this case, appearances are deceptive! I am very, very nervous, everywhere, every time. Because one very much wants to do a good job, and anyone who really cares about doing that tends to worry. It's natural, especially before recitals where one has to face so many different composers and styles.' Borodina has given solo recitals, sometimes accompanied by the brilliant Larissa Gergieva, sister of the conductor Valery Gergiev, at La Scala, Alice Tully Hall in New York, the Théâtre des Champs-Elysées in Paris, the Grand Théâtre de Genève, the Hamburg State Opera, the Accademia di Santa Cecilia in Rome, the Auditorio Nacional in Madrid and at the Edinburgh Festival, to name but a few. She now spends half her time abroad, sometimes with the Mariinsky Theatre, and half at home in St Petersburg.

Borodina describes herself as someone of lethargic temperament, a 'homebody' who loves to potter about the house and cook whenever she gets a chance. On the day of a performance, she tries to have 'an absolutely normal day. I eat, talk, walk, and do what I would normally do. After the performance, I feel very steamed up. I want to go out, eat, talk to people, discuss the evening and so on.'

What are her dreams for the future? 'I have had a very slow progress,' she says – surprisingly for someone whose career hit top gear at just over thirty. 'My career didn't develop suddenly or rapidly, but moved gradually, progressively upwards. I am grateful for this because the quicker you hit the top, the harder it is to stay there. And it hurts so much to fall down! I really don't want that to happen to me. So I never jump at anything that is offered me without first thinking about it very carefully. Dreaming doesn't enter into the picture! For example, although I love some soprano roles and would love to be able to sing them, I understand that I shouldn't. So every time anyone suggests such a thing, I sit down and think about whether this would be a good thing and how it would affect my voice. And my answer is always "no". As you mentioned dreams, my dreams would be to be able to sing

Desdemona. I think it's *my* part: I feel it, I love it, it's inside me. I love both the story and the music. But my voice and I know that it's not for us. So, I limit myself to humming it around the house.'

When asked about her interests or hobbies away from the musical and operatic world, she sighs: 'I have a family [A twelve-year-old son Alexei from her first marriage, a baby boy born in early April 1998 by her second husband]. They absorb a lot of time and energy. I am lucky to be able to leave Alexei with my mother when travelling abroad, otherwise I couldn't have any peace of mind. I like forests, I like water, and I like fishing which combines proximity to both. I love many other things, but I never have time for them. A singer's life demands a lot of sacrifices. Sometimes I feel like I want to chuck it all and live like a normal human being.

'But, now that I have not been working for two months [Borodina was at the last stages of her pregnancy at the time], I catch myself thinking that I can't live without singing. I am tired of not singing. I miss it terribly. I miss this thing pouring out of me and, especially, I miss the giving, which is, perhaps, the most marvellous aspect of singing. All of us have a lot in life and singing is definitely my lot. Sometimes, for instance, I feel totally listless, as if I have no energy at all. Yet the moment I walk onstage, I feel this something, this force coming to me from somewhere above; and suddenly I exude so much energy that it's enough for each of the two thousand or so people out there. So I must conclude that singing is my purpose in life.'

SUSAN
GRAHAM

SUSAN GRAHAM IS a perfect example of the new generation of
American singers. She combines a creamy, seamless high lyric
mezzo voice with tall, slim, alluring good looks; her outgoing, instantly
likeable personality is matched by a very high degree of professional
integrity. Even the most pernickety of critics would find it hard to fault
her, for her self-knowledge is so accurate and her self-critical faculty
so acute that she has, so far, avoided any mistakes in her choice of
repertoire. She is well-known in trouser roles such as Cherubino,
Octavian, the Composer, Chérubin, Cecillo (*Lucio Silla*) and Sesto (*La
clemenza di Tito*), and has also sung Dorabella, the title role in
Alexander Goehr's restructured version of Monteverdi's *Arianna* and
French parts such as Charlotte (*Werther*) and Marguerite (*La damnation
de Faust*). She is also a thrilling concert singer and a budding recitalist.

'She comes from that perfectionist, confident American background
and is a very hard worker,' remarks Peter Katona, Artistic Administrator
of the Royal Opera, Covent Garden. 'She can do anything, has learnt
everything, is always excellently prepared, her languages are good, in
fact all the elements that go to make a well-rounded artist are there.
She cannot be thrown by any crisis but can cope with any unforeseen

circumstances with a most un-primadonna-ish attitude. This American professional ethos makes her a delight to work with and much loved by conductors and directors. At the same time, she has a nice, characterful edge.'

I first met Susan Graham in December 1997 during rehearsals for the Paris Opéra's production of *Der Rosenkavalier*. The public and critical acclaim that followed the premiére came as no surprise to those who knew Graham's portrayal of Octavian from the Welsh National, the Vienna or the Bavarian State Opera, or who witnessed the touching vividness with which she experienced the character.

'I see Octavian as an amalgamation of Cherubino and Don Giovanni,' says Graham. 'He's still young enough to have his feelings hurt and to cry, yet old enough to think he can change the world and to see himself as a huge gift to womankind! We all carry our own lives and experiences inside us all the time and I find that, depending on the circumstances and the colleagues I'm working with, I bring out slightly different qualities in Octavian, qualities I've experienced in people in my own life. Of course, the freedom to do this has come only after doing so many performances of the role with so many different casts. And after going through so many revolving doors and cast lists, all you are left with is your relationship with the character. Which means that, for me, Octavian is the kind of boy I would like to have dated. And as such I want him to be dashing and heroic and kind of cavalier, but underneath it all very sensitive, very giving, affectionate and well able to take care of women; and at the same time very playful and active and bursting with youthfulness, athleticism and sense of fun.'

Crucial to the success of any production of *Der Rosenkavalier* is the interplay between the three principal characters, the Marschallin, Octavian and Sophie. The Opéra Bastille had assembled a dream cast, with American sopranos Renée Fleming and Barbara Bonney as the Marschallin and Sophie, partnering Graham's Octavian – surely this generation's answer to Munich's dream combination of the late 1970s and 80s of Gwyneth Jones, Lucia Popp and Brigitte Fassbaender.

Indeed, the performances turned out to be vocally stunning. But, as both Renée Fleming and Barbara Bonney explain in their respective chapters, the cast felt that some of the human element so crucial to this opera was missing from Herbert Wernicke's production, set in some indeterminate part of the 20th century. They found it too detached and overly formal, and tried hard to introduce some warmth and humanity themselves.

'There *has* to be real human warmth between the three main characters in this opera, who have to relate to each other in very distinct ways. This is especially true of Octavian who, above all others, *has* to be human because the action of the opera depicts his growing-up period. The way he relates to the Marschallin has to be different from the way he relates to Sophie. With the Marschallin he's very much the child but with Sophie he is a grown-up. He is the nurturer, the one who takes care of her and supports her when she's so overcome with emotion. And although, like Barbara Bonney, I think the relationship may run into trouble in the future, for *that moment* it's magic: he's wallowing in it and it's the only thing he's thinking about. That's why I linked him to Don Giovanni. At that moment Octavian believes that it will last forever. In fact, both of them believe this passionately, and this total conviction must be conveyed to the audience.'

Graham first opened the score of *Der Rosenkavalier* in 1981 when she was studying music at Texas Technical University, a college specializing in Engineering and Agricultural Sciences but also boasting an excellent music department. (Bruce Ford is another alumnus.) Part of the course was a very ambitious 'scenes' program, for which Graham had to perform the Act I Finale from *Così fan tutte* and the Act II Trio from *Der Rosenkavalier*. 'I remember thinking that this was the hardest music ever written, with all the different metres and everybody singing something different – which, of course, is what makes it so great – and having to sustain your line in the midst of this mayhem. But, after finally learning it I felt, "Wow, this is like flying". It's an incredible thing to be part of, and the way the three voices are interwoven is amazing.'

Although she as fascinated by *Der Rosenkavalier*, she had no reason to learn the whole role because nobody was going to ask her to sing Octavian at that stage. The parts she was busy with at the time were Cherubino, Dorabella, Siébel (*Faust*) and Stéphano (*Roméo et Juliette*). After graduating from Texas and moving on to the Manhattan School of Music on a scholarship, she won yet another award that enabled her to participate in the San Francisco Opera's Merola Program for young singers, and spent a whole summer learning Octavian.

'This was in 1991, when I was in that 'Zwischenland' between being a masterclass student and a young professional. I went on to coach the role with Christa Ludwig, Elisabeth Söderström and Evelyn Lear – all three marvellous people. I well remember an incident from an Evelyn Lear masterclass in New York. She asked me to perform the opening duet from Act I. While I was singing "Wie du warst", she became the Marschallin and showed me how to throw her back on the bed. And at the point where I sing "Ich bin dein Bub" she (as the Marschallin) kept whispering into my ear "Kiss me, kiss me", to which I kept whispering back "I can't, not in front of all these people". But she insisted and when I finally managed it, she exclaimed "*That's* how it goes!"

'Everything is there in the score, and the only way of doing it is simply to let it unfold. For instance, you cannot mess with the moment Octavian and Sophie first set eyes on each other at the Presentation of the Rose. It's just a Holy Moment and as such is described by the music which is quite, quite breathtaking. Other Holy Moments? The end of the opening duet in Act I, when the birds start chirping, and light pours into the Marschallin's bedroom, and Octavian sings "Warum ist Tag" and they go back to bed; the spot in Act II where, after Octavian tells the Marschallin that he doesn't understand anything anymore, she replies "gar nichts" – that she can't either; the Marschallin's "ja, ja," in response to Faninal's remark about young people being what they are; the interplay between the Marschallin and Sophie after the former's entry at the inn and the little *nichts*, so graphically described in the music – "ra ta *tum*, ra ta *tum*, hmm, you're quite attractive, my dear"; and the very end where the Marschallin has a tear in one eye and a smile in the other.

'All these Holy Moments are so accurately described in the music that you simply cannot interfere. This is why so many contemporary directors will not go near it. They realize they cannot make their mark on it.' Carlos Kleiber, for many years the conductor of the classic Otto Schenk Munich production in which everything seemed to flow out of the music, remarked to the director at their first meeting that he wished him to be 'the translator of the music in terms of staging and acting', a task at which the latter succeeded brilliantly. Graham sang Octavian in this production in 1995, shortly after performing it, also with great success, at the Vienna State Opera. But she is thankful for the fact that her first chance to sing the role – at the Welsh National Opera in Cardiff in May 1994 – gave her a long rehearsal period, starting from scratch, and the opportunity to 'get it into my bloodstream'.

'There are far too many theatres in Europe where a singer just turns up, goes on stage and sings their part without ever *experiencing* it, unless, of course, they've sung it before. Barbara Bonney, for instance, sang her first Sophie under such circumstances. But it's far from ideal, especially for a role as long as Octavian. In fact the only difficulty in Octavian – a very well-written and comfortable role – is its length, and the fact that he has to be on stage virtually all the time.

'There is a break during the *levée*, but that's no help because I'm changing into Mariandel's clothes, then back into Octavian's, fixing the hair and make-up in my dressing room and then running back on stage for "Du bist traurig". The only real respite comes in Act II during Ochs's soliloquy, where he's reading the letter, and right up to the end of the act. And, would you believe, Wernicke here in Paris wanted me to stay on stage even then! But I said, no way! This is when I go to my dressing room and sit down. Because if I don't, I'll never make it to the third act. As Tatiana Troyanos used to say, the key to surviving the role of Octavian is to have your rest at the end of Act II! She was dead right.

The Act III trio is vocally one of the trickiest moments in the whole role to sustain because (a) it comes right at the end of a long evening and you are exhausted, (b), my line goes right through the passaggio, and (c), it's doubled by French horns. I always feel the urge to compete with the French horns which is stupid because there are five of them and one of me. So I'm torn between wanting to outblow them or lying back and letting the other two sing the passage with me just gliding above them. Needless to say, the latter is the smartest choice because there are still a lot of delicate things for me to sing after the trio. So I can't afford to give in to the temptation to try to outblow the French horns at that moment. But it's not easy to resist, because it's such an emotional climax that you just want to throw all your blood and guts into it. But if you did, you'd be shot out at the end.

'Act I presents no problems, it rides very well. Dramatically, you have to be able to see what's going wrong in Octavian's relationship with the Marschallin. Musically, the greatest moments come in the second half of the act. For me, one of the tenderest, most gorgeous lines, both musically and dramatically, is "Mein schöner Schatz". Because I don't have a boomy voice but a voice that I can scale back and float at the top in a way that makes me very happy – a facility I want to use as much as possible and as long as I can. I relish this moment in Act I, which is a perfect opportunity to do just that. It's up on G and F sharp, very high and floaty. And I love to turn everything around at that moment, because the Marschallin is wailing about stopping all the clocks. Just before Octavian launches into his passionate outburst, "nicht heute, nicht morgen", there is a moment where he shows a touch of such tender sensibility and vulnerability, where he *wants* to understand what she's going on about, he *wants* to be there for her, to be the cushion she can fall onto. She doesn't let him. But Sophie does, and this is why, through her, he becomes a man.'

Surprisingly, Graham explains that for her the hardest, 'most terrifying bits' of the role are the Mariandel scenes, where she has to be woman playing a man playing a woman, because there is no real singing. She just has to 'speak and act' in a silly voice and pretend to be drunk. There is pressure to be funny, 'and the funny bits are usually so overdone that it's hard to make it fresh enough to be funny again.' Despite this, and despite the role's length, Octavian is not a part she now feels nervous about before singing. 'I just feel there's a very big mountain there to climb every night. But the role almost flows by itself.' She feels far more nervous before singing her other famous Strauss trouser role, the Composer in *Ariadne auf Naxos*, which feels like 'climbing the Matterhorn!' This role, though much shorter than Octavian, is difficult because it is higher. 'Being that bit higher makes all the difference. So, although it amounts to about 45 minute's singing, at the end I feel as if I've been singing for four hours. This makes me feel much more nervous before the performance than I ever do about Octavian. As well as being higher, there is the added difficulty of having the big aria at the end, by which time – unless you've paced yourself very carefully in the big scenes with Zerbinetta and Ariadne and in the passionate outburst immediately before – you would be so exhausted that you could easily find yourself screaming instead of singing'. She points out that, as if this aria was not hard enough to sing on the ground, in Tim Albery's Munich production she was asked to sing it standing precariously on a tilted platform after having climbed a ladder! But Graham relished the challenge. 'I love thinking "this is impossible" and in the next breath "I'll do it!" I suppose it comes from being a double Leo (Sun and Moon) with Aquarius Ascendent!'

Graham considers the Composer a harder role, both dramatically and vocally. 'He is a much darker, more complex and tormented character than Octavian. He is an artist, a creator with an artist's demons inside. At the same time, he wants those demons exorcised by Zerbinetta, and pins all his hopes on her being his muse. But it doesn't quite work out that way. So I see him as brooding – not as sexual as Octavian – and tormented, sitting in a Parisian garret at a messy table full of scores, stacks of paper, cigarette butts and glasses of whisky – not wine, definitely whisky, it's more unhealthy. Although he does have moments of youthful optimism, it's harder for him to relate to others or to reality itself. He's a real "Weltfremder", a stranger to the world and its ways. His youthful idealism causes him to explode when his mentor points out that he has to go with the show "for the ducats", and makes him spit out that he doesn't care about *that*. I would say that this youthful idealist in his garret in Paris is definitely the hardest of all my trouser roles.' Graham's cool, clear-headed self appraisal – a quality seldom found to such a degree among singers – means that she is harder on herself that the public or critics ever give her cause to be. Of the Munich production of *Ariadne auf Naxos* the critic of *Opera Magazine* wrote: 'It was worth the trip for the Composer of Susan Graham, whose beautiful fresh, free mezzo has a top of soprano-ish ease and freedom, which makes her a marvellous exponent of the role.'

Trouser roles suit this willowy brunette, who oozes allure and walks tall. She moves beautifully, with a confident spring that probably stems from her healthy, athletic childhood and adolescence in New Mexico and Texas, where she used to play games and climb trees with the boys. Graham has often dwelt on the piquancy of playing those boyish male characters. She is intrigued both by the physical challenge – the different way of moving and walking – and by the challenge of under-standing the psychology from a male point of view.

Her most famous trouser role is Cherubino in *Le nozze di Figaro*, which she first sang as a student and has now performed worldwide. In 1995 and 1996 she sang Cherubino at the Salzburg Festival, where her portrayal was hailed as 'a Cherubino that will surely be talked about years hence' (the *Sunday Telegraph*), while *Die Welt* remarked that 'Susan Graham's touching Cherubino outshone all.'

'Cherubino is the best role in all opera! He gets to sing two great arias, that great Act IV Finale, and he gets the whole of Act III to sit in his dressing room and learn other roles – which I've done many times. He's also a great character: he gets to do comedy, he gets to be a seducer, he has some heartbreaking moments, in fact he has everything. And he's not very hard work. The arias are so brilliantly written that they almost sing themselves. And the whole Cherubino–Count relationship is very interesting. I feel he's still a child and very scared of the Count – although because of my height, I play a slightly more imposing and hormonally advanced Cherubino. In fact sometimes I'm taller than the singer playing the Count! Dmitry Hvorostovsky, for instance, had to pull himself to his full height when facing me – so I could show off! But with Counts such as Thomas Hampson I'd have to stand on a chair to be taller than him! The only time we sang *Figaro* together was in 1991, my first season at the Met, when I was covering Cherubino for Flicka [Frederica] von Stade, a singer I have always admired so wholeheartedly that I consider her one of the reasons I wanted to be in this profession. And, angel that she is, she secretly told me two weeks before that on such and such a date she was going to miss the performance, and to be very well prepared. So, this was the occasion I stood on a chair! But seriously, just for this role I regret not being five foot five. It can be kind of cute if Cherubino is the same height as the girls. There are some roles, such as Zerlina and Hänsel, which I haven't sung since my first season as a professional in Oregon and would love to sing again, but for which I'm almost too tall.'

Graham sang Cherubino shortly after our conversation at the Lyric Opera of Chicago in February 1998. The *Chicago Sun Times* commented that 'Graham is tall and her Cherubino had the sweetly klutzy air of a handsome young teen whose body – not to mention his hormones – are getting away with him. His Act I paean to Love's marvels ("Non so più") was full of breathless delight'.

Mozart's Cherubino is not Graham's only encounter with this mischievous hero, whom she has also sung in *Chérubin*, Massenet's tribute to Beaumarchais. 'In the libretto Chérubin is supposed to be three years older than Cherubino. He's seventeen – in fact the action takes place on his seventeenth birthday – the same age as Octavian. But Chérubin is more of a merry prankster. He is not yet interested in being too serious or taking life really seriously. He is less mature and poised than Octavian – at least the Octavian of the end of *Der*

Rosenkavalier — and can have his heart broken more easily; and he does, by Ensoleillad, whom he idolizes, before he, too, ends up with the "girl next door", Nina. In this sense there is a similarity between Chérubin and Octavian, who also both believe that this new-found love will last forever. But we *know* he's going to dump Nina. In Octavian and Sophie's case, it's not quite so obvious. But with Chérubin and Nina it's a mathematical certainty. We *know* she's going to have her heart broken by this little scamp!'

Chérubin was Graham's first French role, and she identified with the French culture and language right from the start. Her French diction was singled out for praise in most of the rave reviews that followed *Chérubin*: 'Her rich and wonderfully focused high mezzo was matched to crisp words and a very physical portrayal of the ardent adolescent', wrote John Allison in *The Times*. She subsequently made her début at La Scala as Marguerite in *La damnation de Faust* under Seiji Ozawa in 1995, and the following year sang Charlotte in *Werther* in Amsterdam in a production conducted by Edo de Waart and directed by Willy Decker. In the very early stages of her career she had already sung this role in Saint Louis in English, and she will sing it again at the Metropolitan Opera in the autumn of 1998.

'Charlotte is by far the most challenging role in my repertoire right now,' she stresses. 'Vocally it's high, it's low, it's soft, it's loud and both musically and dramatically it's so emotionally intense. Act III is a killer, in every sense of the word. The character is also very difficult for me because she is so contained that she imposes an almost classical corset on you. She is a woman constrained by duty, obligation and social convention, who denies herself what she most wants in life. She keeps quashing her true feelings, and that's a difficult state for me to project because I'm such a typically extrovert Leo character. Charlotte, on the other hand, I would put down definitely as a Virgo character. (Now that – the Astrology of Operatic Characters – would make an interesting book!) And for this reason it's hard for me to find the balance between her restraint and the bridge that leads to her great emotional outpouring, and to show what makes her finally go to him and want to save him. But of course, she's too late. Her feelings about this, on so many different levels, are so overwhelmingly intense that this scene is almost too much, too emotional. On top of this you have the music, which at that point is almost hysterical. "Seigneur Dieu" is just about the last straw – it's pain of an almost unbearable degree. You feel she's only a step away from committing herself to an asylum. Then there is the prospect of a future too awful to contemplate that hangs over the whole scene . . .

'Willy Decker in Amsterdam addressed this point very starkly and interestingly: as Werther dies and there is this last musical passage, the back wall of the stage opened and you saw the whole community with their backs to the audience and to us on stage. Then, very quietly, Charlotte walked back – staggeringly – perhaps without any feeling, yet knowing she has no other option, and joined them. Somehow she manages to pull herself together, away from the abyss, and join the townsfolk and children, her father and all those people who had been pointing fingers at her. And just before that, while Werther lay dying, Decker did another brilliant thing: he had Albert walk in and confront me silently, looking straight into my face, as if to ask why I chose to come to him, why I was there, why Werther shot himself and what was going on between us. In effect, he was saying "I know everything".'

Marguerite in *La damnation de Faust*, on the other hand, is what she calls a 'short and sweet' role, difficult only in that there is very little time for the artist to put the character across. 'You only have "Un Roi de Thule", "D'amour l'ardente flamme" and the trio, of which the most difficult is definitely "D'amour l'ardente flamme" because it has such a wide range. And the things that have always been the most challenging for me are not the roles or arias with the highest tessituras but those with the lowest. For this reason I would never venture into Dalila and think very carefully about Carmen, maybe in a very classical French way. I don't have a meaty voice so those are my scary areas – I would never risk sacrificing my easy top, which might be a very real risk if I took on those roles.

'I consider my greatest gift to be the fact that I have a very *natural* voice and voice production. I never had to *discover* a technique, it was always there. What was not there, and which I owe to my present teacher, Marlena Malas, was seamlessness. When I first went to her I had three different voices, bottom, middle and top. Now I have it unified from top to bottom so that it sounds seamless. I'm a very strong believer in going with what feels vocally right. I am very grateful for my top and the way I can slim the voice down when I have to, and I don't want to give that up for anything. As a singer you are what you are, and you should flow with that. Because of my easy top, about six people a day come and tell me I'm a soprano. But I'm not. And I'm not, nor could I ever be, a Verdi mezzo. [The only Verdi role she has sung is Meg Page in *Falstaff* at Salzburg and the Metropolitan.] I would never attempt either Eboli or Amneris. I don't think I can sing that low. That is why I'm not an Italian singer, full stop. Although I *can* sing Rossini. I don't think my Rosina was horrible or anything like that, but that's not where I live, vocally, temperamentally or spiritually. And Rossini *serio*, what I call Marilyn Horne-ville, is also out, because again that requires a lot more meat at the bottom than I'm comfortable with.'

Graham's repertoire also includes Dorabella in *Così fan tutte*, which she has performed at many venues, among them the Metropolitan Opera, the Paris Opéra (for the re-opening of the Palais Garnier) and at Covent Garden in the entertaining production directed by Jonathan Miller with costumes by Giorgio Armani. 'Susan Graham is a very special presence and an electrifyingly funny actress,' says Jonathan Miller. 'In fact one of the few opera singers who could walk straight off the operatic stage and into the movies. She belongs to the world of Diane Keaton: ironic, witty, a real New York American funny girl. Working with her was pure pleasure.' Surprisingly, she considers Dorabella 'one of the most ungrateful roles in my repertoire. You're on stage all night, you have great music, but you're always a third below, you're always singing below Fiordiligi. She gets "Come scoglio" and "Per pietà", while all Dorabella gets is "Smanie implacabili" for three minutes – which is sort of yelling and pulling your hair out – and "È amore un ladroncello", which is difficult and often cut. The rest of her music is wonderful but it's a long, exhausting role. You're on stage all the time but without the usual payoff – except for Mozart's music which is always a payoff in itself – in the sense that, like Guglielmo, you're always second banana to Fiordiligi. You're second banana all night long, and it takes an awful lot of work!

'As a character, Dorabella is interesting. She's a real sensualist, much earthier and more human than Fiordiligi'. (The late Karl Böhm used to say that one could tell by the excitement in the strings that she would be the first to give in.) 'I always imagine her as sloppier, more untidy than her sister, and I like playing her with a sense of humour and a spark in my eye, especially in that delightful little scene just before "È amore un ladroncello" where she says in the recitative: "Okay, sister, if we do it your way, if we don't go with these Albanians, what have we got? A handful of nothing! And you know, by the time those other guys come back, we'll be married to these sexy Albanians and miles away!" I call this little scene Dorabella's coming of age. And I like to show that little bit of anger and backbone at this point, and also a little touch of pain. You can play this scene in a confrontational and snappy way, and usually if someone is confrontational and snappy it's because they're hurt, they're in pain. Here I get the chance to show that real moment of pain in Dorabella. Yet, for the reasons I explained, one Dorabella every few years is plenty!'

Graham, whose delightful and sunny nature combines European sophistication with a touch of American wholesomeness, is both a sports addict and a computer freak who can spend an entire evening in front of her screen. The fact that she appears to have no hang-ups perhaps explains why she can be as clear-headed about her future as she is about her vocal attributes. She is interested now in further exploring the

Baroque and classical repertoires, and also taking on more French roles.

'I see myself as in between Flicka von Stade and Tatiana Troyanos. I love the Classical sensibilities of Handel and Gluck, and feel they would be perfect for me. I would also like to sing Idamante [*Idomenea*] and Poppea in Monteverdi's *L'incoronazione di Poppea*. I also *love* the classical world of Berlioz. I have just put Didon in *Les Troyens* in the calendar for after the Millennium. I might even stretch as far as Mignon.' Graham has already performed and recorded Berlioz's song-cycle *Les nuits d'été* (for Sony Classical), and has also released a solo album of French arias. '*Les nuits d'été* has taken a very special place in my heart and head and soul. I don't know what it is about this piece, but from the first moment I learnt it, it seemed as if I'd known it all along. Ravel's *Shéhérazade*? It's coming . . . I *love* the French style. And I always feel strangely at home here in Paris – it feels so *right*. And I'm utterly enthralled by French culture, that whole Versailles thing. Not just the gilding and so on. I would love to go back in time and live in the Louvre for a week: the dresses, the art, walks through the garden with a parasol and so on. That European decadence fascinates me.

'Come to think of it, it's strange. I'm a girl from New Mexico. There was nothing in my background or growing up to suggest that I would live a life like the one I'm living. Except, perhaps for the fact that I was always very extrovert and theatrical – again, typically Leo – always performing and showing off and standing on top of sofas to demonstrate my latest trick. I remember that when I was nine we had to do a book report at school and I chose a Sarah Bernhardt as a subject. My mother helped me dress up as Sarah Bernhardt and I stood up in the middle of the school theatre and did my little show. My mother, who would have loved to have lived a life like mine, was very supportive. She's very artistic, but she grew up in the wrong place and time, in a ranch in New Mexico, and never had a chance to explore or tap her talents.

'I know that many artists come from dysfunctional families, but my background was very stable, secure and normal. My eldest sister was more academic and shy. She was a good pianist but never liked the limelight or the stage. My brother was a star athlete. Both have been married for twenty-five years and have kids. My parents have been married for fifty years, all very normal. And here am I, thirty-eight years old and chasing around the world!

'There is a side of me that feels homesick for a place of my own. I have a place in New York where my furniture lives, but I don't see it very often: I'm *so* thankful I don't have any children! When I see colleagues who do, I know that if I did I'd be tortured. Look at what Flicka von Stade went through. I remember her flying back on Concorde for birthdays between performances of *Le nozze di Figaro* at the Paris Opéra. Torture! So I have a dog instead, Libby, whom I dote on and who travels with me to most places, except England, of course, because of quarantine. She's here in Paris right now, and was meant to be in the *levée* in *Der Rosenkavalier*, which is her best role! Though she did brilliantly in the orchestral pre-general rehearsal, she was sacked, would you believe, because she didn't have a union card and is not a "French professional animal actor"!'

DENYCE
GRAVES

'WHAT IMMEDIATELY IMPRESSED me about Denyce Graves, aside from her obvious vocal and physical beauty, was an aura of the dramatic about her', says Placido Domingo, of this sensational mezzo with 'a voice like spun gold' who went on to become *the* Carmen of this decade. Indeed, Domingo's only misgiving is that 'as Carmen she is *so* good that the world might want her exclusively for that. This would be a shame, because she has very much to offer in other parts.'

As usual, Domingo has hit the nail on the head. Firstly, because there has not been a Carmen such as Graves in a very long time; secondly because for a while it did indeed seem as if the operatic world wanted Graves only for her Carmen – one review even ran the title 'Denyce Carmen Graves'; and thirdly because she is equally impressive in other roles, such as Dalila (*Samson et Dalila*), Charlotte (*Werther*) and Giulietta (*Les contes d'Hoffmann*).

Graves points out that it was Carmen who came to her rather than vice versa. 'Carmen found *me*. And you can say she's been chasing me around now for a long time. My first experience of her was at a student workshop, where everyone was saying that if only I could come out of myself, I would make a great Carmen. I didn't agree with them and, in some ways, I still don't, even though Carmen and I have had a long walk with each other by now. Why? Because I'm more reserved, a lot shyer, less courageous and less assertive than she is. I wish I had more of this liberated attitude of hers, more of her free spirit that doesn't give a damn about what people think. All these are things I aspire to. I think Carmen may have come into my life for this purpose – to show me the things I need to acquire in my own life.' But at that time, the conductor and director at this workshop were throwing up their arms and wondering how they were going to cajole Graves out of her shell. The baritone singing Escamillo kept begging her to 'give a bit more' in their scenes, and she kept promising she would try.

Carmen did eventually force Graves's real artistic self to come out. But this did not happen until she sang it in Minneapolis in 1991, after the beginning of her career. The production was by the British director Keith Warner, and the designer was Jeanne Marie Lecca, who became a close friend. 'The production was so extreme that it forced me to stretch myself as an artist. It was very naked, very bold, very sexual and very violent. I had nothing to lean on, nowhere to hide. There was just a bare stage with a white wall and a couple of chairs. All the focus was on the music and the relationships, which were very clear, although stretched to extremes. I had no experience of Carmen as yet, no points of reference, but I knew that what was happening – venturing out of myself further than I ever had, or thought possible – was something very important. In fact, I would rank this as one of the three landmark productions of *Carmen* in my career.'

The next came nearly three years later, by which time Graves had sung the role triumphantly in San Francisco, Los Angeles (to Domingo's Don José), Vienna, Genoa, Berlin, Florence, Paris, Geneva, Covent Garden (again with Domingo), Zürich and Munich. It was Franco Zeffirelli's production in Verona in 1994–5 and it totally changed her view of the role. 'By then I had a vast experience of the part, in all sorts of different stagings. I was very open and keen to discover new things about her all the time. Within five minutes of our first meeting, Franco had turned my face in a different direction and changed my perspective forever. After agreeing that neither of us much cares for Habanera, which he called "a musical theatre number", and for which everyone has their own idea about how it should be sung, Franco added that he thought it a very *cynical* song. In the next breath he asked if I thought of Carmen as a happy woman. I replied that I did. But he went on to say that he thinks of her as a very *un*happy woman. I was astounded! I never imagined Carmen as unhappy, but as a carefree spirit who prized and wanted freedom above all. Franco replied this was precisely the reason for her unhappiness: because what she *fears* most is *loss* of freedom, the loss of control that goes hand in hand with being in love. He added that in his view Carmen is *desperately* in love with Don José. But because of this fear she tries to make herself as terrible as possible in his eyes. Being a kind of witch who sees into people's souls, she realizes something very powerful and magical is happening between them. And she's *afraid*: afraid of her feelings, afraid of what this can do to her, of what surrender would mean for her. Even *thinking* about her in this way, opening up my imagination and letting it flow with this idea, changed my entire perspective about Carmen.'

The third landmark production was Ann-Margret Pettersson's in Washington D.C. Graves says that this 'got rid of every stereotype about Carmen anyone might have had in their minds and gave her an extra twist. There were no gypsy skirts or anything like that. Just a vest and a black skirt. Everything hinged on projection of the character.'

Naturally, crucial to the shaping of any portrayal of Carmen is the tenor singing Don José, who necessarily brings out different facets of her character. Graves is not the same Carmen with Neil Shicoff that she is with Domingo. 'There's no way I could be. Placido is a very *gentle* Don José, while Shicoff is much more violent and confrontational. He hits out a lot – I even get bruises on my arms when I sing with him, not only as Carmen but also as Baba the Turk in *The Rake's Progress* [which she was then singing at the Met]. So, it's very hard to say who "my" Carmen is.'

That said, Graves adds that there are certain things about her portrayal of Carmen that remain, no matter who she's singing with or who is directing the show. 'First and foremost, the fact that she is a free spirit, a liberated woman, very much in charge of her life, very much in charge of her sexuality. A woman who prizes freedom above all. In the Habanera, she tells exactly who she is and what she thinks about love. She is also a fatalist. She feels this inexplicable attraction, this strange connection to Don José. Maybe because she sees in this passionate man – who we know has killed someone in his native Navarra – a reflection of her own wild self, which can be very exciting. That's one version. Another is that she sees him as a complete innocent, and finds this intriguing in a situation where all other men are throwing themselves at her which doesn't interest her.

'But whichever of these two views you prefer to believe, Carmen is never a whore or a loose woman, she never gives love for money. She is simply the undisputed queen of her environment. When she finds herself in chains, she does what she has to do in order to free herself. This often tends to be misunderstood. Once José frees her, she owes him a debt. In the version with spoken dialogue, she actually says that gypsies always pay their debts. Then, when she offers him this very special gift of singing and dancing for him – something very intimate and personal which she doesn't do for everybody, but a genuine gift to him – his rejection hits her like a slap in the face. I think that if José's superior officer hadn't arrived to try and court Carmen, that would have been it. Basta. I don't think she would have taken him back after such an insult. But then, when the superior officer comes, José shows another side of himself. When ordered back to barracks, he becomes insane with jealousy. Carmen finds this sudden switch interesting. You see, there are so many layers to this piece and so many different ways of seeing the character that it's dangerous to arrive for a production with preconceived ideas. You should arrive open, willing to allow yourself the freedom to recreate a new Carmen with each company. Then you make beautiful discoveries along the way and grow with it, and the piece also grows with you. Otherwise, especially when you do as many Carmens as I, you risk becoming stultified.

'Vocally, Carmen is no big deal. Like her spiritual twin Don Giovanni, who also dies rather than lose his freedom, the role does not stand or fall by vocal performance alone, although of course it needs to be well sung. Equally important are personality, presence and pizazz. You never have an occasion to sing, I mean *really* sing. Micaëla and Don José both have wonderful arias, but Carmen doesn't. The Habanera is sung with the chorus, the Seguidilla with Don José, the Gypsy Song with the girls, while the Card Scene, which is the nearest thing Carmen has to a proper aria, also starts off with Frasquita and Mercédes. So there's always some interpolation. So it's not really a very *gratifying* part.[1]

'At the same time, it's very difficult vocally because it doesn't give you much opportunity to get into the voice. The Habanera demands delicate singing the moment you walk on stage. This is always difficult because it takes time for you to get over your nerves and the adrenaline rush you experience when you walk on. For this reason singing something loud is easier at this point than something as delicate as the Habanera. In the Seguidilla, after you've sung the first verse, Don José butts in, so again you don't have the chance to get into your voice properly. Same in Act II, the Gypsy Song. You keep getting flickers of singing which are always interrupted. The longest uninterrupted singing you have is in the Card Scene, but by then we're already into Act III! And you've had that killer of an Act II when you've had to dance and jump on tables and run out of breath! So, much though I love performing Carmen, I have to state that vocally it's both ungratifying and difficult.'

---

[1] Grace Bumbry made precisely this point about Carmen in *Diva: Great Sopranos and Mezzos Discuss their Art*.

Graves's journey from the shy, introverted youngster of that first workshop production to 'the definitive Carmen of our age' (Martin Feinstein, former director of the Washington Opera), was not all that long. She rose to prominence quite quickly after her professional début in 1990-91. But the journey was exceptionally hard. She was born in one of the most deprived black neighbourhoods in the States: Galveston Street, Washington D.C. Southwest, a place of acute misery and helpless despair – no escape, nowhere to go – where violent crime is a way of life. Home was a tenement block near the sewage treatment plant and the District of Columbia car pound.

Memories of that childhood still haunt her, and she has never been back. One day, she recalls with a shudder, a friend of her brother was shot as he left their apartment. They never found out why. On another occasion as she made her way home from choir practice by bus, a man trying to get on at a bus stop was gunned down on the spot. Terrified, the driver and passengers leapt screaming from the still moving bus. 'I remember leaping over the body out into the night, in the rain, and just running, running and running in the dark. I didn't know where I was, and I didn't know where I was going. I just knew I had to get away from there, as far, far away as I could get.'

Graves's family could easily have become what is known as 'dysfunctional'. Her father was an abusive alcoholic who beat her mother so hard that the doctor, desperate that she should leave her husband, said he would be glad if next time he killed her. Denyce's father vanished leaving her mother pregnant with her younger sister. Denyce was then one and her brother three. The fact that the family produced not only a world-class diva but also two other well-adjusted people in good jobs, is entirely due to Denyce's mother, Dorothy Graves, a woman of exceptional vision, faith and pluck. Only years later did she admit that at times she was overwhelmed, and wondered how she was ever going to cope: 'I didn't want the children to know I was discouraged.' It is painful even to try and imagine what it must have been like for a woman alone to bring up three children in these circumstances. She took a job at the Federal City College (now the University of the District of Columbia), first as a laundress, then as a typist. She now works in the Registrar's office there. She was determined that her kids would stay off the crime- and drug-infested streets, and rise above the ugliness and despair around them. In this she was sustained by her passionate and unshakeable faith in God. The church and Gospel singing were part of daily life: she sang hymns every day with the children – the first song Denyce ever heard was 'Jesus Loves Me' – and would get so carried away that one day she let the pressure cooker explode, spreading greens all over the walls and ceiling.

She told Denyce that 'God has kissed your vocal cords', and always tried to push her to the front of the choir at their local Baptist church. This was part of a morale-boosting campaign aimed at keeping the childrens' spirits high. 'Every day she would line us up and tell us we were the most beautiful, clever and gifted children in the world', remembers Denyce. To keep their minds occupied and their bodies off the streets, she invented different tasks for them to perform each day and have ready for her when she came home from work.

Denyce was a shy, serious, highly motivated child who felt deeply ill at ease in her surroundings. Her mother described her as 'the most disciplined young person I've ever known'. She wanted out of Washington Southwest and into the great wide world. This did not endear her to her classmates or the neighbourhood kids, who perceived her as an 'oddball'. They made fun of her love of acting by calling her 'Hollywood', and taunted her with the ultimate insult: 'You want to be *white*'.

Her saviour was her music teacher at elementary school, Judith Grove Allen, her 'guardian angel'. Grove Allen was immediately struck by this 'different' child: 'Her voice was nice but not yet overwhelming in those very young days. What was impressive was her attitude: she was more interested, more committed – she was a go-getter'. Teacher and pupil became inseparable, right through junior High School. Then Miss Grove Allen announced that the only place for

Denyce was the Duke Ellington School for the Arts in located in the exclusive Georgetown neighbourhood in Washington Northwest. The school only admitted pupils on audition, something her teacher suggested she try. Wearing a brand new dress bought for the occasion, she sang the well-known Gospel song 'You Light Up My Life', and was accepted. Though she did not yet know it, this school would be her passport out of Galveston Street.

Immediately, she felt at home: 'Finally, I felt I could *breathe*. This school was heaven: an explosion of music, of people who loved and were passionately committed to whatever it was they were studying. All of us would make a habit of turning up early, before the doors were even open. Just standing outside, in the garden, made you feel special. There was one boy practising the trumpet, a girl balancing her leg in a ballet extension against a tree. Everyone was *fired* with enthusiasm and showed commitment to what they were doing.' To top it all, Judith Grove Allen became the principal, and watched over Denyce's musical progress. This was when she saw her first opera – the dress rehearsal of *Fidelio* at the Kennedy Center. She found the experience overwhelming, but as yet had no definite plans to become an opera singer – that came after hearing a recording of Marilyn Horne singing *Cavalleria rusticana*. Judith Grove Allen had already made up her mind that Graves was going to be 'the next Leontyne Price'.

On graduation from Duke Ellington, Graves won a partial scholarship to the distinguished Oberlin Conservatory in Ohio. But as the money was not sufficient Grove Allen coaxed the members of the Zion Baptist Church in Northwest Washington into organizing a fund-raising recital for Graves that provided enough money for her first year. Her mother, although proud of Denyce as the first member of the family ever to attend college, was uncomprehending: 'You're going to college to learn how to *sing*? You already know how to sing!'

So Graves headed for Ohio, out of the squalor of Washington Southwest forever. At Oberlin Conservatory she was again lucky in her voice teacher: Professor Hodden, who was so good that when she moved to New England Conservatory in Boston, Graves and a host of other students followed suit. Both in Ohio and Boston, life was very hard for Graves. To make ends meet, she did all sorts of jobs around the clock: waiting at tables, cleaning dormitories, baking doughnuts, washing dishes, assembling tacos or working as a night-time telephone operator in a Boston hotel, where she once had to put through a wake-up call to the famous bass Samuel Ramey. This meant she sometimes averaged no more than a couple of hours sleep. She also sang in the local church choir on Sundays for forty dollars. 'What didn't I do to make money', she remembers with a sigh!

Her voice was fast developing into the sensuous, velvety instrument we now know, and at her teacher's suggestion she entered the 1986 New England Metropolitan Opera auditions, which everyone expected her to win. 'I *had* to win! I was four months behind with my rent and couldn't even pay for the rented dress I was wearing.' She won. After graduating from New England Conservatory in 1987 she was supposed to go to New York for the final auditions. But the strain, and the long hours of overwork during the last seven years in Ohio and Boston took their toll. Her voice failed her. 'It was a disaster', she recalls. A curable thyroid condition was diagnosed as the cause, but Graves was so demoralized that there and then she decided to quit singing, and took a secretarial job.

However, her excellent performance in the preliminary local auditions meant that word about her had spread. The Houston Opera got in touch, inviting her to participate in its newly established pro-gramme for young artists. She was still so discouraged that she declined on the spot. But they kept ringing. The third time they called, Graves's friends persuaded her to look upon it as an omen and to accept.

Graves moved to Houston in the autumn of 1988 and stayed for two seasons, which proved the making of her career. Her first big part was the title role in *Hänsel und Gretel* but, most importantly, while she was learning the main repertoire in the studio programme she was also per-forming small roles in the main house. One of these was in a

production of *Otello* (with Domingo in the title role), in which she sang
Emilia. Domingo was impressed, and was to prove an important force
in launching her career. Graves herself was by now fiercely motivated
and 'incredibly competitive'. In 1989 she was awarded the Richard F.
Gold Career Grant by the Houston Opera; and in 1990, at the end of
her apprenticeship, she won just about every major American musical
award there is: the Marian Anderson Award (presented by the great
lady herself), the much coveted George London Career Grant and a
Jacobson Study Grant from the prestigious Richard Tucker Music
Foundation, which invited her to perform at its 1990 gala concert,
always a very major musical event in the States. In the wake of this
cascade of American awards came the Grand Prix du Concours
International du Chant de Paris!

Her personal life was happy, too. In 1989, while still apprenticed at
Houston, she met her husband, guitarist and lutist David Perry, at one
of her first professional engagements – as the Sorceress in Purcells's
Dido and Aeneas – with a Virginia-based company called Wolf Trap. He
was playing the lute in the orchestra, and that was it. She was twenty-
four, he thirty-nine. His family, which is full of musicians, was instantly
welcoming. Hers were 'less fantastic', and some even refused to come
to the wedding. Her mother, who was not surprised at this inter-racial
marriage, having always felt that Denyce would marry out of the race,
accepted it. She sensed that David was the right man for her daughter.
And, so far, she has been proved right.

Perry is a concert guitarist and tenor, and manages their production
company, Carmen Productions. He is the sort of husband every diva
dreams of but seldom finds. Calm, unflappable, unusually empathetic
in both joy and disappointment and, being a musician, a first rate pair
of ears for her.

'I could go on forever about my husband. He's my greatest support
system and rock. He gets even more excited than I do about the good
things that happen to me and even more upset about the bad ones! You
say that you feel diva-husbands are the unsung heroes of your book.

This is so true! Because much as I love this profession – I would never want another – it comes with its price. And you pay. You *do* pay. You give up a life of normalcy, sometimes your family, sometimes your relaxation, holidays – sometimes it seems as if you give up *life*. You're always working. And in your work you give so much of *yourself* away, so much energy, so much *juice*, that there is very little left for yourself. It takes a very special person to put up with all of this. I thank God every day for David.' The couple, who now live in a luxurious, six-bedroom, six-bathroom Georgian mansion in Leesburg, Virginia, have a pact never to be apart for longer than two weeks at a time.

So Graves began her career well armed both professionally – with all those awards – and emotionally. In 1990–91 she sang in the production of Carmen in Minneapolis already mentioned and in 1991–2 began a string of important débuts: at the San Francisco Opera, the Los Angeles Music Centre (with Domingo as Don José), the Vienna State Opera and the Teatro Carlo Felice in Genoa. She was also invited to sing her first Dalila in a concert performance at the Ravinia Festival, conducted by James Levine and with Domingo as Samson. Graves loved the role of Dalila from the word go. 'It's the polar opposite of Carmen, a gorgeous sing from A to Z with wonderful, long lines which suit my voice: a wonderful role for a mezzo. Her arias are sublime. Two of them are in Act II, where you sing from start to finish. And, of course, you're the only woman in the opera, which is exciting and fun. Vocally it's challenging but, unlike Carmen, enormously satisfying. You use your voice in a sinuous, cantabile way that feels good while you're doing it. The tessitura is middle and middle-high, ideal for a mezzo. It also gives you the chance to sing a couple of high notes, which is always thrilling. The only danger lies in getting totally carried away. You have to watch this because the music really *pulls* you and you have to force yourself to remember to stay grounded.'

Graves finds Dalila's first aria, 'Printemps qui commence', the most challenging vocally. 'Like the Habanera, it's very delicate and comes shortly after your entry, when you are still charged with adrenaline and

settling down. In such circumstances, it's easier to have to sing something with full voice than having to paint with a fine brush.' Dalila's first
aria in Act II, 'Amour! viens aider', is difficult in a different way, and
requires stamina. 'It has a force, a certain *drive*, a vocal drive, leading
up to that B flat. This needs meticulous control. The next aria, "Mon
coeur s'ouvre à ta voix" after Samson's entry, is your reward. It's just
exquisite and makes you feel privileged to sing it. Its only drawback is
that its Samson who gets to finish it.'

At that first performance in Ravinia Domingo made Graves promise
to save her first staged Dalila for him. She took him to heart: after
many other concert versions at which she kept begging him, 'I'm
ready, come on let's *do* it,' they finally did, at the Metropolitan Opera
in February 1998. My meetings with Graves took place shortly before
this, and she said that she had not been 'so excited about anything in a
long while!' The reviews were excellent: 'Graves sang vibrantly,
enlivening the opera's longueurs with a vivid stage presence.' (*The
Times*)

Graves had already begun to heed Domingo's advice not to let herself be typecast as Carmen, and started to diversify. Apart from Dalila,
the next couple of seasons saw her singing the title role in Honegger's
Antigone at the Teatro Massimo in Palermo (1992–4) and returning
there the following season for Giulietta in *Les contes d'Hoffmann*, a
gorgeous role for her; she also made her début at the Teatro Bellini in
Catania as Leonora in Donizetti's *La favorite*. In 1996 she added
Dorabella in *Così fan tutte* to her repertoire at the Philadelphia Academy
of Music. She fully realized that a steady diet of Carmens was vocally
far from healthy: the voice *needs* bel canto singing in between, to
restore its elasticity, line and evenness of tone.

'Mozart and bel canto make your voice much better. They're
difficult, especially for a voice like mine, which is broad, *fat*. I need to
work to line it up and make it skinnier. With Carmen you have to
watch out. It's too theatrical. It can easily take the sheen off the voice
and get it out of line, make it hard.' Graves works with New York-based

coach, Edward Zambara, who, she says, has helped with breath control, top notes and diction. 'There are so many facets, so many details to think of and worry about: specific notes or entire passages that need to be worked at and got right. You take them to your teacher and try to fix them. But once I'm on stage, I've decided to leave any technical worries behind. This is the moment for the thing to happen, so let it happen.'

One of the most exciting events of Graves's career – sandwiched between international appearances – was her début at the Metropolitan Opera in October 1995. It was a highly emotional occasion. Her mother and her old teacher, together with about one hundred friends and family had arrived from Washington by car, coach and train to witness her big moment. All the great international theatres she had already sung in meant little to them, but singing at the Met proved that the little girl from Galveston Street, Southwest, had really made it to the top. Recognizing that her story was a living embodiment of the American Dream, CBS Television's famous programme *60 Minutes* was there to record the occasion. 'This was not just a move for myself, but for my people, my family,' Graves told *The New York Times*, whose critic chronicled her triumph: 'Ms Graves has a classic mezzo voice with dusky colorings and a wide range, from her chesty low voice to her gleaming top notes. She is a compelling stage actress who exuded the sensuality that any Carmen must have but few do . . . Ms Graves had the Met audience enthralled . . . and received a tumultuous standing ovation.'

More new roles followed during the following seasons: Adalgisa in *Norma* at the Zürich Opera (1996–7), Marguerite in *La damnation de Faust* and Cuniza in *Oberto* (Verdi's first opera), in a concert performance at Covent Garden. At the time of our encounters, she had just sung Charlotte in *Werther* in Genoa which she adores.

'*Werther* is a different world from anything I've done so far, and Charlotte one of my most favourite heroines, totally different from the two seductresses, Carmen and Dalila. *Werther* as an opera really belongs to the tenor. But Charlotte has some very big moments. I enjoy playing this kind of repressed character – I find it very stimulating and very sexy. Making this *real* is quite a challenge. There is all that anguish and torment inside, but it has to be masked by a veneer of tranquillity. I find this very interesting, because most of my other heroines are very straightforward, very upfront. Dalila is more emotionally calculating than Carmen, with whom what you see is what you get. Still, like those two, Charlotte is a woman of great passion – but it's all squashed. She has so many responsibilities weighing on her – the children, the promise she made at her mother's deathbed, her duty to Albert – that she has learnt to put herself last on the list. Surrendering to her own desires is just not on for her. In fact, Charlotte only finally discovers herself as a woman through Werther's eyes. But this happens while she's married to Albert, so there is no opportunity for her to explore this side of herself. At the end, you are left with a terrible sense of *waste*.'

Vocally the role lies very well for her voice. But Act III is still a very difficult sing because there are three arias, one after another. First there is the Letter Scene, then the 'Air' and then 'Seigneur Dieu!', which, Graves says, is 'emotionally almost more than one can bear and vocally absolutely terrifying. The range does make it difficult. It's written above the passaggio, all on G and A, and hovers on this zone repeatedly, again and again, with no chance to have a break, or take a breath or get back to the low part of the voice. By the end I feel utterly exhausted. But I like that, because it helps me stay in the character. This is a kind of physical sensation I like in all of my roles.'

As an example of this, she mentions that the other day she was working with a coach who remarked on a gasp of disgust she had let out during a performance of *Carmen*, when Don José was talking about his mother in Act III: 'At this point Don José really makes *me*, Denyce, very angry. I get so *annoyed* with his whining, I think it's so unattractive and so unmasculine! So I have to do something physical to let my disgust out of my body. I like feeling this kind of physical sensation in my body while performing, even when I'm being hit, as I am in some operas, because it makes me *physically* angry. And when I, Denyce, feel joy or pain, I stay engaged in the character. The same is true of exhaustion which I feel as Charlotte at this point in the last act.

'I feel physically and emotionally spent, drawn, sucked into the character at "Seigneur Dieu!" – drained of all energy and about to collapse. Then, at Werther's arrival, I feel physically energized again. Whereas before his entry the knowledge that there's this big scene looming makes me feel even more tired. When Werther arrives, fresh and in good voice, having had a chance to rest in his dressing room, this energizes me – unless, of course, you have a flat performer.'

This, she explains, is the main difference between a good and a bad performer: 'There are people who raise your level of performance and people who pull you down and sap energy from you. This is something I didn't know as a student because you only learn it from experience. That's why I've now become quite discriminating about who I sing with. The fact is that the moment you walk on stage, you have so much against you anyway that you need to stack the cards in your favour wherever you can. And if there are people who strengthen, excite and help you to stay in character, people whom you admire artistically and who, through an exchange of energies throughout the evening, raise the level of your performance, then there's nothing greater! It's total joy, total ecstasy. But there are others who make it seem just a job, a chore and a bore . . .'

The kind of performers Graves likes working with are those she calls *organic*, those of her colleagues who throw something at her in mid-performance which she can use to her advantage. 'That's *exciting* – it means the two of you are creating something spontaneous up there, on the spot. Colleagues apt to do different, spur-of-the-moment things at every performance. This is magic, it's electrifying, it makes you want to run to the theatre to get there early, impatient, itching, *hungry* for the performance, the moment when you can get up there on stage and *do* it.'

VESSELINA
KASAROVA

'OF ALL THE wonderful singers who emerged in the 1990s, Vesselina Kasarova is perhaps the most remarkable,' says Jonathan Miller, who directed this marvellous lyric mezzo in productions of *Anna Bolena* in Munich, *Idomeneo* in Florence and *Mitridate, re di Ponto* in Salzburg. 'She has an amazing, extraordinarily wide-ranging voice – all the way from Chaliapin to Yma Sumac – and is one of the most expressionistic actresses on the operatic stage: an explosive, original, oblique dramatic presence whose passionate body language is something I haven't encountered in any other singer I've worked with. She could compete with the German expressionistic actresses of the 1920s anytime, especially in trouser roles – she is an electrifying 'boy' on stage. And by the way,' added Dr Miller, rushing out of the door into a waiting taxi, 'she also happens to be an enchantingly modest young woman.'

'For me singing has to do with honesty,' says the thirty-three year old Kasarova. 'My aim is to communicate joy to my public, and that cannot happen if I am not absolutely honest – if I don't become each of the characters I play, rather than just offering versions of myself. That's why I think acting is as important as singing – not only stage acting, but also vocal acting. For each role I try to bring out different colours in my voice, maybe even a different timbre.

'Body language is also crucial, because singing is an expression of one's whole body. One of the most important lessons I learnt from my teacher at the Sofia Conservatoire, Ressa Koleva, was to be aware of my body. If you know and understand your body and its rhythms, you will also know how to use it expressively, in the same way that a pianist will exploit the expressive characteristics of a particular instrument.'

It was as a pianist that Kasarova began her musical education in her native town, Stara Zagora in southern Bulgaria (also the birthplace of the soprano Anna Tomowa-Sintow). She learnt the piano from the age of four, encouraged by her parents and especially her father, who although a driver by profession loved playing and listening to music. Through all sorts of tortuous means he managed to bypass the draconian Communist bureaucracy and succeeded in getting Vesselina a good piano from East Germany. She studied the piano for twelve years at a special music school, to which all gifted children were sent by the regime ('They spent a lot of money on musical education and sport', she explains.) At the age of eighteen she was awarded her recital diploma, but stunned her parents by announcing that she wanted to be a singer. She had discovered in the school choir that she had a good voice, and as she had always loved opera she determined to try her luck and audition for the Sofia Conservatoire, where such famous singers as Tomowa-Sintow, Ghena Dimitrova and Raina Kabaivanska had studied.

At first her parents were fearful at the prospect of her launching herself into such a precarious and volatile profession, but in the end they relented. After a couple of months' preparation Kasarova auditioned for the conservatoire and was accepted. Here she was lucky enough to fall into the hands of the right teacher straightaway. This was important because, as she points out, Bulgaria's operatic tradition is based on Puccini and Verdi. Promising young voices are often pushed into this repertoire and are prematurely ruined. The fact that Kasarova was not given Amneris, Eboli and Azucena to sing at this stage was due entirely to her teacher Ressa Koleva, whose background was in concert and chamber singing rather than opera. She consequently handled her young pupil's amazing voice with care and sensitivity, steering her towards Mozart and Rossini, whose works were comparative rarities in Bulgaria at that time. She also tried to get hold of as many western recordings as possible — not easy either — to find out what was happening in the outside world and get an idea of different styles of singing.

The training at the Conservatoire, though free, was nonetheless very rigorous and thorough. There were daily voice lessons, classes in musical theory, lessons in movement and so on, all at a relentless pace. With hindsight Kasarova has come to appreciate the discipline and resilience instilled in her by this system, though at the time her self-discipline was inspired by fear of failure. During the last two years of her five-year course she also began performing at the National Opera House: Rosina in *Il barbiere di Siviglia*, Preziosilla in *La forza del destino* and, for her graduation exam, Dorabella in *Così fan tutte*.

Shortly before her graduation, Kasarova was selected along with other promising young singers to perform at a concert attended by a Western agent Luisa Lasser-Petrov who specialized in bringing singers out of Eastern Europe. Petrov was so impressed that she sent a tape of Kasarova to Karajan. A few months later an invitation came to audition for the great maestro in Salzburg. This was in the summer of 1989, during rehearsals for *Un ballo in maschera*. Karajan was so enthusiastic he offered her a concert of Bach's *Mass in B minor* in the following year for which he also engaged Cecilia Bartoli for the higher mezzo part. But this was not to be. A few days later Karajan was dead. Kasarova still treasures the memory of that meeting.

At about the same time, the director of the Zürich Opera, Christoph Groszer, was visiting Sofia as part of the jury for a singing competition in which Kasarova was taking part. He arrived tired, settled into his seat and prepared to be bored. As indeed he was, until Kasarova came on stage. So stunned was he by a voice of such calibre in the midst of mediocrity that there and then he offered her a two-year contract as a company member in Zürich. But, this being a Communist country, it was some months before he could obtain an exit visa for her.

So, in autumn 1989, at twenty-four years of age and speaking not a word of German, Kasarova found herself in Zürich, not just a new country but a whole new world for someone from Eastern Europe. 'It was a complete culture shock, a very difficult time for me,' she remembers. 'You cannot imagine the loneliness, the sense of being lost, unable to communicate with anyone. I was so homesick, the only thing that sustained me during those first months were my daily calls to my parents. They gave me the courage to go on. Yet this was the time and place where everything began for me, where I took my first steps onto the stage.' She was helped at this time by Nadine Schlegel, who was her interpreter, surrogate mother and friend. Schlegel describes Kasarova, or 'Vessi', as 'a simple, very shy girl from a poor country, who rejoiced at the prospect of a new pair of shoes'.

She was also helped by the entire staff of the Zürich Opera, who took to this very lovable person. The impression of inner purity and spiritual health is very strong to anyone meeting Kasarova even now, when she is a world star in the operatic firmament. There is the sensation of being in the presence of someone very natural, fresh and healthy, in all senses, 'like a fresh apple', as a German paper put it. 'I hope she'll always remain that way', says Jonathan Miller.

Having the kind of nature that makes everyone be on your side is a very great blessing, and right from the start it helped Kasarova get the best out of the colleagues, conductors and directors she worked with. Zürich was the springboard from which her career was launched, and where, she says. She learnt all the basics of the profession. 'It was the ideal place to do this. Although at the beginning it was very hard, with me speaking no German – which is such a complicated language – or any other language except Russian. My interpreter was always at my side, but I felt very insecure and nervous. Imagine my consternation when I was told that my very first roles were to be the Second Norn and Wellgunde in *Götterdämmerung*. They are small parts, to be sure, but in a very important work. The production was conducted by Ralf Weikert, who was enormously helpful and kind, as were all my colleagues and the entire administrative staff of the opera house. I shall never forget that.' Soon, as she began to learn German and acclimatize to her new life, she came to feel very much at home in this theatre. It became her artistic home, and in a way remains so to this day. During her first season there, she was entered for the Bertelsman New Voices Competition in Gütersloh, Germany, and won first prize.

Zürich not only gave Kasarova her first real stage opportunities, but also the most thorough training a young singer could hope for. 'There always seemed to be *time* to prepare new roles in both depth and detail. This was crucial for a young singer like me, who was singing everything for the first time, to whom everything was new. But it's also very important even for great and famous singers, who seem to choose Zürich to try out new roles. This is not, as most people think, just because the theatre is small. It's because here they can really learn their parts in an atmosphere conducive to *quality*. And so I found myself working side by side with such artists as Francisco Araiza and Edita Gruberová, and learning so much from them. Singing the small part of Alisa in *Lucia* with Edita Gruberová in the title role, or Annio with Ann Murray as Sesto in *Clemenza* was the best kind of lesson.' (Kasarova became friends with both, and now gives concerts with Gruberová.) Other parts she sang at that time include Stéphano in *Roméo et Juliette*, Anna in *Les Troyens* and Olga in *Eugene Onegin*.

The role of Olga was extremely important for her future, for through it she met and married her husband, Roger Kaufmann. A native of Zürich, he had fallen in love with her when he saw her performing at a charity concert. Already besotted, he attended all eighteen performances of *Onegin* as well as half the performances of a piece by John Cage, adding 'That's true love'. His ardour won her over: they are now married and live in a suburb of Zürich.

Of all the parts Kasarova sang in Zürich the most important was undoubtedly Annio in a production of *La clemenza di Tito* by John Dew conducted by Nikolaus Harnoncourt, whose insights and inspiration instilled in her a lasting passion for Mozart. 'Mozart is the most difficult, the most beautiful and expressive of all composers. On top of that, his music has a naturalness and simplicity which, I believe, is the reason for its everlasting popularity. All his operatic characters have one thing in common: their music is permeated by purity, humanity and *truth*. They are all delineated much more through the music than through the action or the libretto, and so it's through their music that they can best be understood. It's surprising, but if one were to attempt to analyse a Mozart character only through the libretto, one could actually end up misunderstanding them. They are shaped through their music, and in this sense Mozart is the most dramatic of all composers. But in Mozart drama is not tantamount to sheer volume. On the contrary, a characteristic of his genius is that he often marks some of the most dramatic passages *piano* or *pianissimo*, because what he demands from you is not volume but *intensity*.' (Carol Vaness makes similar points in her chapter, about Elettra in *Idomeneo* who, she feels, can only really be understood through her music, and apropos of Donna Anna, who demands *piano* singing.) 'This is why, if you are musical, Mozart is the easiest of all composers to understand,' continues Kasarova. 'His wishes almost leap out of his score, spontaneously. Other composers may be open to more than one way of interpretation. But there is only *one* way of singing Mozart's music, *his* way. His music, both in *opere serie* and *opere buffe*, is so pure and natural that it only sounds right when you sing it the way he wants you to.'

In 1991, after two years in Zürich, Kasarova joined the Vienna State Opera where she remained for a further two years. Her time there was valuable in that it raised her professional stakes, and also gave her a chance to expand her repertoire, adding Rosina (her début role), Cherubino, Fyodor in *Boris Godunov*, Pauline in *The Queen of Spades* and Meg Page in *Falstaff*, the last two under Seiji Ozawa. She found that the preparation at Vienna was not nearly so thorough as it has been in

Zürich, for it is a repertory theatre and many of her roles were in revivals of existing productions rather than in new ones. For someone as avowedly addicted to rehearsal as Kasarova, this must have been frustrating indeed.

In the same year that Kasarova joined the Vienna State Opera she also made her début at the Salzburg Festival, again in the role of Annio. She returned to Salzburg the following year for further performances as Annio in a new production. Then something totally unforeseen happened which propelled her to international fame almost overnight. Twenty days before the Salzburg Festival was due to stage two concert performances of *Tancredi* – their contribution to the Rossini Bicentenary – Marilyn Horne, who was to sing the title role, cancelled. Mezzos who can sing this gorgeous yet fiendishly difficult role are very few and far between (in fact the only other distinguished interpreter of the part who springs to mind is the late Lucia Valentini-Terrani). In despair the management asked the young Kasarova if she would attempt to learn the part in the remaining two and a half weeks. 'I just reeled from shock when they asked me! Had it been today, I would probably have said no. But in those days I was too inexperienced to imagine the consequences if things went wrong – which they easily could have done.'

But fortunately nothing went wrong, and Kasarova was pronounced 'The Sensation of the Season'. She had managed to learn the part by heart by herself at the piano before working at it with her Salzburg coach, Giancarlo Andretta. Nobody suspected just how 'new' the role was for her! She fell in love with Tancredi, which she considers 'one of the most fulfilling roles in the entire mezzo repertoire. The tessitura is perfect for a mezzo and gives you the chance to use your entire range. It's also a deeply rewarding role to play: a true "romantic" whom I consider to be a sort of emotional ancestor to Massenet's Werther.' Kasarova has now recorded *Tancredi* for RCA (about which the *Sunday Times* wrote that 'The main reason for acquiring it is Vesselina Kasarova's fabulous singing of the title role'). She would later make a triumphant New York début at Carnegie Hall in a concert performance of this opera in November 1997 conducted by Eve Queler.

As Kasarova had already discovered when she sang her first Rosina in Vienna the previous season, Rossini suits her voice. 'I always think of him as balm for the voice. His roles seem to lie well for my voice, and whenever I sing them I experience a sensation of physical well-being. I don't agree with those who consider him less "serious" than Mozart by claiming he is the more "Mediterranean" of the two. I think this is a facile judgement that shows a misunderstanding of Mozart and at the same time underestimates Rossini. Both composers were tremendous innovators and both have their serious and comic sides – their *opere serie* and *opere buffe*. Dramatically, Mozart is more "political", more socially aware. Musically, both are extremely demanding. Mozart requires finesse and the utmost precision, while Rossini demands a prodigious ability for coloratura – indeed without agility you *cannot* sing Rossini. Yet it's essential not to view these coloraturas as mere vehicles for virtuosic vocal displays, but to search for the *dramatic* reason for them and to sing them as expressively as you can.'

The Salzburg performances of *Tancredi* which launched Kasarova's international career were perhaps the only occasions when she suffered from stage-fright. 'Normally I'm a very calm and serene kind of person – I love my work, and enjoy performing. Even as a child, when I played the piano in concerts, I experienced a great thrill from the proximity of the public. But this time, with such a short period to learn the role, I did feel nervous.' Making such a success of *Tancredi* would have been a towering achievement in any circumstances for any singer tackling such a difficult role at the age of twenty-seven. But to have done so with twenty days' notice in a completely new role comes close to performing a miracle. And that only three years after graduating from the Sofia Conservatoire and moving to the West.

The operatic world duly stood up and took notice. Invitations began pouring in for a string of important international débuts: At Covent Garden and Florence as Rosina and at the Bergenz Festival as Fenena in

Nabucco, all in 1992, and in 1994 as Dorabella under Muti and Pippo in
La gazza ladra in Barcelona. She was also immediately invited back to
the Salzburg Festival for Zerlina in a new production of *Don Giovanni* in
1995 (and for its revival the following summer) under Daniel
Barenboim and directed by Patrice Chereau.

Working with Chereau was a stimulating experience, although she
recalls that the first week was awful, fraught with tension because
Chereau was so impatient. 'But then, he's a genius,' she adds with an
indulgent smile. 'I learnt a great deal about the role from him. Zerlina
is one of Mozart's most "political" characters in the sense that her actions
are mostly determined by the social position she's trapped in. This
factor is often overlooked in productions that concentrate merely on the
erotic, seduction factor between Zerlina and Don Giovanni. And by the
way, I think the sensuality of the role is greatly enhanced when it is sung
by a mezzo! But it's a fact that in the eighteenth century and even up to
the end of the nineteenth, members of the aristocracy and the *haute
bourgeoisie* seduced women of lower birth with promises of marriage. In
most cases this led to ruined lives and illegitimate children. Occasionally
it also led to deaths, because in order to avoid social disgrace some
women resorted to primitive abortions. So, it's not just Don Giovanni's
sexuality or indeed her own naiveté that tempts Zerlina into his arms,
but a very real desire to jump at an opportunity to better her social position. But the nice thing about Zerlina is that after Don Giovanni is
unmasked she manages to find a way back to Masetto to the man she
loves. She is happy to have survived Don Giovanni's attentions without
lasting harm and lucky to have landed safely back in reality. The three
women in the opera – Donna Anna, Donna Elvira and Zerlina – are
from different backgrounds and are all heading into different futures.'
('A magical, resolute Zerlina', wrote the *Wiener Zeitung* of Kasanova's
portrayal, while *Opera Now* called it 'enchanting'.)

The following autumn Kasarova made another important début.
She sang a major bel canto role, Giovanna Seymour in Donizetti's *Anna
Bolena*, at the Bavarian State Opera in Munich with Edita Gruberová in

the title role. This was a new departure point from which she intends to continue (she has subsequently also portrayed Romeo and Adalgisa), as she explained to Richard Fairman. 'It's an extension of the styles of Mozart and Rossini, building on the *piano* writing of Mozart and the coloratura of Rossini, then using the shaping of the bel canto line to make its own demands over and above those.' For these reasons, as she explained to me, Giovanna Seymour was a very difficult role. 'The main vocal difficulty is its very high tessitura. In her duet with Bolena, for instance, Giovanna sings in the highest reaches of the mezzo register. The dramatic difficulty is that although Giovanna is a central character in the opera, you are given few moments in which to put her across and communicate her plight to the audience: the knowledge that, although not directly responsible, she is nevertheless the cause of Bolena's death.' The production was Kasarova's first with Jonathan Miller with whom she forged a strong rapport. It was a spectacular success, and is still revived at regular intervals. 'In her one experiences a complete blending of technique and emotion, something missing from many a "coloratura-diva",' wrote *Opernwelt*. 'Nothing sounds calculated or manufactured, every phrase rings true. This rich and fruity voice is sheer bliss – the height of luxury.' She has now repeated the role at Munich a number of times.

Kasarova and Miller came together again the following spring in Florence for *Idomeneo*, in which Kasarova sang Idamante, a role which she has proceeded to make uniquely her own. She finds the role vocally difficult and dramatically very interesting because of Idamante's development through the course of the opera. 'You have to show his growth from young prince to the new king both in your acting and in your singing. Vocally it's difficult because it's very, very high – sometimes even higher than Ilia, who is a soprano! His most important moments are not, as one might imagine, the two arias in Act I, but the recitatives and ensembles in the later acts. Jonathan Miller was marvellous because he didn't try to impose an interpretation on me – that's not his style. He just threw ideas at me, allowed them to sink in and let me create my own portrayal.' Julian Budden wrote in *Opera* that Kasarova was 'an admirable Idamante, every inch the *jeune premier* with clear, bright, soprano-like tone and a beautiful legato line'. (Even more enthusiastic was the public and critical acclaim that followed Kasarova's American début in this role at the Lyric Opera of Chicago in October 1997.)

1996 was indeed a landmark year for Kasarova, in which she added three more major new roles to her repertoire. One is speechless with admiration at how she managed this with such distinction in every case. Adalgisa (*Norma*) and Charlotte (*Werther*) in Zürich, and Romeo (*I Capuleti e i Montecchi*) for her début at the Paris Opéra in October under Evelino Pido.

Kasarova has a special affection for the French repertoire. She considers it to be one of the richest of the mezzo voice. 'What fascinates me most in French music is its special colour, its overall elegance and very particular "perfume".' Charlotte immediately became one of her most favourite parts, because of its vast palette of expressive possibilities. 'It allows you to use every part of your register and show all the colours in your voice. It's lyrical, dramatic and romantic in turn, which makes it more comfortable for a young singer. Vocally, I feel very comfortable in this role. Physically, from the point of view of stamina, it's extremely demanding. In Act III, for instance, Charlotte is almost constantly on stage. Psychologically, the role is also immensely demanding and draining, because Charlotte is a character imprisoned in her situation from which there is no escape. She sacrifices herself to duty, but Werther's death, to my mind, also signifies her own death, spiritual and emotional, if not actual. Although I haven't experienced anything comparable in my own life, I identify with Charlotte to an incredible degree, because the emotions expressed through her music mirror my own to a very large extent. It's an ideal role for a mezzo, both vocally and because of the range of emotions. It suits me to a point where during rehearsals I actually had to restrain myself a couple of times in order not to burst into tears. This is what I meant when I said it's a part that weighs on me psychologically – Charlotte's fate touches me deeply.' After first singing the role at Zürich, Kasarova repeated it with great success at the Deutsche Oper in Berlin in the summer of 1997.

She was almost as overcome by emotion during the opening night of *I Capuleti e i Montecchi* in Paris, at the moment when Romeo, believing Juliet dead, bids farewell to her in 'Deh, tu bell anima'. There was a pause during which not only Romeo, but Kasarova herself seemed overwhelmed by the emotion of the situation. When asked by the critic of *Opernwelt* whether one can plan or calculate such moments she replied that one could not, that she was totally surprised by the almost uncontrollable tide of emotion that nearly overcame her: 'It was as if something were coming to us from above', says Kasarova (who is a profoundly religious person and always wears an Orthodox Cross around her neck), 'and it affected us both. The soprano singing Juliet also sensed it and cried at this point . . . I was very disturbed that something like this should happen to me on stage, and brooded about it all night.'

Kasarova had worked on the role of Juliet meticulously for over a year, examining every phrase, every expressive point, so that she could understand the role and feel it becoming part of her. She listened to every recording – 'not in order to copy anyone but to become aware of the various ways one could mould it' – and then began to study the libretto. 'I asked myself what I could do with the text, with the recitatives which are very free and very emotional. I think that, despite meticulous preparation, you can never do things exactly the same way every time. Every performance was slightly different, with subtly new nuances here and there.' This was one of the very few occasions when Kasarova was slightly nervous before the premiére. But she need not have worried: such was her concentration on the character that, combined with her vocal prowess, it ensured that the evening was a spectacular success.

By now Kasarova was beginning to ride the crest of a wave in her career, culminating in more outstanding successes in 1997. She has risen quickly to the peak of the profession, without ever giving one performance that fell short of top quality.

The year began with a production of *Mitridate, re di Ponto* at the Mozart Week in Salzburg, directed by Jonathan Miller, in which she had been offered the choice of singing either Sifare or Farnace: 'I chose Farnace because he is such a rich, complex personality. At first sight the part looks vocally difficult because the tessitura is mostly very low. Personally I think the vocal difficulties are exaggerated by the way he tends to be portrayed dramatically: most people nowadays tend to show only his "bad" side. I don't believe Farnace is "bad", but just a very strong, powerful personality. In any case Mozart characters are never black and white, good or bad, but very rich, complex, many-sided people. Again, what I like about Farnace is that like Sesto and Idamante he evolves a lot through the course of the opera. In his first aria, "Venga pur, minacci e frema", your voice has to show strength of character through the right colours and expression. Mozart's orchestration supports you all the way at this point, showing through both its sheer tension and energy a very resolute character indeed. But there is also another side, which is typical of Mozart. Even his "bad" characters are written with a certain elegance, which is never kitschy but designed to win our sympathy. This was the third production I had done with Jonathan Miller, and by now our rapport was almost telepathic. We had exactly the same ideas about the character.'

The production was repeated in that year's Salzburg Summer Festival, and constituted a double triumph for Kasarova, also the star of *La clemenza di Tito*, in which she sang Sesto for the first time. Her heart-rending portrayal, which won rave reviews across Europe, reflects her deep love for this character. 'Sesto is one of the most thrilling roles in the entire mezzo repertoire. There is something extra-special about him. You can sense by the way he is delineated musically that Mozart loved this character most particularly.'

Peter Katona, Artistic Administrator at Covent Garden, found Kasarova's Sesto 'absolutely mesmerizing'. This is all the more interesting because, unlike most, he had not been particularly impressed by Kasarova's Tancredi in 1992. 'I had found it vocally very impressive, but not individual or exciting enough. Of course, the fact that it was only a concert performance may have had something to do with it. But this time I was sitting on the edge of my seat, reflecting on how wrong one's first judgements can sometimes prove to be. It was a fantastic, astonishing and totally commanding performance.' He immediately invited Kasarova to sing this role for the opening of the new theatre at Covent Garden in January 2000.

Sesto was Kasarova's fourth Mozart trouser role, and as Jonathan Miller pointed out, she is a riveting 'boy' on stage. Asked whether there is anything special about portraying trouser roles, she replied: 'I love transforming myself on stage and always seek to immerse myself totally in the characters I portray, whether they are female heroines or trouser roles. The latter do demand a special aesthetic presentation, with reduced gestures and far greater concentration, because I can't use my own natural body language and movements. In this sense my trouser roles have helped me develop and taken my acting skills a step further. I can't say I ever played a character in which I could recognize myself, although certain characters like Charlotte, Romeo, Tancredi and Sesto do contain elements with which I strongly identify. Generally I draw on elements of myself that correspond to each character. I suppose the happier heroines are closer to my own character, but this may be why the tragic or "bad" characters fascinate me more.'

Kasarova had a chance to sing something altogether lighter when in February 1998 she took part in the Zürich Opera's production of Offenbach's *La Périchole*, conducted by Harnoncourt. This was a different Kasarova: sparkling, vocally brilliant and dominating every inch of the stage from the moment she walked on. Like Offenbach's *La belle Hélène* which she had sung in Zürich in 1994, also with Harnoncourt, *La Périchole* proved her a natural comedienne.

The summer of 1998 found Kasarova portraying the title role in *La Cenerentola* at the Rossini Festival in Pesaro, while her future plans extend into 2002. Among her new roles or important débuts are: Marguerite in *La damnation de Faust* at the 1999 Salzburg Festival, her début at the San Francisco Opera as Idamante in autumn 1999, Dorabella in a production of *Così fan tutte* at the Salzburg Festival in 2000, her first Octavian at the Metropolitan Opera in 2001 and an opera by Gluck in Zürich in 2002.

Other parts she would like to tackle eventually include Carmen and also Eboli, which she considers to represent the absolute frontier of the dramatic mezzo repertoire for her: 'I will never sing Azucena or Amneris, although would you believe, I was asked to sing the latter by a very important conductor back in my early days in Zürich! They thought my Slavic temperament was right for those roles! I don't know how, but I found the strength to say no. You *have* to do this some- times. You have to follow "the will of your voice" and go only where it wishes to take you. Personally I like to keep my voice light by return- ing to Mozart – the test is always Cherubino's two arias – and by singing Lieder recitals between operatic performances. I have always loved Lied since my days as a pianist, and I relish the intimacy of the communication with the audience.'

Kasarova, who will undoubtedly prove to be one of the greatest mezzo voices of this era, is a typical product of her generation in that she is both good looking and a great singing actress. She is well aware of how dramatically the operatic profession has changed in the past couple of decades. 'Today everything is more dynamic, more competitive, more intense at all levels and demands far greater concentration. Stagings tend to be freer, more open to ideas and scenically more bare, and it's therefore up to us as artists, to fill them out with our own personalities and expressive possibilities. The public also concentrates more on our plusses and minusses. All of which demands strong nerves and self-control.' She declared shortly after her Paris début.

When asked how she copes she answers, 'Oh, thanks to my Slavic soul, I suppose.' On top of that her name – Vesselina – means 'the happy one' in Bulgarian. One left this truly lovable young woman wishing her to remain so all her life. The birth of her first baby in November will certainly enhance her happiness.

JENNIFER
LARMORE

'DIVAS ARE A little bit like witches. Just as there are black witches and white witches, so there are bad divas and good divas. A good diva is someone who is professional, always well prepared, punctual, doesn't cancel on a whim, cares for her colleagues and, most important, for the music she sings. If you throw all these ingredients into a melting pot and add a good voice, the result would be a good diva. Mind you, it's the public who ultimately decides who is and who is not a diva, because another chief characteristic of this elusive breed is the capacity to arouse extreme reactions, vociferously pro or anti, and to command throngs of truly *fanatical* fans,' declared the American lyric mezzo Jennifer Larmore during our meeting at the charming riverside Paris apartment she was renting during the run of the Paris Opéra production of *L'italiana in Algeri* in spring 1998.

It is, indeed, to France that Larmore owes the launch of her career and diva status. For it was Pierre Medecin of the Opéra de Nice who in 1986 discovered the young Georgia-born mezzo, then fresh from her vocal studies, in an audition in New York. Medecin hired her on the spot. Larmore is quick to acknowledge her enormous debt of gratitude to France. 'This country has been good to me. That's why I always come back here. I have a deep affection for it and for the French. I spent the first four years of my career in Nice, where I learnt most of my repertoire – at a rate of about ten roles a year!' It was in Nice that she also learnt her excellent French, spoken without an American accent. (Yet another example of the love affair between American divas and the French!)

As anyone who watched the 1996 Olympics – where Larmore sang the Olympic Hymn – must know by now, she was born in Atlanta, Georgia, to music-loving parents. Her writer-actor father was also an amateur singer, and her mother a nurse. Her paternal grandmother used to play the piano in silent movie theatres. Larmore's father inherited his mother's musical talent and sang in local choirs and operatic productions. So, as far back as Jennifer (one of four children – three girls and a boy) can remember, there was always music at home. She even used to sing phrases like 'I'm going to the kitchen' operatically, rather than speak them.

When she went to school she turned out to be the kid with the loudest voice in class. Her teachers always sent her home with little notes around her neck telling her parents that she had a wonderful voice and loved music so much that she should be encouraged in every possible way. 'Of course, my parents were thrilled. In fact they made my brother, sisters and me listen to the Metropolitan Opera weekly radio broadcasts which, of course, at the time we hated. They also took us to the Atlanta Symphony Concerts, for which they held a subscription, and to any visiting opera or ballet company. They took me to my first opera – *La traviata* – at the age of ten, and that's when I fell in love with opera. In retrospect, I was lucky to have had parents who enstilled in me a love of the arts early on.'

By the time she was fourteen, she seemed to have what she calls 'a natural voice', complete with coloratura, or rather 'the kind of voice made for coloratura' – one with an inbuilt capacity for agility. But, she stresses that it was 'very young and very sweet and very refined and very small'. Her first lucky break came at the age of seventeen when a friend asked her to stand in for her in a solo at their local church. A wealthy couple who were patrons of the arts, Mr and Mrs William Dalrymple, happened to be present and were so impressed by the budding young talent they discerned in this young singer that they offered on the spot to subsidize her musical education. 'They told me I could choose any school I wanted.'

Her parents' reasoning, she says, was that she was still 'too young, innocent and protected and not at all world-wise – I had never yet been out of Georgia except to North Carolina, which is the same thing – to be sent to a big city. They decided on Westminster Choir College at Princeton, New Jersey, where she would have more opportunities than in a large university'. The prestigious Westminster Choir is one of the best know choirs in the States and regularly sings with the New York Philharmonic. So before completing her studies, 'with emphasis on Vocal Production' *cum laude*, Larmore had the opportunity to sing in concerts conducted by Bernstein, Mehta and Leinsdorf.

Another of the privileges of the Westminster Choir was to be the choir-in-residence at the annual Festival of Two Worlds both in its birthplace in Spoleto, Umbria and in its American version at Charleston, North Carolina. During one of those residences Larmore was chosen by Menotti to sing the Old Beggar Woman in his one act opera *The Egg*. 'I went to the open auditions for the part of the Old Beggar Woman in Menotti's new opera, *The Egg*. When it was my turn, he asked, "How well can you suffer?" I pulled up my long hair and began suffering like I'd just lost my dog and he said, "she's the one!"' It was also there that she met her future husband, the bass-baritone William Powers, who has proved a great partner throughout their marriage. She realizes exactly how lucky she is to have one of the few good operatic marriages around. 'I have been blessed and lucky beyond my wildest dreams, and it would have been sad if I hadn't had someone to share it all with. I can't imagine life without Bill. He's a sounding board, a support and a great friend as well as being my husband. I can call him and just say, "hello" and he'll say: "What's wrong?" It's

wonderful to know someone that well.' Since they first married, two
years after their meeting in Spoleto, they've made it a rule never to be
apart for more than a month. 'While at Westminster, I studied with Dr
Robert McIver. He saw that I had a fine vocal instrument without any
major problems, and decided to let my voice continue developing
naturally. Our lessons were filled with encouragement, pedagogy,
studies of language, interpretation, style and deportment. Every young
singer should have a teacher like him. I left his studio with a wonderfully
well-rounded knowledge.'

It was at his suggestion that, soon after graduating from Westminster
Choir College, Larmore eschewed graduate school and at her
husband's insistence went to study instead with John Bullock (the father
of Hollywood actress Sandra Bullock), a formidable teacher of vocal
technique, who was then based in Arlington, Virginia, just outside
Washington D.C. While at the college, she had never really studied
technique as such. 'My teacher there stressed that I had a natural voice
and that he didn't want to fool with that. But of course, although he did
help me with languages and interpretation, there were basic things I
needed help with, such as the fact that I didn't have an upper extension
to my voice.'

John Bullock, with whom she studied for three years, was to fix all
that. 'We did nothing but work on technique for three whole years. He
taught me everything there is to know about musculature, about the
physiological basis of the voice: how it all works, what happened, for
example, when my voice cracked. He started off by asking me to make
baby noises [she demonstrates the slightly nasal baby cry], which I
thought very weird. Yet he pointed out that when we grow up, we
forget what it's like to be that strong, to have that kind of power in our
voice – which is what makes it possible for babies to he heard from a
great distance. They do it because they use specific muscles in the neck
and diaphragm. Of course everything in singing starts with breath control, we all know that. If you don't have good breath control, you can't
do anything. So we worked on that for a long time. He also fixed, in just

one lesson, a problem I had with my jaw, which used to lock, and helped me acquire that much needed upper extension – how to get up to a high C, for instance, which a mezzo should be able to reach easily. To do that, I indulge in a little visualization: I visualize myself opening up, which prevents me from looking strained or uncomfortable, because the audience are there to enjoy themselves and not to see singers suffer! At the time I could flip up to those C sharps in *La Cenerentola*, for instance, but not hold them. To do that, I need to be absolutely still, as if someone were holding something against my head. How do I manage to convince directors to *allow* me to stand still at that point? I'm afraid I just insist!'

Larmore feels that understanding the physiology of singing is something very few singers are lucky enough to be taught at an early age. Some of them have to discover it by themselves, later, while others never do. Yet it is the most accurate and secure method of acquiring a technique. 'Let's face it, after being born with a voice, technique is the most vital thing there is. It's everything, an edifice on which you build your whole craft and career. I was thinking about this just recently, because during this run of *L'italiana in Algeri* in Paris I got really ill, first with pharyngitis and then with bronchitis. I even had to cancel two performances, something I never do. I have to be practically on my deathbed to cancel and I must say it felt almost as bad as that. I sang the remaining performances still feeling below par, and *that's* when you really need our technique. Boy, was I grateful to John Bullock.'

After three years with John Bullock, Larmore felt ready for a career and said so to her husband. She took part in the Metropolitan Opera auditions but nothing happened there for her because, as she explains, 'all they were looking for was a Cherubino'. Then, her husband's management arranged an audition for him in which those responsible for casting in three opera houses were to be present: Augusta (Georgia), Syracuse (New York) and Nice. The management conceded that if time permitted, Jennifer would also be allowed to audition at the end. 'I had thought that maybe Augusta would take me, being a Georgia girl, but they didn't, and neither did Syracuse. It was Nice, France, which I had dismissed as the theatre least likely to be interested, that came up trumps! Pierre Medecin came up with seven contracts spread over four years.'

So, in autumn 1986, she went off to Nice where she was to spend four crucial formative years. She made her début as Sesto in *La clemenza di Tito* during her first season. On the evenings she was not singing Sesto, she was singing Annio, the other trouser role, which she found 'too high'. She much preferred Sesto, 'who is like a tonic for the voice and more comfortable to sing than Annio because of the tessitura.' As she mentioned earlier, Nice is where she learnt most of her reper- toire, including 'what not to sing, what my limitations were, something a singer should learn as early as possible'.

Her next roles were Zerlina and Giovanna Seymour in *Anna Bolena*, a high tessitura role that reduced her to a nervous wreck: 'I thought I was going to *die*! I lost ten pounds, I was sick and so nervous that I fantasized about running on stage and shouting "Stop the show, I want to get off!" I remember that in Act II I needed to go faster during my duet with Henry VIII. So I tapped the tempo on the shoulders of Evgeny Nesterenko, who was singing Henry. He understood and immediately went with me. But the conductor had other ideas. He very distinctly beat *his* tempo with his baton. Evgeny and I went to the front of the stage and *glared* at him. The audience started edging to the front of their seats and when we were finished, they went wild with applause! They mistook my abject terror for intensity.'

This conductor obviously lacked flexibility: what James Levine, one of the most exemplary conductors ever to run a great theatre such as the Metropolitan Opera, declared to be one of the essential attributes of an operatic conductor. 'Say I am performing an aria with a singer who can make every conceivable expressive point at a tempo just one split hair slower or faster than I originally wanted. Would I not be an idiot to force him? All that would happen is that we would lose all those expres- sive points and not get what I wanted, either! That doesn't mean that I would take any deviation from my mental image of the work lying down. Not at all. But one must work at it, and shape it exactly as if one were working with clay, and try to bring out the singers' best assets and diffuse their liabilities. And every singer, every conductor, every human being has liabilities! Composers were looking for artists who were empathetic with their creations, and you don't help achieve this empathy by putting square plugs into round holes or by working in a dictatorial, high handed way.'[1] (One knows that every operatic singer alive would wish those lines pinned inside the door of every conductor's dressing room in all the world's opera houses.)

Jennifer credits James Levine with some wonderful musical moments when they performed *La Cenerentola* at the Metropolitan Opera together. 'James Levine breathes with me when I sing and makes me feel totally at east, confident and capable. He smiles at me when he's conducting and genuinely seems to enjoy what I do. This is not only rare but allows the singer a sense of liberty and creative freedom.'

Larmore's next parts in Nice were Isolier in *Le comte Ory* and Angelina in *La Cenerentola*. During the same period she was allowed to travel to Lyons, Strasbourg and Bonn (1988) for her third Rossini role, Rosina in *Il barbiere di Siviglia*, and to Marseilles for Mélisande in 1990.

It was in the 1990s that Larmore's international career began in earnest, with her débuts at Covent Garden as Rosina, (1991, 'one of the sexiest Rosina's Covent Garden has seen in decades'), La Scala as Isolier, Turin as Isabella in her first production of *L'italiana in Algeri* and the Paris Opéra as Rosina (all in 1992). During the same year she made two important recordings – *Semiramide* for Deutsche Gramophon and *Il barbiere di Siviglia* – for Teldec. Less successful was her début at the Salzburg Festival in 1993, as Dorabella, for which she blames the production. 'I made a very successful vocal début at the Salzburg Festival in 1993 as Dorabella in *Così fan tutte*, but the production was marred internally, and as a result, all the performers were frustrated and

[1] H. Matheopoulos: *Maestro: Encounters with Conductors of Today*

visually the show suffered severely. A wonderful cast of first rate singers was assembled for a production that didn't belong at a festival of this prestige.'

Amazingly, it was not until 1994, eight years after the beginning of her career in Europe, that her native America first had the chance to hear Larmore, in a concert performance of *I Capuleti ed i Montecchi* in which she sang Romeo under the baton of Eve Queler at Carnegie Hall, and which led to her winning the Richard Tucker Prize. The following year, she made a triumphant Metropolitan Opera début as Rosina. 'Her performance lived up to her billing in every respect. her stage presence was as charming as her vocal production was gorgeous', wrote the *New York Times*. Larmore returned to the Met for equally successful appearances in the title roles in *Hänsel und Gretel* (1996) and *La Cenerentola* (1997). Since 1994, Larmore has had an exclusive contract with Teldec, with which company she has recorded all her major roles from Angelina, Rosina and Isabella to Orfeo and Carmen, as well as a string of delectable solo albums.

By the time of the Metropolitan *Cenerentola* Larmore had become renowned worldwide for her interpretation of Rossini, a composer with whose 'ebullience and sense of humour' she strongly identifies. 'Of course, to sing Rossini the most essential thing is the ability to sing coloratura. The music of Rosina, Angelina and Isabella is full of it. But this is not meant just as a display of vocal virtuosity. There is always a reason behind coloratura singing. In Rosina's "Una voce poco fa", for instance, you have to convey her happiness as well as her cunning and cleverness to the audience, which takes a lot of concentration and energy. The thing about Rosina is that, because the singing has to appear effortless, people tend to think that you just open your mouth and it pours out! But it's not at all like that. It's a lot of work and every bit as difficult as going up there and singing Wagner! We just make it look a little easier because Rossini's music has a sunny quality, at least in his comedies, which are full of energy, both in the sense of stamina and emotional energy. To sing Rossini, you've got to be someone who's not afraid to go up there and give it your all. *And* be comic with it. And let the sun shine through your singing.' Something which Larmore, with her extrovert personality and dark good looks, appears to relish. 'Of course, Rossini *serio* is completely different, a big mental journey from the comedies. The singing has much more line to it and those *opere serie* are full of long, meaty duets, such as Arsace's with Semiramide, for instance.'

The easiest by far of her Rossini roles is Isabella in *L'italiana in Algeri*, which also happens to be her favourite character: 'I really love this woman! I wish I could become a little more like her. She takes control of everything in her life, and I like that. She would probably make a great businesswoman or run a country any day. She also manages to feel good in any circumstances and turn every situation to her advantage. She has a sense of humour, but she also takes a lot of things seriously. Her love for Lindoro, for instance, she takes very seriously. Even when she finds out that he is supposed to marry Elvira, the Bey's wife, as part of the latter's plan to get rid of his wife, and she gets upset. Her first reaction, almost a reflex, is to try and figure a way of salvaging the situation. I like that kind of woman – strong and able to take control of things. I think she's a great character.

'Vocally she's relatively easy to sing, by Rossini standards, because the tessitura is low and also because she has quite a few lines to speak and declaim. Of course she has quite a lot of coloratura and fast movement in the voice, but she also gets music with a beautiful line – as, for example, in "Per lui che adoro", my favourite moment in the opera – which is something you don't get in either Rosina or Angelina. I did fight to get this moment to be absolutely still, because at this point, the audience needs it, I need it, we all need it. Especially because in this production by Andrei Serban, one of the best I have ever sung in, there was a lot of movement. Working with him was sheer joy, because he was brimming with ideas, had a great sense of humour but was also clever enough to allow you a measure of freedom.' Larmore, dressed in spectacular costumes and wearing a long Cleopatra wig, sparkled throughout, and despite some difficulties with the highest notes, due no doubt to her recent severe illness, won a huge ovation. Isabella's first aria, 'Cruda sorte', she considers to be comparatively easy. 'Not like going on stage and having to sing "Una voce poco fa" – an aria difficult because of its tessitura – without a chance to warm up. With "Cruda sorte" you can wake me up at three in the morning and ask me to sing this aria and it will most likely sound fine. Whereas "Una voce poco fa" would take a little work . . .

'Having to go on stage and sing this very difficult aria "cold" is one of the most difficult things about *Barbiere*. *And* knowing that everyone has a favourite interpretation of this aria in their minds and ears. It's a little daunting, to say the least, especially when you are singing the role for the first time. Yet even now, with so many performances of Rosina under my belt, I still have butterflies in my stomach whenever I have to sing it. It's still a challenge. Another challenge, and this is also true of all the roles you sing very often, is how to make it a little bit different every time. That's when the actress in you has to come to your aid.

'Another key moment in *Barbiere* is the Lesson Scene, "Contro un cor". It can be a fantastic comic moment. It's a joke, so you have to be a bit of a clown, a very good comic. What is not easy is making it work as a comedy while singing it as well as you can. Musically it's quite difficult: it's low, it's high, and then again it's low and high again. The audience doesn't know what's coming next, and this element of surprise and danger almost makes them seem to enjoy it all the more. I don't think one should think of Rosina as a diva role. If you go on stage with the attitude that "this is my second aria", then you're lost! It is a scene where each singer plays a crucial comic role. It is fiendishly difficult to sing, but I find that if I am really involved in the comedy and am reacting to my colleagues, then any technical difficulty goes right out the window! *Barbiere* is basically an ensemble piece in which the tenor and the baritone are equally important, so you shouldn't prance about and expect people to look only at you.'

Angelina in *La Cenerentola* (which like her other Rossini roles

Larmore has sung all over the world) is easier, precisely because it does give the singer a chance to warm up. 'Her showpiece aria, the rondo "Non più mesta", comes at the finale, whereas Isabella and Rosina get theirs right away. But, apart from "Naqui all' affanno", Angelina doesn't get all that much to sing, even though towards the end she has to switch gears. But by the time you get to the rondo, both you and the audience are ready for it, for audiences always *grow* into a performance, I find.'

Larmore stresses that the best possible preparation for Rossini were the Baroque operas she sang during her Nice years: two Monteverdi roles, Silvia in *Orfeo* and Ottavia in *L'incoronazione di Poppea* which she first sang in Bologna and later recorded for Harmonia Mundi, along with the title role in Handel's *Giulio Cesare*, which she first sang in Baune, and then Paris, Cologne, Berlin, Brussels, Madrid and will sing again at the Met in 2000. 'Handel and Monteverdi are a wonderful preparation for Rossini. Both have a lot of coloratura. Handel, of course, is more of a tour de force, with all those endless da capo arias and *fioriture*. The main difference, though, between Rossini and Baroque composers lies precisely in the ornamentation. I am greatly looking forward to singing *Giulio Cesare* again at the Metropolitan Opera with Sylvia McNair as Cleopatra.'

She looks forward to repeating some of her bel canto parts: Giovanna Seymour in *Anna Bolena* and Romeo in *I Capuleti ed i Montecchi* and maybe taking on the title roles in *Maria Stuarda* and *La Favorita* and Adalgisa in *Norma*. She might also try Eboli, having already had a taste of Verdi as Maddalena in *Rigoletto* and Dalila. She took her first step in that direction by singing her first Carmen at the Hollywood Bowl under John Mauceri, a role she will repeat in Los Angeles. Her recording of Carmen certainly whets the appetite, and her views on the role are interesting. Like all prospective interpreters of the role (compare Olga Borodina's chapter), she wishes her Carmen *different*. 'I would like my Carmen to have an Iberian flavour, but to be subtle yet at the same time different. I disagree totally with a colleague who states that

Carmen is "an opera for tourists". I believe she is an amazingly magnetic woman who loves freedom and life. I don't want to play her in a vulgar way. She can be sweet and vulnerable in one moment and then turn around and be hard and calculating. But the question I like to ask myself is: what kind of woman would make a man give everything up for her? Obviously not a tart paid by the hour. That sort of fling would soon be over. What I find particularly interesting is the fact that in Act IV, despite her infatuation with Escamillo and her being at the bullfight as his guest of honour, she is still wearing Don José's ring. She sings "cette bague que tu m'avais donné" and throws it back at him after their argument, but she did arrive wearing it. Escamillo could have showered her with jewels but she's still wearing this bauble. So I really believe she fell in love with Don José. But then she became completely disillusioned with him. This is a guy who says all the wrong things at the wrong time. He never says anything right or at the right time. We all know people like that. The two of them are completely mismatched, but I do believe she loved him.

'Vocally, Carmen is an easy sing, apart from Act IV, where the final duet has some very heavy orchestration. That's a place where you can run into trouble because her music at this point is very low. It would be much easier if one had the tenor singing lower and Carmen singing higher, above his line. But Bizet has written precisely the opposite, and that's why most people find it necessary to push at this spot. But there's no need to push.

'So, with the roles I mentioned, I think there's a future for me out there. I'll do the *ingénue* Rossini parts as long as I can, as long as they keep inviting me and as long as I think I'm viable for them. I've already asked some people to tell me as soon as I start sounding bad, because you are not always the best judge of yourself in these things. It may be hard to let go . . .'

After the hectic first decade of her career, Larmore now takes things more easily and has more time off – almost five months a year – to relax in the beautiful house she and her husband bought and decorated to a 'state of the art' standard. They live in the suburbs of Chicago, 'real horse country' where they are almost the only people without a horse. They call their house 'The Resort', because for them 'the perfect vacation is going home'. The house is inspired by Frank Lloyd Wright, and is 'all high ceilings, a house where you can feel comfortable and happy'. They've turned all the spare bedrooms into libraries and closets for Jennifer's concert gowns. 'Deer come right up to the windows,' she says. 'My husband has built a secret lodge in the garden where we can sit out in the summer and just think. It's a real haven from the business side of life.'

Two years ago, they acquired a Schnauzer puppy, Sophie, whom they both dote on and who travels with them all the time. She is very conscious that it takes the place of the child she has chosen not to have because of the demands of her career. Sophie, who has already made her stage début in the San Francisco Opera's production of *Barbiere* as Dr. Bartolo's dog, was at hand to welcome her mistress the moment she walked off stage at the Palais Garnier in Paris, and rushed to climb onto her lap before her awaiting fans had a chance to monopolize her. That brings us to another attribute of being a good diva in which Larmore believes passionately – being genuinely nice to your fans afterwards. 'You have to give a lot to those fans who fall in love with you, or rather with what you do, and go on giving to them after the performance, because this is also part of the communication that begins while you're up there on stage.'

DOLORA ZAJICK

'DOLORA ZAJICK'S VOICE is the only one existing today without any competition in the world', declared the legendary soprano Birgit Nilsson in 1991. As usual – because Nilsson's acumen, wit and forthrightness are as proverbial as her voice – she hit the nail on the head. For American-born Dolora Zajick is, indeed, the only authentic dramatic mezzo to emerge in the last decade. Her full, rounded, richly coloured voice is seamless throughout its impressive range – normally from G below the stave to a thrilling high C, but able also to reach up to the Queen of the Night's top F *in full voice*. Her sound possesses both ample power and that exciting cutting edge that enables it to pierce through the orchestra and to hold its own in any ensemble. From the dramatic point of view, although Zajick was always a commanding presence on stage, her acting until recently tended to be undistinguished. Yet even before she improved significantly in this domain, this presence, combined with her sweeping vocal excellence, ensured that her portrayals were in a class of their own.

Zajick's vocal prowess rests on rock solid foundations. She is a formidable technician, who understands the voice better than most voice teachers and voice doctors and she has worked very long and hard to achieve this total mastery over her voice. This means that she brings to her portrayals an instrument so finely honed and in tune with her mind and will that it allows her total freedom of interpretation. This, indeed, seems to be the essence of her artistic credo. 'When you are connected technically, you empty out all the energy that is in you – that *is* you. All the anguish, joy, everything. *That's* what people pay to see', she told *Opera News* a few years ago. And this is indeed what they get when they see Zajick in any of her great roles, especially her great Verdi roles such as Azucena, Eboli and Amneris. It's very hard for her to choose the one she loves most. 'For the sheer singing, Eboli. From the dramatic point of view, Amneris. There is an energy in you that comes out when you perform. When you sing Amneris, you have the opportunity to follow her evolution, and so something comes out that I can't fully explain. I always feel connected to the universe, as if some- one had plugged me into it. And I feel grateful that I've been given this gift, grateful for the opportunity to run into the right people who could teach me how to use it and grateful for the musical ability to execute what I'd learnt. Because singing is not just about voice and vocal tech- nique. There is a musical side to it that you have to understand.'

Zajick's path to self-discovery was unusual. Born in Oregon, she moved to Nevada at a young age. She was the eldest of five children in a music-loving family. She suggests that her eldest brother could have been a Wotan, but then draws a line to discussing her family. In fact Zajick hails from Bohemian Gypsy stock, her great grandfather having emigrated to the United States from Czechoslovakia. She had no intention of pursuing a musical career, but enrolled at Nevada State University to study medicine. For fun, she also enrolled in a singing class. 'I had a natural voice. But it was so hidden by how I sang when I first started, that no-one could have guessed I had a voice. In fact when I first turned up for voice lessons they put me in the class, as opposed to giving me personal tuition. As I was doing it just for fun in those days, I didn't take this for an insult. But then I started learning and developing so fast that the instructor who taught the class put me in

touch with Ted Puffer, Director of the Nevada Opera Association, and
the man who taught me how to sing. He started working with me and
soon asked me to sing alto in the Nevada Opera Chorus. After a while
I graduated to small roles.

Zajick's decision to drop medicine for music came to her while she
was still in pre-Med. In the middle of a chemistry class she realized that
this was not the kind of grind to which she would like to devote the
rest of her life. As it happened, after class she had to go straight to a
chorus rehearsal. 'Suddenly I became aware that this was exactly where
I wanted to be. So I thought, well, I'll take my chances. I knew by then
that I had a voice. But I had no idea how far I could take it. In addition,
I was starting late in every conceivable way. But once I had made up my
mind I got on pretty fast. I kept my nose clean, went after what I had
to go after and kept on improving until, one day, somebody noticed
me.

'Luck does come into it, of course, because it's hard to find a good
teacher. On the other hand, it's also hard to find a good student. When
the two come together the results can be fabulous'. They obviously
came together in the case of her and Ted Puffer, with whom she continues to study to this day, in New York where he is now on the faculty
of the Manhattan School of Music. Puffer started off teaching her the
basic technique of singing, before getting on to the finer points. This
basic technique, as Zajick rightly affirms, is the most important thing
for a singer. 'I'm a firm believer that if you start off with a technique
first, you can then grow into everything else. But if you start from
other areas and don't have an understanding of technique, no matter
how famous you may become or how big your career, it's an edifice
built on quicksand. Some people don't have what it takes to have a
vocal technique, and some even know it. They can have great careers
for a while. They can go at it while they last but, believe me, they
won't last long.'

Few people are better qualified to describe what makes up a good
technique than Zajick, who brings to the subject her medical student's

analytical mind and an awesome capacity to dissect the process. 'Let's start from the beginning. As I already mentioned, having a voice is one thing. Being musical is another. Having an ear for languages is yet another. It's connected to but not the same as being musical. Yet another thing is what my teacher calls vocal intelligence, and I call kinesthetic empathy. To illustrate exactly what I mean I would use as an example a pianist who is able to go to a concert, close his or her eyes, listen to the concert and *know* that, for instance, the right shoulder of the pianist on stage is a little tight or that there is a little tension in a specific part of his hands. A good pianist will *hear* and *know* this with-out even looking.[1] For a singer, the equivalent is to hear another singer and know exactly what they're doing technically, because you start to feel it yourself. This ability to *know* when it's the right sound, and when it's not *why* it's not, this is vocal intelligence or what I call kinesthetic empathy. And it's just as important as having a voice. I know some people who have incredible voices, are incredible musicians and actors, but who don't have vocal intelligence.'

Having vocal intelligence makes it easier for a singer to acquire a basic technique, which is the most important thing for them and 'something you don't often hear', says Zajick. 'When I do, I get excited'. She goes on to explain that once you know what to do, tech-nique is 'complex in its simplicity, like yoga. One of the first things is to build up the diaphragm and the muscles in your abdomen. When trying to support the voice, many people use a great many muscles they don't need in trying to find the ones they do. But once you learn to isolate only the muscles that are absolutely necessary for vocal sup-port, you are on your way. Because the muscles you sing with are the same muscles that you laugh, cry hard or vomit up with. Now, how-ever unpleasant it might be to visualise what it feels like when you're

[1] Conductors can also have this kind of empathy. Adrian Boult once commented: 'When I listen to the wireless, I can often *hear* a conductor's gestures and say to my wife, "Listen to that beggar's elbow!"'

vomiting, what it boils down to is a spasm in the diaphragm. Laughing is a small contraction and throwing up is a big contraction. And the reason why a person has that involuntary contraction is to push on the stomach so that poisonous food is ejected. (Incidentally, this is why I don't like to eat big meals or heavy food before singing. Because when you're really using your diaphragm, pushing down on your stomach, the last thing you want is heavy food that is going to make your organs work extra hard. I eat only something very simple, like bananas, whole grains, maybe a little tinned fish, but basically carbohydrates for energy that don't put a lot of strain on the stomach. Plus a little apple juice, water, and absolutely no acids.) Once you have learnt to isolate the muscles necessary for supporting the diaphragm all you have to do is habituate it so that it becomes automatic.'

She stresses that this is true of all the technical things she does on stage. 'I went through a phase when I had first to learn how to do them and *then* make them a habit, from doing them over and over again. For example, trills, which I needed for *Il trovatore*. I learnt how to do them. It took a long time. It was in the back of my mind since my student days. So I fiddled with exercises my teacher gave me until I worked it out. The same is true for the *pianissimo* high C I needed for Adalgisa. I worked and worked until it was securely there. But I could do all this because I had my basic technique. This is what saved me.'

Zajick studied with Ted Puffer throughout her years at the University of Nevada, from where she graduated with both a Bachelor's and a Master's Degree in Music. One of the many things she is grateful to him about is the fact that he soon understood that she was a Verdi mezzo and that, as such, she needed to be protected. 'The biggest mistake that people make with Verdi mezzos is that they try to turn them into sopranos. That's the first, but potentially fatal mistake. For although one might have a good top, that doesn't necessarily mean one is a soprano. The tessitura is different and the breaks are different. The mezzo's break is half to a whole step lower than the soprano's, and a soprano's chest voice and passaggio are half to a whole step higher than a mezzo's. So, having high notes doesn't make one a soprano. It all depends on where the voice is centred. I can pop an occasional high note, but I can't hang there.' Despite her high notes, and the fact that at the opposite end of the scale she has also sung the contralto part of Ulrica in *Un ballo in maschera* with distinction, she classifies herself as a high mezzo.

After graduating from Nevada State University, she envisaged a cosy life singing small roles in Ted Puffer's Nevada Opera Company. But he thought otherwise and urged her to go to New York. So, with a one-way plane ticket paid for by her grandparents so she wouldn't chicken out, two hundred dollars and a suitcase, she arrived in New York. She was turned down by the Juilliard but accepted by the Manhattan School of Music, where she studied with Helen Vanni and Lou Galtiero. She was virtually penniless, and supported herself by singing for the First Presbyterian Church Choir. She does not deny that for most of her first year she slept on a bench in Central park, an astonishing sacrifice for the sake of financing her education.[1]

In 1982 Zajick decided to try for the Tchaikovsky Competition in Moscow. She had no idea where the money would come from but started coaching with Donald Hall nine months before the competition. With a fortnight to go she still had no money. In despair, she approached the director of the Presbyterian Church Choir, who organized a collection from the congregation. The board of the Manhattan School of Music gave her an additional $300 for clothes. She returned from Moscow with a bronze medal, the first American to win anything at this competition for twelve years. On her return, she came to the attention of Terence McEwen, General Director of the San Francisco Opera, who has been responsible for launching many of today's top American singers. He accepted her into his company's Merola Program

[1] Azucena's words 'ed e il miotetto il ciel' – my roof is the sky – seem particularly pertinent.

for young artists. Zajick spent three intensive years there perfecting her voice and singing small roles.

By 1986, she was considered ready for her début in a big role: Azucena in the company's production of *Il trovatore*, revived especially for her at the opening of the summer season. In Terry McEwen's words, 'Zajick walked off with the show'. The local press concurred: 'San Francisco Opera's Summer Season will be remembered for Dolora Zajick. She is fabulous as Azucena in the Company's *Il trovatore*. The shouting would not stop when she came on stage to take her final bow', wrote the *San Francisco Examiner*, while the *San Francisco Chronicle* remarked: 'Zajick's voice was full, strong, focused and vital in tone throughout the extraordinary Azucena register to the thrilling high C that Verdi demands.'

In the autumn of the same year, Zajick returned to New York and won the coveted Richard Tucker Award, a landmark in the career of some of America's most distinguished singers. At the gala concert, she sang alongside colleagues such as Alfredo Kraus, Samuel Ramey, Paul Plishka and Eva Marton. She was just over thirty and now definitely on her way. The Metropolitan Opera immediately engaged her for Azucena, with which she made her début there in 1988 and which can perhaps, be seen as her talisman role.

Zajick sees Azucena as a very interesting character. 'She is the key to the whole opera. If you get a director who doesn't understand what's really wrong with Azucena, then the whole of *Il trovatore* becomes a joke. You *have* to understand what this opera is really about, which, more often than not, is missed. But, like the original play by Gutiérrez on which it is based, it's a statement against superstition: the superstition of the gypsies, the superstition of the Catholic Church and the Inquisition, the superstition in everybody's minds in Spain at the time. In fact, right from the beginning, Ferrando uses the fear induced by superstition to keep his soldiers awake for their watch. For this reason there should always be soldiers on the brink of falling asleep onstage when Ferrando sings "Alerta, alerta". In those days any soldier caught sleeping while on watch would be killed. That's why Ferrando tells them the story of Azucena's mother, and exaggerates it for effect, knowing that this will keep them awake. Ferrando is, in fact, the only one in the plot who knows what Azucena looks like. And how does he know? probably because he was a soldier on watch at the time who didn't do his job properly. So he feels guilty and is after the woman who, in his eyes, is evil. But his real motive is guilt.

'Azucena herself is superstitious. She believes, as gypsies did in those days and some still do, that the snapping and crackling of evening camp fires are the souls of their ancestors talking to them. Verdi and his contemporaries knew this and that's why "Stride la vampa" made sense to them but is different to interpret today. So when Azucena first appears and sings "Stride la vampa" she "hears" her mother talking to her and asking her to avenge her. But today, as we live in a different culture and don't understand how superstitious people were in those days, it's very hard to put this across. The way I want my Azucena to come across is as a woman tortured by flashbacks, hallucinations. But I don't want her to seem schizophrenic. In our culture and society, the diagnosis for her condition would be post-traumatic stress disorder. What triggers off her hallucinations or flashbacks is often fire. And this is the significance of fire as a protagonist in *Il trovatore*. It is the trigger for Azucena's hallucinations, in which she "sees" and "hears" something that's not there. One of the greatest difficulties in interpreting her is how to indicate, through your voice and acting, when she is hallucinating and when she is not.'

Like all great writers, Guiterrez was accurately writing about a psychiatric disorder there was no diagnosis for at that period in history. Freud had not even written his 'Interpretation of Dreams' at that point. Verdi, was insistent that Azucena not be portrayed as insane. By this he meant that he wanted her hallucinations to be the result of flashbacks and not schizophrenia, for which there also wasn't a term. The librettist, Cammerano wanted to put a Mad Scene for Azucena in the last act, but thankfully, Verdi won.

'The reason why she's having these flashbacks, or symptoms of a post-traumatic stress disorder, is that she witnessed the brutal death of her mother and, while in a distressed state had murdered her own baby by mistake instead of the intended victim, and because she hasn't yet avenged her mother. She has had masses of opportunities to kill Manrico, but she couldn't do it because it would be like killing her own son all over again. So the only way she can wreak her revenge is by having him kill his brother. But of course, if he knows that Luna is his brother, he won't do it. This is why, when Azucena is captured, she doesn't tell the Count "I have your brother". Instead, she calls for Manrico to save her, so that he *has* to be caught. When Manrico shoots off to rescue Leonora, Azucena figures that if she can't have him kill his brother, then she will have to have *him* killed by his brother instead. Because this – avenging her mother – is the only way that she can be freed from the torment of those recurring hallucinations which she believes are sent by her mother to punish her.'

Zajick, who brings to the understanding of the opera plots the same analytical mind with which she approaches the physiology of the voice and the acquisition of a technique, explains that there are two clues to Azucena's real motive and plan for revenge: 'One is in the recitative, where she tells Manrico, "you owe me this", to kill di Luna. The subtext of her reply is: "I could have let you die then, and if I had I wouldn't be having these horrid visions anymore!" But she can't actually say this because she wants him to kill his brother. The second clue is when they're in prison. Again, she could tell him he's the Count's brother and thus save him, and perhaps herself. But then she has a vision again. She "sees" her mother and cries, "who will save me from this terrible vision?" Then Verdi has her fall asleep. But she knows that her visions will only stop after she has wreaked the ultimate revenge and can turn to the Count and say, "Now *you*'ll have to live with the fact that you killed your own blood as I was made to kill mine". But, alas, few people ever seem to make an effort to understand *Il trovatore*. Because they see a witch or a disturbed creature they feel they can write the entire opera off, in dramatic terms.

'Vocally, the role is the most wide-ranging of my three Verdi heroines, and contains a high C. But nowadays most people leave that out and claim that Azucena is really a contralto part. But it isn't. Ulrica in *Un ballo in maschera* [which Zajick first sang at the Metropolitan in 1994] is a contralto role. But if you really look at that high C in Azucena's duet with Manrico, you get a very clear idea of the kind of voice Verdi had in mind. But possibly because Azucena is an old woman – or at any rate middle aged – and not a glamorous part, people have started labelling her a contralto role. Yet she has the widest range of all the great Verdi mezzo roles, the lowest and the highest notes. There is no high C in Eboli or Amneris whereas there *is* in Azucena, almost mirroring her nerves, which are stretched like an elastic band and in a state of extreme inner tension all the time. For this very reason, Verdi also makes extensive use of the chest voice. He really knew how to capitalize on expression through vocal register. He was exceptionally gifted at this.'

Zajick's triumph as Azucena at the Met was as great as the one she had scored in San Francisco. 'She commanded the range of the role easily, from the chest notes at the bottom to the high C, which is usually left out,' wrote the *New York Times*. 'But Miss Zajick hit it square on with no apparent effort. Moreover, she successfully accomplished the trills and turns of "Stride la vampa". These were standard accomplishments in the nineteenth century but more recent dramatic singers have not been up to them; since they are essential to the character of the song, it was good to have them in Dolora Zajick's portrayal of the part.'

This triumph was due in equal measures to Zajick's exceptional voice and to her phenomenal technique, which enabled her to stretch up to that high C with no apparent effort. In working on her range Zajick has deliberately extended her head voice below its usual break into chest voice, and extended her chest voice some way into the 'head' register, giving herself additional strength and variety of tone.

There is both a recording and a live telecast of *Il trovatore* from the Met with Pavarotti, Eva Marton and Sherril Milnes, conducted by James Levine, in which Zajick's admirers and all students of the art of singing can savour the vocal magnificence of this portrayal. As a passionate lover of *Il trovatore* since my mid-teens, I can confirm that I have never heard or seen an Azucena of this quality in the past quarter century.

Zajick made her début at the Vienna State Opera in spring 1989, again as Azucena. Shortly before that, in December 1988, she made her first appearance at the Lyric Opera of Chicago as Amneris, her favourite role and one which she has since sung all over the world, including the Metropolitan and the Vienna State Opera and at Covent Garden, where she made her début in 1994.

The reason why she finds it 'a wonderful and very interesting role' is because 'Amneris evolves a great deal during the course of the opera. It's not a gradual development, it's a day-night evolution. She is the Pharaoh's daughter, all powerful, the most important woman in Egypt. But the problem is that by the time she has learnt her lesson it's too late and the man she loves is dead. Many people identify more with her than with Aida because she points to the foibles all of us are capable of. The bottom line is that we all change, we grow, we evolve. And Amneris does grow. But she pays a terrible price for it.

'She starts off as a young woman who, because of her position, is used to having her way and who is by nature impulsive. That's her main trait. She's used to snapping her fingers and everything she wants gets done. She just assumes that because of who she is, Radames will automatically want to marry her, because in ancient Egypt if you married the Pharaoh's daughter you became the next Pharaoh. This is the first time in Amneris's life that she encounters rejection – and on what scale! The whole opera is about trying to make someone love you who doesn't, and doesn't *want* to. Of course, it's impossible. But Amneris doesn't understand that. Remember, she's not only Pharaoh's daughter, but in her belief a goddess. In Egypt if a slave as much as looked at the Pharaoh's daughter, he was executed – there are records showing just such a scene. So the distance Amneris travels, psychologically, when she repents and tries to save Radames is immense. The fact that she could even *reach* this point is amazing. But she cared enough for him to feel this total repentance and, through it, to change.'

Zajick regrets that, in purely dramatic terms, there isn't enough time to register Amneris's evolution. Some productions do not even allow her to put across this change in the little time allotted in the action. Directors usually just have Amneris standing over the tomb and singing 'Pace t'imploro'. Zajick says that the best production she ever did was in Verona: 'I just threw myself on Radames's tombstone and sang my last lines prostrate. The priests, who were positioned higher, rolled the stone and threw him in. Ugh! And for me, as Amneris, to throw myself on the tombstone is quite something. For the daughter of the god-King that was Pharaoh to move from this position to that of throwing herself on Radames's tombstone is extraordinary. But it's also her salvation, because she will have to live with the consequences of her action for the rest of her life.'

Zajick laments the fact that *Aida* is usually staged in a very static way that deprives it of its acutely human dimension. Essentially it is a very intimate opera, a love triangle, interrupted by the Triumph Scene. But when it is staged simply as a grand spectacle, it makes it very difficult for any singer playing Amneris to bring movement to her portrayal. 'Usually you end up standing there like a statue. You can only break loose from that in the Judgement Scene, of course, but the rest of the time, unless you have a very good director, you don't get much opportunity for real acting.

'This is a shame because the Bedroom Scene [Act II, scene 1] is very important. It's vital to show both the pain and the anger of both women. There is a very telling line where Aida says, "You have all of Egypt, and all I have is this love". She doesn't say "this man" but "this love". That's when Amneris becomes so furious. She wouldn't become this furious if she were really happy in her situation with Radames. Of course, this confirms her worst suspicions. And the whole point of setting up Aida is to find out if those suspicions are true or not.'

The main reason Amneris is the most difficult of the three Verdi mezzo roles is the tessitura, to sing every note as written, to soar through the high As, B flats, Bs, and Cs continuously in the triumphal march, then to cut through the thick orchestration of the Judgement Scene and have enough steam for the climaxes requires a great deal of stamina, especially for the numerous high notes. The tessitura is higher than for the other two roles, which is why some dramatic sopranos are able to handle Amneris. The lower part of the voice may not be as rich than for a mezzo, but the high notes will soar as they were meant to.

She stresses that Amneris is the most difficult of her Verdi mezzo roles, vocally and dramatically. 'Amneris is not like Eboli, who plays a sort of chess game all the time. The only game Amneris plays is in the Bedroom Scene, when she tries to find out if Aida loves Radames. That's the only time she indulges in deception. When she does find out, at first she reckons she's triumphant because she knows that, after Radames's victory, her father will designate him as her husband. So there is joy at this point, as the trumpets herald his victory. But it's a hollow triumph. For as she finds out in the Judgement Scene, when she tries to save Radames from the priests and he replies that he'd rather die than marry her, you cannot *make* somebody love you. But she goes on hoping to convince him to defend himself. He refuses, and when she asks why, he replies that with Aida dead he has no wish to live. She tells him that Aida is alive, but that he must promise not to see her again. But he won't . . . Like Eboli in *Don Carlos*, Amneris is an anti-heroine: both are women rejected in love.'

Zajick first sang Eboli in 1992 at La Scala, where she had in 1987 made her début in Verdi's *Requiem*. Since then, she has sung the role at the Metropolitan, the Lyric Opera of Chicago and the Vienna State Opera, and will sing it again at the 1998 Salzburg Festival. Vocally, she considers the role to be easier than Amneris: 'It's a low-lying role. In the trio, for instance, Eboli sings lower than the tenor. And if you really sing that trio as written, there's a very interesting combination of colours, with the three voices and you singing underneath the tenor lines, providing this colouration. Musically, it's very difficult to coordinate everybody and make this trio work. The Veil Song and its coloraturas are no problem. Of course, it's just an entertainment, a song out of character. Eboli is bored, and wants to amuse herself by singing this Saracen song. But, unbeknownst to her, it's a play on what happens later, in the Garden Scene, when *she* takes off her veil and is faced with that horrible rejection. The joke is ultimately on her, because what she was singing about earlier suddenly happens to her in earnest. Up to then, she held all the trump cards. And suddenly, the tables are turned. This is why it's so important to set up the scene where she sings the Veil Song so skilfully, in order to show this irony. She does regret her actions, eventually and curses the vanity that got her into trouble in the first place. So she does evolve, but only up to a point, unlike Amneris who goes from day to night.

'Musically, the role is written in a very interesting way. She does get plenty of line, of course, but Verdi purposely made a lot of her music very snappy. When she does sing a line – as in the middle of "O don fatale" – it is very beautiful. Basically, she gets a line when she is elegant – when she is exchanging pleasantries with Rodrigo, for example. But the rest of the time her music is very choppy, and it's intended to be: there's something very bold about Eboli, very *carefully* bold, but bold nevertheless. The risk she takes with Don Carlos is quite breathtaking. It's all the more surprising when one considers that she has had to be very careful all her life, unlike Amneris, who was born into her position. It's hers automatically, whereas Eboli *wants* to be there, she wants to be powerful or near the source of power, and connives for it in every way she can. She becomes the king's mistress and she loves the king's son. If she can't have the king's son, she doesn't want anybody. But she has had to be very roundabout to get all the things she sets her mind to.

'She's much more complicated than Amneris, probably a lot older and much more experienced: a sophisticated woman who has been around and is a really cunning survivor at court. In fact in this respect she and Rodrigo, otherwise polar opposites, are of the same ilk because of all the politically astute people at court they are the *most* politically astute, the ones who really know what's going on. As I said before, it's a chess game. Eboli is ecstatic, for instance, when the queen's lady-in-waiting is sent back to France because now *she* will be the lady-in-waiting. It's a step closer to the source of power for her, a little gift from King Philip. This woman is a real operator and very dangerous, as indeed she proves to be in Act IV.

'But there is also a softness and womanliness about her, which I detected only after I took on the role of Lady Macbeth, which brought a new level of maturity to all my other Verdi parts. Of course, Eboli is very different from Lady Macbeth. But there is something very saucy about her, about the way she wears her hat, the fact that she asks Rodrigo about the fashions in Paris. She is a very *charming* woman. And you have to float about the stage in a way that puts that across. The fact that she is entertaining the court when the queen is absent means that she must also be very clever at making people feel comfortable and happy. There is that lightness of touch about her as well as all the rest. A truly complex character.'

Zajick's portrayal of Lady Macbeth – which she first sang in Barcelona in 1996–7 and in Hamburg in autumn 1997 – helped her to make giant dramatic strides and to evolve theatrically. It is, as she points out, not an easy role to act. 'Macbeth is pretty straightforward. He lives through his wife until there comes a point where there is a separation between them because there simply is no meaning to life anymore. So his role is very straightforward, while hers is very tricky. She starts off with a bang and goes out with a whimper, while he starts off with a whimper and goes out with a bang. In their respective evolution, there is one point where they cross. But from then on he is dominant and she disintegrates. She has her Mad Scene, which is very powerful. But the problem here is that you have to put across that "lostness", but always in a *hard* not a fragile way.'

Surprisingly, Zajick explains that she learnt most about how to portray Lady Macbeth from watching Bette Davis on film, especially in *Whatever Happened to Baby Jane*. 'When Lady Macbeth disintegrates, she actually becomes childlike, but in an *evil* way, just like Bette Davis in that film. There is always a sinister dimension. So I thought I must bring something similar to my portrayal of Lady Macbeth, because she is a very treacherous lady. It took me a few performances, but finally I felt I had grasped who and what she was.

'The lives of Lady Macbeth, Amneris and Eboli all revolve around power: who has it and who wants it. Amneris has it implicitly, by reason of her birth, Eboli positions her way around it. But Lady Macbeth's outlook is different, because she is not just an ambitious woman, she feels she is *entitled* to be queen. The historical background backs this up because it was Macbeth, rather than Duncan, who was supposed to be king. And, indeed, there is something about Lady Macbeth that suggests that she feels that the crown is hers by right. But she can only achieve this through her husband, because in those days that was the only way.'

One of the key factors in the opera, according to Zajick, and one which is always underplayed, is the role of the witches. 'You have to look at the historical period Shakespeare was dealing with, and bring out the spookiness that permeated people's feelings towards witches. People had only recently converted to Christianity, and the witches were those who practised the old religion. And if you diminish the role of the witches you cannot explain why both the Macbeths accept their word so unquestioningly, and why Lady Macbeth goes for it as soon as she hears their prophecy. If you don't show this, you fail to understand the piece. Verdi hints very strongly through his music that there's witchcraft involved. In fact Verdi is a master of the *double entendre*. In *Il trovatore*, for instance, just about everything that Azucena utters is a *double entendre*, but it's lost on the others because she is the only one who knows the whole story.

'In the case of Lady Macbeth, her famous phrase "Unsex me here", when she calls on the spirits, means that figuratively she would like to be a man, so that she can do all the things a man can do and that literally the witches will aid her. This is a particularly tricky moment to play. You should really show her making up her mind to go after her goal. In the Hamburg production they did something very clever: they gave her a letter opener for Macbeth's letter which, from the moment she makes up her mind to kill Duncan, becomes a knife. This was the right sort of detail to emphasize because it immediately implies that there is going to be murder, there's going to be death, there's going to be blood . . .

'I think that one of the reasons why Lady Macbeth seems to break down so suddenly is that there doesn't seem to be any evolution from the ferociously determined woman of the Letter Scene to the wreck of the Sleepwalking Scene. Yet I believe that she already starts to break down at the Banqueting Scene. What I did at that point was to stare down at my hands which, in my hallucination seemed covered in blood, before I walked off stage.

'Of course, by then Lady Macbeth has completely lost control of her husband. And whether one calls him evil or not, the fact remains that, of the two, Macbeth is the one who evolves and reaches some sort of existential maturity at the end, by realizing the meaninglessness of everything he has achieved. Life has lost all meaning for him and he knows exactly why. He has learnt a great life-lesson before he dies. Still, he dies fighting, trying to survive. She, on the other hand, dies without ever having faced her demons. Of course, talking about all this is one thing and conveying it on stage is another.'

It is precisely in this context that Zajick, during her performances in Hamburg, had a revelatory experience that had a marked effect on her acting ability and brought a new dimension to the interpretation of her other Verdi heroines.

'There were people there whom I trust and who came to all the performances. They all said that I *sang* the role better in the first two performances, but that I was a little too pale dramatically. Then, before the third performance, I got sick. This proved the greatest blessing that ever happened to me. Because I didn't want to let the Intendant down, as it was important to him that I sing the last performance, I had to go on stage with only 50 per cent of my voice. And this for a role like Lady Macbeth, which happens to be one of the most vocally treacherous in the repertoire. Now, I had never sung that sick in my life. I had sung with 80 per cent or even 75 per cent of my voice, but never with half. Interestingly enough, I did manage the *pianissimo* high D at the end of the Sleepwalking Scene, but in many other spots my voice was not as focused as it should be and I found myself thinking that this must be the worst singing I had ever done in my life. It was correct *technically*, but the pipes weren't doing what they are supposed to do.

'To compensate for this, I broke out dramatically in a way I had never done before in my life, because I thought that the only way to save this performance was with theatricality. I thought I must go out there and wow them. And I succeeded in bringing the house down. And the odd thing was that people who don't know much about voices came up to me and said they had never heard me sing better, so fooled were they by what I did on stage! And I find this a very interesting thing about our craft. Let's be honest: I started off my career singing a lot better than I could act. But I have definitely evolved and people who now come to my performances notice that. But I guess it takes time for some people to catch up with my progress . . . The way each of us uses what makes us special to please the audience is different. But thank goodness I do have a presence on stage. Taking on Lady Macbeth helped me evolve beyond that. But I vowed that I will limit the number of times I sing this role. Why? Because I'm not a soprano. If I were to sing Lady Macbeth too often, it would burn me out.'

Lady Macbeth is a role that many dramatic mezzos – such as Grace Bumbry and Shirley Verrett – have sung from time to time, probably because most parts written for a dramatic soprano require a very solid middle voice (on which to built the top notes), and this is exactly what a high mezzo has by nature. Another soprano role attempted by dramatic mezzos is Santuzza in *Cavalleria rusticana*, which is also in Zajick's repertoire. I wondered exactly why this is a role that many mezzos can sing comfortably.

'I don't think they can sing it *comfortably*,' she replied. 'I don't think it's a comfortable role for anybody, be they a mezzo or a soprano, because it's written right on the crack, although it veers slightly more towards the soprano than the mezzo tessitura. The mezzos usually have difficulty with the "Inneggiamo" while sopranos have trouble with Santuzza's duet with Turiddu, which is duck soup for mezzos. But the "Inneggiamo" usually kills mezzos. Because I'm not a soprano, I had to work extra hard to ensure that it felt right vocally. And when I listened to recordings by some other mezzos, even some of the greats, to see how they handle this spot, I can hear a barely perceptible discomfort at this point. To your question of whether Santuzza is a rewarding role, I would answer: only up to a point. It's not a role I'd like a steady diet of. I first sang it in Reno, Nevada when I was too young and too stupid to know I shouldn't be doing it at that age.'

A role Zajick would really love to add to her repertoire is Arsace in Rossini's *Semiramide*. She had hitherto avoided Rossini, thinking that even Rossini *serio* might be too difficult for a heavy voice such as hers. But Lady Macbeth proved *so* much more difficult than any Rossini role could be that she thought taking on Arsace might be a lot of fun. 'I love singing coloratura and ornaments anyway, and it will be interesting for me to find out if I can rise to the challenge, with so many coloratura mezzos around at the moment. But it would have to be with a conductor who understands heavy voices, who understands the difference between Semiramide's voice and a voice like mine and is prepared to be flexible enough about tempi to allow for the weight of a voice such as mine, and thus make it possible for me to sound *manly*. There is one spot in particular where Semiramide and I have to charge on like gang-busters and here the conductor's tempo would make all the difference . . . As a composer, Rossini is, of course, diametrically different from Verdi. Verdi is a very masculine, very visceral composer. He evolved a great deal. Early Verdi is not like late Verdi because, apart from anything else, he became a lot more experienced in his vocal writing.'

At the time of our New York encounters Zajick, who had already sung her first bel canto part – Adalgisa – in Bilbao and Barcelona in 1996, was about to expand further into this repertoire with Leonora in Donizetti's *La favorita*. In terms of style, she considers this part 'almost a precursor to Eboli, although in terms of character it's a little bit different. I often wonder if this opera was not the seed for Verdi's *Don Carlos* because there are some similarities between the two, such as the way "O don fatale" is written – a bit like "O mio Fernando". Vocally the two parts are very similar although the orchestration is, of course, thinner in the Donizetti work. As a character Leonora is a king's mistress too, but unlike Eboli who is an anti-heroine, a villainess, she is a heroine. Both ladies, however, are tempered with humanity. Which of the two is the more rewarding? Playing villainesses is always more interesting. However, I must say that I quite enjoyed singing Adalgisa, which is an *ingénue* role.

'Of course, not all bel canto is interesting. A lot of it is very good and a lot of it is not very strong. It still has a very beautiful vocal line but not an awful lot of substance. The singer practically carries the whole evening, which is why conductors don't want to do bel canto operas. They do have a point, because orchestrally a lot of bel canto is certainly not interesting. In fact, unless you have a cluster of singers able to do justice to the vocal line, there is little point in mounting these operas. Even in *Norma*, one of the greatest bel canto works, there are parts I like and parts I find boring, like every time those Romans keep marching on stage. I wish Bellini could come back and edit it a little bit. Verdi, on the other hand, rarely writes a single note too many.'

When asked to define the characteristics of bel canto singing, Zajick explains that it implies a slightly different use of the voice, 'a smoother transition from the head to the chest voice. It's not more difficult than singing Verdi, just different. Of course, there is usually a lot more coloratura, which is fine because I like to sing coloratura. This smoother vocal writing is very soothing for the voice.' She adds that she might like to try Giovanna Seymour in *Anna Bolena* one day.

She has also been asked to sing some Wagner and says she might consider Erda one day. Fricka she never wants to do because she does not like the character, and the same is true of Ortrud. In any case, she says she is tired of 'screaming' roles: 'I want to *sing*. I want to make music. As everybody knows, I already have vehicles for the volume of my voice. I know there aren't all that many more roles for my type of voice – the Kostelnička in *Jenůfa* is a tantalizing possibility – but I need to go out and do something for the fun of it, like Ježibaba the Witch in *Rusalka*, which was terrific fun'. She sang this role with great success at the Metropolitan Opera, and recently recorded it for Decca under Sir Charles Mackerras, with Renée Fleming in the title role. Sir Charles confirms that Zajick had many interesting even eccentric ideas of her own to bring to the part: 'She loved that witch character and brought a lot of humour to the part. A lot of these witch characters, such as the one in *Hänsel und Gretel*, for instance, *should* be both humorous and sinister.'

Her repertoire also includes French parts such as the title role in Massenet's *Hérodiade*, which she first sang in San Francisco and has also recorded for Sony, and Saint-Saëns's Dalila, which she will sing for the first time in spring 1998. 'It's a great role, a gorgeous sing, and the orchestral writing is brilliant. You have a cushion under you all the time. All her arias are beautifully written, but "Mon coeur s'ouvre à ta voix" is just spectacular.' Like many of her American colleagues she particularly enjoys singing in French and studies her French parts with the leading French coach, Janine Reiss. 'French is a fun language to sing in. It was not easy to learn, but once I got the grasp of it, it came very fast.'

It came as no surprise to discover that Zajick's method of learning new roles is extremely methodical and analytical. 'Every score is like a gold mine, with treasure to divulge,' she explained with obvious relish.

'But there is an awful lot of work to be done before you can get to that treasure. I prepare a word-by-word translation into English of the libretto of my part, as well as that of the characters she interacts with. Then I go through it with a language coach to make sure I get the pronunciation, the phrasing, the projection of the words and the stresses right. The next step is starting to speak it in rhythm, memorizing the rhythms and the words. Then I start working on the vocal side. Technically I never set out to memorize my roles, but because I'm so thorough in my learning process, it happens automatically.'

Every step of her preparation is entered into a little black book – she has one for each of her roles – which contains a word-by-word translation of the libretto into English, and a phonetic transcription in the symbols of the International Phonetic Alphabet. It also contains the score, complete with any markings she has made during her preparation but without the pages that have nothing to do with her role, 'because I travel a lot and don't need all that extra weight'.

How long does this intricate procedure take? 'I like taking my time with a new score. The spadework of looking up every word can take any length of time. You can do it in a week or in five months. I prefer to take my time. The singing side is a different story. It takes six months to work a new role into your voice, and that's that. It's like clockwork, no matter what you do. The point is that you want the role to become second nature. So I would say that the entire process of learning a new part takes me about eight months.'

She would also like to include some recitals into her schedule. Indeed she was preparing a recital programme for San Francisco and Dresden at the time of our meetings, consisting of some of Arsace's music from *Semiramide* and songs by Poulenc, 'because the poetry is gorgeous', Brahms and Wolf.

But her problem she acknowledges, is having to rein herself in. 'I have so many interests that don't even have anything to do with music but which I like to spend a lot of time on.' In fact Zajick, a formidably intelligent and many-sided woman – almost uniquely so among singers – is also a gifted painter and poet. She is also busy writing a book on the cognitive and neuromuscular aspects of singing. How does she find time for all this as well as a busy international operatic career?

'My mind is racing all the time. I can't rest. I'm either thinking up poems or paintings or planning a book, or reading everything I can lay my hands on, everything from medicine to chimpanzees. I really enjoy reading. Going to bed without a book is impossible for me.'

She does take time off between engagements, however, to relax at her home in Reno, Nevada, where she tends her flower garden with its pond brimming with frogs, about which she is passionate. She travels with pictures of her garden and relishes the peace it obviously provides her.

Having spent some of the most riveting hours ever in a singer's company, I left her with the comment that her breadth and variety of interests must surely make her one of the best balanced and least neurotic of singers. 'I think so . . . I enjoy singing. It's hard work, though . . . but it's worth it.'

INDEX

The more important references are indicated by **bold** figures; '*n*' refers to a footnote; '*q*' stands for quoted. Use has been made of the following abbreviations: spr – soprano; mspr – mezzo-soprano; tnr – tenor; bar – baritone; bsbar – bass-baritone; bs – bass; accomp – accompanist; adm – administrator (including opera house intendants and managers); cdr – conductor; dir – director or producer; tchr – teacher.

Abbado, Claudio, cdr 60–1; *Elektra* 162, 170; *Figaro* 61; *Otello* 68; *Tristan und Isolde* 193; Verdi *Requiem* 69; *Wozzeck* 181

Adler, Kurt Herbert, adm 212–13, 215

Adriana Lecouvreur (Cilea) 93: Adriana 85

Affiliate Artist Program, *see* San Francisco Opera

Agrippina (Handel), 249

Aida (Verdi) 9; Aida 69, 102, 114, 116–17, 119, 242, 250, 271, 344, 345; Amneris 271, 285, 333, 342, 343, 344–5; Amonasro 69; Priestess 215; Radamès 33, 271, 344

Alagna, Roberto 74, 75, 76, 80–1, 84, 85, *q*86, 87, 88, 89, 173

Albery, Tim, dir: *Ariadne auf Naxos* 280

Alceste (Gluck), 34

Alcina (Handel): Alcina 37, 206

Alden, David, dir: *Macbeth* 157–8; *Makropoulos* 157

Alexandrov, Yury, dir: *Betrothal in a Monastery* 96

Allen, Judith Grove, tchr 295–6

Allen, Thomas 12
Allison, John q283
Alvarez, Marcelo, tnr 134
Alzira (Verdi): Alzira 234, 240

144
Amsterdam: *Queen of Spades* 101;
   Werther 283
Andrea Chenier (Giordano): Maddalena
   de Coigny 105, 106, 118, 242
Andretta, Giancarlo, tchr 310
Andromeda (Mozart–Paisiello), 259–60
L'anima del filosofo (Haydn): Euridice
   248, 249
Anna Bolena (Donizetti) 304: Anna
   Bolena 85, 242, 313; Giovanna
   Seymour 312, 313, 324, 326, 329,
   352; Henry VIII 324
Antigone (Honneggar): Antigone 300
Appellation 198n
Arabella (Strauss): Arabella 15, 36,
   163; Zdenka 10, 15, 16
Aragall, Giacomo 235
Araiza, Francisco 308
d'Arcangelo, Ildebrando 53
Argento, Dominick, *Voyage of Edgar
   Allen Poe* 202,
Argyris, Spiro, cdr 184
Ariadne auf Naxos (Strauss): Ariadne
   24, 280; Composer 274, 280, 281;
   Naiad 10; Zerbinetta 202, 280
Arianna (Goehr): Arianna 274
Armani, Giorgio 285
Armida (Haydn): Armida 249
Armida (Rossini): Armida 37, 40, 44,
   52–3
Arts Florisants, Les 249
Askonas, Lies 178
Aspen: *Così* 237
Athens Megaron 121: *Don
   Giovanni*, 122–5, 129, 130

Athens National Opera 125, 128;
   Entführung 129; *Schauspieldirektor*
   129
Athens State Opera: *Entführung* 124
Atlantic Richfield 213
Attila (Verdi): Odabella 100, 105,
   112–13, 228
Auger, Arleen, spr 18, 41
Australian Opera: *Ballo* 225

Bach, Johann Sebastian, *Mass in B
   minor* 252, 306
Baden-Baden: *Traviata* 121, 130, 133
Balabanova, Inga, mspr 127
ballo in maschera, Un (Verdi) 306:
   Amelia 105, 109, 211, 215, 225;
   Renato 109; Riccardo 109; Ulrica
   109, 271, 339, 342–3
barbiere di Siviglia, Il (Rossini): Rosina
   61, 108, 109, 202, 208, 225,
   252–3, 255, 285, 306, 310, 311,
   325, 326, 328, 329
Barbu, Mia, tchr 77, 78, 86
Barcelona, Teatre del Liceu: *Così* 236,
   237; *Gazza ladra* 312; *Macbeth* 346;
   Norma 351
Barenboim, Daniel, cdr 252; *Don
   Giovanni* 312
Barstow, Dame Josephine, spr 31n
Bartoli, Cecilia, mspr 26, 64, 74, 93,
   247–62
Battle, Kathleen, spr 145
Baudo, Pippo 251–2
Baune: *Giulio Cesare* 329
Bayreuth: *Meistersinger* 50, 51; *Parsifal*
   193; *Ring* 184, 186, 187, 189
Beatrice di Tenda (Bellini): Agnese 58
Beaumarchais, de Pierre 77, 282
Behrens, Hildegard, spr 152
Belford, Robert xxiv
belle Hélène, La (Offenbach) 317

Bellini, Vincenzo 22, 34
Bergamo, Donizetti Festival 58
Berganza, Teresa xxvii, 252
Bergenz Festival: *Nabucco* 311, 312
Berghaus, Ruth, dir 182
Berlin: *Carmen* 290; *Giulio Cesare* 329;
    Tosca 105, 112
Berlin, Deutsche Oper: *Bohème* 238;
    Madama Butterfly 147, 148; *Werther*
    314–15
Berlin State Opera: *Elektra* 185, 189;
    Rigoletto 201
Bernacus, David, bar 208, 209
Bernhardt, Sarah, 287
Bernstein, Leonard, cdr 76, 321
Bertelsman New Voices Competition
    308
Betrothal in a Monastery (Prokofiev):
    Clara 96, 102
Bilbao: *Norma* 351
Bizet, Georges 293n
Bogachov, Vladimir 271
Bogachova, Irina, tchr 265
bohème, La (Puccini): Mimì 4, 11, 37,
    58–9, 74, 78–9, 80–1, 83, 125,
    203; Musetta 163, 166, 178, 235;
    Rodolfo 81
Böhm, Karl 286
Bolshoi Theatre, *see* Moscow
Bologna: *Cenerentola* 255, 258; *Falstaff*
    69; *Giulio Cesare* 329; *Poppea* 329
Bondy, Luc, dir: *Don Carlos* 162, 171,
    172–3; *Don Giovanni* 170; *Salome*
    152
Bonn: *Barbiere* 327; *Guarany* 240;
    Traviata 239
Bonney, Barbara, spr xxiii, **3–19**, 37,
    39, 275, 276, 278
Boris Godunov (Musorgsky): Fyodor
    309; Marina Mniszek 266
Borodina, Olga, mspr 93, 94, 98,

329, **263–73**
Borovsky, Victor 102–3
Boulevard Solitude (Henze): Manon
    142
Boult, Sir Adrian 335n
Brahms, Johannes 195, 353
Britten, Benjamin 21
Brussels, Théâtre de la Monnaie:
    Figaro 166; *Giulio Cesare* 329;
    Meistersinger 166–7; *Otello* 67, 68
Budden, Julian 314
Buenos Aires, Teatro Colón: *Otello*
    242; *Simon Boccanegra* 166; *Tosca* 99
Bullock, John, tchr 322–3
Bumbry, Grace 293n, 349
Burchuladze, Paata, bs 108

Caballé, Montserrat, spr xxii, 48, 203
Cage, John 308
Callas, Maria, spr 33, 34, 54, 70, 75,
    105, 111, 203, 247, 252
campanello di notte, Il (Donizetti):
    Serafina 127, 237
Canetti, Giovanna, tchr 57–8
Canning, Hugh q3–4, q96, q163
cantatrice villane, Le 258
Cappuccilli, Piero, bar 9
Capriccio (Strauss) 36
Capuleti e i Montecchi (Rossini): Juliet
    315; Romeo 314, 315, 317, 326,
    329
Cardiff Singer of the World 165, 173
Carmen (Bizet): Carmen 257, 269,
    284, 289–94, 299, 300, 301, 302,
    318, 329–30; Don José 60, 82,
    290, 291, 292, 293, 302, 332;
    Escamillo 290; Frasquita 293;
    Mercédes 293; Micaëla 59–60, 74,
    82, 125, 293
Carolis, Natale de, bsbar 60, 65, 71–2
Carreras, José, tnr xx, 9, 75

Carsen, Robert, dir: *Lohengrin* 173, 174

Caruso, Enrico, tnr 93

Catania, Teatro Bellini: *favorita, La* 300

Cavalleria rusticana (Mascagni): Santuzza 24, 95, 106, 111, 114, 119, 349–50; Turiddu 350

Cavalli, Francesco 249

Cavani, Liliana, dir: *Pagliacci* 85

Celibidache 89

Cenerentola, La (Rossini): Angelina 248, 255–6, 268, 270, 328–9

Central City, Colorado: *Falstaff* 144

Chaliapin, Fyodor 264, 304

Chereau, Patrice, dir: *Don Giovanni* 312

Chérubin (Massenet): Chérubin 274, 282–3; Nina 74, 82

Cheryov, Vladimir 135

Chicago Lyric Opera xxi, xxv, 20, 141, 142, 167, 175, 188; *Aida* 344; *Don Carlos* 344; *Falstaff* 202; *Faust* 47–8; *Figaro* 43, 144, 282; *Fledermaus* 10; *Gioconda* 34; *Idomeneo* 314; *Lulu* 154; *Makropoulos* 154; *Parsifal* 159; *Rake's Progress* 202; *Ring* 28, 29, 30, 31; *Tosca* 105, 112; *Traviata* 207; *Tristan und Isolde* 34–5; *Voyage of Edgar Allan Poe* 202

Chicago Sun Times, The q282

Chicago Tribune, The 249

Christie, William, cdr 249; *Alcina* 37

clemenza di Tito, La (Mozart): Annio 274, 309–10, 311, 324; Servilia 144; Sesto 215, 257, 309, 316–17, 324; Vitellia 70, 211, 214, 215, 219–20, 221, 224

Colbran, Isabella, spr 40, 257

Coliban, Sorin 122n

Cologne: *Elektra* 193; *Giulio Cesare* 329

Coltellini, Celeste, mspr 258

Columbia Artists xxi, xxii, 123, 178

comte Ory, Le (Rossini): Isolier 325

Connell, Elizabeth, mspr 219

contes d'Hoffmann, Les (Offenbach): Antonia 144, 148; Giulietta 289, 300

Copley, John, dir: *Bohème* 74; *Orlando* 204–5

corsaro, Il (Verdi): Medora 68, 242

Così fan tutte (Mozart) 55; Despina 11, 198, 199, 202, 248, 254–5; Dorabella 62–3, 255, 274, 277, 285–6, 300, 306, 318, 325; Ferrando 62–3, 224, 340–1; Fiordiligi 4, 11, 25, 36, 43–4, 60, 62–5, 67, 163, 166, 167, 211, 220, 224, 226, 230–1, 236–7, 285–6; Guglielmo 63

Cossotto, Fiorenza, mspr 109, 215

Cotrubas, Ileana, spr 165

Covent Garden, *see* London, Royal Opera House

Cox, John, adm 219

Daily Telegraph, The q271

Dallas: *Lucia Lammermoor* 202

Dalrymple, Mr and Mrs William 321

Damnation de Faust, La (Berlioz) 268, 270; Marguerite 274, 283, 284, 301, 317

·*Dangerous Liaisons* (Susa): Tourvel 37

Daphne (Strauss) 36

Darmstadt, State Theater 8–9, 10; *Elektra* 184; *Figaro* 15; *Idomeneo* 15; *lustige Witwe* 16; *lustigen Weiber von Windsor* 9

Davis, Sir Colin, cdr: *Clemenza* 310; *Damnation de Faust* 268

de los Angeles, Victoria, spr 47

Decker, Willy, dir: *Werther* 283, 284

Delfici, I 249

Dew, John, dir: *clemenza* 309

Diadkova, Larissa xvii, 93

Dialogues des Carmélites 211

Dido and Aeneas (Purcell): Sorceress 298

Dimitrova, Ghena 305

Dohnányi, Christoph von, cdr: *Salome* q153, 154; *Wozzeck* 181

Domingo, Placido, tnr xx, 22, 23, 51–2, 58, 60, 68, 75, 82, 105, 116, 118, 121, 123, 133, 136, 154, 176, 194, 226, 232, 238–40, 241, 267, 271, 289, 290, 298, 299, 300

Don Carlos (Verdi): Don Carlos 172, 347; Eboli 228, 270–1, 285, 319, 329, 333, 344–6, 353; Elisabeth de Valois 69, 100, 108, 162, 170, 171–3, 175, 177, 178, 226, 228–9, 242; King Philip 172, 173, 346; Rodrigo 173, 347, 346

Don Giovanni (Mozart): Don Giovanni 11, 12, 46, 65–6, 80, 122, 170, 216, 218, 255, 275, 276, 293, 312; Don Ottavio 45–6, 216; Donna Anna 20, 24, 27, 36, 43, 45–6, 51, 65, 66, 80, 122–4, 125, 129, 163, 166, 167, 176, 211, 212, 216–19, 220, 230, 232, 309, 312; Donna Elvira 24, 36, 45, 60, 65, 66, 80, 129, 163, 166, 167, 178–9, 211, 217, 218, 225, 255, 312; Masetto 313; Zerlina 11, 45, 74, 79–80, 125, 129, 202, 254, 255, 282, 312

Don Pasquale (Donizetti): Norina 199

Donizetti, Gaetano 10

donna del lago, La (Rossini): Malcolm 257

Dorn, Dieter, dir 182

Dresden: *Tristan* 193

Drese, Dr Claus Helmut, dir 122

due Foscari, I (Verdi) 105, 110

Eaglen, Jane, spr **20–35**, 71, 112

Eda-Pierre, Christiane, spr 145

Edinburgh Festival 98, 263

Egg, The (Menotti): Old Beggar Woman 321

Elektra (Strauss): Chrysothemis 162, 170–1, 173, 175, 185; Elektra 184–5, 189, 191, 193; Klytemnestra 170

L'elisir d'amore (Donizetti): Adina 10, 74, 199, 202, 203

Enchantress, The (Tchaikovsky): Kuma 95, 100–1

English National Opera, *see* London

Entführung aus dem Serail, Die (Mozart): Blonde 145; Constanze 14, 42, 124, 129, 133, 142, 145, 202

Epstein, Matthew, adm xxi, qxxii, xxv, qxxvi–xxvii, 142, q146, 147, 160, 175, 188

Ernani (Verdi): Elvira 105, 106, 112, 113, 119, 204, 242

Eschenbach, Christoph, cdr: *Arabella* 15; *Rosenkavalier* 38

Eugene Onegin (Tchaikovsky) 94; Olga 308; Tatiana 95–6, 102, 163, 178

Evening Standard (London), *The* q74

Ewing, Maria, mspr 153

Eyre, Richard, dir: *Traviata* 82, 135, 136

Faggioni, Piero, cdr 69, 232; *Tosca* 110–11

Fairman, Richard 313

Falstaff (Verdi): Alice Ford 69; Meg Page 285, 309; Nannetta 10, 74, 142, 144, 199, 202

Farina, Franco 138

Fassbaender, Brigitte, mspr 275

Faull, Ellen, tchr 236

Faust (Gounod): Marguerite 36,
47–8; Siébel 265, 277

favorita, La (Donizetti): Leonora 300,
329, 353

Fedora (Giordano): Fedora 106,
118–19; Loris 118; Vladimir 118

Feinstein, Martin, adm q294

feldeltà premiata, La 249

Ferrara: *Figaro* 61

Fidelio (Beethoven): Leonore 34, 175,
184, 185–6; Marzelline 10

Fiery Angel, The (Prokofiev): Renata
91–2, 98, 100, 103, 142, 159, 160;
Ruprecht 91

Financial Times, The q74, q91, q193–4,
q256

Fischer, Adam, cdr: Nina 259

Fledermaus, Die (Strauss): Adele 10;
Rosalinde 163

Fleming, Renée, spr xxii, xxvi, 5, 15,
17, **36–54**, 188, 198, 275, 276, 352

fliegende Holländer, Der (Wagner):
Senta 142, 159, 175, 183–4

Florence, 193; *Barbiere* 311; *Bohème*
59; *Carmen* 290; *contes d'Hoffmann*
144; *Don Giovanni* 232; *Giuoco del
batone* 58; *Idomeneo* 305, 313, 314;
Norma 33; *Trovatore* 58

Ford, Bruce 276

forza del destino, La (Verdi) 108; Carlo
101; Leonora xxiii, 68, 101, 211;
Preziosilla 306

Fra Diavolo (Auber): Zerlina 127

Francesca da Rimini (Zandonai):
Francesca 85

Frankfurt Opera 10

Freeman, David, dir: *Fiery Angel* 98

Freiburg: *Fidelio* 185; *Tristan* 193

Freischütz, Der (Weber): Aennchen 10;

Agathe 163, 166

Freni, Mirella, spr 9, 203, 251

Freud, Sigmund 339

Frittoli, Barbara, spr xxiii, **55–72**,
22n

Gall, Hugues, dir 10

Galtiero, Lou, tchr 337

Galuppi, Baldassare 259

Gardiner, John Eliot, cdr: *lustige
Witwe* 16

Gatti, Daniele, cdr: *Falstaff* 69

Gavanelli, Paolo 138

Gavazzeni, Gianandrea, cdr: *Ballo in
maschera* 109

gazza ladra, La (Rossini): Pippo 312

Gelsenkirchen: *fliegende Holländer* 184

Geneva, Grand Théâtre: *Carmen* 290;
Così 199, 202; *Don Pasquale* 202;
Falstaff 10; *Figaro* 43; *Puritani* 202;
Simon Boccanegra 166

Genoa, Teatro Carlo Felice 58, 299;
Carmen 290; *Werther* 302

George London Foundation xxiv

Gergiev, Valery, cdr xxiii, 96, 97–8,
99, 270, 272; *Queen of Spades* 105

Gergieva, Larissa, accomp 272

Gheorghiu, Angela, spr xx, 37n, 57,
73–89, 94, 125, 138

Ghosts of Versailles, The (Corigliano):
Rosina 37

Gilbert, Sir W. S. 24

Gioconda, La (Ponchielli): Gioconda
27, 34

Giulio Cesare (Handel): Cleopatra 11,
124, 130, 134, 136–7, 206, 329;
Giulio Cesare 329

giuoco del batone, Il (Bucchi) 58

Glasgow Herald, The q263

Glinka, Mikhail 94

Glinka Competition 95, 107

Glyndebourne Festival Opera:
Clemenza 215; *Così* 55, 62, 63–5,
220, 224; *Don Giovanni* 65, 66,
220; *Figaro* 43, 44; *Idomeneo* 220,
221, 223; *Simon Boccanegra* 225
Goehr, Alexander: *Arianna* 274
Gorchakova, Galina, spr xxv, **91–103**,
116
Götterdämmerung (Wagner):
Brünnhilde xxi, 20, 22, 27–31, 34,
184, 186–7, 189, 190–1, 193; Erda
354; Fricka 354; Second Norn
307–8; Wellgunde 308
Graham, Susan, mspr xxiv, 17, 37,
47, 82, **274–88**
Graham, Tom 178
Graves, Denyce, mspr xxiv, **289–303**
Graz: *Armida* 249
Green, Alan 123, 132
Griselda, La (Scarlatti) 249
Groszer, Christoph 306
Gruberová, Edita, spr 308, 312
Guleghin, Mark, bar 105, 108, 116,
119, 120
Guleghina, Maria, spr 93, **104–20**,
228, 271

Hadzinassios, George 128
Hagegård, Håkan, bar 13, 18
Haitink, Bernard, cdr: *Così* 224; *Don
Carlos* 100, 171; *Don Giovanni* 219;
Idomeneo 220
Hall, Donald, tchr 337
Hall, Sir Peter, dir: *Don Giovanni* 216,
219; *Aida* 116; *Bohème* 238; *Don
Giovanni* 167; *Eugene Onegin* 178;
Fiery Angel 98; *Jenůfa* 177;
Khovanshchina 270; *Macbeth* 348;
Rigoletto 201; *Tosca* 105, 112
Hamburg State Opera 10: *Bohème*
238; *Fiery Angel* 98; *Jenůfa* 177;

Khovanshchina 270; *Macbeth* 346,
348–9; *Rigoletto* 201; *Tosca* 105,
112, 238
Hamlet (Thomas): Ophélie 204
Hampson, Thomas 12, 85, 173, 204,
282, 250, 329
Handel, G. F. 11, 25, 133, 137, 205
Hänsel und Gretel (Humperdinck) 326,
352: Gretel 10, 144; Hänsel 282,
298, 319, 326
Harewood, Lord 167
Harnoncourt, Nikolas, cdr: *anima del
filosofo* 249; *Armida* 249; *Clemenza*
309; *Don Giovanni* 255; *Figaro* 11,
253, 254; *Périchole* 317; *Trionfo*
249
Hartmann, Irmgard, tchr 182, 187,
188, q189, q190, q194
Hasse, Johann Adolph 259
Helsinki, National Opera House:
Figaro 165; *Simon Boccanegra* 166
Heppner, Ben 34
Hérodiade (Massenet): Hérodiade 352;
Salomé 36, 39–40, 48
Herzog, Werner, dir: *Guarany* 240
Higgins, John q86–7
Hodden, Prof., tchr 296–7
Hofmannsthal, Hugo von 38
Hogwood, Christopher, cdr: *Rinaldo*
249
Holl, Helmut, tchr 41
Holland Festival: *Figaro* 144
Hollywood Bowl: *Carmen* 329
Holowid, Stephen 144–5, 148
Hong Kong: *Queen of Spades* 101
Horne, Marilyn 146, 285, 296, 310,
311
Horres, Kurt, cdr 10; *Meistersinger*
167, 169
Houston Grand Opera xxiv, 52; *Attila*
112–13; *Cenerentola* 255; *Figaro* 42;

Houston Grand Opera – *continued*
   Hänsel und Gretel 297; *Macbeth*
   157–8; *Otello* 157, 297–8;
   Rosenkavalier 38, 39
Houston Opera, Richard F. Gold
   Career Grant 298
Houston, Whitney 20
Hugo, Victor 201
Humperdinck, Engelbert 10
Hvorostovsky, Dmitry 269, 282

Iasonidou, Medea, tchr 123, 128, 129
Idomeneo (Mozart) 304: Elettra 70,
   211, 214, 220, 221–3, 309;
   Idamante 222, 257, 287, 313–14,
   317; Ilia 10, 14–15, 163
IMG 18, 178
L'incoronazione di Poppea (Monteverdi)
   143, 160; Ottavia 329
Iolanta (Tchaikovsky): Iolanta 98, 107
L'italiana in Algeri (Rossini): Isabella
   252, 271, 319, 325, 326, 327, 328,
   329; Lindoro 329
Ivanov, Evgeny, tchr 107

Jacobs, Arthur q144
Jenůfa (Janáček): Jenůfa 163, 177;
   Kostelnička 352
Joel, Nicholas, dir: *Lucia di
   Lammermoor* 202
Johnson, Beverley, tchr 41, 42
Jonas, Peter, adm 136
Jones, Gwyneth, spr 275
Jones, Richard, dir: *Götterdämmerung*
   191; *Walküre* 28
Joy of Music, The (TV series) 76
Juan Carlos of Spain, King 172n
Judge, Ian, dir: *Norma* 31–2

Kabaivanska, Raina, spr 305
Kaipainen, Jouni 179

Karajan, Herbert von, cdr xxiii, 184,
   252, 306; *Aida* 9; *Bohème* 59;
   Rosenkavalier 38–9; *Trovatore* 69
Kasarova, Vesselina, mspr xx, 135,
   304–18
Kát'a Kabanová (Janáček) 178
Katona, Peter, adm xxvi, qxxvii, q55,
   q73, 78–9, 80, 82–3, q87, q101,
   q123–4, q125, 129, q130–1, q136,
   q137, q139, q263, q274, 316–17
Kaufmann, Roger 308
Kelessidi, Elena, spr **121–39**
Khovanshchina (Musorgsky) 270;
   Marfa 127, 265, 266, 267, 270
Kirov, *see* St Petersburg, Mariinsky
   Theatre
Kleiber, Carlos, cdr: *Bohème* 59;
   Rosenkavalier 4, 6–7, 10, 278
Koenig, Lesley, dir: *Così* 254
Koleva, Ressa, tchr 305, 306
Krainik, Ardis, dir xxv, q142
Kraus, Alfredo, tnr 148, 204, 338
Kuhn, Gustav, cdr 130
Kupfer, Harry, dir 182; *Damnation de
   Faust* 270; *Ring* 186, 191

Lady Macbeth of Mtsensk
   (Shostakovich): Lady Macbeth 105,
   106, 142, 159
Lappeenranta Singing Competition
   165
Larmore, Jennifer, mspr qxix, **319–31**
Lasser-Petrov, Luisa 306
Lear, Evelyn 277
Lecca, Jean Marie: *Carmen* 290
Leech, Richard 150, 206
Legend of the Invisible City of Kitezh, The
   (Rimsky-Korsakov): Fevroniya 95,
   98
Lehár, Franz 10–11, 16
Lehnhoff, Nikolaus, dir 182

Leinsdorf, Erich, cdr 321

Lemnitz, Tiana, spr 167

Leningrad, *see* St Petersburg

Levine, James, cdr q xx–xxi, xxiv,
xxv, q52, 178, 324–5; *Cavalleria
rusticana* 106; *Cenerentola* 256, 325;
Così 254; *Don Giovanni* 202; *Figaro*
257; *Idomeneo* 223; *Lohengrin* 175;
Lucia q202; *Meistersinger* 162, 170;
Samson et Dalila 299; *Tosca* 106;
Trovatore 342

Lewis, Henry, cdr 146–8

Lewis, Keith 216

Lievi, Cesare, dir: *Cenerentola* 256;
Nina 258, 259

Lindsley, Charles, tchr 212

Linko-Malmio, Liisa, tchr 164, 165

Lipp, Wilma, spr 122, 123

Lisbon: *Don Giovanni* 66

Lock, James 89

Lohengrin (Wagner): Elsa 22n, 71,
162, 173, 174–5, 176, 177, 191;
Ortrud 352

London, Albert Hall: *Traviata* 121,
135

London, Barbican Hall: *Bohème* 59;
Ernani 106, 112, 113

London, English National Opera 24,
27; *Ariadne aux Naxos* 24; *Cavalleria
rusticana* 24; *Don Giovanni* 24; *Mary
Stuart* 24, 25, 26; *Moses* 24;
Trovatore 24

London, Festival Hall: *Così* 44; *Don
Giovanni* 45; *Enchantress* 100–1;
Parsifal 193; *Wozzeck* 181

London, Royal Academy of Music
19

London, Royal Opera House, Covent
Garden xxvi, 55, 73–4, 78–9, 102,
344; *Alzira* 240; *Barbiere* 311, 327;
Bohème 74, 84, 88, 125, 166, 178;
Carmen 60, 74, 82, 125, 267, 290;
Cenerentola 268; *Chérubin* 82;
Clemenza 219; *Così* 62, 63, 163,
166, 285; *Damnation de Faust* 268,
270, 301–2; *Don Carlos* 162, 171,
173; *Don Giovanni* 79, 125, 216,
217, 218; *Elektra* 171, 185; *Ernani*
242; *Eugene Onegin* 96; *Falstaff* 69;
Fedora 106; *Fiery Angel* 91, 98;
Figaro 144; *Forza* 101; *Freischütz*
166; *Giulio Cesare* 134, 136–7;
Götterdämmerung 191; *Lohengrin*
173, 174; *Madama Butterfly* 150;
Médée 44; *Nina* 125; *Norma* 32;
Oberto 301–2; *Rondine* 84–7;
Rosenkavalier 3, 10; *Salome* 152;
Samson et Dalila 270; *Semele* 204,
205–6; *Simon Boccanegra* 44; *Tosca*
99; *Traviata* 74, 82, 87, 121, 125,
129, 130–3, 136; *Trovatore* 225–6;
Turandot 34, 81, 125; *Viaggio a
Reims* 45; *Walküre* 189

London, Wigmore Hall 19, 271

London, George, bsbar xxiii, xxiv,
42, 141, 183

Loppert, Max q247

Lorengar, Pilar, spr 131, 236

Lorescu, Arta, tchr 78

Los Angeles Music Centre: *Carmen*
299

Los Angeles Opera: *Carmen* 290;
Norma 34; *Pagliacci* 240

Lott, Felicity, spr 6, 7

Louise (Charpentier): Louise 36, 46,
79

Lucia di Lammermoor (Donizetti) 80;
Alisa 308; Arturo 202; Lucia 85,
197, 202–3

Lucio Silla (Mozart): Cecilio 257, 274

Lucrezia Borgia (Donizetti): Lucrezia
37, 54, 85, 242

Ludwig, Christa, mspr qxxii,
    qxxiv–xxv, 277
Luisa Fernando 234
Luisa Miller (Verdi): Luisa 69, 137–8;
    Miller 138; Rodolfo 138
Lulu (Berg): Lulu 154
lustigen Weiber von Windsor, Die
    (Nicolai): Anna 9
lustige Witwe, Die (Lehár): Danilo 16,
    177; Hanna Glawari 10–11, 16,
    163, 177
Lyons: *Barbiere* 325

Macauley, Alistair q91–2, 100
Macbeth (Verdi): Lady Macbeth 70,
    71, 100, 113–14, 119, 157–8,
    346–49; Macbeth 348
McEwen, Terence, adm, xxv, 198,
    337, 338
McIver, Dr Robert, tchr 322
Mackerras, Sir Charles, cdr qxix, xx;
    Don Giovanni 218; *Figaro* 56, q61–2;
    Makropoulos q151, 157; *Orlando* 204;
    Rusalka 131, 352; *Semele* 204–5
McNair, Sylvia 329
McTeague (Bolcom) 143
Madama Butterfly (Puccini) xxi;
    Butterfly xxi, 25, 95, 99, 142, 146,
    147, 148, 149–50, 151, 152, 160,
    238, 241–2; Pinkerton 150
Madrid: *Eugene Onegin* 178; *Giulio
    Cesare* 329; *Idomeneo* 15
Mahler, Gustav 71, 195
Makropoulos Affair, The (Janáček):
    Elina Makropoulos 141, 151, 152,
    154, 155, 156; Emilia Marty 152,
    156
Malas, Marlena, tchr 285
Malfitano, Catherine, spr xxii, xxvi,
    140–61
Mannheim: *Götterdämmerung* 186

Manon (Massenet): Des Grieux 49;
    Manon 10, 36, 39–40, 47, 48–9,
    51, 54, 85, 142, 145, 147, 157, 160,
    206, 207, 208
Manon Lescaut (Puccini): Manon
    99–100, 101, 118, 163, 178
Mansouri, Lofti, adm 269
Maria Stuarda (Donizetti): Elizabeth I
    24, 25; Maria 85, 329
Marian Anderson Award 298
Mariinsky Theatre, *see* St Petersburg
Marin, Constantin 77
Marin, Ion, cdr 77
Marton, Eva, spr 338, 342
Mass in B minor (Bach, J. S.), 252, 306
Massé, Denise, tchr 194
Massenet, Jules 10
Mattila, Karita, spr xx, **162–80**, 188,
    217
Mauceri, John, cdr: *Carmen* 329
Mazeppa (Tchaikovsky) 102
Mazzonis, Cesare, adm 108–9, 110
Meat Loaf 20
Medecin, Pierre 319, 326
Médée (Cherubini) 44; Médée 32, 33
Mehta, Zubin, cdr 321; *Figaro* 43;
    Tristan und Isolde 193
Meistersinger von Nürnberg, Die
    (Wagner): Eva 36, 50, 51, 162,
    166–9, 170, 173, 179; Hans Sachs
    167, 168–9; Walther 168
Mentzez, Suzanne 215
Menuhin, Lord: *Otello* 137
Merida Festival: *Carmen* 267;
    Salammbô 267
Merola Program, *see* San Francisco
    Opera
Metropolitan Opera House, *see* New
    York
Michigan: *Manon* 206
Mikhalski, Nicolai, tchr 95

Milan, La Scala 20, 102; *Ballo* 105;
　Beatrice di Tenda 58; *Comte Ory* 327;
　Damnation de Faust 283; *Don Carlos*
　344, 346; *due Foscari* 105, 110; *Fiery*
　Angel 91–2, 98, 100; *Forza* xxiii;
　Lady Macbeth 106; *Lucrezia Borgia*
　37, 54; *Macbeth* 114; *Madama*
　Butterfly 150; *Nabucco* 108–10,
　115–16; *Norma* 34; *Ring* 30; school
　108; *Tosca* 105, 110–12; *Zauberflöte*
　10, 13, 18
Miller, Jonathan, dir q65, q88, q89,
　q307, q308, 318; *Anna Bolena* 313;
　Bohème 59; *Così* 62, 63, q177, 285;
　Don Giovanni q232; *Figaro* 11–12,
　61; *Idomeneo* 313–14; *Mitridate* 316;
　Traviata 88–9
Milnes, Sherrill, bar 342
Minneapolis: *Carmen* 290, 299
Minnesota Opera Company 144
Minsk Opera 107, 108
Mitridate, re di Ponto (Mozart):
　Farnace 316; Sifare 60, 63, 257
Moffo, Anna 47
Moll, Kurt 7
Monaco, Giancarlo del, adm 240
Monde, Le q48
Monitz, Andrei 127
Monte Carlo: *L'amico Fritz* 85;
　Francesca da Rimini 85; *Macbeth* 114
Monteverdi 86, 249, 274, 329
Montreal: *Don Carlos* 242
Mortier, Gerard, dir 67
Moscow, Bolshoi Theatre, 97, 103,
　265; *Tsar's Bride* 127
Moses (Rossini): Sinaïde 24
Moses und Aron (Schoenberg) 202
Moshinsky, Elijah, dir qxxv–xxvi,
　q101–2; *Forza* 101–2; *Lohengrin*
　173, q174–5; *Makropoulos* 141;
　Samson et Dalila 267, 270

Mozart, W. A. 8, 15, 27, 53, 70, 94,
　173, 198n, 259, 260, 309, 313, 316;
　Requiem 235
Mulgan, Diana 178
Munich, Bavarian State Opera 20;
　Aida 116; *Anna Bolena* 305, 312;
　Ariadne 281; *Ballo* 105; *Carmen* 290;
　Cenerentola 255; *Don Giovanni* 216;
　Entführung 202; *Forza* 101; *Lulu*
　154; *Rosenkavalier* 10, 275, 278;
　Traviata 136, 138
Munich Festival: *Meistersinger* 166, 169
Murray, Ann, mspr 219, 308
Music Magazine 102–3
Muti, Riccardo, cdr 60–1, 68;
　cantatriei 258; *Cenerentola* 258; *Così*
　62–5, 312; *forza* xxiii; *Macbeth* 114;
　Norma 33, 34; *Pagliacci* 85; *Trovatore*
　68; Verdi *Requiem* 69

Nabucco (Verdi): Abigaille 100, 105,
　106, 108–10, 114, 115–16; ; Fenena
　114, 115, 311–12; ; Ismaele 114, 115
Napa Valley: *Così* 213
Naples: *Bohème* 58; cantatrie villane
　258; *Don Giovanni* 65
Nelson, John, cdr: *Faust* 48
Neschling, John, cdr: *Guarany* 240
Nesterenko, Evgeny, bs 324
Netherlands Opera: *Moses und Aron*
　202
Nevada Opera Company 336
New York, Carnegie Hall 179, 180;
　Armida 37, 52–3; *Capuleti e i*
　Montecchi 326; *Norma* 34; *Tancredi*
　311
New York City Opera 144; *Clemenza*
　215; *Don Giovanni* 216, 219; *Traviata*
　220
New York, First Presbyterian Church
　337

New York, Metropolitan Opera House, xxi, xxiv, xxv, 20, 42, 49, 79, 102; *Aida* 116; *Andrea Chenier* 106; *Arabella* 10, 15; *Ariadne* 10; Auditions 233, 236, 297, 323; *Ballo* 343; *Barbiere* 202, 328; *Bohème* 59, 74, 178, 237; *Boris Godunov* 266, 268; *Carmen* 301; *Cavalleria rusticana* 106; *Cenerentola* 255, 256, 325, 326; *Clemenza* 215, 224; *Contes d'Hoffmann* 148; *Così* 224, 248, 254, 285; *Don Carlos* 346; *Don Giovanni* 46, 202, 217; *Elektra* 170; *Elisir d'amore* 202; *Entführung* 145; *Falstaff* 285; *Faust* 47–8; *Fiery Angel* 98; *Figaro* 13, 43, 44, 202, 224, 257, 282; *Forza* 101; *Giulio Cesare* 329; *Hänsel und Gretel* 144, 326; *Idomeneo* 223; *Jenůfa* 177; *Lohengrin* 175; *Louise* 47; *Lucia Lammermoor* 202; *Madama Butterfly* 99, 150, 151; *Makropoulos* 141, 151, 157; *Meistersinger* 162, 170, 179; *Otello* 51–2; *Parsifal* 189, 193; *Puritani* 204; *Queen of Spades* 101, 105, 163, 178, 268; *Rake's Progress* 291–2; *Rigoletto* 201, 204; *Rinaldo* 223; *Roméo et Juliette* 75, 202, 206; *Rosenkavalier* 319; *Rusalka* 51, 352; *Samson et Dalila* 300; *Thaïs* 47; *Tosca* 106; *Traviata* 238, 142n; *Tristan und Isolde* 35; *Trovatore* 341–2, 343; *Turandot* 34, 196, 202, 208; *Werther* 283; *Zauberflöte* 132
New York Times, The, q34, q206–7, 301, q341
Newsweek 247
Nilsson, Birgit, spr xxii, 332
Nina (Paisiello): Lindoro 259; Nina 125, 248, 254, 258–61, 262
Norma (Bellini): Adalgisa 215, 301, 313, 314, 329, 338, 353; Norma 20, 22, 23, 26, 27, 29, 30, 31–4, 119
Norman, Jessye, spr xx
Novosibirsk, opera house 93
nozze di Figaro, Le (Mozart) 69, 198n; Cherubino 10, 12, 15, 225, 253, 254, 255, 257, 274, 275, 277, 281–2, 310, 319; Count 12, 13, 61, 253, 282; Countess 4, 11, 12, 36, 42–3, 44, 56, 60, 61–2, 66, 163, 211, 224–5, 229, 253–4; Figaro 12, 13, 253; Susanna 9, 10, 11–12, 13, 23, 25, 43, 61–2, 79, 142, 144, 197, 198, 202, 253, 254, 255, 257
Nucci, Leo, bar 109
nuits d'été, Les (Berlioz) 287
Nunn, Trevor, dir: *Idomeneo* 220

Oberon (Weber): Reiza 163
Oberto (Verdi): Cuniza 301
Olmi, Paolo, dir: *Otello* 68
Onassis, Aristotle 75
Opera 160, 164, 167, 218, 225, 247, 281, 314
Opera de Nice 319; *Anna Bolena* 324; *Cenerentola* 325; *Clemenza* 324; *Comte Ory* 325; *Don Giovanni* 324; *Orfeo* 329; *Poppea* 329
Opera News 41, 103, 212, 333
Opera Now 37, 40, q51, 312
Opernwelt 313, 315
Orfeo (Monteverdi) 326; Silvia 329
Orlando (Handel): Shepherdess 204
Otello (Rossini): Desdemona 121, 137
Otello (Verdi): Cassio 67, 227; Desdemona 37, 50, 51–2, 60, 67–8, 80, 178, 211, 225, 226–7, 229, 242, 273; Emilia 298; Otello 51–2, 67, 226–7, 298
Otter, Anne-Sofie von, mspr 7
Ovation 231

Oviedo: *Così* 236
Oxburg: *Siegfried* 186
Ozawa, Seiji cdr 309; *Damnation de Faust* 283

Packwood, Mark, tchr 125
Pagliacci, I (Leoncavallo): Canio 85, 240–1; Nedda 85, 144, 237, 240–1
Palermo, Teatro Massimo: *Antigone* 300; *Contes d'Hoffmann* 300
Palumbo, Donald q141
Panaki, Elena, spr 127
Pappano, Antonio, cdr: *Don Carlos* 171; *Otello* 67
Paris, Châtelet: *Arabella* 163; *Don Carlos* 171; *Elektra* 189; *Louise* 46; *Mitridate* 63
Paris, Opéra and Opéra Bastille, 20, 102; *Alcina* 37; *Barbiere* 325; *Boris Godunov* 266; *Capuleti e i Montecchi* 314, 315; *Carmen* 290; *Così* 166, 285; *Don Carlos* 170, 229; *Don Giovanni* 66; *Elektra* 185; *Entführung* 145; *Faust* 47–8; *Figaro* 10, 198n, 202, 288; *Giulio Cesare* 206, 329; *Italiana in Algeri* 319, 3235; *Lohengrin* 173, 174; *Lustige Witwe* 177; *Macbeth* 119; *Manon* 145, 206; *Nabucco* 105, 115; *Norma* 34; *Pagliacci* 144; *Rigoletto* 204; *Rosenkavalier* 3–7, 17, 37–9, 275, 288; *Traviata* 88–9; *Walküre* 176
Paris, Palais Garnier: *Don Giovanni* 45
Parsifal (Wagner) 100; Gurnemanz 194; Kundry 142, 159–60, 189, 191, 193–4; Parsifal 159, 193, 194
Patience (Gilbert and Sullivan): Lady Ella 24
Pavarotti, Luciano, tnr xx, 34, 57, 75, 105, 109, 230, 247, 341
Pavarotti Competition 236

Pavlov, Prof., tchr q126–7
pêcheurs de perles, Les (Bizet): Leila 125
Pelléas et Mélisande (Debussy) 325
périchole, La (Offenbahc) 317
Perry, David 298–9
Perth: *Così* 25; *Madama Butterfly* 25; *Tosca* 24
Pesaro: *Armida* 37, 52–3; *Cenerentola* 319
Petrov, Luisa Lasser 78–9
Pettersson, Ann-Margret, dir: *Carmen* 291
Philadelphia Academy of Music: *Così* 300
Piccinni, Nicola 259
Pido, Evelino, dir 314
Pilou, Jeanetta, spr 122, 123
pirata, Il (Bellini): Imogene 52
Plishka, Paul, bs 338
Pola, Bruno, tchr 57
Polaski, Deborah, spr xxvi, 171, **181–95**
Ponnelle, Jean-Pierre, dir 225; *Cenerentola* 270; *Figaro* 253
Ponselle, Rosa, spr 93
Popp, Lucia, spr 4, 6, 83, 165, 169, 275
Poulenc, Francis 8, 353
Powers, William, 321
Previn, André 37
Price, Dame Margaret 32
Price, Leontyne, spr xxii, 36, 48, 57, 92, 116, 209, 211, 296
Prince Igor (Borodin): Yaroslavna 95
Pritchard, John, cdr: *Norma* 32
Puccini, Giacomo xx, 59, 100, 102, 118
Puffer, Ted, tchr 334, 336, 337
puritani, I (Bellini) 124: Elvira 202, 204, 215; Enrichetta 215
Puttnam, Ashley, spr 220

Queen of Spades, The (Tchaikovsky) 93, 94, 96; Lisa 95, 96, 101, 102, 105, 163, 178; Pauline 309

Queler, Eva, cdr 52; *Capuleti* 326; *Tancredi* 311

Raeburn, Christopher 252

Raimondi, Ruggero, bs 9, 12, 68, 80, 122, 123, 130, 154, 225

Rake's Progress, The (Stravinsky): Anne Trulove 202; Baba the Turk 291–2

Ramey, Samuel, bs xxii, 47, 216, 223, 297, 338

Ravenna Festival: *Norma* 33, 34; *Pagliacci* 85

Ravinia Festival, 19; *Samson et Dalila* 299

Reiss, Janine, tchr qxxi, 47, 194, 352

Requiem (Verdi) 31, 69–70, 344

Rifa, José qxxvii

Rigoletto (Verdi) 80, 94; Countess Ceprano 107; Duke 138, 201; Gilda 10, 80, 85, 113, 117, 124, 128, 130, 138, 197, 199–201, 204, 242; Giovanna 201; Maddalena 329; Rigoletto 138, 200–1

Rinaldo (Handel) 249: Armida 223

Ring des Nibelungen, Der (Wagner): Brünnhilde xxi, 20, 22, 27–31, 34, 184, 186–7, 189, 190–1, 193; Erda 352; Fricka 352; Second Norn 308–9; Sieglinde xxi, 175, 176; Siegmund 29, 176; Wellgunde 308; Wotan 29

Rise and Fall of the City of Mahagonny, The (Weill) 158–9

ritorno d'Ulisse in patria, Il (Monteverdi): Penelope 287

Rizzi, Carlo, cdr: *Lucia di Lammermoor* 202

Rodriguez, Andres, dir 235

Rome Opera, 93, 250; *Aida* 197; *Barbiere* 252; *Lady Macbeth* 105; *Macbeth* 113–14; *Tosca* 119

Roméo et Juliette (Gounod): Juliette 128–9, 148, 202, 204, 206–7; Roméo 206; Stéphano 277, 308

Ronconi, Luca 52–3

rondine, La (Puccini): Magda 84–8

Rosenkavalier, Der (Strauss): 'American' 3; Faninal 5, 277; Mariandel 278, 279; Marschallin 3, 4, 6, 7, 36, 37–9, 51, 61, 71, 275–6, 279, 277; Nina 283; Ochs 7, 39, 278; Octavian 3, 5, 6, 7, 274, 275–6, 277–80, 282–3, 319; Sophie **3–7**, 15–16, 39, 275–6, 277, 278, 279, 283

Rosenthal, Harold 167

Rosmonda d'Inghilterra (Donizetti) 52

Ross, Rick 41, 49

Rossini, Gioacchino 311, 328–9

Rostropovich, Mstislav 267

Rouen: *Walküre* 186

Rozsa, Vera, tchr q165–6, 171

Rudel, Julius, adm 215

Rusalka (Dvorak): Jezibaba 352; Rusalka 36, 51

Ruslan and Lyudmila (Glinka): Lyudmila 95, 98

Ruta, Tina, tchr 125

Rysanek, Leonie, spr xxii

Sadko (Rimsky-Korsakov) 98

St Louis: *Werther* 283

St Petersburg, Mariinsky Theatre xxiii, 96, 97, 98, 99, 102, 103, 265; *Boris Godunov* 268; *Faust* 265; *Fiery Angel* 98; *Forza* 101–2; *Khovanshchina* 265; *Queen of Spades* 105, 268

Salammbô (Musorgsky) 267

Salome (Strauss): Herod 152–3;
  Salome 142, 146, 151, 152–3, 154,
  158, 175
Salzburg xix; *Ballo* 306; *Clemenza* 144,
  215, 310, 316, 317; *Contes
  d'Hoffmann* 144; *Così* 261, 318, 325;
  Damnation de Faust 319; *Don Carlos*
  344; *Don Giovanni* 46, 66, 167, 312;
  Elektra 162, 185; *Entführung* 42;
  Falstaff 285; *Figaro* 56, 61–2, 281;
  Jenůfa 177; *Mahagonny* 158;
  Mitridate 304, 316; *Moses und Aron*
  202; Mozarteum 8–9; *Otello* 68;
  Salome 152; *Stone Guest* 268;
  Tancredi 310, 312; *Traviata* 87–8;
  Tristan 193; *Troyens* 194; *Wozzeck*
  181
Samson et Dalila (Saint-Saens) 270;
  Dalila 267–8, 270, 271, 284, 289,
  299–300, 302, 329, 352; Samson
  267, 299–300
San Francisco Chronicle, The q269, q338
San Francisco Examiner, The q207; q338
San Francisco Opera xxv, 20, 198,
  Adler Fellow 199; Affiliate Artist
  Program 213; *Aida* 215; *Barbiere*
  331; *Bohème* 238; *Carmen* 269, 290,
  299; *Cenerentola* 268; *Clemenza* 214;
  Così 199; *Dialogues des Carmélites*
  211; *Fiery Angel* 98; *Figaro* 43;
  Hamlet 204; *Hérodiade* 48, 354;
  Idomeneo 15, 139, 318; *Lohengrin*
  162, 173; *Louise* 36, 47; *Lucia* 202;
  Manon Lescaut 163, 178; Merola
  Program xxiv, 199, 277, 337–8;
  Orlando 204; *Parsifal* 159; *Rigoletto*
  199–201; *Roméo et Juliette* 206;
  Tosca 112; *Trovatore* 3380; *vespri
  siciliani* 228
Santa Fe: *Figaro* 288
Santi, Nello, cdr: *Tosca* 230

Santiago Opera 235, 239
Schaaf, Johannes, dir: *Don Giovanni*
  79, 218; *Figaro* 166
Schauspieldirektor, Der (Mozart):
  Madame Herz 129
Schenk, Otto, dir: *Rosenkavalier* 278
Schiff, Andras 247
Schlegel, Nadine 308
Schlesinger, John, dir: *Rosenkavalier* 3
Schubert, Franz 15
Schumann, Robert 8
Schwarzkopf, Elisabeth, spr 41–2, 48
Sciutti, Graziella, spr 122
Scott, David, tchr 212
Scottish Opera: *Don Giovanni* 166;
  Norma 31–4; *Walküre* 28
Scotto, Renata, spr 235
Seattle Opera 20; *Norma* 34; *Otello*
  225; *Tristan und Isolde* 34
Secunde, Nadine xxi
Semele (Handel): Semele 197, 204,
  205–6
Semiramide (Rossini) 325: Arsace 327,
  350, 353; Semiramide 208
Serban, Andrei, dir: *Italiana* 327;
  Turandot 82
Seville: *Norma* 119
Shicoff, Neil, tnr xxii, 291
Siegfried (Wagner): Brünnhilde xxi,
  20, 22, 27–31, 34, 184, 186–7,
  189, 190–1, 193; Erda 352; Fricka
  352
Sills, Beverly, spr xxiii, 47, 213, 215,
  220, 221, 230
Simon Boccanegra (Verdi): Amelia 37,
  44, 163, 166, 176, 211, 225
Simone, Roberto de: *Così* 62–5, 258
Sinodinos, George, dir 128
60 Minutes 301
Skovhus, Bo 12, 16, 177
Söderström, Elisabeth, spr 277

Sofia, National Opera 306

Solti, Lady q44

Solti, Sir George, cdr 51, q82; *Così* 44; *Don Giovanni* 45; *Rigoletto* 85; *Rosenkavalier* 3, 4, 10; *Traviata* 82–4, 133–4

sonnambula, La (Bellini) 52; Amina 52, 54, 124

South Bank Show, The 247

Spectator, The q74, 191, q194

Spencer, Charles 195

Stade, Frederica von, mspr 287, 288; *Figaro* 282

Stanislavsky, Constantin, dir 126

Stein, Peter, dir: *Wozzeck* 181, 182

Stone Guest, The (Dargomïzhsky) 268

straniera, La (Bellini) 52

Strasbourg: *barbiere* 327

Strauss, Richard 15, 38, 71, 176, 195

Stravinsky, Igor 8

Streetcar Named Desire, A (Previn): Blanche 37

Sullivan, Sir Arthur 24

Sumac, Yma 304

Sun-Times, The (Chicago) q43

Sunday Correspondent 232

Sunday Telegraph, The 263, q267, q281

Sunday Times, The q3, q96, q153, q171, q173, q185, q312

Suor Angelica (Puccini): Suor Angelica 241

Susannah (Floyd): Susannah 37

Sutherland, Dame Joan, spr xxii, 203

Sverdlovsk (Yekaterinburg) opera 95, 96

Swenson, Ruth Ann, spr xxiv, 82, **196–209**

Tancredi (Rossini): Amenaide 208, 252; Tancredi 257, 310–11, 316

Tanglewood 19

Tanner, Michael, q191

Tate, Jeffrey, cdr: *Clemenza* 219, q220

Tchaikovsky, P. I. 94, 102

Tchaikovsky Competition 108, 337

Te Kanawa, Dame Kiri, spr xx, 36, 83, 165

Tebaldi, Renata, spr xix, 93, 203

Terfel, Bryn 152

Thaïs (Massenet): Athanaël 48; Thaïs 36, 39–40, 48, 160

Times, The q74, q86–7, q91, q131, q185, q206, q267, 283, q300

Titus, Dickson, tchr 198

Tokyo 18; *Ballo* 119; Suntory Hall 121

Tomlinson, John 194

Tomowa-Sintow, Anna, spr 305

Tosca (Puccini): Angelotti 111, 155; Cavaradossi 154–5; Scarpia 111–12, 154–5, 227; Shepherd-Boy 250; Tosca 24, 85, 99, 105, 117, 117, 119, 146, 154–5, 160, 211, 229–31, 242

Traviata, La (Verdi) 80, 94; Alfredo 133, 135, 136, 228, 238; Germont 118, 135, 138, 239; Violetta 37n, 74, 75, 78, 81, 82–4, 87–8, 117–18, 121, 122, 124, 125, 129–31, 132–3, 134, 135, 136, 138, 142, 144, 157, 203, 207, 211, 220–1, 227–8, 238–9, 240

trionfo del tempo e del disinganno, Il (Handel): Pleasure 249

Tristan und Isolde (Wagner) 100; Isolde 27, 34, 35, 193

trovatore, Il (Verdi): Azucena 271, 306, 333, 336, 338–42; di Luna 26, 227, 342; Ines 58; Leonora 24, 26, 68–9, 211, 225–6, 227; Manrico 58, 342, 343

Troyanos, Tatiana, mspr 215, 278, 287

Troyens, Les (Berlioz): Anna 308;
Cassandra 194; Didon 194, 270,
271, 287
Tsar's Bride, The (Rimsky-Korsakov):
Lyubasha 266
Tsouchlos, Nicos, dir 122
Tucker, Richard, tnr xxiii, xxiv
Turandot (Puccini) xx, 119; Calaf 34;
Liù 74, 82, 95, 125, 196, 202, 203,
208, 238; Turandot 20, 25, 27, 29,
34, 99
Turin, Teatro Reggio: *corsaro* 68;
Italiana in Algeri 325; *Mitridate* 63
Tyler, Bonnie 20

Ulrich, Alan q199, q207–8

Valentini-Terrani, Lucia, mspr 310
Van Dam, José, bar 167, 173
Vaness, Carol, spr xxiv, xxvi, 138,
210–32, 309
Vanity Fair 247
Vanni, Helen, tchr 337
Varady, Julia 215
Varnay, Astrid 191
verbena de la Paloma, La 234
Verdi, Giuseppe 26–7, 37n, 52, 69,
70, 80, 94, 95, 100, 102, 117, 118,
173, 226–8; *Requiem* 31, 69, 70
Verona Arena: *Aida* 116, 119; *Carmen*
290; *Nabucco* 106
Verrett, Shirley, 349
vespri siciliani, I (Verdi): Elena 52,
100, 112, 211, 228
viaggio a Reims, Il (Rossini): Contessa
di Foleville 45
Vick, Graham, dir q62, q65; *Così* 55,
62, 63–5; *Don Giovanni* 65, 66,
166; *Mitridate* 63
Vienna, Musikverein: *Trionfo* 249
Vienna, Theater an der Wien: *Anima*

del filosofo 248, 249; *Così* 258
Vienna Festival: *Così* 62–5; *Don
Giovanni* 170; *Figaro* 11–12, 61;
Otello 121, 137
Vienna State Opera 20, 79, 189; *Aida*
271; *Andrea Chenier* 105; *Barbiere*
309; *Bohème* 59, 74, 83; *Boris
Godunov* 309; *Carmen* 59–60, 290,
299; *Don Carlos* 344; *Don Giovanni*
66, 167, 216; *Elisir d'amore* 74;
Ernani 119; *Falstaff* 309; *Figaro* 43,
310; *Lustige Witwe* 10–11, 16;
Norma, 34; *Queen of Spades* 101,
105, 309; *Rigoletto* 201; *Ring* 29;
Rosenkavalier 7, 10, 275, 278; *Tosca*
105; *Traviata* 144; *Trovatore* 342;
Vespri siciliani 228
Villarroel, Veronica, spr **233–43**
Vivaldi, Antonio 249
Vogue q75
Voigt, Deborah xxiv
von Rhein, John 50, q249–50
Voyage of Edgar Allen Poe (Argento) 202

Waart, Edo de, cdr: *Werther* 283
Wagner, Richard xx, 22, 23, 26, 27,
34, 50–1, 100, 176, 189, 195
Wagner, Wolfgang 50–1
Walküre, Die (Wagner): Brünnhilde
xxi, 20, 22, 27–31, 34, 184,
186–7, 189, 190–1, 193; Erda 354;
Fricka 352; Sieglinde 175, 176;
Sieglinde xxi; Siegmund 29, 176;
Wotan 29
Ward, Joseph, tchr 21–2, q23, 25, 28
Warner, Keith, dir: *Carmen* 290
Warren, Leonard, bar 101
Washington Opera: *Carmen* 291, 294;
Don Giovanni 166, 178; *Lucia* 202
Weaver, William 247, q256
Weber, Carl Maria von 10

Weikert, Ralf, cdr: *Götterdämmerung* 309
Welsh National Opera 175; *Rosenkavalier* 275, 278
Welt, Die q281
Wernicke, Herbert, dir: *Rosenkavalier* 3–7, 276, 278; *vespri siciliani* 228
Werther (Massenet): Albert 284, 301; Charlotte 271, 274, 283–4, 289, 301–2, 314–15, 318
Wheen, Francis 252
Whittaker, Matthew 18
Wiener Zeitung q312
Winbergh, Gösta, tnr 175, 216
Wolf Trap 298
Wozzeck (Berg) 154: Marie 181, 193

You 262
Young, Simone, cdr: *Traviata* 134–5

Zajick, Dolora, mspr xxiv, 69, 108n, 188, **332–54**

Zambara, Edward, tchr 301
Zarzuelas 234
Zauberflöte, Die (Mozart) 10, 255; Pamina 10, 13–14, 15, 142, 163, 166, 196, 197, 198; Papageno 13, 14; Queen of the Night 334; Sarastro 14; Tamino 14
Zeffirelli, Franco, dir: *Carmen* 290–1; *Pagliacci* 240; *Tosca* 119; *Turandot* 196
Zürich Opera 307, 308: *Armida* 249; *belle Hélène, La* 317; *Carmen* 290; *Clemenza* 308, 309; *Così* 255; *Don Giovanni* 255; *Eugene Onegin* 308; *Figaro* 11, 253; *Götterdämmerung* 309; *Hänsel und Gretel* 319; *Iphigénie* 319; *Lucia* 309; *Nina* 248, 254, 258, 261; *Norma* 301, 315; *Périchole* 317; *Roméo et Juliette* 308; studio xxiv; *Troyens* 308; *Werther* 314–15